"Written by four of the world's leading assessment psychologists, *Therapeutic Assessment with Children: Enhancing Parental Empathy Through Psychological Assessment* provides a roadmap for implementing the innovative Therapeutic Assessment (TA) model in clinical work with children and their families. Blending clinical wisdom with rigorous empirical evidence, this compelling book illuminates the human side of psychological assessment, reminding us that the purpose of assessment is to understand people, not test scores. For those already familiar with TA, *Therapeutic Assessment with Children* will provide profound insight into the psychological functioning of children within the family system. For those not yet familiar with TA, this book will change the way you think about and conduct psychological assessment. Of interest to early career psychologists and seasoned professionals alike, this important book should be on every clinician's shelf."

Robert F. Bornstein, *Ph.D., University Professor,*
Derner School of Psychology, Adelphi University, New York

"This volume exquisitely details Therapeutic Assessment with Children (TA-C), a developmentally, culturally, and contextually sensitive relationship-based approach to psychological assessment of children and families consistent with attachment theory. Loaded with clinical examples, the volume elegantly articulates the background and guidelines for multi-method assessment that fosters 'heart-to-heart communication' with children and their parents and will aid in their attachment. Lucid and insightful, I recommend this book highly for practitioners seeking a sophisticated, conceptually- and empirically-grounded handbook on planning and conducting child assessment."

Carol George, *Ph.D., Professor Emerita, Distinguished Research Fellow,*
and Infant Mental Health Program Director, Mills College, California

Therapeutic Assessment with Children

Therapeutic Assessment with Children presents a ground-breaking paradigm of psychological assessment in which children and families collaborate with the psychologist assessor to understand persistent problems and find new ways of repairing their relationships and moving forward with their lives.

This paradigm is systemic, client-centered, and culturally sensitive and is applicable to families from many different backgrounds who often feel misunderstood and disempowered by traditional assessment methods. In this book, the reader will find a step-by-step description of Therapeutic Assessment with Children (TA-C), with ample teaching examples to make each step come alive. Each chapter includes detailed transcripts of assessment sessions with Henry, a ten-year-old boy, and his parents as they progress through a Therapeutic Assessment and find new ways of appreciating each other and being together. The combination of didactic and clinical material will give even new clinicians a groundwork from which to begin to practice TA-C. The volume demonstrates how the core values of TA-C—collaboration, respect, humility, compassion, openness, and curiosity—can be embedded in psychological assessment with children and families.

Therapeutic Assessment with Children will be invaluable for graduate assessment courses in clinical, counseling, and school psychology and for seasoned professionals wanting to learn the TA-C model.

Deborah J. Tharinger is Professor Emeritus at the University of Texas, a Licensed Psychologist in Austin, Texas, and a Founding Member of the Therapeutic Assessment Institute (TAI).

Dale I. Rudin is a Licensed Psychologist in Austin, Texas, and a Founding Member of the TAI. She currently serves on the Board of Directors of TAI.

Marita Frackowiak is a Licensed Psychologist in Austin, Texas, and a Founding Member of the TAI. She currently serves on the Board of Directors of TAI.

Stephen E. Finn is a Licensed Psychologist in Austin, Texas, and Founder and President of the TAI. He is also a Clinical Associate Professor at the University of Texas.

Therapeutic Assessment with Children

Enhancing Parental Empathy Through Psychological Assessment

Deborah J. Tharinger,
Dale I. Rudin,
Marita Frackowiak, and
Stephen E. Finn

NEW YORK AND LONDON

Cover image: © Getty Images

First published 2022
by Routledge
605 Third Avenue, New York, NY 10158

and by Routledge
4 Park Square, Milton Park, Abingdon, Oxon, OX14 4RN

Routledge is an imprint of the Taylor & Francis Group, an informa business

Library of Congress Cataloging-in-Publication Data
Names: Tharinger, Deborah J., author.
Title: Therapeutic assessment with children : enhancing parental empathy through psychological assessment / Deborah J. Tharinger, Dale I. Rudin, Marita Frackowiak, Stephen E. Finn.
Description: New York, NY : Routledge, 2022. | Includes bibliographical references and index.
Identifiers: LCCN 2021046945 (print) | LCCN 2021046946 (ebook) | ISBN 9780367429263 (hbk) | ISBN 9780367429270 (pbk) | ISBN 9781003000174 (ebk)
Subjects: LCSH: Psychological tests for children. | Family psychotherapy.
Classification: LCC BF722.3 .T48 2022 (print) | LCC BF722.3 (ebook) | DDC 155.4/1828--dc23/eng/20211217
LC record available at https://lccn.loc.gov/2021046945
LC ebook record available at https://lccn.loc.gov/2021046946

ISBN: 978-0-367-42926-3 (hbk)
ISBN: 978-0-367-42927-0 (pbk)
ISBN: 978-1-003-00017-4 (ebk)

DOI: 10.4324/9781003000174

Typeset in Goudy
by MPS Limited, Dehradun

We dedicate this book to all the children and parents who have trusted us with their stories and their struggles over the years. Each of these families helped us grow as psychologists and as people, and this book truly could not have happened without their courageous decision to be vulnerable and let us into their lives.

Contents

Figures

Tables

Boxes

Foreword

It is a delight and a privilege to write in support of a book as consequential to the field of psychology as *Therapeutic Assessment with Children: Enhancing Parental Empathy Through Psychological Assessment.* The authors of this book—Steve Finn, Deborah Tharinger, Dale Rudin, and Marita Frackowiak—have, consistent with the values of Therapeutic Assessment, generously shared their gifts of practical experience, scholarship, and clinical wisdom with humility and respect. They have also made a great contribution to the child clinical field. This book will be extremely useful for those with a background in Therapeutic Assessment, but it also works well as an introduction to Therapeutic Assessment and as a practical guide for those who wish to enhance their clinical work with children and families.

Therapeutic Assessment with Children locates Therapeutic Assessment within the much broader landscape of psychological and developmental theory. It then links these foundational concepts to child clinical practice, helping clinicians work more effectively with families closer to the time when clinically concerning patterns of adaptation first emerge. In this way, it makes it possible, often in real time, to attenuate the effects of developmental compromise and promote a more healthy and adaptive developmental trajectory for the child and parents. The ability to thoughtfully conceptualize complex child cases is an important clinical skill. This book will deepen and strengthen the reader's ability to do so. But it will also demonstrate how to use Therapeutic Assessment to help the child client directly while also engaging parents with respect and empathy.

When I first encountered the Therapeutic Assessment model, I felt as if I was coming home. Its component pieces were consistent with my academic background in clinical and developmental psychology, as well as clinical training that emphasized the close relationship between assessment and therapy. I heard similar sentiments from many colleagues when they were first introduced to the principles and practice of Therapeutic Assessment. How can it be that something so innovative could feel so familiar to so many? Perhaps it is due to the eclectic influences from which the theory of Therapeutic Assessment is derived, or the way in which Therapeutic Assessment has been democratized in practice and training. These are important reasons why clinicians from varied backgrounds and from across the world so readily connect to the Therapeutic Assessment approach. But there is, I think, even more. I believe that the success of Therapeutic Assessment in helping clinicians use the assessment process in the service of meaningful therapeutic change is of central importance as well. To encounter a clinical approach that values both assessment and therapy in a cohesive manner is to be reminded of why we aspired to do this work in the first place. By reconnecting us to our own reasons for choosing a clinical career, Therapeutic Assessment, in a very real and personal sense, brings us home again. And for those of us whose clinical careers focus on working with youth and families, this book carries that message to us directly.

To be fair, I should note that there are personal, as well as general, reasons for my resonance to this model, first developed by Steve Finn. Like Steve, my graduate and clinical training were at the University of Minnesota and Hennepin County Medical Center in Minneapolis. Additionally, I have the singular honor of having been the first postdoctoral fellow to be supervised by Steve during my rotation on an adult psychiatric inpatient unit. What I recall most clearly about that early training experience was Steve's fierce commitment to respecting the dignity and individuality of each client we assessed, his fundamental belief that the assessments we conducted were in the service of understanding the client, and his emphasis on communicating what we learned with fidelity. In both the work of his career and that of the clinicians he has taught and inspired, Steve has extended, but never lost focus on, these guiding principles. As has been true with every extension of the Therapeutic Assessment model to additional settings and populations, these principles are evident throughout this book.

It was some years after Steve left Minnesota for Texas that I reconnected with him as he began to develop, research, practice, and teach Therapeutic Assessment. This led to my introduction to the larger group of thoughtful and talented psychologists working together in Austin, Texas to refine the practice of Therapeutic Assessment. That cohort included several individuals with the vision, focus, and interest to adapt Therapeutic Assessment to child and adolescent clinical practice. The co-authors of this book have been critical to that mission. They have deeply influenced my teaching, research, and writing. Through their scholarship, workshops, and consultations I have learned a great deal from each of them about how to apply the Therapeutic Assessment model in my own work with children and adolescents. I am excited that this book creates that opportunity for so many more clinicians to learn from them as well.

Therapeutic Assessment with Children demonstrates in practical and actionable ways how to work collaboratively with children and parents. Richly described examples illustrate the development of meaningful clinical questions linked to relevant assessment data. It shows how to incorporate these into working hypotheses which engage both children and parents. In addition to providing a guide for how to conduct culturally and developmentally informed assessment, the authors also demonstrate developmentally-appropriate assessment feedback techniques for young children including, for example, the use of stories and fables. A central theme of this book is that for change in the life of a child to be sustained, parents must come to a new understanding of their child's dilemmas. That is what the Therapeutic Assessment process provides. Skillful assessment brings into focus for the clinician, child, and parent the challenges interfering with healthy development. The therapeutic relationship formed during the assessment supports change by promoting parental empathy, understanding, and agency. This book stands as a single source to guide the application of the Therapeutic Assessment to work with children and families, to teach the skills required to do so successfully, and to adapt the Therapeutic Assessment process to varied settings. That is a remarkable accomplishment and exactly what those of us in the child clinical field need. In choosing this book you have chosen well.

Michael F. Troy, Ph.D., LP
Medical Director, Behavioral Health Services Science Director, Behavioral
    Health Services
Associate Medical Director, Neuroscience Institute
Children's Hospital – Minnesota

Author of:

Davies, D. & Troy, M. (2020). *Child Development: A Practitioner's Guide* (4th ed.). New York: Guilford.
Parritz, R. & Troy, M. (2018). *Disorders of Childhood: Development and Psychopathology* (3rd ed.). Boston: Cengage.

Preface

We are delighted to invite all of you into a world where psychological assessment of children is conceived of as a collaborative effort among the assessor, the child, *and* the parents; where change (or the desire not to change) is viewed as happening within a family system and a culture, and not centrally within the child; where the value of an assessment is judged by how useful it is to the family in feeling understood and validated in their experiences; and where the assessment is, in and of itself, a therapeutic experience for the family. Welcome to Therapeutic Assessment.

Stephen Finn coined this term, "Therapeutic Assessment (TA)," in the late 1980s to describe a structured model of collaborative assessment that was proving clinically to have a major impact on people's lives. Since then, research has documented the efficacy of TA, and interest in TA has grown exponentially, including TA applied to children and their families. Finn and Deborah Tharinger· researched and refined Therapeutic Assessment with Children (TA-C) at the University of Texas between 2002 and 2015 and published a number of articles and chapters on its methods and underlying principles. J. D. Smith added to the literature with a series of innovative time-series analyses of TA-C. Also, faculty from the Therapeutic Assessment Institute (TAI), including Marita Frackowiak and Dale Rudin, have conducted training workshops on TA-C and done supervision with hundreds of clinicians around the world. As a result, TA-C is now practiced in the USA, Canada, Italy, France, Japan, Australia, Brazil, Argentina, Mexico, Sweden, Denmark, Finland, and perhaps other places as well. This proliferation has led to other published case studies of TA-C and to additional research studies. At this point in time, TA-C continues to expand and be modified for use in many types of settings.

While the success of TA-C is exciting, what has been missing up until now is a complete published description and illustration of TA-C from start to finish—a sort of "handbook," if you will. At a Board meeting for the TAI in 2017, the four of us—Deborah Tharinger, Dale Rudin, Marita Frackowiak, and Stephen Finn—decided to undertake such a project. We all felt this was a "dream team," as Deborah and Stephen had written about TA-C before, and Marita and Dale had years of experience working with children and families and in teaching and supervising TA-C. The tome you hold in your hands is the result, and our goal is that it helps professionals and graduate students feel into the underlying attitude of TA-C and begin to try out its methods. As we will repeat many times in the ensuing pages, you do *not* have to incorporate every part of TA-C for it to be effective, and we encourage you to "pick the low hanging fruit" from this volume and see what happens. And for those of you who wish to learn the full model and perhaps become certified in TA-C, this book is a basic map that will help you get started.

We strongly believe that TA is best practiced in a community, and this book would not exist without the many people who have supported us in its development. We cannot acknowledge everyone here, but we especially want to thank the other members of the Board of the TAI, all of whom have contributed to our work and inspired us: Filippo Aschieri, Hilde de Saeger, Francesca Fantini, Jan Kamphuis, Hale Martin, Noriko Nakamura, Pamela Schaber, and J. D. Smith. Former TAI Board members Lionel Chudzik, Diane Engelman, Melissa Lehmann, and Lena Lillieroth also supported us in important ways. Diane Santas and Sharon Witkin read and provided useful comments on earlier drafts of the book. Donald Viglione reviewed our R-PAS coding. Hal Richardson helped with our Figures and artwork. Lionel Chudzik crafted our genogram. Mike Troy generously agreed to write the Foreword. And last but not least, "Henry" and his parents graciously consented to Dale's sharing details of their TA-C so that other people could learn the model. We are especially grateful to them for this brave and invaluable gift.

Our greatest hope is that this book will help change psychological assessment with children and families around the world to be more collaborative, respectful, compassionate, systemic, and culturally attuned. We realize this is a tall order, but to use a common term from Therapeutic Assessment, we are content for this book to be a half-step toward this end.

Author Biographies

Deborah J. Tharinger, Ph.D., is a Licensed Psychologist in Texas. She attended the University of California at Berkeley for her graduate education and training. Dr. Tharinger is Professor Emeritus in the Department of Educational Psychology at the University of Texas at Austin (UT), where she was an active faculty member for 35 years. UT was her first and only academic position. Dr. Tharinger maintained a small private practice for most of her years at UT. She met Stephen Finn at UT and became enamored with Dr. Finn's orientation to psychological assessment and jumped right in, integrating the values and methods of Therapeutic Assessment (TA) into her course and practicum on child assessment. She also initiated, with Dr. Finn, a research project on the effectiveness of TA with children and adolescents. She is a faculty and founding member of the Therapeutic Assessment Institute and a member of its Board of Directors. Dr. Tharinger has published over 50 articles and chapters, with the most current ones focused on Therapeutic Assessment with children, adolescents, and families, many published with Dr. Finn and her graduate students. She resides in Austin, Texas and is affiliated with the Center for Therapeutic Assessment.

Dale Rudin, Ph.D., is a Licensed Psychologist as well as a Licensed Specialist in School Psychology who practices at the Center for Therapeutic Assessment in Austin, Texas. In 1975, she obtained a Master's in Deaf-Blind/Multi-handicapped education from Boston College, eventually becoming a teacher and then principal at the Texas School for the Blind and Visually Impaired in Austin. Dr. Rudin received her doctorate in Educational Psychology from the University of Texas in 1992. She is passionate about the need to consider the whole family when one of its members is differently abled. Dr. Rudin has conducted numerous workshops for parents of children with special needs, teachers, and other professionals. In addition to providing assessment services, her private practice focuses on psychotherapy with individuals, couples, and families. Dr. Rudin has a multi-theoretical approach, working from Kohutian, Systemic, and Emotionally Focused Therapy perspectives. She is a founding member of the Therapeutic Assessment Institute, serves on its Board, and consults to clinicians around the world interested in learning Therapeutic Assessment. Dr. Rudin is certified in Therapeutic Assessment with adults, adolescents, and children.

Marita Frackowiak, Ph.D., is a licensed psychologist in private practice at the Center for Therapeutic Assessment in Austin, Texas. She is a founding member of the Therapeutic Assessment Institute, a member of its Board of Directors, and an international lecturer on Therapeutic Assessment. Dr. Frackowiak attended the University of Texas at Austin for her graduate education and training, where she first met Dr. Stephen Finn. She was one of the first post-doctoral supervisees of Dr. Stephen Finn and at that time provided supervision for clinical cases on the Therapeutic Assessment Project, directed by Dr. Deborah Tharinger. Since then, Dr. Frackowiak has worked with Dr. Stephen Finn for almost two decades providing clinical services, conducting research, publishing articles and chapters, presenting at national and international conferences, and providing trainings on Therapeutic Assessment. She is the author of a therapeutic fable, *Little Bear's Cup and Saucer,* and is currently working on publishing additional therapeutic fables. Her current professional focus, in addition to clinical work, is lecturing internationally and offering consultation to clinicians around the world. Dr. Frackowiak is certified in Therapeutic Assessment with adults, children, adolescents, and couples.

Stephen E. Finn, Ph.D., founder of the Center for Therapeutic Assessment, is a licensed clinical psychologist in practice in Austin, Texas, a Clinical Associate Professor of Psychology at the University of Texas at Austin, Senior Researcher and Director of Training at the European Center for Therapeutic Assessment at Catholic University of Milan, Italy, and Director of Training at the Asian-Pacific Center for Therapeutic Assessment in Tokyo, Japan. He has published 90+ articles and chapters on psychological assessment, psychotherapy, and other topics in clinical psychology, and is the author of *In Our Clients' Shoes: Theory and Techniques of Therapeutic Assessment* (Erlbaum, 2007) and *A Manual for Using the MMPI-2 as a Therapeutic Intervention* (1996, University of Minnesota Press). Dr. Finn also co-edited, with Constance Fischer and Leonard Handler, *Collaborative/ Therapeutic Assessment: A Casebook and Guide* (Wiley, 2012). In 2011, Dr. Finn was awarded the Bruno Klopfer Award from the Society of Personality Assessment for distinguished lifetime contributions to the field of personality assessment. In August 2017, he received the award for Distinguished Contributions to Assessment Psychology from Section IX (Assessment) of the Society for Clinical Psychology (Division 12 of the American Psychological Association). In 2018, he received the Carl Rogers Award for an outstanding contribution to theory and practice of humanistic psychology from the Society for Humanistic Psychology (Division 32 of the American Psychological Association).

1 Introduction to Therapeutic Assessment with Children

Once upon a time, there was a little Coo-Coo Chuck named Henrietta. Henrietta was soft and pink and cute, and she lived with her mother and little brother, Tarzan, in a big hole in a tree. At first, things went pretty well and Henrietta was happy. But then, when she was little, her mother started using drugs, and she couldn't take good care of Henrietta and Tarzan anymore. For a while, she even left Henrietta alone with Tarzan, and Henrietta had to dress and clean Tarzan and feed him and keep him out of trouble. This was a really hard and scary job for a little Coo-Coo Chuck. Luckily, Henrietta was a very special Coo-Coo Chuck and was remarkably brave.

Henrietta's Aunty loved her and her brother a lot, so she took them to live with her and her friend, Sue, in another tree in a different part of the forest, while Henrietta's mother went to the animal hospital to get well. Although Henrietta's dad couldn't take care of her, he called every week and sent money. No one realized at the time that Henrietta's mom was very, very sick, and that Henrietta and Tarzan would end up living with Aunty and Sue for quite a long time.

Now one thing you should know is that Coo-Coo Chuck mommies usually teach their babies to talk about how they feel and what they need so that other people can understand and help them. Sadly, Henrietta's mother wasn't able to teach Henrietta how to do this before she had to go to the hospital. So when Henrietta and Tarzan went to live with Aunty and Sue, there were a lot of things that happened that they didn't understand, and Henrietta wasn't able to explain. This made everyone unhappy, and it got in the way of their playing and having fun together.

For example, Henrietta was really hurt inside that her mother had used drugs and left her alone with Tarzan. It felt like her heart was ripped up and torn open. But Henrietta didn't know how to talk about this and let other people know how she was feeling. So, one day, she took some crutches from her Aunty, and brought them to school, where she pretended to have a hurt foot. Everyone was very nice to her and this made her feel better and not so hurt about her mother. But Aunty and Sue were very upset when they found out. Henrietta had no way of explaining why she had made up this story.

DOI: 10.4324/9781003000174-1

Henrietta also felt really empty inside, like there was a big hole in her heart that could never be filled up. Deep down, she really wanted lots of hugs and kisses, but she was afraid to even hope for these things because it would remind her of her mom and be too painful. So, instead of asking for hugs, she kept taking food she wasn't supposed to have, like ice cream, cookies, and pie. When she ate these things, the hole inside felt smaller for a little while, and Henrietta didn't feel so scared anymore.

But again, Aunty and Sue were upset and confused. Why did Henrietta steal food, and why didn't she ask for what she wanted? They didn't know that her mother hadn't taught her how to say what was going on inside. They got angry, and yelled, and punished her and Tarzan. They still loved Henrietta, but they didn't know how to help her.

Another problem was that Henrietta was kind of bossy with Tarzan and tried to make Tarzan do his chores after school when Tarzan didn't want to. Tarzan and Henrietta would end up in big fights, with Tarzan saying, "You're not in charge of me. You're not my mother!" Aunty and Sue kept telling Henrietta not to worry about Tarzan's chores and not to fight with Tarzan. But Henrietta couldn't explain that she'd always been in charge of Tarzan when her mother was sick, and she wasn't sure she wanted to give up that job. After all, suppose Aunty and Sue got sick one day. Tarzan would still need Henrietta to take care of him.

So, one day Aunty and Sue decided to go see some owls in another tree in the forest, who knew a lot about baby Coo-Coo Chucks and why they did things. The owls talked to Aunty and Sue, and they had Henrietta tell stories, draw pictures, and look at some inkblots. They listened carefully to everyone, and thought about what should happen to help Henrietta and her family.

Finally, they had a meeting with Aunty and Sue, and the owls explained how Henrietta never learned to talk about how she was feeling, how empty and hurt she was inside, why she made up the story of the hurt foot, and why she kept stealing food. The owls said,

> Henrietta needs lots of laughing and playing, and lots of love to help her get over being left alone by her mother. And it's really important that you not yell at her. When Henrietta gets scared, her brain freezes and she can't think straight. When that happens, she can't learn anything new, like how to talk about how hurt and empty she feels.

The owls also met with Henrietta and they told her,

> You aren't a bad Coo-Coo Chuck, you just don't know how to talk so other people can understand you. This isn't your fault, but it is confusing and frustrating for other people. There are some owls we know who can teach you the things your mother couldn't teach you, and who can help Aunty and Sue understand some of the things you do.

Also, you've done a great job of taking care of Tarzan, but now you can trust Aunty and Sue to do that. This is your time to be a little Coo-Coo Chuck, whose job is to play, have fun with friends, and learn.

After this, Henrietta went back to the home tree with Aunty, Sue, and Tarzan. Things began to go better almost immediately, but Aunty and Sue decided that they still wanted to see the owls that had been recommended for them and Henrietta. They began to go every week to the new owls. Sometimes Henrietta would go alone and play and practice talking about how she felt. Sometimes Aunty and Sue would go alone and talk about how not to yell at Henrietta and Tarzan. And sometimes the whole family would go and play games and talk together. As time went on, the family grew stronger and happier and safer for everyone.

Sarah

The Coo-Coo Chuck's name is Sarah and she was ten years old when this fable was written for her. Like many children, when she realized the fable was about her, her face lit up with surprise followed by delight and the joy of feeling understood. An independent girl, she chose to read it aloud to herself, her aunts, and her two assessors. She looked up at various points to see how others were reacting. Everyone smiled back at her and felt good that she liked the fable. The session was moving, peaceful, and connecting. The adults and this child held a shared narrative about their life together. It made sense; it was painful, honest, loving, and hopeful—all at the same time.

Three months earlier, Steve had received a call from a desperate woman "at the end of her rope" wondering if the child she had brought into her home just four years earlier needed to be sent away to a different relative. The woman, named Laura, stated that she and her female partner were completely overwhelmed by the demands of parenting Sarah and her seven-year-old brother, and they were not sure they could continue. Laura and her partner were caring for the two children since they were found alone in winter in an apartment after their mother abandoned them. Their mother, Laura's sister, was struggling with serious drug addiction. Laura had no idea when she agreed to care for the two children that it was going to be a long term, highly demanding, painful, and stressful situation. Laura was referred to Steve's practice for an assessment of Sarah to see what might be the best progression for her. Laura's partner was concerned that Sarah might have a serious emotional disturbance and parenting her would be beyond their capacity.

Just like the Coo-Coo Chuck in the fable, Sarah stole food, lied to her aunts, and angrily bossed around her little brother. She had controlling and angry outbursts, and when engaged by others she would shut down, stay silent, or run to her room. She did not show gratitude or affection. She stayed distant and reserved with her aunts; they felt rejected, taken advantage of, and very tired. Parenting Sarah was extremely demanding and unsatisfying.

With other ongoing stressors in the family, the parenting challenges began to erode their own relationship as well as impact their personal health. Although they were educated and caring people, their own histories of trauma and neglect got in the way of their understanding of how Sarah's unstable early years contributed to the problems they were experiencing now. Both women were tough survivors, and they did not want to give up easily, but the demands of their situation were clearly too much for them.

As you read in the fable, the owls agreed to help. Steve and his co-assessor completed a two-assessor model of comprehensive Therapeutic Assessment with Children (TA-C) with Sarah and both her aunts to help them better understand Sarah's puzzling behaviors. The aunts watched Steve's testing sessions with Sarah through a video feed in another room, accompanied by the other assessor. This setup allowed for constant discussion of their observations with the second assessor, allowing Sarah's aunts to begin to think like psychologists about her various disturbing behaviors.

In one of the testing sessions, Steve and Sarah did the Fantasy Animal Drawing Game (Handler, 2007). That's when the Coo-Cook Chuck was created. Sarah drew a fantastic creature and named it "the Coo-Coo Chuck." Talking about it with Steve, she revealed how sad and worried the little Coo-Coo Chuck felt and how much it wanted to be cared for. The rest of the assessment findings consistently showed a child with deep attachment wounds and developmental trauma, who used distancing and dismissing defenses to cope with deep underlying feelings of insecurity and pain. This was obvious to the clinicians; the challenge was to make it understandable to non-psychologist, exhausted, and overwhelmed aunts. Ideally, Steve's and his co-assessor's goal was to help Sarah's aunts tap into the care and compassion they felt when they first took Sarah and her brother into their home. Also, the assessors hoped to help the caregivers understand that they needed support from professionals to develop more effective parenting strategies focused on emotional regulation, bonding, and limit setting. They also needed to hear that it was important for them to take care of themselves so they would have emotional and physical energy to carry on. The stakes were high as they were ready to send Sarah away.

This scenario is not unique to Sarah or unfamiliar to us, as we routinely encounter heartbreaking and complex family dilemmas in our assessment work with children. However, what is unique is the way assessors trained in TA-C approach families. Using theory, underlying principles and values, collaborative methods, and findings from tests and other activities, we creatively and compassionately help families change their views of their problems in living. We work with parents and caregivers to help them develop a more coherent, accurate, compassionate, and useful understanding of their children—a new story or narrative. We then use this new understanding to help them shift their direct interactions and responses to their children's emotional expressions, behaviors and needs. We believe that once parents "change the viewing," they will "change the doing."

Starting at the End

Perhaps you were surprised that we began this book with fable, which is the last step in a TA-C, with the exception of a Follow-up Session that takes place several months later. We also wonder if you were delighted that we began the book this way, as writing individualized stories for our child clients is fresh, engaging, creative, and effective. We have to remind ourselves that it wasn't that long ago when most psychologists routinely provided little or no feedback to children following a psychological assessment.

We decided to lead with a fable for several reasons. First, we wanted to illustrate the uniqueness and creativeness of TA-C. And second, we wanted to illustrate, by example, how we communicate what we figure out about children and their families in a way all, children *and* their parents, can relate to and keep in mind. As you likely experienced reading the *Fable for Sarah*, this was a story for the whole family that captured what they had experienced, what they now understood, and how they could move forward.

Although the fables may be our favorite way of giving feedback to children, they are just one piece of the feedback we give to parents. Prior to presenting the fable to Sarah and her aunts, we discussed our findings with the aunts, answered their Assessment Questions, and collaborated on suggestions of how to best move forward. We also sent the aunts a caregiver-friendly letter summarizing what was discussed at that meeting. In other situations, if required for third parties, we provide a formal report, infusing a therapeutic approach into our report writing. However, for those of us experienced with TA-C, the stories are often our proudest achievement, as they communicate from our hearts to the hearts of our clients. To have this experience yourself, we invite you to invest in all that follows, as the only way to get to the ending is to start at the beginning.

We now turn to Chapter 2, the beginnings, and emerge ourselves in the foundations: the comprehensive model of TA-C with its phases and steps, how it developed over time, its guiding theoretical frameworks, and research findings. We then continue to Chapters 3 through 10 for in-depth coverage of the full TA-C model, one phase or step at a time, illustrated by a case study of a ten-year-old boy and his parents. Each of these chapters has a comprehensive teaching component to guide the reader to prepare and conduct the phase or step presented. To illustrate the "how to," the applicable portion of the case study is presented in detail in each of these chapters, corresponding to the teaching component just reviewed. For example, after the guidance on planning and conducting the Initial Meeting with the Parents, corresponding case material on that step is presented. This method continues throughout Chapters 3–10, giving the reader the opportunity to follow a case from beginning to end.

In Chapter 11, we address and illustrate adapting the procedures of TA-C to practice with particular clients in varied circumstances and settings, as the case study followed in the book reflects assessing a child in an outpatient, independent practice using the full TA-C model. These adaptations include brief TA-C; TA-C done remotely; TA-C in inpatient and residential treatment facilities; TA-C in outpatient community mental health centers; and TA-C bridged to schools and school assessments. In Chapter 12, we discuss pragmatics, logistics, and support for beginning to practice TA-C: the nuts and bolts. In Chapter 13, the final chapter, we share our sense of where TA-C fits in the ongoing development of psychological assessment and our thoughts about future directions.

Reference

Handler, L. (2007). The use of therapeutic assessment with children and adolescents. In S. Smith & L. Handler (Eds.), *Clinical assessment of children and adolescents: A practitioner's guide* (pp. 53–72). Mawah, NJ: Erlbaum & Associates.

2 Basic Steps, Development, Theory, and Research

Full Model of Therapeutic Assessment with Children

As previewed in Chapter 1, Therapeutic Assessment with Children (TA-C) is a semi-structured model of psychological assessment that engages primary caregivers and their children in a collaborative process leading to new understandings and ways of handling persistent problems in living. TA-C is primarily designed for pre-adolescent and latency-aged children (e.g., ages 4–12) and their parents, but it can be applied to older children (ages 13–14) if their developmental age is younger. Similarly, certain 11- to 12-year-olds are mature enough that we use the model of Therapeutic Assessment with Adolescents (TA-A), aimed at children ages 14 and older (Tharinger et al., 2013). Also, Therapeutic Assessment has been adapted to assessments of infants and children under the age of 4. For details, see the article by Gart et al. (2016).

Figure 2.1 shows a flowchart of the semi-structured TA-C model as it has evolved to this point in time. We consider this flowchart to be a general guide that *must* and *should* be adapted to each client and setting, and we implore you to always prioritize the needs and well-being of your clients over any fixed idea of how a TA-C should unfold. On the other hand, this flowchart is an expression of the ways we have found, based on our research and clinical experience, to maximize the therapeutic impact of child/family psychological assessment. Thus, we urge you to study and understand the flowchart and to think carefully when you choose to deviate from it.

We now briefly describe each step of TA-C with the goal of providing an overview. The 13 steps are grouped into 5 phases. Again, every TA-C may not include all these steps, and we discuss specific instances of appropriate modifications as we go through each step.

Phase I: Initial Sessions (Chapter 3)

Step 1: Initial Phone Contact with Parents

Typically, a TA-C begins when parents/caregivers call the assessor to inquire about having their child assessed. (If referring professionals call us first, we

DOI: 10.4324/9781003000174-2

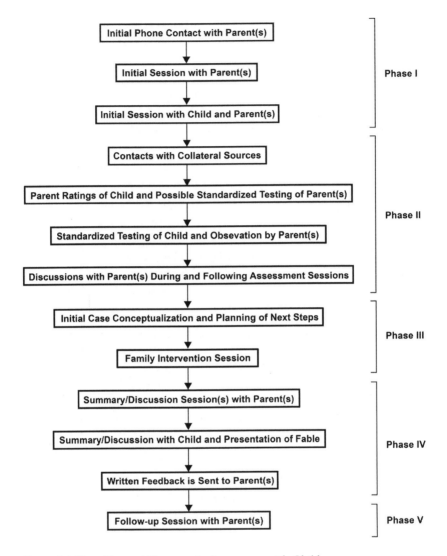

Figure 2.1 Flow Chart of Therapeutic Assessment with Children.

discuss the assessment with them and then ask them to have the parents call us.) The assessor tells the parents about TA-C, addresses any questions about the procedures, cost, etc., and asks about the parents' major concerns. If the parents are ready, we then schedule the initial session of the TA-C—with the parents alone. After the phone call, we send parents a detailed information sheet about TA-C and urge them to contact us again before the first meeting if they have any important questions.

Step 2: Initial Session with Parents

In the first meeting, we build the collaborative working relationship with the parents by exploring their goals for the assessment and co-constructing individualized Assessment Questions that capture their concerns, puzzlements, and challenges regarding the child and family. Typically, the child is not invited to this initial session so that parents can speak freely with the assessor(s). As we discuss and collect background information on the family's struggles, we model openness, lack of judgment, and compassion, fostering a positive working alliance. Last, we propose a plan for the TA-C, including the number of sessions, types of testing to be done, cost, and tentative completion date, and fine-tune this with the parents. Again, we address any questions and concerns the parents may have. If the parents wish to move forward, we schedule the next session, in which they will bring the child, and we coach the parents on how to talk to their child about the assessment.

One other matter typically discussed in the initial session is the involvement of other professionals already involved with the child and family. If there is a therapist, psychiatrist, or physician who has recommended the TA-C, typically parents want assessors to discuss the child with those professionals and possibly even to collect Assessment Questions from them. Occasionally, parents say they want an "independent" second opinion on the child and request that we do not talk to collateral professionals. Of course, if this is true, we adhere to their wishes.

Step 3: Initial Session with Parents-Child

In this session, we help orient the child to the assessment, begin to build a positive relationship with the child, and observe the parents and child interact. Often, early on the assessor asks the child what they understand about the TA-C. The assessor helps parents address any confusion or questions the child has, and invites the child to come up with her/his own Assessment Questions. (Often, younger children do not offer questions at this point.) Then, depending on the age of the child, the assessor may ask the family open-ended questions to get to know them better (such as, "What do you do as a family to have fun together?" "If you could change something about the family, what would it be?" "What would you *not* want to change in the family?"). Alternately, the assessor may ask the family to engage in a low-stress activity, such as drawing a map of their house or their neighborhood. In the latter part of the session, the assessor often engages the child in an individual assessment task (such as drawings) or in play. Parents may watch from within the room or from behind a one-way mirror or over a video link. If parents observe from outside the room, the child is shown how the parents will view subsequent assessment sessions.

Phase II: Data Gathering/Testing Phase (Chapter 4)

Step 4: Contacts with Collateral Sources

As mentioned earlier, depending on the Assessment Questions agreed upon for the TA-C, it may be useful for the assessor to communicate with collateral sources of information, such as therapists, psychiatrists, pediatricians, teachers, occupational therapists, or even other family members, such as aunts or grandparents. Of course, these people are only contacted with the permission of the parents, and the assessor always tells parents the main points of what was discussed and learned. When another professional has been instrumental in referring the family for the TA-C, and it is clear that the clients most likely will continue working with that therapist or psychiatrist, often the contact is more extensive. For example, we may schedule a meeting at a therapist's office, where we share the Assessment Questions already developed with the clients, discuss initial impressions, and collect Assessment Questions from this professional that will be shared with the parents and explicitly addressed at the end. Many parents are comforted by the idea that the TA assessor will collaborate with other important professionals and become part of the child and family's "team" of helpers.

Parents are also involved at Step 4 by gathering relevant records, such as previous assessment reports or school records. They may already have these documents in their possession, or they may contact other professionals and agencies to collect them. Many parents are pleased by the opportunity to become co-"sleuths" with the assessor, working to explore the answers to their Assessment Questions.

Step 5: Parent Ratings of Child and Standardized Testing of Parents

Quite often, early in the assessment process, we ask parents to complete a standardized rating form about their child. Such ratings tell us how parents see the child at the beginning and how similar their views are. In many assessments, we also invite parents to take a standardized personality test that we think will be useful in addressing their Assessment Questions.

Step 6: Standardized Testing and Observation by Parents

In the middle phase of the assessment, we administer standardized psychological tests to the child that will provide information relevant to the parents' Assessment Questions. We educate parents about these tests and invite them to collaborate in making sense of the child's test responses, behavior, and reactions. Also, some portions of child assessment sessions are devoted to non-standardized activities, such as drawings or play. We invite parents, if at all possible, to observe the child assessment sessions, either from within the assessment room, behind a one-way mirror, or over a video link. Sometimes there are two assessors who work as a team and take part in the initial session(s); then one works with the child during the testing sessions while the other sits with the observing parents to discuss what they see and offer support. When it is not possible for parents to observe sessions or when we wish to be more thoughtful about what parents see, we videotape the assessment sessions and then show excerpts to parents at a later time.

Step 7: Discussions with Parent(s) During and After Assessment Sessions

Typically, it is very useful for the assessor to meet with parents alone at various points during the middle phase of the assessment. For example, early on, you may collect a detailed developmental history of the child, perhaps asking parents to bring in family photos or a baby book if they have one. Also, if the child can tolerate being alone for short periods in the waiting room, you may check in with parents at the beginning of child assessment sessions or ask them to stay afterward to discuss what they observed each day. If the child cannot be alone, we may ask parents to talk later from home by phone. Also, not infrequently, as new understandings of the child and family emerge, we ask parents to meet with us for one or more sessions to discuss these new ideas and get their input and reactions.

If a referring professional is involved in the TA-C in a major way, the assessor also typically updates this person as the assessment proceeds: sharing important events, asking for input, and checking out emerging hypotheses. If the referring professional has had contact with the child and family during the assessment, they may also share any comments or impressions gathered from the family.

Phase III: Case Conceptualization and Family Intervention Session (Chapters 5 and 6)

Step 8: Tentative Case Conceptualization and Planning of Next Steps

When we have completed the middle phase of the assessment, we take time apart from the family to pull together the information we have gathered. We develop a tentative case conceptualization based on our theoretical and practical knowledge, and we think about how to help the parents reach a more coherent, accurate, compassionate, and useful understanding of their child. We use this initial case conceptualization to plan the subsequent steps in the assessment.

Step 9: Family Intervention Session

In the Family Intervention Session (FIS), we ask the parents and child to participate in some activity that will help test out and clarify our initial case conceptualization and bring the parents along to a new understanding of the child and family. Sometimes parents already have a new view of the child as a result of the previous assessment sessions; then the FIS may focus on helping them practice a new way of being with the child. Often by the end of the FIS, parents can begin to answer many of their own initial Assessment Questions.

Phase IV: Presentation and Discussion of Results (Chapters 7–9)

Step 10: Summary/Discussion Session(s) with Parent(s)

Summary/Discussion Sessions are the occasions for assessors and parents to collaborate in answering the Assessment Questions and to lay out the next steps for addressing the challenges that brought the family for the TA-C. Assessors carefully prepare for these sessions, choosing how they will high-light various findings from the psychological testing. Not uncommonly, if a referring professional is involved, the assessor meets with that person first to share the assessment results and get their comments and questions. Then—with parents' permission—this professional may attend the Summary/Discussion Session to support parents and help "translate" what the assessor says. During the actual session, the assessor stays open to parents' input, asking them to confirm, modify, or reject the assessors' ideas. Also, the assessor (and referring professionals, if present) helps support parents emotionally as they react to the new understandings emerging through the assessment. Finally, the assessor and parents discuss how and what feedback will be given to the child in the subsequent session.

Step 11: Summary/Discussion Session with Child and Presentation of Fable

The assessor and parents provide appropriate information to the child about what they have learned via the assessment and support the child's reactions. Depending on the age of the child, assessment feedback may be provided directly, for example by answering the child's Assessment Questions (if there were any). For most children, we present them with a fable that captures in metaphor the new understandings that have emerged from the assessment. Such fables are tailored to the developmental level and particular interests of the child, and children are invited to modify the fables in this session. Then the fable is printed and is given to the child to take home. The assessor acknowledges the ending of the assessment with the child and says goodbye (unless the assessor will continue working with the child and family in ongoing treatment).

Step 12: Written Feedback Is Sent to Parent(s)

Two to four weeks after the parent Summary/Discussion Session, the assessor mails a written summary of the assessment process and findings, typically in the form of a letter that directly addresses the parents' Assessment Questions. Parents are invited to note places that are unclear or conclusions they see differently, and to either contact the assessor at that point or bring these up in the Follow-up Session. If other forms of written feedback are also needed (e.g., a formal report for the child's school), these are always shared with parents for comment before they are sent. Typically, with parents' permission, the written feedback is shared with any referring professional and with other professionals involved in ongoing services with the child and family. In most cases, parents are also sent two forms to fill out to give feedback to the assessor about the TA-C: (1) the Parent Experience of Assessment Scale (PEAS; Austin et al., 2018), and (2) the Parent Feedback Questionnaire. They may send these back before the Follow-up Session, bring them to the Follow-up Session, or complete them after the Follow-up.

Phase V: Follow-up (Chapter 10)

Step 13: Follow-up Session with Parent(s)

Parents are invited to meet with the assessor several weeks after they receive the written assessment feedback to continue discussing: the assessment results, the written feedback, their experiences trying to implement next steps, and how the child and family are doing post-assessment. The assessor and parents discuss their feelings about the TA-C and say goodbye.

We hope this provides you with an overview of the TA-C model. As promised, in Chapter 3, we begin going through each step, in detail, and continue through Chapter 10. Before doing that, however, we wish to give you a more ample understanding of the development of TA-C, as well as the concepts and theories that have shaped our work.

History of Collaborative/Therapeutic Assessment and TA-C

If you are reading this book, you probably know that, until relatively recently, psychological assessment has been viewed primarily as a tool to diagnose mental disorders/deficits and measure different attributes of people (e.g., degree of extraversion, level of verbal expressive abilities). Assessment in clinical settings has been done to facilitate communication between professionals, plan interventions, and/or evaluate the success of an intervention (Finn, 2007). Our sense is that this traditional "information gathering model" of psychological assessment is still predominant around the world.

In 1997, Finn and Tonsager published a now famous article contrasting the "information gathering model" with a "therapeutic model," in which psychological assessment was recognized as a potentially beneficial intervention with clients and the important people in their lives. Finn and Tonsager asserted that tests could still be used for the same purposes as in the traditional model, but that they were also "empathy magnifiers" that could help clients and others to better understand their persistent life difficulties. How did the therapeutic model develop?

Early Efforts

In fact, the seeds of this model were visible in the mid-1900s. For example, Bellak (1951) devoted an entire chapter of his classic textbook on picture-story tests to the use of the Thematic Apperception Test (TAT; Murray, 1943) in psychotherapy. Bellak explained that by engaging a client in discussing her/his test responses the clinician could "help the patient to gain some 'distance' from himself and to establish the psychotherapeutic attitude" (p. 143). (In modern terminology we might say such discussions help the client to "mentalize" (Allen et al., 2008)). Luborsky (1953) was enthusiastic also about the potential therapeutic benefits of self-interpretation of the TAT. And Harrower (1956) outlined an approach she called "projective counseling," in which she asked adult clients to free associate to their Rorschach percepts, sentence completion responses, and TAT stories to gain new insights into their conflicts and problems. Harrower's method was quite collaborative, and she detailed several case examples where it helped clients "come to grips, sometimes surprisingly quickly, with some of [their] problems" (p. 86).

Over time, even within the realm of traditional assessment, there began to be more recognition that psychological testing was a complex interpersonal process with potentially important impacts on clients. This was especially true of psychologists working in or trained at the Menninger Foundation in Kansas, many of whom wrote influential papers in which they tried to deepen psychologists' understanding of the "psychodiagnostic process," e.g., Aronow and Reznikoff (1971), Berg (1985), Mosak and Gushurst (1972), and Pruyser (1979). Among these writers, Allen (1981) went so far as to say that "one cannot diagnose without treating" and that psychological testing "might be viewed as the treatment process in microcosm" (p. 251).

Although the aforementioned efforts all focused on adult clients, starting in the mid-1980s several distinguished family therapists wrote about psychological assessment of children as a potentially effective family systems intervention. For example, Fulmer et al. (1985) explained how giving parents feedback about a child's psychological test results could foster systemic goals such as reframing, promoting differentiation, de-triangulation, and creating engagement. Ziffer (1985) strongly urged family therapists not to reject psychological testing as inevitably tied to pathologizing individual family members. He recommended that assessment psychologists create a "team" with the family therapist and parents, and consider letting parents view videotapes of the child testing process. Williams (1986) and Pollak (1988) also provided specific guidelines about how to provide therapeutic feedback from assessments to adolescents and parents.

Constance Fischer and Leonard Handler

An important milestone in the development of TA-C and families was the publication of *Individualizing Psychological Assessment* by Constance Fischer in 1985. Although Fischer had been writing for some years about collaborative assessment practices rooted in phenomenological psychology (Fischer, 1970), it was in this book that she laid out a coherent theoretical rationale as well as detailed instructions for how to involve clients as "co-evaluators" in their assessments. In her vivid case excerpts, Fischer also demonstrated several innovative practices that greatly influenced TA-C: (1) conducting home visits where she had parents observe standardized testing of a child, and then interviewed them afterward about their observations, and (2) giving assessment feedback to a child via an individualized fable. Fischer's book was republished in 1994 and is still widely cited and read. Her influence on our work and on the field of Collaborative/Therapeutic Assessment cannot be overstated.

Another important pioneer of collaborative assessment methods with children was Leonard Handler. Handler experimented for years with innovative ways of engaging adult clients in their assessments. For example, he developed a set of creative probes to be used in querying clients about their Rorschach responses, such as, "If this mushroom could talk, what would it say?" (Finn et al., 2012). However, Handler is best known for his collaborative assessment methods with children, described in an influential chapter he published in 2007. Among these methods, Handler refined collaborative storytelling approaches used in child psychotherapy (Mutchnick & Handler, 2002) and invented a now widely used technique called the Fantasy Animal Drawing Game (Handler, 2012). We teach readers about this method in Chapter 4. An important part of all of Handler's work with children was to use assessment materials to help parents understand and become more empathic to their children.

Stephen Finn and the Center for Therapeutic Assessment

Besides their own publications and work, Fischer and Handler also contributed to TA-C through their collegial and personal relationships, first with Stephen Finn, and eventually with all the authors of this book. Finn took a faculty position at the University of Texas at Austin in 1984, after finishing his doctorate at the University of Minnesota. There Finn began to develop what he initially called an "interpersonal model of psychological assessment," consciously referencing the work of Harry Stack Sullivan (Finn, 2008), and he and his students conducted controlled research on the therapeutic impact of psychological assessment on adult clients (Finn & Tonsager, 1992) and provided guidelines for how to integrate collaborative assessment into managed care (Finn & Martin, 1997). Finn met Constance Fischer in 1993, through his involvement with the Society for Personality Assessment, and around this same time, he left his full-time faculty position at the University of Texas to found the Center for Therapeutic Assessment (CTA). As evident in the name of the new Center, Finn now called his model "Therapeutic Assessment," and at the CTA he and a group of colleagues (including Dale Rudin, one of the co-authors of this book) began to develop and refine the use of collaborative assessment with adult clients, couples, adolescents, and children and families. In 1994, Fischer and Finn met Leonard Handler at an SPA meeting, and the three became friends and began to share ideas and give presentations together. Finn also began to do trainings in the USA and abroad on TA-C, and in 1995 he did the first "live assessment" workshop at the CTA in which participants observed over a video link an entire child/family assessment *in vivo*.

In 1997, Finn presented a paper at the annual meeting of the Society for Personality Assessment entitled "Collaborative Child Assessment as a Family Systems Intervention" (Finn, 2008). In it, he laid out the basic structure of TA-C as it had been developed at that point in time. The model included the following features: (1) asking parents to help define the goals of the psychological assessment of their child, (2) inviting parents to observe the child testing sessions and discuss their observations with the assessor afterward, (3) inquiring if parents were willing to be tested as part of their child's evaluation, (4) incorporating family sessions as part of the child's assessment, (5) encouraging parents to corroborate and modify assessment findings presented throughout the assessment, (6) asking parents to review reports for schools, therapists, or other referral sources, and (7) involving parents in giving oral or written feedback to the child, such as co-writing a therapeutic fable for the child. As you will see later, these elements are part of the TA-C model we describe in this book.

The early part of the second millennium witnessed several important developments in TA-C. Finn began to do more presentations on TA-C, including with his friend, Carol V. Middelberg, a skilled family therapist who was previously a faculty member at the Chicago Family Therapy Institute. Middelberg had expertise in object-relations family therapy (Middelberg, 2001) and helped Finn understand how projective identification might explain patterns he had noticed in children and families referred to the CTA for psychological assessments. In 2005, Finn and Middelberg conducted the second live TA of a child and family at the University of Texas with over 60 participants observing. This assessment is summarized at the beginning of Chapter 1, and the "Coo-Coo Chuck" fable that opens this book is drawn from this TA-C. This live TA workshop and several others during this period were organized by Mary McCarthy, a member of the CTA, who worked at the University of Texas at Austin under a grant from the University Affiliated Program.

The Therapeutic Assessment Project at the University of Texas

In 2002, Stephen Finn and Deborah Tharinger, his colleague at the University of Texas, began a multi-year research study on TA-C and on TA-A. Funded by the Hogg Foundation for Mental Health and the ECG

Foundation, utilizing the talented graduate students in the School Psychology Training Program at the University of Texas, and supported by clinical supervisors such as Carol Middelberg and Marita Frackowiak (who did her post-doc training with Finn and is one of the co-authors of this book), Tharinger and Finn studied and refined the methods of TA-C. TAP eventually led to a series of influential publications that included the first empirical study of TA-C (Tharinger et al., 2009), a series of case studies with diverse multi-problem families (Austin et al., 2012; Hamilton et al., 2009; Tharinger et al., 2007, 2012), and articles explaining core steps of the model, such as inviting parents to observe child testing sessions (Tharinger et al., 2012), the use of play (Tharinger et al., 2011) and drawings (Tharinger & Roberts, 2014) during assessment sessions, FISs (Tharinger et al., 2008), giving assessment feedback to parents (Tharinger et al., 2008), writing therapeutic feedback fables for children (Tharinger et al., 2008), and using TA-C in schools (Tharinger et al., 2011). This series of publications introduced many psychologists around the world to TA-C.

WestCoast Children's Clinic

TA-C also matured and developed in new ways due to Finn's collaboration with a community mental health center in Oakland, California named WestCoast Children's Clinic (WCC). Staff at WCC are committed to providing mental health services to children and families in their area who seek their services. Often these clients are economically disadvantaged, of diverse racial and ethnic backgrounds, and have experienced significant trauma. WCC received funding to treat foster children and their families. Finn began to do trainings in TA-C at WCC starting in 1993 at the invitation of Barbara Mercer, the Assessment Director there. Besides teaching WCC psychologists about TA-C and TA with Adolescents, Finn did a number of live assessment workshops at WCC that were attended by psychologists from around the world. Finn's co-presenters for these workshops were Carol Middelberg, Barbara Mercer, and Caroline Purves, herself a pioneer of CTA who had written about collaborating with clients referred for involuntary assessments (Purves, 2002). The clinicians at WCC have taken the lead in adapting the methods of TA-C to culturally diverse, traumatized child and family clients, and in underlining the importance of holding our clients' cultural, ethnic, and racial contexts in mind as we attempt to serve them. We highly recommend the groundbreaking publications on TA-C that have come out of WCC (Finn, 2011; Guerrero et al., 2011; Haydel et al., 2011; Lipkind and Mercer, 2019; Mercer, 2011, 2017; Mercer et al., 2016; Purves, 2012, 2017; Rosenberg et al., 2012). As we lay out the steps of TA-C in this book, we will highlight insights and modifications learned from the clinicians at WCC.

The Therapeutic Assessment Institute

Other important developments in TA and TA-C were the founding of the Therapeutic Assessment Institute (TAI) in 2009; the European Center for Therapeutic Assessment (ECTA) in Milan, Italy in 2010; and the Asian-Pacific Center for Therapeutic Assessment (ACTA) in Tokyo, Japan in 2014. The TAI Board established certification procedures for TA-C (and other TA models) and it oversees training and certification in TA around the world. Starting in 2010, the TAI has sponsored "Immersion Courses" in TA that have introduced many clinicians around the world to TA-C, and also Advanced Trainings, where clinicians have conducted TA-Cs with actual clients under close supervision. Both ECTA and ACTA provide TAs for clients and sponsor trainings on TA. Clinicians from ECTA have also made important contributions to the case literature on TA-C (e.g., Aschieri et al., 2012; Fantini et al., 2013).

Another significant event in 2009 was the creation by the TAI of a website on Therapeutic Assessment: *www.therapeuticassessment.com*. Here clinicians and others around the world can gain information and download articles on TA, read the TAI newsletter, *The TA Connection* (first published in 2013), view certification requirements, and communicate with each other through a member list serve. The development of the website was also the occasion for us to articulate in a clear way the core values of TA (Finn, 2009): collaboration, respect, humility, compassion, openness, and curiosity (Box 2.1).

Foundational Theories and Core Constructs

As discussed previously, TA-C developed gradually and somewhat organically over the last 30 years, with influences from many people with different theoretical backgrounds, experiences, and perspectives. In fact, our experience and belief is that the general procedures and steps of TA-C can be used regardless of a clinician's theoretical background, and (as we will discuss in Chapter 5) it is often helpful to conceptualize a particular child's and family's strengths and struggles using different psychological points of view. However, currently, there is a group of core concepts and theories that ground the thinking and practices of many of us who practice TA-C. Before proceeding with our in-depth explanation of how to practice TA-C, let us briefly summarize these foundational theories.

Attachment Theory

We are greatly influenced by work published over the last 50 years by Ainsworth (1967), Bowlby (1969), George and West (2012), Schore (2001), Sroufe (1996), Trevarthen (1993), Tronick (1989), and others regarding *attachment theory* and the larger field of *interpersonal neurobiology*. To put it

Box 2.1   Core Values of Therapeutic Assessment*

Collaboration

Psychologists practicing Therapeutic Assessment believe and have evidence that assessments are most useful and their results are most accurate when clients are engaged as full collaborators. Clients help set the goals for their assessments, assist in collecting relevant background information, give their thoughts about the meaning of test results, and verify assessment findings by tying them to real-life examples. Clients also have input into recommendations and review and comment on any written documents that result from an assessment.

Assessors also collaborate with referring professionals and, when appropriate, with other important people in clients' lives, such as family members, physicians and psychotherapists, teachers, judges, and employers.

Respect

The procedures of Therapeutic Assessment are grounded in respect for our clients and the belief that assessors should treat clients as they would wish to be treated. Thus, assessors who practice Therapeutic Assessment carefully explain assessment procedures to clients, help them make informed choices about whether to participate, ask for their input as the assessment proceeds, and involve them in designing "next steps" at the end of the assessment. Clients are seen as "experts on themselves" who work together with assessors to better understand stuck points or dilemmas in their lives.

Therapeutic Assessment is also suited to clients of different cultures, in that assessment procedures are adapted to specific cultural contexts. In addition, assessors have no fixed assumptions about the meaning of test scores, and clients are asked to help assessors understand how assessment findings relate to the clients' particular cultural backgrounds.

Humility

Assessors practicing Therapeutic Assessment are acutely aware that they bring their own perspectives and biases to their work with clients and that they can never fully understand another person's inner world. They are also knowledgeable about the limitations of psychological tests and do not see them as providing infallible "Truths" about clients. Test scores and interpretations are seen as starting points for discussions about clients' lives and as tools for generating hypotheses that may assist clients in discovering new options.

Assessors using Therapeutic Assessment are trained to "find their own versions" of the struggles experienced by their clients. We are reminded of the words of Harry Stack Sullivan: "Everyone is much more simply human than otherwise." We are humbled by how often our clients' struggles mirror our own, and we are aware that all of us are growing, struggling human beings, generally doing the best we can given our backgrounds and resources.

Compassion

In Therapeutic Assessment, assessors use their empathy and their psychological tests to "feel into" clients' lives, and to help understand puzzles, behaviors, and patterns that are incomprehensible to others. This often results in clients' feeling more compassion for themselves and in their receiving more acceptance and support from important others. Very often, as compassion increases and shame decreases, clients find they are able to make life changes that formerly eluded them.

Openness and Curiosity

Assessors practicing Therapeutic Assessment aspire to conduct each assessment with openness to learning about themselves, the world, and the amazing resourcefulness of human beings to adapt to challenging circumstances. We are genuinely curious about each person who comes for an assessment, and we find that our curiosity often inspires clients to step back and see themselves and their life circumstances in new ways.

We believe we are still developing the potential of Therapeutic Assessment. We are open and curious about what our clients will teach us about how to improve our methods and evolve our concepts.
Note: *Taken from Finn (2009).

succinctly, we believe that human beings are "wired" for love and connection, and that it is essential to hold this capacity in mind in order to understand children and families.

Attachment theory describes a biologically based system in humans that promotes survival of the individual and the species by ensuring that parents, extended family, and "tribe members" have an investment in protecting and caring for children and important others and helping to regulate their emotions. Research on human attachment has shown that children's early experiences with caregivers have a profound and far-reaching influence on the development of their personality, sexual and social relationships, and mental health (Howe, 2011). When children are raised with caregivers who are appropriately protective, responsive, empathic, and emotionally attuned, they develop a *secure attachment*, which is associated with many positive outcomes later in life (Sroufe, 1996). In recent years, it has also become clear that early attachment relationships have a profound influence on children's ability to understand and manage their emotions in a healthy way (Schore, 2001; Tronick, 1989).

In our experience, many of the children who are referred to TA-C have *insecure attachments*, in spite of the best efforts of their caregivers to love and provide for them. Not surprisingly, many of the caregivers we see also come from a background of insecure attachment. And frequently, insecure attachment (of both child and caregiver) plays a crucial role in why the caregivers are worried, frustrated, or puzzled about and seeking expert advice about what to do. Thus, in almost all cases, we have found it crucial to consider both child and adult attachment and to be able to explain to caregivers how to respond to children's attachment needs in the best way.

One other place where we hold attachment theory in mind during TA-C is in the relationship we aspire to build with the child's caregivers. From its inception, TA practitioners have understood that most clients are more open to changing their narratives when they feel "held" by a person who has their best interests in mind, is emotionally attuned, sees them as unique individuals with their own needs, feelings, and ideas, and tries not to needlessly cause them shame or anxiety. Another way to think of this is that the assessor aspires to become an "auxiliary attachment figure" (i.e., "tribe" member) for the parent. Finn (2008) posited that when clients "feel felt" by an assessor, this meets a basic human longing to be understood, which then sets the stage for therapeutic change during an assessment. Recent evolutionary theory further elaborates how this kind of relational experience moves the assessor into the position of being a "privileged source" of information who is more likely to be believed by the client (Kamphuis & Finn, 2019). One final reason we aspire to demonstrate attuned, responsive, protective, authentic relationships with parents in TA-C is that this creates a parallel process where we model what we hope caregivers will provide for their children.

Trauma and Adverse Childhood Experiences

Another major impact on Therapeutic Assessment has been research over the past 25 years concerning the effects on children and families of *trauma* and *Adverse Childhood Experiences* (ACEs). In our experience, many of the families that seek TA-C have been exposed to trauma, and we strive to keep the following scientific findings in mind:

1. Stressful and threatening life experiences that are accompanied by insufficient interpersonal support can have long-term debilitating effects on many aspects of human functioning. This is true not only for severe trauma, abuse, and neglect but also for potentially less overwhelming events, such as divorce, witnessing domestic violence, having a family member with drug or alcohol problems, or a household member going to prison. A term now used to encompass all these different types of childhood traumatic events is *Adverse Childhood Experiences* (ACEs).

2. ACEs are common in the USA. The National Survey of Children's Mental Health reported that approximately 68% of children aged 0–17 had at least one ACE (Blodgett & Lanigan, 2018). Another study found that compared to a child with no ACEs, one who had four or more ACEs was 32 times more likely to be diagnosed with a behavioral, emotional, or cognitive problem (Plumb et al., 2016). Also, a large study of adults who retrospectively reported ACEs and then were followed over time found a strong relationship between the number of ACEs and numerous health, social, and mental health outcomes over the lifespan (Anda et al., 2006).

3. ACEs are so impactful because they alter the structure and physiology of the developing brain and the biochemistry of the neuroendocrine systems, thereby affecting multiple human functions and behaviors (Teicher, 2000). And as we will describe later, if children are traumatized early in their lives, the effects are compounded when they reach later developmental stages.

4. For various reasons, many parents underestimate the effects of trauma on their children (McNally, 1993). In our experience, this means parents often have incomplete or inaccurate understandings of their traumatized child's behavior, emotional, and cognitive struggles, and attribute these to individual characteristics of the child rather than to trauma.

5. Assessing, naming, and documenting the effects of trauma on children can help parents see their children more accurately and compassionately. Psycho-education about childhood trauma is an important part of the Therapeutic Assessment process that can reduce shame, lead to helpful next steps, and provide needed hope.

6. Although ACEs are significant, they do not inevitably lead to lifelong dysfunction in children and families. We have been repeatedly impressed by the resilience and wisdom we have encountered among our traumatized clients, and our experience is that TA-C can help families and children build resilience after trauma.

Systems Theory

From our reading and professional travels, it appears that the majority of psychological assessments of children done around the world predominantly take an *individual* perspective on each child. By this, we mean that parents are involved in a limited way, and the children are often seen alone for the assessment situations. Such assessments typically address such questions as, "What are this child's strengths?" "Does this child have a learning disability?" or "What is this child's diagnosis?" These are important and valid questions and they might also be addressed through TA-C, but there is a fundamental distinction in how TA assessors think about such matters.

We believe that children can only be fully understood within the context of the important systems in which they are embedded: their family, their school, their community, and their culture. This perspective is a fundamental aspect of *systems theory*, a multi-disciplinary set of theories that has influenced fields such as psychology, anthropology, environmental science, economics, and medicine. If one takes a systems perspective, the aforementioned assessment goals might shift dramatically. Instead of simply asking, "What are this child's strengths?" we might ask, "In what contexts does this child show strengths and are these strengths the same in different contexts? What aspects of the environment help or deter this child from showing her/his strengths?" In addition to asking, "Does this child have a learning disability?" we might ask, "What learning environments/approaches help this child learn the best?" and "How do family attitudes shape this child's learning?"

Family systems theory, which is most pertinent to TA-C, makes assertions such as the following:

1. There is a normal and expected interaction effect where children influence their families and families influence children.
2. We can only comprehend children's strengths and struggles if we also consider their families.
3. Attempts to help or change children's ways of being will inevitably impact their families, and may lead to *change-back behaviors* (Hecker & Wetchler, 2003), where family members will make "countermoves" to get children to change back and re-establish the previous family homeostasis.
4. Intervention efforts involving children are most effective when their families are also considered and involved as collaborators.

There are many different schools/refinements of family systems theory. One version that has influenced TA-C a great deal and that will be described in detail below is *object relations theory*. Another important point is that although we attempt to think systemically in TA-C, we do not deny that children have important individual differences, traits, temperaments, or disorders that greatly impact them and their families. Nevertheless, we are most interested in how children's families and systems respond to these in-dividual challenges.

Diversity and a Multicultural Perspective

One important systemic/contextual variable that has received increasing attention in recent years is that of clients' diversity in terms of religion, race, culture, sexual orientation, gender, and gender identity. Collaborative as-sessment was actually at the forefront of thinking in this area (Dana, 1993, 1997), and multiple recent publications have summarized how TA is un-iquely suited to considering and respecting clients' diverse backgrounds (Finn, 2016; Macdonald & Hobza, 2016; Martin, 2018; Mercer et al., 2016). These recent writings include a special section of the *Journal of Personality Assessment* entitled "Cultural Considerations in Collaborative and Therapeutic Assessment" (Smith, 2016). To review major points included in these publications:

1. TA does not consider psychological test scores as measures of "Absolute Truth" about clients, but as signs of how clients act and feel in particular contexts at certain points in time. This helps TA assessors consider the influence of cultural variables on clients' lives. For example, Tharinger et al. (2007) described a research TA-C case involving two Mexican-American grandparents and their 11-year-old granddaughter. At one session during the assessment, the grandparents brought food they had prepared for the entire clinical and research teams. Instead of possibly interpreting this action as a sign of "poor boundaries" or of the grandparents trying to "win the assessors over" to their point of view, the clinicians saw it as a culturally appropriate expression of the grandparents' gratitude and a way for them to proudly share their culture with the predominantly Anglo clinicians and researchers. By accepting and enjoying the gift of food for what it was and thanking the grandparents the team further strengthened their alliance with the family.

2. The relationship between assessors and clients is prioritized in TA, and assessors seek to empower clients by inviting them to collaborate at each step of an assessment, especially regarding the goals of the assessment. Some clients from minority cultural backgrounds report this is the first time in their lives that they have felt respected by a medical or mental health professional (Macdonald & Hobza, 2016). In addition, the TA core values of *curiosity*, *humility*, and *openness* set the stage for clients of diverse backgrounds to feel accepted, understood, and validated. For example, in Finn's (2016) chapter about how to use TA with clients seeking gender-affirming medical interventions, he emphasized the need for assessors to be transparent and humble about their role as potential

"gatekeepers" and to minimize this power differential as much as possible.

3. One of the aims of TA is to reduce clients' shame, which is often prominent in clients from non-dominant cultures. For example, Rosenberg et al. (2012) described the TA of 13-year-old Mexican American girl with academic difficulties and her family. The Anglo assessor had some knowledge of Spanish, which was useful in her communications with the girl and her family, but she frequently made grammatical mistakes and was aware of her own struggles with perfectionism. The assessor's ability to talk about the discomfort she felt created a bond and a healing opportunity for the girl, who often felt "less than" in school because of her learning difficulties. The assessor's transparency also created an opportunity for the family and girl to "help" the assessor with her Spanish, which reduced the power imbalance in the assessment and created safety.

4. TA assessors are aware that their own backgrounds and experiences necessarily influence their perspectives and they seek to learn about people from other backgrounds as a way of being open to other points of view. They also work to avoid naïve or misguided conclusions about what it means to be part of a certain cultural group. Martin (2018) emphasizes that TA works to avoid stereotyping by staying close to the client's experiences and the meaning of those experiences to the client. This is done by inquiring, listening, and believing the client.

Complexity Theory and Dilemmas of Change

Another multidisciplinary systems theory that is highly relevant to TA-C is *complexity theory* (and its close cousin, *chaos theory*), including a related concept from family systems theory, *dilemma of change*. Complexity theory has been articulated in the last 50 years and attempts to explain and understand the characteristics of complex, dynamic, multivariate systems such as the weather. Prior to complexity theory, the unpredictability of multi-faceted phenomena like the weather was attributed to randomness (i.e., widely divergent conditions of relatively equal probability). Complexity theory showed that apparently random events could be predicted in certain systems if one understood their non-linear (interactive) properties. For example, one important feature of complex systems is that small changes in one part of the system can sometimes produce large changes in the whole system. This has led to the coining of the famous "butterfly effect," where a butterfly flapping its wings in one part of the world possibly influences the weather all over the world.

As applied to children, families, and other multifaceted human systems, complexity theory helps us understand how these systems grow and change and why they appear to resist change. The following are implications of complexity theory:

1. Children and families are naturally predisposed to grow and develop toward increasing complexity and adaptation; we don't need to "instill" or "inspire" our clients to grow and change. There is a normal, inherent set of *driving forces* that will lead to change over time.

2. There are also natural and helpful *restraining forces* that keep children and families from developing too quickly and that protect their stability, identity, and health. Some of these restraining forces are internal, such as physical limitations on a child's growth and development. Others are external. For example, if a child begins to change too quickly or in ways that challenge family traditions or established roles, parents may interrupt a psychological intervention they see as producing that change. In many areas of clinical psychology, restraining forces have been labeled as psychological "resistance" on the part of children and families, typically with a pejorative connotation. In TA-C, we recognize that too rapid change can disorganize children and families, lead to psychological symptoms, and even to family break-ups. Thus, we take a much more benign view of restraining forces—seeing them as essential as driving forces.

3. When driving and restraining forces are optimally balanced, children and families grow and develop naturally and flexibly, unless there are external forces (such as illness or trauma) that interrupt this process. When restraining forces greatly exceed driving forces, this can lead to blocked growth and feelings of shame and hopelessness in children and families. In this situation, children and families face what has been called a *dilemma of change* (Papp, 1994), where the normal process of development cannot unfold because it would lead to overwhelming anxiety, pain, or disintegration in one or more family members or in the family as a whole. Many of the children and families who come to mental health professionals seeking psychological assessment and intervention face dilemmas of change that are not immediately apparent. For example, a school may refer a child for an assessment complaining that parents have been "resistant" to the child getting tutoring after school. It may turn out that the child is needed at home in the afternoons to help care for younger siblings, so that the mother may work and continue to support the family. In addition, many referring professionals send clients for TA-C because they do not understand clients' dilemmas of change and are therefore feeling puzzled, frustrated, and/or impatient.

4. Identifying, understanding, and naming children's and families' dilemmas of change often is a first and sometimes sufficient step in helping them get unstuck and move forward. Much of TA-C is focused on collaborating with children and families to develop an empathic understanding of their blocks to change and how those blocks serve them now or did so in the past. We also look for "tipping points" where small changes in how parents view their children can sometimes produce

large and positive shifts in both children and families—a kind of psychological "butterfly effect."

A Developmental Perspective

TA-C also attempts to maintain a *developmental view* of children and families. Lifespan development theory posits that children, couples, and families go through a series of normal, somewhat predictable developmental stages, each with different characteristics, challenges, and objectives (Feldman, 2014; McGoldrick et al., 2010). Later developmental stages are influenced by what happens in earlier stages, and therefore, disruptions in earlier life phases inevitably affect later ones (Parritz & Troy, 2017). This helps explain why early stresses and traumas can have such a profound, wide-ranging impact on children's development, and why problems may erupt as families and relationships mature. For example, we have seen children with early medical traumas that interfered with their early social development (perhaps because they were unable to attend school or participate in sports or other activities). These children may appear to do fairly well until they reach adolescence, when suddenly they have serious problems separating from their parents and developing close relationships with peers. This may be because certain problems from the earlier traumas (e.g., a lack of confidence) were not that important until the children had to function more independently from their parents and develop close relationships on their own. As alluded to earlier, developmental theorists believe that not only children go through life stages but also families and couples, and that these also inevitably affect children. For example, some committed couples come together without one or more of the partners successfully individuating from their families of origin—a developmental task of early adulthood in Western societies (McGoldrick et al., 2010). This situation can cause conflict, either within the couple or between one or both members of the couple and the grandparents, and the children are almost inevitably affected by this conflict.

Narrative Identity, Phenomenological Psychology, and Self-verification Theory

Narrative identity is "the internalized, evolving story of the self that each person crafts to provide their life with a sense of purpose and unity" (Adler, 2012, p. 367). This construct overlaps and is consistent with the field of *phenomenological psychology*, which led to Fischer's (1985/1994, 2017) groundbreaking work (described earlier) at Duquesne University on *collaborative individualized assessment*. Phenomenological psychology starts with the basic premise that human beings are "meaning makers" who are constantly trying to comprehend the world around them. The procedures and theory of TA-C are based on this idea: that the "stories" families and children weave about themselves and each other have a profound influence on their relationships and how they act in and experience the world. Imagine Billy, a boy who struggles in school, and how his parents might respond differently depending on whether they viewed him as (1) lazy, (2) depressed, or (3) learning disabled and doing the best he could. In TA-C, we would explore how the parents saw Billy, try to understand how their narrative developed, and assess if it were the most useful and accurate way of viewing the boy. If not, we would collaborate with the parents in examining and possibly revising their narrative, expecting that (as an old family therapy maxim says): "if you change the *viewing*, you change the *doing*." This goal is consonant with many other forms of psychological intervention, including Cognitive-Behavior Therapy, psychodynamic psychotherapy, and in particular, Narrative Therapy (White & Epston, 1990).

TA was also influenced by *self-verification theory*, developed by Finn's and Tharinger's colleague at the University of Texas at Austin, William Swann (Swann, 1996, 1997). Swann's theory goes beyond others that are similar in explaining: (1) how inaccurate narratives are maintained, and (2) why they are so resistant to change. Swann has presented evidence that once a narrative is developed, people "screen out" information that contradicts their narrative and "screen in" information that confirms it. People also seek out people and environments that confirm their core narratives and avoid others and situations that disconfirm them. For example, if Billy's parents see him as lazy, most likely they will spend more time at the school open-house talking to teachers who also see Billy as lazy, and they will be less likely to remember any comments from other teachers who might believe that Billy is "trying the best he can." Swann goes on to explain that if people receive information that contradicts their existing narratives and cannot easily dismiss or forget it, they often become anxious, or—in extreme cases—may become disoriented, feel something is terribly wrong, and that they are falling apart (Swann, 1997). This is a distressing state that Kohut (1984) called *disintegration anxiety*. If we were doing a TA-C with Billy's parents, we would be very attentive not to challenge their existing view of him too quickly and instead, to involve them in gradually constructing a new more accurate narrative.

The Zone of Proximal Development and Scaffolding

Two other core TA concepts that are related to self-verification theory are Vygotsky's *zone of proximal development* (ZPD; Zaretskii, 2009) and *scaffolding* (Bruner, 1978). Vygotsky recognized that all learning occurs in a social context; the ZPD is that threshold of learning people can achieve with interpersonal support, as opposed to (1) skills they already can do on their own, and (2) skills that are too difficult to grasp even with the help of others. Scaffolding is when we provide just enough active support to help learners achieve their next steps, but no more or less. When scaffolding is well done, it leads people to have the highest rate of learning.

In TA-C, when we are seeking to help parents change the narratives/ working models they have about themselves and their children, we scaffold by using "half-steps" in our comments and questions. For example, Sean was a nine-year-old boy whose parents strongly believed that he had ADHD and that this explained his overactivity and inability to do homework at home. Sean's teachers reported that he was "an angel" in school and could work for long periods without interruption, but the parents were suspicious of this information. During the TA-C, the parents observed Sean doing a number of different tests, and the assessor and they collaborated in discussing what they observed. Here is brief excerpt from the conversation that occurred at the end of one session:

Assessor:	What did you think about the session today?
Mother:	We were relieved that you got to see him getting worked up and not following the rules, like he does at home.
Assessor:	Yes, he got really antsy during that last test, didn't he? And he kept trying to get out of doing it. Is that similar to what you see at home?
Father:	Exactly. That happens all the time, like when we ask him to do his chores.
Assessor:	And what did you think about how Sean was at the beginning, when I did that other test with him where he had to draw the lines between the letters and numbers (the Trails Test)?
Mother:	He was fine then. In fact, I thought he did really well.
Father:	Me too.
Assessor:	That's right. I'll score it, but I think he scored high and was really focused when he did it. ... When do you think his behavior began to change?
Father:	After the break—when you asked him to tell the stories to those cards.
Assessor:	Yes, the TAT.
Mother:	He sure didn't want to do those.
Assessor:	I agree, and his behavior seemed to break down. Do you think?
Both parents:	Yes!
Assessor:	He was almost like a different child! I wonder what happened?
Mother:	I think he was just getting tired.
Assessor:	That could be ... Dad, do you have any thoughts?
Father:	Well, it was a different kind of test too. Like more emotional.
Assessor:	Hmmmm....That's true. The other one was more cognitive. And could you hear the stories he told? (*Parents nod "yes."*) Let me read them back to you and see what you think. (*Reads three stories.*) Any thoughts?
Father:	Gosh, they're all really sad!
Mother:	They are! What does that mean? Do all kids tell stories like that?

Assessor: Not usually ... so it made me wonder if Sean is feeling sad a
                     lot. And if the challenging behavior we saw after he told
                     those stories was related to that sadness somehow ...

Here you can see how the assessor contained what she was thinking, listened
carefully, and gently guided Sean's parents with her comments and questions
to begin thinking about an emotional basis for his "bad behavior." This kind
of scaffolding takes focused attention and attunement, and it is not uncommon for assessors to sometimes "go too fast" and to have to back up and
or repair. But by attempting to stay in the parents' ZPD regarding the new
narrative, the assessor helps the system shift in a safe way.

   TA assessors use scaffolding in all phases of TA-C, from Initial Sessions to
Summary/Discussion Sessions. Especially in the later sessions of TA-C, there
is another core concept that is helpful to keep in mind: Levels of
Information.

Levels of Information

In an early exposition of Therapeutic Assessment, Finn (1996) recommended
that assessors consider "Levels of Information" when aspiring to help clients
change their existing narratives via psychological assessment. As shown in
Box 2.2, Levels of Information is a way for assessors to think about self-
verification and disintegration anxiety when working with clients, and to
become empathic to parents' and families' dilemmas of change. This schema
also helps assessors practice scaffolding in various parts of the TA-C process,
with Level 2 Information often specifying where the ZPD is for any given
family system.

Control-Mastery Theory

As Finn (2007) described, TA and TA-C were influenced by a relatively new
psychodynamic model called *Control-Mastery theory* (Weiss, 1993). This
approach posits: (1) clients' problems in living stem from unconscious pathogenic beliefs about themselves that they developed based on previous
experiences, and (2) clients avidly and continuously seek to "disconfirm"
these beliefs in their interactions with others so they can become more independent, happy, and secure. This view is quite different from the earlier
Freudian concept of "repetition compulsion," where people are doomed to
repeat past traumas over and over again until they are remembered and resolved (Laplanche & Pontalis, 2018). Control-Mastery theory is useful in
TA-C in helping assessors and parents view puzzling and troubling behaviors
of children as possible "tests" that the children hope others will "pass,"
thereby disconfirming their pathogenic beliefs. For example, a child may
unconsciously believe: "I am not that important to others and no one will
protect me." The child may then gradually harm herself in an escalating

---

Box 2.2   Levels of Information in TA-C*

Level 1 Information

Information that verifies parents' usual ways of thinking about their child and themselves. Generally parents are not threatened by this information and find it validating and comforting if it is confirmed by the assessor. Parents generally say, "This sounds exactly like my child/me."

Level 2 Information

Information that is slightly different from parents' usual ways of thinking about their child and themselves, but that does not cause a great deal of emotional distress if presented by the assessor. Parents often say, "I've only begun to think about my child/myself this way, but I can see how it fits and is useful."

Level 3 Information

Information that is so novel or different from parents' usual ways of thinking about their child and themselves that they are likely to reject it and/or to feel distressed if it is presented by the assessor. Parents might react saying, "This is absolutely not true of my child or of me!" or "I can't bear to think that what you are saying is true."
    Note: *Adapted from Finn (1996).

---

manner—first making small cuts to her feet, then to her legs, arms, and face—until her parents take note and step in to do something. Another child may believe, "My anger is terrifying and no one can help me control it," and so may fly into anger outbursts secretly hoping that his parents will step in and contain him, thereby demonstrating that they are not shocked and terrified by his anger. By helping parents see their children's unconscious tests of them, assessors can often give parents a way to be more successful in their interactions with children.

Shame

When we aspire to help caregivers develop new, more helpful ways of thinking about themselves and their children, another important potential restraining force we hold in mind is *shame*—an inner sense "that one is fundamentally bad, inadequate, unworthy, or not fully valid" (Mason & Fossum, 1986). Shame is one of the most painful human emotions (Malatesta-Magai, 1991) and it has been called "the sleeper in psycho-pathology" (Lewis, 1987) because so often it is an unrecognized contributor to the problems experienced by clients seeking mental health services.

In the families we see for a TA-C, shame can play an important role in multiple ways:

1. Often, parents and children feel shame about the problems that bring them to seek our help, believing that these difficulties show that they are less worthy or competent than other families. For example, when parents ask, "Why is our child depressed?" they may secretly fear that we will conclude they are inadequate parents and that their child's mood struggles are because of terrible mistakes they have made. Such shame can interfere with their developing new understandings of their child's depression or with learning new ways of being with their child that will alleviate the depression. Children also may believe that they are "bad" because they cannot feel or behave the way their caregivers wish they would, and such feelings may be related to their struggles. For example, many years ago Finn assessed a 12-year-old boy who had tried to commit suicide by putting his head in the family's gas oven. During one assessment session, the boy explained that he had heard his parents fighting about him frequently and believed he was the cause of their unhappiness. Believing everyone would be happier if he were gone, the boy had decided to take his own life.

2. Caregivers' shame can also influence their parenting, which then can have a major influence on children. For example, a mother with severe shame about her own sexuality may react with panic and anger if she finds her child masturbating. The child may then either become inhibited sexually or, sometimes, begin to act out sexually. In another family we know, the parents believed desires for affection and reassur-ance were signs of "neediness" and that everyone should be "strong and independent." They were exasperated with their emotionally sensitive son, who in turn became increasingly anxious and tearful.

3. Shame exists in all cultures that have been studied (Gilbert & Andrews, 1998), but different behaviors and traits are considered socially unac-ceptable depending on the culture. Clinicians working with TA-C need to be sensitive to these issues when working with families from cultural backgrounds different than their own. For example, Guerrero et al. (2011) described the TA-C of an 11-year-old African-American girl, Lanice, and her family. At one point, the Caucasian assessment team was caught off guard when Lanice's mother strongly objected that her daughter was being treated too laxly during the observed testing sessions (e.g., being allowed to lay across the table while she completed the Rorschach). The mother believed Lanice was being taught that she

didn't have to listen to adults and that this was causing her to be more disrespectful at home and school during the assessment, a dangerous outcome for an African-American girl. Fortunately, the assessment team was able to repair this disruption and was more sensitive afterward to the mother wanting Lanice to show respect to adults in authority.

4. As mentioned earlier, an explicit goal of TA-C is to help families develop more coherent, accurate, useful, and *compassionate* stories about their problems in living. Thus, a major focus of every step of TA-C is to help parents and children have less shame. This requires clinicians to be aware of how to avoid eliciting shame in clients and also how to intervene if it arises.

Object Relations Theory and Projective Identification

Object relations theory is a set of psychoanalytic theories developed by Fairbairn (1952), Guntrip (1968), Klein (1976), Winnicott (1958), and others that attempt to explain how early relationships shape the behavior and personality of children, and how families and couples develop and maintain patterns of emotional expression and behaviors. Object relations theory posits that humans develop mental models/images of themselves and of important people in their lives through psychological processes like *splitting* (e.g., seeing yourself or others as "all good" or "all bad"), *projection* (i.e., seeing others as possessing characteristics you cannot accept in yourself), and *introjection* (i.e., coming to see yourself as others see you). For example, in TA-C we sometimes encounter parents who see their children as "selfish" when the children are simply exhibiting an appropriate level of self-focus for their age. To us it often seems that such parents are denying their own egocentrism and attributing it to their children—an example of *projection*. And over time the children may come to believe that they are selfish and increasingly begin to act that way (*introjection*). Another important concept from object relations theory is *projective identification*, which attempts to explain how complementary/reciprocal roles develop within families and couples. The idea is that because it is difficult to integrate/balance certain emotions and traits within ourselves (e.g., the part of us that enjoys working hard and being productive with the part of us that wants to rest and play), some families unconsciously "divide" these complementary traits between different family members, with some members becoming "over-functioning" hard workers, and others "under-functioning" slackers. While not necessarily pathological, projective identification can help explain why some children and parents seem stuck in "role-locks" that they cannot break. This theory also provides guidance about what would be necessary for the family to relate more adaptively. This leads us to a discussion of common relational patterns we have seen among families presenting for TA-C.

Prototypical Patterns among Families Presenting for TA-C

The families who seek Therapeutic Assessments for their children are diverse in many ways, and each is unique, with its own history, challenges, and ways of expressing love and care. As we meet each new family, we find ourselves curious, touched, inspired, and humbled to learn from them and appreciate how they have approached the task of raising children. Nevertheless, over the years we have also noticed certain patterns among the families we have seen, and we found that identifying and thinking about these patterns has proven useful in our work. Our hypotheses about these patterns were influenced by the work of Slipp (1984), an object relations family therapist who wrote extensively about projective identification within families. The prototypes we describe below are simplified versions of Slipp's more detailed models. Before going further, we should also acknowledge that no family ever perfectly "fits" within these prototypes, and many families show a mixture of these patterns. Still, in the rest of this book, we attempt to demonstrate the usefulness of holding these prototypes in mind when practicing TA-C.

Scapegoated Child

In families fitting this pattern the caregivers typically see the child as willfully "bad" and disobedient—often since early in life—although the specific complaints may vary from the child's being angry, impulsive, vengeful, selfish, lazy, untruthful, and/or needy (Figure 2.2). In the classic scapegoating pattern, the parents strongly agree that the child is "the problem," and typical Assessment Questions are some version of "Why is our child so bad?" and "What can we do to control this problem child?" Very often the children do exhibit some kind of acting-out behavior (e.g., angry tantrums, stealing, lying, aggression toward siblings), and careful interviewing of the family often reveals harsh or inconsistent limit setting on the part of caregivers.

How can we understand this family pattern? Object relations theory posits that scapegoating parents are projecting negative traits on the child that come from one or more sources: (1) their own personalities (e.g., a father who is engaged in a secret extra-marital affair accuses his son of being a "liar"), (2) their own families of origin (e.g., a mother who cannot see her own parents' egocentrism and wishes to remain close to them accuses her child of being "selfish"), and/or (3) their partner (e.g., a husband has no apparent anger about his wife's doing little around the house, yet calls his daughter "lazy" when she doesn't pick up her plate after dinner). When parents are united in scapegoating the child, they feel better about themselves, closer to each other, and avoid facing hard realities about their families of origin. The scapegoated child in turn takes in (or "introjects") the parents' negative perceptions, comes to believe them, and acts them out. In this way, the child helps the parents avoid emotions that would be destabilizing, protects the parents' relationship, and keeps the family together.

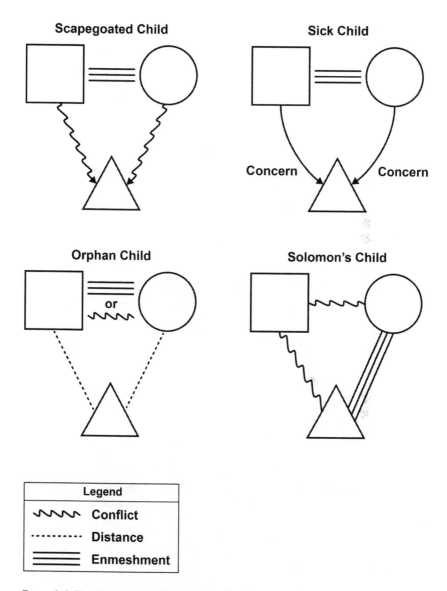

Figure 2.2 Four Prototypes of Families Seeking TA-C.

In our experience, scapegoated children often appear depressed and full of shame on psychological testing (especially performance-based tests) and this fits with the theory that such children are "holding" depression and shame that their parents cannot integrate. As might be expected, on structured rating scales such as the Behavior Assessment System for Children (BASC; Reynolds & Kamphaus, 2015) or the Child Behavior Checklist (CBCL;

Achenbach & Rescorla, 2001), the parents typically describe the child as impulsive, aggressive, selfish, needy, or lacking a conscience. There is some variation, but sometimes, scapegoated children are extremely well-behaved when alone with the assessor, and it is important that assessors not over-emphasize this in discussions with parents (who may feel invalidated). Instead, it is important to look for opportunities to join with parents about the child being difficult, puzzling, or challenging. The most common assessor countertransference in these assessments is to feel compassion for the child and anger at the parents. The most successful approach is typically to use the TA-C process to reframe the child as "sad" or "hurt" instead of "bad," but without blaming the parents for the child's problems. It is very important to take half steps in this work with the parents so they do not become over-whelmed.

Sick Child

In this prototype, parents are typically united in expressing concern about their child who is seen as sick, depressed, fragile, highly sensitive, anxious, and/or in need of special care (Figure 2.2). As with the scapegoated child, the focus of caregivers' attention is typically on the child, but with concern ra-ther than anger. However, there may be anger at other important adults (e.g., teachers, babysitters, coaches) who do not understand how "carefully" the child needs to be treated. Typical Assessment Questions are "How can we help our child be less anxious?" and "How can we help others recognize that our child is sensitive?" These children may show a variety of internalizing symptoms (e.g., generalized anxiety, irrational fears, sleep difficulties, enur-esis) or externalizing behaviors (e.g., temper tantrums), all of which are in-terpreted by the parents as signs of the child's delicate temperament. Typically, the clinician is struck by the parents' inability/refusal to contain the child or set appropriate limits. Sometimes the "sick" child may have an actual medical condition (e.g., asthma, cancer), and careful interviewing may reveal that the family is not following treatment procedures that previously have been recommended and perhaps were effective.

Object relations theory hypothesizes that in this family pattern, parents are projecting their own fears, anxieties, and dependency needs onto the child, and they refrain from setting appropriate limits. Often such parents had harsh, tyrannical, or abusive parents themselves, and in compensation they bend over backward to accommodate their child's needs. This "power va-cuum" frightens children because they don't feel contained and protected. Some react with increased anxiety and fearfulness, often controlling the whole family with their anxiety. For example, a child may need elaborate, lengthy bedtime rituals in order to sleep or special accommodations when-ever asked to leave the house. Other children become strident and grandiose as if begging their parents to contain them, but the parents do not because they see the child as "delicate" and do not wish to be "mean." Typically, the focus on the child as an identified patient also protects the parents from unresolved marital issues.

The major unintegrated affect states in "sick child" families are anger and positive entitlement, and performance-based testing of the children often reveals that they are containing a great deal of anger. The most common countertransference with this family pattern is for assessors to feel frustrated with both parents and children and to wish to "shake" them. Modeling appropriate limit setting with the children in assessment sessions can be very helpful to parents. Also, typically, after testing limits with the assessor in early testing sessions, the children often seem to feel relieved and settle down. The most successful approach is typically to use the TA-C to gradually reframe the child from being "delicate" to being "stronger than is apparent" and "needing containment." As the assessor encourages parents to experiment with being firm, generally they need lots of support. And parents typically feel guilty and need lots of reassurance as they focus more on their own needs.

We should mention that in some cases fitting this pattern, the "sick" child actually is ill, for example, with diabetes, asthma, a physical anomaly, etc. We recognize that it is common and natural for parents of medically ill children to become somewhat overprotective or to lean toward overindulgence. However, we contend that a medical illness alone does not lead to the full "sick child" prototype unless the other psychological factors we mentioned previously are present.

Orphan Child

With this prototype, parents typically seek an assessment at the urging of other important individuals (e.g., teachers, school principals, police) sometimes after their child has dramatically acted out in an aggressive or self-destructive way, such as an incident of public vandalism or a dramatic suicide attempt (Figure 2.2). Other times a previously academically successful child suddenly starts getting failing grades at school. Very often the child was not seen "a problem" before, and may even have been exceptionally independent and high achieving. Parents often seem puzzled and/or exasperated at having to focus on the child, and ask Assessment Questions like "Why did our child behave this way right now?" and "How quickly can we get back to the way things were?" Very often the assessor feels that the parents are overinvolved with each other because they are in a mutually idealizing relationship. At other times, the parents are not focused on the child because they are "at war." In yet other cases, the parents have been greatly distracted by another child in the family with serious medical or mental health problems, or with another ill family member (such as a grandparent) and have not been able to give the referred child enough parenting. Careful interviewing often reveals that the child has been treated as overly adult and independent—left alone for long periods of time or expected to perform self-care activities (e.g., cooking, laundry, caring for younger siblings) that are not typical for his/her age. Orphan children themselves are typically pseudo-mature, i.e., they act much older than their chronological age.

Object relations theory hypothesizes that parents in this family prototype are out of touch with the normal needs of their children for affection, care, and attention—typically because they did not have secure attachments themselves as children. Sometimes parents will explicitly state their beliefs that needing others is a character flaw and that "after a certain age, children should take care of themselves emotionally." With mutually idealizing parents we often find a great emphasis on achievement in the family; the child's past good grades, success in extracurricular activities, etc. have been taken as signs that "everything is fine." Such parents are typically quite caught off-guard when the child sends an important signal that all is not well. Not infrequently, the child has to use increasingly more severe tactics (e.g., from saying she is sad, to cutting, to making a serious suicide gesture) in order to get the parents' attention. With those parents caught in intense marital conflict even dramatic signals from the child may get ignored until an outside party—such as the child's school—insists that the child needs attention.

On formal rating scales, parents fitting this pattern typically rate their child as not having any problems. On standardized testing, the children often show considerable psychological resources (such as high IQ and good reflective capacity); but they appear emotionally over-controlled (e.g., no color determinants on their Rorschach responses). Typically, once the assessor establishes an alliance, these children open up easily and start revealing both their inner distress and the underlying family problems. The most common assessor countertransference is a desire to "adopt" the child and give her affection and care. It is important not to push too quickly for parents to acknowledge the emotional needs the child is bringing in, and to join with how difficult it is for the parents to see the child's distress "because of her excellent psychological resources." Typically, the most successful approach is to use the TA-C to construct a new narrative in which the child is "very capable, but needs more care and attention."

Solomon's Child

The name for this prototype alludes to the story in the Hebrew Bible (1 Kings 3:16-28) of two women who came to King Solomon because they were fighting over which was the mother of an infant child (Figure 2.2). Parents in this situation typically present in open disagreement about how to view and treat their child, asking the assessor to render judgment about "Who is right?" The parents may disagree about whether the child has a psychological problem at all (i.e., "Is this behavior normal or abnormal?"), or often one parent sees the child as "bad" (spoiled, selfish, disobedient) while the other sees the child as "sick" (anxious, depressed, sensitive). Frequently, one parent feels closer to the child (in Western heterosexual families often the other-gender parent) and the second parent feels more distant. Commonly the child acts very differently with each parent, but also the caregivers may show different interpretations/reactions to the same child behaviors. Typical Assessment Questions are those such as, "Does Johnny need more discipline or more affection?" and "Is Susie depressed or manipulative?"

Object relations theory posits that parents in this family configuration are "triangulating" the child, i.e., using the child as a "stand-in" or focus for their own relationship disagreements. For example, a mother may complain that the father is too harsh and cold with the child, while actually the mother feels these things regarding herself but is not assertive enough to say so. Similarly, a father may complain that a mother is "too affectionate and attentive" to the child, when actually he wants more attention from his wife but feels ashamed to ask for it. By arguing about the child, the caregivers focus their disagreements on parenting issues, rather than on the underlying personal and/or marital issues that are more frightening, shameful, or overwhelming. And by maintaining a self-righteous position with each other, the parents each avoid feeling insecure and maintain their self-esteem.

On formal rating scales, parents fitting this pattern often present wildly different views of the child, typically with one seeing the child as internalizing and the other seeing the child as manipulative and/or externalizing. On psychological testing, these children often show signs of disorganized attachment, with a great deal of inner confusion, overwhelming emotions, and distrust of others. They can be difficult to form alliances with until they understand that the assessor is not going to take sides with one parent against the other. Then the children often feel relief and are able to reveal how much they feel caught in the middle of their parents. Since the typical assessor countertransference is to feel triangulated by the parents also, this often helps the assessor find empathy for the child. In general, the goal in TA-C with these families is for the assessor to maintain an alliance with each parent, help both understand how harmful their triangulation is to the child, and use the assessment to weave the narrative that, "Both of you are right! Johnny needs both more affection *and* more firmness." The parents may then be referred for parenting consultation, emphasizing that the child needs the parents to be "on the same page" in how they handle them. Often, we also suggest that each parent has strengths and skills in the way they interact with the child that the other can learn from.

Research on TA-C

As discussed earlier, TA-C is a relatively recent development. However, there already are multiple research studies that have examined its efficacy and feasibility.

Initial Pilot Study of TA-C

The first study was published over ten years ago by two authors of this book, Deborah Tharinger and Stephen Finn, with other colleagues (Tharinger et al., 2009). It had the modest goal of following a group of children and families as they participated in a TA-C, to see if the positive shifts previously reported in published case studies could be documented in a larger clinical sample. The 14 families included 10 boys and 4 girls aged 8–11, all drawn from the waiting list of a local community mental health center. All the families had sought assistance because the children had moderate to severe social, emotional, or behavioral concerns. Ten children were White and four were of mixed ethnicity.

The TAs consisted of eight 1.5-hour sessions conducted approximately weekly over three months, for an average of 12 hours of direct service. The clinicians for each case were two graduate students in the Therapeutic Assessment Project (TAP) at the University of Texas at Austin (described earlier in the chapter). The two-assessor model of TA-C was used. For sessions focused on the parents, both assessors attended. For testing sessions, one assessor worked with the child while the other sat with the parents behind the mirror or in an adjacent room with a video feed to be available to the parents in discussing their observations. All assessors were being trained in TA-C and were closely supervised by Deborah Tharinger, Stephen Finn, and Marita Frackowiak (among this book's co-authors). The psychological tests used in the TA-C were tailored to each case, and included intellectual and psycho-educational tests and a variety of self-report and performance-based personality measures. Caregivers sat behind a one-way mirror with one of the assessors during the child assessment sessions or watched a live video stream from another room. All of the TAs included a FIS, a Summary/Discussion Session with the caregivers, and the presentation of an individualized fable to the child. There were no Follow-up Sessions as families were promised immediate service after the TA-C at the community mental health center from which they were referred. All of the 14 families completed the TA-C.

Table 2.1 summarizes the major findings of the study. As you can see, consistent with hypotheses derived from published case studies, the eight-session TA-C was accompanied by a significant decrease in child symptomatology, as reported by both mothers and children. Also, both mothers and children said their families were functioning significantly better after the TA-C, as reflected in their ratings on a standardized measure of family cohesion, conflict, and communication. Consistent with the theory that TA-C leads to increased parental empathy and a new "story" about the child, mothers showed greatly reduced negative feelings about their child and moderately increased positive feelings. Last, all the mothers expressed a high degree of satisfaction with the TA-C process, with several making comments that it was "life changing" and "a real blessing." Although this study examined a relatively small sample and it lacks a control group (which would eliminate alternative therapeutic factors such as attention alone or spontaneous remission), it was important in being the first study to document that TA-C can be effective and acceptable to children and families with moderate to severe mental health challenges who are seeking help in a real-life clinical setting. The study is also noteworthy in suggesting that

Table 2.1 Major Results of the Tharinger et al. (2009) Pilot Study of TA-C

Variable	Measure	Result	Effect Size[a]
Mothers' Satisfaction with the Assessment	CSQ-R[b]	Very High	–
Mothers' Ratings of Child Symptomatology Pre- to Post-Assessment	BASC-PRS-C[c]	Mild/Moderate Decrease	$d = .36$
Mothers' Ratings of Family Functioning Pre- to Post-Assessment	SRMFF[d]	Mild/Moderate Increase	$d = .38$
Mothers' Reported Negative Feelings about Child, Pre- to Post-Assessment	PPNEC[e]	Large Decrease	$d = 1.18$
Mothers' Reported Positive Feelings about Child, Pre- to Post-Assessment	PPNEC[e]	Moderate Increase	$d = .58$
Children's Self-ratings of Depression and Maladjustment, Pre- to Post-Assessment	BASC-SRP-C[f]	Large Decrease	$d = .74$
Children's Ratings of Family Functioning Pre- to Post-Assessment	SRMFF-CR[g]	Moderate Increase	$d = .50$

Notes

a Cohen's d (1992).
b Client Satisfaction Questionnaire-Revised (Larsen et al., 1979).
c Behavioral Assessment System for Children-Parent Report Scales-Child (Reynolds & Kamphaus, 2004).
d Self-Report Measure of Family Functioning (Bloom, 1985).
e Parents' Positive and Negative Emotions about Their Child (Tharinger, 2007).
f Behavioral Assessment System for Children-Self Report of Personality-Child (Reynolds & Kamphaus, 2004).
g Self-Report Measure of Family Functioning-Child, Revised (Stark, 2002).

relatively un-experienced clinicians (graduate students) working under close supervision can successfully implement TA-C.

Time-Series Studies of TA-C

When many people imagine research testing a therapeutic intervention, they immediately think of studies that compare outcomes for participants randomly assigned to two groups—an "experimental" group that receives the therapy being tested (e.g., a new medication) and a "control" group that does not (who may receive a placebo or a previously existing medication). Such studies are called *randomized controlled trials* (RCTs), and many experts consider them to be the gold standard method for examining the efficacy of a new intervention.

There is another type of outcome research that also is highly respected, and that has certain benefits not found in RCTs. In these studies, called *time-series analyses*, subjects receiving an intervention serve as their *own* controls (Borckardt et al., 2008). That is, the subjects are followed closely on relevant outcome variables for some length of time *before* the intervention is conducted (the baseline), *while* the treatment is occurring (the intervention), and for a period *after* the treatment has stopped (the follow-up). If the significant therapeutic change occurs while the intervention is happening (as compared to the baseline) these positive results are unlikely to be due to spontaneous remission or regression to the mean, and it is likely safe to conclude that the intervention is effective (Smith, 2012). Besides being less costly than RCTs (because they typically involve fewer subjects), time-series studies have the advantage of allowing one to see *when* and *how* change occurs in response to an intervention, which often provides important insights into its therapeutic factors. At the time this book is being prepared, there are three published time-series studies that have greatly advanced our knowledge of and our confidence in TA-C; all were led by J.D. Smith, a psychotherapy researcher who has special interest and expertise in time-series analysis and has been trained in TA-C.

Smith et al. (2009)

This study examined the TA of a nine-year-old boy, his biological mother, and stepfather. The presenting issue was the boy's aggressive and angry behavior at home. The clinical picture closely fit the prototype of the "Scapegoated Child" as reflected in parents' Assessment Questions ("Why is he so angry?" "Where does his anger come from?" "Why does he direct it at mother?"). The two-assessor model was used, with parents and one assessor observing over a video link from an adjacent room while the other assessor interacted with the boy. Starting immediately after the Initial Session, the parents made daily ratings of the boy's problematic behaviors, giving an eight-day baseline period. Parents continued their ratings over the 62 days of the intervention phase, which involved eight 2-hour clinical sessions: three testing sessions, a developmental history session with parents alone, two FISs, a Summary/Discussion Session with parents, and a Summary/Discussion Session with the child and parents to share the therapeutic fable. A Follow-up Session was held 40 days later. The boy and parents also completed the BASC-2 (Reynolds & Kamphaus, 2004) at the beginning of each clinical session, and at the Follow-up Session parents took an early version of the Parent Experience of Assessment Scale (PEAS; Austin et al., 2018), an assessment feedback/satisfaction form for parents (discussed in Chapter 9).

In brief, the time series analysis of the parents' daily ratings documented a substantial decline in the boy's anger and acting-out behavior over the course of the TA, and these continued to decrease over the follow-up phase. There were some statistical difficulties analyzing the daily ratings because of missing data (the boy was separated from the parents during the follow-up interval) and the low frequency of some of the variables measured (e.g., number of angry outbursts daily). Still, there was a clear decrease in the boy's aggressive behavior over the course of the TA-C. Also, the results of the repeated administration of the child and parent BASC-2 were very useful and indicated a change from many scales being in the clinical range at baseline to only one scale rated by the stepfather being in the clinical range at follow-up. This new view of the child by the parents fit with the results of their PEAS, which showed that both were very pleased with the outcome and process of the TA. Of note, as in the Tharinger et al. (2009) study, the assessors in this study were psychology graduate students without a great deal of clinical experience, working under close supervision.

As mentioned earlier, one of the most useful aspects of the time-series design is that one can track when change occurs during the course of an intervention. With this family, while some improvements were noted during the testing sessions, the first FIS seemed highly clinically significant. This meeting was very moving and involved the parents (with support from the assessors) seeing their role in one of the boy's angry outbursts and then making a repair with him. Post hoc analyses of the daily ratings and BASC-2 scores showed a substantial improvement in the family's functioning immediately after the family session. This particular finding provided the inspiration for a later time-series study we discuss later.

Smith et al. (2010)

The next TA-C study published by Smith et al. followed three pre-adolescent boys and their families as each participated in a nine- or ten-session TA-C conducted by one graduate student assessor. Besides including three cases, this study was unique in that all the boys met the DSM-IV diagnostic criteria for oppositional defiant disorder (ODD). All received the same battery of tests as part of the TA-C, and parents watched over a video link in another room, but without an assessor present. Instead, "mini-consultations" were done with the parents after each of the child testing sessions. All assessments included a FIS, Summary/Discussion Sessions with parents, Feedback/Fable Sessions with the children and parents, and two-month Follow-up Sessions. Outcome variables were parents' daily ratings of problem behaviors during the baseline period (10–49 days), intervention phase (60–70 days), and follow-up period (60–70 days), as well as the parents' and boys' ratings on the BASC-2 at each clinical session. At the end of the Follow-up Session, all parents also completed the PEAS.

The original research report of this study is well worth reading and contains many interesting details about the three families and their TA-Cs. To summarize, all three boys showed clear and significant improvements in their ODD symptoms over the course of the TA-C, with most of the BASC-2 scales going from being clinically significant at baseline to being in the normal range at follow-up. Again, on the PEAS all parents rated themselves at follow-up as highly satisfied with the TA-Cs. What is incredibly interesting about this study, however, is that the three boys and families showed different trajectories of change. Two of the families showed gradual, steady improvement over the course of the TA-Cs, which was then maintained and even increased over the follow-up phase. In contrast, the third family showed only small positive changes over the intervention phase, but a very large change soon after the TA-C was completed, with improvement continuing over the follow-up period. Thus, while TA-C was associated with substantial positive changes in all the families, it appeared that there might be different mechanisms of change in the three families. Again, these kinds of findings regarding the timing of change would never come to light in an RCT and are best documented by time-series studies.

Smith et al. (2011)

The third published time-series study of TA-C focused on the importance of the FIS in producing change. The one-assessor TA-C model was used with the parents observing over a video link to another room. As reported earlier, in their post hoc analyses, Smith et al. (2009) noted a big shift in the daily ratings of the nine-year-old client's aggressive behavior following the FIS with his mother and stepfather. That particular session seemed to be a "tipping point" in the parents' shifting their narrative from one where the boy was "hateful and bad" to a more systemic narrative that included the parents' own role in his angry escalations. Intrigued by this finding, Smith et al. (2011) designed a study where they planned in advance to test the importance of the FIS.

The clients were a 12-year-old boy and his father. The parents were married and lived together but the mother was reportedly unable to participate in the TA-C. The presenting picture closely resembled the "sick child" prototype described earlier. The boy had academic and social problems at school and low self-esteem. The father was very close to the boy and attributed the boy's struggles to his being "gifted" intellectually, bored at school, and creating jealousy in the other children because of his intelligence. In fact, as the testing took place it became gradually clear that the boy had only average intelligence, displayed an overly aggrandized self-image in part due to his father's idealization of him, yet underneath had a great deal of anxiety and shame. It became evident that the boy often rushed through tasks, not giving his best effort, because he expected to be successful without really trying. In the family session, with coaching from the assessor, the father was able to participate in giving realistic feedback to the boy about his intellectual abilities. The boy seemed relieved. The father then coached the boy through the Bender Gestalt Test, containing his tendency to rush, asking more of him, and not giving overly positive feedback. A Summary/Discussion Session with the father followed, as well as a session with the boy and father where the fable was presented, and a Follow-up Session 60 days later. At the Follow-up Session, it was clear that the TA-C had made a very positive impact; the boy was doing better both in school and in his peer relationships, and the father had a better relationship with the boy that was both firm and positive. Both attributed the positive shifts to the TA-C.

The time-series analysis of the boy's daily problematic behaviors confirmed the substantial improvement during the follow-up period. It also showed a very interesting trajectory of change. In this case, there was actually a slight *worsening* of the problem behaviors during the early phase of the intervention period, perhaps related to the undoing of defensive grandiosity in both the boy and the father. But there was substantial improvement in the family functioning after the FIS, and this continued steadily afterward, especially during the follow-up. This provided more evidence of the efficacy of TA-C overall, and in particular, of the potential therapeutic power of FIS.

The Therapeutic Power of Fables

The next study examined a different specific component of TA-C: the provision of a feedback fable to the child and parents at the end of a psychological assessment. Tharinger and Pilgrim (2011) were interested in the impact of child fables on families apart from the rest of the TA-C model. Hence, they approached a well-respected clinic that did traditional neuropsychological assessments of children and proposed a research collaboration. Licensed psychologists working for the clinic conducted their typical complete neuropsychological assessments on 32 children, including a parent feedback session. The children (23 boys and 9 girls with an average age of 9) had been referred for a variety of concerns, including academic difficulties, attention problems and hyperactivity, and social/emotional issues. A very complete standard battery of cognitive and neuropsychological tests was used, all administered in one day by a clinic psychometrist. One to three weeks following the parent feedback session, each child and one of the parents voluntarily returned for a research session of 45–60 minutes. They were assigned to two groups. The *experimental group* received an individualized feedback fable based on the assessment results that had been written by the assessing psychometrist and one of the researchers. Following, dependent measures were administered. Parents completed the PEAS and the Client Satisfaction Questionnaire-8 (CSQ-8; Larsen et al. 1979), and the children completed the Child Experience of Assessment Scale (CEAS; Tharinger & Pilgrim, 2008). (The CEAS is similar to the PEAS but with items that are appropriate for children.) The *comparison group* completed the dependent measures first and *then* were presented with the child fable, which they were anticipating.

The researchers found that clients rated their assessment experiences as significantly better after they were given the feedback fables. Children in the experimental group said they learned more, felt closer to the assessor, felt more included in the assessment, and believed their parents learned more about them than did children in the comparison group. Parents whose children received fables were significantly more satisfied with the assessments, felt their children were closer and better understood by the assessor, and experienced more collaboration. This study is important in suggesting that even if one is unable to implement the full TA-C model, just adding a feedback fable for children at the end of an assessment has a significant impact on both children and parents.

A Study of Modified CTA with Children

A group of Swedish researchers (Hansson et al., 2016) studied the efficacy of a modified TA-C approach that included the collection of Assessment Questions from parents, a comprehensive standardized neuropsychological assessment battery, Extended Inquiries of certain tests with children, parent feedback sessions, written feedback to parents, and feedback to the child, sometimes involving a feedback fable. In almost all cases parents did not observe the child testing sessions, and none of the assessments included a FIS. Clients were drawn from families presenting at a public child and adolescent psychiatric clinic in Sweden, and the children ranged in age from 9 to 16 years. An interesting feature of this study is that besides the CTA group (N = 11) there were two comparison groups: one (N = 11) where parents received five 90-minute support sessions, and another (N = 9) where no services were given but outcome measures were collected. The CTA group had a six-month follow-up session while the others did not. The dependent variables were the children's ratings on the Beck Youth Inventories (BYI; Beck et al., 2001) expressed both as their scores on the instrument's scales (Depression, Anxiety, Self-Concept, Anger, and Disruptive Behavior) and also the number of clinically significant psychiatric symptoms (from 0 to 20) that they endorsed. Outcome data were not collected from parents.

Interestingly children in all three groups showed significantly lower scores on the BYI scales at the end of their assessments, and there were no differences between the CTA group and the two control groups. However, when examining the number of clinically significant symptoms the children endorsed, the CTA showed a very large drop in the six months following the assessment. This is suggestive that CTA had a positive impact, but the data are difficult to interpret because the other two groups were not followed up. The lack of outcome data from parents was also a limitation. And there is one other feature of the study that makes the results difficult to interpret; the clients were not randomly assigned to the three conditions, but were allowed to volunteer for which protocol they preferred. It is possible that clients who were more open to collaboration chose the CTA protocol, which could greatly have impacted the results.

Still, in our minds, the study of Hansson et al. (2016) suggests an important possible finding: even when child psychological assessment aspires to be collaborative, if it is primarily child-focused and does not include systemic aspects of the TA-C model (i.e., parent observation of child testing, a FIS, and a systemic case conceptualization), it may not be that effective in improving family functioning.

Research on TA-C: Conclusions

Although research on TA-C is still in its beginning stages, there is currently enough evidence to establish that TA-C is an effective brief intervention for various types of families struggling with different kinds of child/family problems. In all existing studies, caregivers were very pleased with the experience of TA-C, suggesting that the model's attention to respectful collaboration is quite successful in building a therapeutic alliance. There is also evidence that TA-C is accompanied by decreases in child symptomatology, as rated by both parents and children, and in improvements in family functioning as perceived by both children and parents. As has been noted in research on other versions of TA (e.g., with adult clients), the effects of TA-C appear to persist and even grow after the assessment is completed, perhaps even as far out as six months. And as best as we can tell, TA-C appears to be effective both for children with internalizing problems and those with externalizing problems. The specific therapeutic mechanisms of TA are still not understood, and the trajectory of change can be different between particular families. However, there is evidence that FISs often provide an important tipping point in client change, and that even if no other features of TA-C are used, the provision of written feedback in the form of a fable can enhance assessment experiences for both children and parents.

Clearly, more research needs to be done, both randomized control trials and time-series analyses. These two types of research appear to complement each other well, and both can contribute to our knowledge. It would be useful to have studies that focus on clients from diverse populations, as well as research that examines the therapeutic impact of other specific features of TA-C (e.g., gathering Assessment Questions, parent observation of child testing, and parent feedback letters).

We now turn to an in-depth exposition of the first phase of TA-C and introduce you to the case study that we will follow across all five phases.

References

Achenbach, T. M., & Rescorla, L. A. (2001). *Manual for the ASEBA school-age forms & profiles.* Burlington, VT: University of Vermont.

Adler, J. M. (2012). Living into the story: Agency and coherence in a longitudinal study of narrative identity development and mental health over the course of psychotherapy. *Journal of Personality and Social Psychology, 102,* 367–389.

Ainsworth, M. D. S. (1967). *Infancy in Uganda: Infant care and the growth of love.* Baltimore: Johns Hopkins University Press.

Allen, J. G. (1981). The clinical psychologist as a diagnostic consultant. *Bulletin of the Menninger Clinic, 45*(3), 247–258.

Allen, J. G., Fonagy, P., & Bateman, A. W. (2008). *Mentalizing in clinical practice.* Washington, DC: American Psychiatric Publishing.

Anda, R. F., Feletti, V. J., Bremner, J. D., Walker, J. D., Whitfield, C., Perry, B. D., Dube, S. R., & Giles, W. H. (2006). The enduring effects of abuse and related adverse experiences in childhood. *European Archives of Psychiatry and Clinical Neuroscience, 256,* 174–186.

Aronow, E., & Reznikoff, M. (1971). Application of projective tests to psychotherapy: A case study. *Journal of Personality Assessment, 35,* 379–393.

Aschieri, F., Fantini, F., & Bertrando, P. (2012). Therapeutic Assessment with children in family therapy. *Australian and New Zealand Journal of Family Therapy, 33*(4), 285–298.

Austin, C. A., Finn, S. F., Keith, T. Z., Tharinger, D. J., & Fernando, A. D. (2018). The Parent Experience of Assessment Scale (PEAS): Development and relation to parent satisfaction. *Assessment, 25*(7), 929–941.

Austin, C. A., Krumholz, L. S., & Tharinger, D. J. (2012). Therapeutic Assessment with an adolescent. Choosing connections over substances. *Journal of Personality Assessment, 94,* 571–585.

Beck, J. S., Beck, A. T., & Jolly, J. (2001). *Manual for the Beck youth inventories of emotional and social impairment.* San Antonio, TX: The Psychological Corporation.

Bellak, L. (1951). *A guide to the interpretation of the Thematic Apperception Test* (revised). New York: Psychological Corporation.

Berg, M. (1985). The feedback process in diagnostic psychological testing. *Bulletin of the Menninger Clinic, 49*(1), 52–69.

Bettelheim, B. (1947). Self-interpretation of fantasy: The Thematic Apperception Test as an educational and therapeutic device. *American Journal of Orthopsychiatry, 17*(1), 80–100.

Blodgett, C., & Lanigan, J. D. (2018). The association between adverse childhood experience (ACE) and school success in elementary school children. *School Psychology Quarterly, 33*(1), 137–146.

Bloom, B. (1985). A factor analysis of self-report measures of family functioning. *Family Process, 24,* 225–239.

Borckard, J. J., Nash, M. R., Murphy, M. D., Moore, M., Shaw, D., & O'Neil, P. (2008). Clinical practice as natural laboratory psychotherapy research: A guide to case-based time-series analysis. *American Psychologist, 63*(2), 77–95.

Bowlby, J. (1969). *Attachment and loss, vol. 1: Attachment.* New York: Basic Books.

Bruner, J. S. (1978). The role of dialogue in language acquisition. In A. Sinclair, R. J. Jarvelle, & W. J. M. Levelt (Eds.), *The child's concept of language.* New York: Springer-Verlag.

Dana, R. H. (1982). Communication of assessment findings. In R. H. Dana (Ed.), *A human science model for personality assessment with projective techniques.* Springfield, IL: Charles C. Thomas.

Dana, R. H. (1993). *Multicultural assessment perspectives for professional psychology.* Needham Heights, MA: Allyn & Bacon.

Dana, R. H. (1997). *Understanding cultural identity in intervention and assessment.* Thousand Oaks, CA: Sage.

Fairbairn, W. R. D. (1952). *An object relations theory of the personality.* New York: Basic Books.

Fantini, F., Aschieri, F., & Bertrando, P. (2013). "Is our daughter crazy or bad?" A case study of Therapeutic Assessment with Children. *Contemporary Family Therapy, 35*(4), 731–744.

Feldman, R. S. (2014). *Discovering the lifespan* (3rd ed). New York, NY: Pearson.

Finn, S. E. (1996). *A manual for using the MMPI-2 as a therapeutic intervention.* Minneapolis: University of Minnesota Press.

Finn, S. E. (2007). *In our clients' shoes: Theory and techniques of Therapeutic Assessment.* Mawah, NJ: Erlbaum.

Finn, S. E. (2008, March). *Empathy, intersubjectivity, and the longing to be known: Why personality assessment works.* Paper presented at the annual meeting of the Society for Personality Assessment, New Orleans, LA, as part of a symposium, "Conceptual Innovations in Personality Assessment," C. G. Overton, Chair.

Finn, S. E. (2009). Core values of Therapeutic Assessment. Downloaded from www.therapeuticassessment.com on December 1, 2009.

Finn, S. E. (2011). Therapeutic Assessment "on the front lines": Comment on articles from WestCoast Children's Clinic. *Journal of Personality Assessment, 93*(1), 23–25.

Finn, S. E. (2016). Using Therapeutic Assessment in psychological assessments required for sex reassignment surgery. In V. Brabender & J. L. Mihura (Eds.), *Handbook of gender and sexuality in psychological assessment* (pp. 511–533). New York, NY: Routledge.

Finn, S. E., Fischer, C. T., & Handler, L. (2012). Collaborative/Therapeutic Assessment: Basic concepts, history, and research. In S. E. Finn, C. T. Fischer, & L. Handler (Eds.), *Collaborative/Therapeutic Assessment: A case book and guide* (pp. 1–24). Hoboken, NJ: Wiley.

Finn, S. E., & Martin, H. (1997). Therapeutic Assessment with the MMPI-2 in managed health care. In J. N. Butcher (Ed.), *Objective psychological assessment in managed health care: A practitioner's guide* (pp. 131–152). Oxford: Oxford University Press.

Finn, S. E., & Tonsager, M. E. (1992). Therapeutic effects of providing MMPI-2 test feedback to college students awaiting therapy. *Psychological Assessment, 4,* 278–287.

Finn, S. E., & Tonsager, M. E. (1997). Information-gathering and therapeutic models of assessment: Complementary paradigms. *Psychological Assessment, 9,* 374–385.

Fischer, C. T. (1970). The testee as co-evaluator. *Journal of Counseling Psychology, 17,* 70–76.

Fischer, C. T. (1985/1994). *Individualizing psychological assessment.* Mawah, NJ: Routledge.

Fulmer, R. H., Cohen, S., & Moncao, G. (1985). Using psychological assessment in structural family therapy. *Journal of Learning Disabilities, 18*(3), 145–150.

Gart, N., Zamora, I., & Williams, M. E. (2016). Parallel models of assessment: Infant mental health and Therapeutic Assessment models intersect through early childhood case studies. *Infant Mental Health Journal, 37*(4), 452–465.

George, C., & West, M. (2012). *The adult attachment projective picture system: Attachment theory and assessment in adults.* New York: Guilford.

Gilbert, P., & Andrews, B. (1998). *Shame: Interpersonal behavior, psychopathology, and culture*. London: Oxford.

Guerrero, B., Lipkind, J., & Rosenberg, A. (2011). Why did she put nail polish in my drink? Applying the Therapeutic Assessment model with an African American foster child in a community mental health setting. *Journal of Personality Assessment, 93*, 7–15.

Guntrip, H. (1968). *Schizoid phenomena, object relations, and the self*. London: Routledge.

Hamilton, A. M., Fowler, J. L., Hersh, B., Hall, C., Finn, S. E., Tharinger, D. J., Parton, V., Stahl, K., & Arora, P. (2009). "Why won't my parents help me?" Therapeutic Assessment of a child and her family. *Journal of Personality Assessment, 91*, 108–120.

Handler, L. (2007). The use of therapeutic assessment with children and adolescents. In S. Smith & L. Handler (Eds.), *Clinical assessment of children and adolescents: A practitioner's guide* (pp. 53–72). Mahwah, NJ: Erlbaum & Associates.

Handler, L. (2012). Collaborative storytelling with children: An unruly six-year-old boy. In S. E. Finn, C. T. Fischer, & L. Handler (Eds.), *Collaborative/Therapeutic Assessment: A case book and guide* (pp. 243–266). Hoboken, NJ: Wiley.

Hansson, A., Hansson, L., Danielsson, I., & Domellöf, E. (2016). Short- and long-term effects of child neuropsychological assessment with a collaborative and therapeutic approach: A preliminary study. *Applied Neuropsychology: Child, 5*(2), 97–106.

Harrower, M. (1956). Projective counseling—A psychotherapeutic technique. *American Journal of Psychotherapy, 10*(1), 74–86.

Haydel, M. E., Mercer, B. L., & Rosenblatt, E. (2011). Training assessors in Therapeutic Assessment. *Journal of Personality Assessment, 93*, 16–22.

Hecker, L. L., & Wetchler, J. L. (2003). *An introduction to marriage and family therapy*. New York: Hayworth Press.

Howe, D. (2011). *Attachment across the lifecourse: A brief introduction*. London: Palgrave.

Kamphuis, J. H., & Finn, S. E. (2019). Therapeutic Assessment in personality disorders: Toward the restoration of epistemic trust. *Journal of Personality Assessment, 101*(6), 662–674.

Klein, M. (1976). *Love, guilt, & reparation*. New York: Random House.

Kohut, H. (1984). *How does analysis cure?* Chicago: University of Chicago Press.

Laplanche, J., & Pontalis, J. B. (2018). *Compulsion to repeat: The language of psychoanalysis*. Abington-on-Thames: Routledge.

Larsen, D. L., Attkisson, C. C., Hargreaves, W. A., & Nguyen, T. D. (1979). Assessment of client/patient satisfaction: Development of a general scale. *Evaluation and Program Planning, 2*, 197–207.

Lewis, H. B. (1987). *The role of shame in symptom formation*. Hillsdale, NJ: Erlbaum.

Lipkind, J., & Mercer, B. L. (2019). Integrating Therapeutic Assessment and community mental health. *The TA Connection, 7*(2), 10–16.

Luborsky, L. (1953). Self-interpretation of the TAT as a clinical technique. *Journal of Projective Techniques, 17*, 217–223.

Macdonald, H., & Hobza, C. (2016). Collaborative assessment and social justice. In B. L. Mercer, T. Fong, & E. Rosenblatt, E. (Eds.), *Assessing children in the urban community* (pp. 69–78). New York, NY: Routledge.

Malatesta-Magai, C. (1991). Emotional socialization: Its role in personality and developmental psychopathology. In D. Cicchetti & S. L. Toth (Eds.), *Internalizing and externalizing expressions of dysfunction: Rochester symposium on developmental psychopathology*, Vol. 2 (pp. 203–224). Hillsdale, NJ: Erlbaum.

Martin, H. (2018). Collaborative/Therapeutic Assessment and diversity: The complexity of being human. In S. R. Smith & R. Krishnamurthy (Eds.), *Diversity sensitivity personality assessment* (pp. 278–293). New York: Routledge.

Mason, M. J., & Fossum, M. A. (1986). *Facing shame: Families in recovery*. New York: Norton.

McGoldrick, M., Carter, B., & Garcia-Preto, N. (2010). *The expanded family life cycle: Individual, family, and social perspectives*. Boston: Allyn and Bacon.

McNally, R. J. (1993). Stressors that produce PTSD in children. In J. R. T. Davidson & E. B. Foa (Eds.), *PTSD: DSM-IV and beyond* (pp. 57–74). Washington, DC: American Psychiatric Press.

Mercer, B. L. (2011). Psychological assessment of children in a community mental health clinic. *Journal of Personality Assessment, 93*, 1–6.

Mercer, B. L. (2017). Making unbearable feedback bearable: You can't "half-ass" attachment. *The TA Connection, 5*(1), 14–18.

Mercer, B. L., Fong, T., & Rosenblatt, E. (Eds.) (2016). *Assessing children in the urban community*. New York, NY: Routledge.

Middelberg, C. V. (2001). Projective identification in common couple dances. *Journal of Marital and Family Therapy, 27*(3), 341–352.

Mosak, H., & Gushurst, R. (1972). Some therapeutic uses of psychological testing. *American Journal of Psychotherapy, 26*, 539–546.

Murray, H. A. (1943). *Thematic Apperception Test manual*. Cambridge, MA: Harvard University Press.

Mutchnick, M. G., & Handler, L. (2002). Once upon a time …: Therapeutic interactive stories. *The Humanistic Psychologist, 30*, 75–84.

Papp, P. (1994). *The process of change*. New York: Guilford.

Parritz, R. H., & Troy, M. F. (2017). *Disorders of childhood: Development and psychopathology* (3rd ed). Boston, MA: Cengage Learning.

Plumb, J. L., Bush, K. A., & Kersevich, S. E. (2016). Trauma-sensitive schools: An evidence-based approach. *School Social Work Journal, 40*(2), 37–60.

Pollak, J. M. (1988). The feedback process with parents in child and adolescent psychological assessment. *Psychology in the Schools, 25*, 143–153.

Pruyser, P. W. (1979). The diagnostic process: Touchstone of medicine's values. In W. R. Rogers & D. Barnard (Eds.), *Nourishing the humanistic in medicine: Interactions with the social sciences* (pp. 245–261). Pittsburgh: University of Pittsburgh Press.

Purves, C. (2002). Collaborative assessment with involuntary populations: Foster children and their mothers. *The Humanistic Psychologist, 30*, 164–174.

Purves, C. (2012). Collaborative Assessment of a child in foster care: New understanding of bad behavior. In S. E. Finn, C. T. Fischer, & L. Handler (Eds.), *Collaborative/Therapeutic Assessment: A casebook and guide* (pp. 291–310). New York: Wiley.

Purves, C. (2017). Collaborative Assessment with adolescents in juvenile hall and group homes. *The TA Connection, 5*(2), 13–17.

Reynolds, C. R., & Kamphaus, R. W. (1992). *Behavior Assessment System for Children*. Circle Pines, MN: American Guidance Service.

Reynolds, C. R., & Kamphaus, R. W. (2004). *BASC-2: Behavior Assessment System for Children* (2nd ed.). Circle Pines, MN: AGS Publishing.

Reynolds, C. R., & Kamphaus, R. W. (2015). *Behavior Assessment System for Children* (3rd ed.). Bloomington: Pearson.

Rosenberg, A., Almeida, A., & Macdonald, H. (2012). Crossing the cultural divide: Issues in translation, mistrust, and co-creation of meaning in cross-cultural Therapeutic Assessment. *Journal of Personality Assessment, 94*(3), 223–231.

Schore, A. N. (2001). Effects of a secure attachment relationship on right brain development, affect regulation, and infant mental health. *Infant Mental Health Journal, 22*(1), 7–66.

Slipp, S. (1984). *Object relations: A dynamic bridge between individual and family treatment.* New York: Jason Aronson.

Smith, J. D. (2012). Single-case experimental designs: A systematic review of published research and current standards. *Psychological Methods, 17*(4), 510–550.

Smith, J. D. (2016). Introduction to the special section on cultural considerations in Collaborative and Therapeutic Assessment. *Journal of Personality Assessment, 98*(6), 563–566.

Smith, J. D., Handler, L., & Nash, M. R. (2010). Therapeutic Assessment with preadolescent boys with oppositional defiant disorder: A replicated single-case time-series design. *Psychological Assessment, 22*(3), 593–602.

Smith, J. D., Nicholas, C. R. N., Handler, L., & Nash, M. R. (2011). Examining the potential impact of a family session in Therapeutic Assessment: A single-case experiment. *Journal of Personality Assessment, 93*(3), 204–212.

Smith, J. D., Wolf, N. J., Handler, L., & Nash, M. R. (2009). Testing the effectiveness of family Therapeutic Assessment: A case study using a time-series design. *Journal of Personality Assessment, 91*(6), 518–536.

Sroufe, L. A. (1996). *Emotional development: The organization of emotional life in the early years.* New York: Cambridge University Press.

Stark, K. D. (2002). *The self-report measure of family functioning–child revised.* Unpublished manuscript, University of Texas at Austin.

Swann, W. B., Jr. (1996). *Self-traps: The elusive quest for higher self-esteem.* New York: Freeman.

Swann, W. B., Jr. (1997). The trouble with change: Self-verification and allegiance to the self. *Psychological Science, 8,* 177–180.

Teicher, M. H. (2000). Wounds that time wouldn't heal: The neurobiology of childhood abuse. *Cerebrum, 2,* 50–67.

Tharinger, D. J. (2007). *Parents' positive and negative emotions about their child.* Unpublished manuscript. University of Texas at Austin.

Tharinger, D. J., Christopher, G., & Matson, M. (2011). Play, playfulness, and creative expression in Therapeutic Assessment with children. In S. W. Russ & L. N. Niec (Eds.), *An evidence-based approach to play in intervention and prevention: Integrating developmental and clinical science* (pp. 109–148). New York: Guilford Press.

Tharinger, D. J., Finn, S. E., Arora, P., Judd-Glossy, L., Ihorn, S. M., & Wan, J. T. (2012). Therapeutic Assessment with children: Intervening with parents "behind the mirror". *Journal of Personality Assessment, 94,* 111–123.

Tharinger, D. J., Finn, S. E., Austin, C., Gentry, L., Bailey, E., Parton, V., & Fisher, M. (2008). Family sessions in psychological assessment with children: Goals, techniques, and clinical utility. *Journal of Personality Assessment, 90,* 547–558.

Tharinger, D. J., Finn, S. E., Gentry, L., Hamilton, A., Fowler, J., Matson, M., Krumholz, L., & Walkowiak, J. (2009). Therapeutic Assessment with children: A pilot study of treatment acceptability and outcome. *Journal of Personality Assessment, 91*, 238–244.

Tharinger, D. J., Finn, S. E., Hersh, B., Wilkinson, A., Chistopher, G., & Tran, A. (2008). Assessment feedback with parents and children: A collaborative approach. *Professional Psychology: Research and Practice, 39*, 600–609.

Tharinger, D. J., Finn, S. E., Wilkinson, A. D., DeHay, T., Parton, V. Bailey, E., & Tran, A. (2008). Providing psychological assessment feedback with children through individualized fables. *Professional Psychology: Research and Practice, 39*, 610–618.

Tharinger, D. J., Finn, S. E., Wilkinson, A. D., & Schaber, P. M. (2007). Therapeutic Assessment with a child as a family intervention: Clinical protocol and a research case study. *Psychology in the Schools, 44*, 293–309.

Tharinger, D. J., Fisher, M., & Gerber, B. (2012). Therapeutic Assessment with a 10-year-old boy and his parents: The pain under the disrespect. In S. E. Finn, L. Handler, & C. T. Fischer, *Collaborative/Therapeutic Assessment: A casebook and guide* (pp. 311–333). Hoboken, NJ: John Wiley.

Tharinger, D. J., Gentry, L. & Finn, S. E. (2013). Therapeutic Assessment with adolescents and their parents: A comprehensive model. In D. Saklofske, C. R. Reynolds, & V. L. Schwean (Eds.), *Oxford Press handbook of psychological assessment of children and adolescents* (pp. 385–422). New York: Oxford University Press.

Tharinger, D. J., Krumholz, L. S., Austin, C. A., & Matson, M. (2011). The development and model of Therapeutic Assessment with children: Application to school-based assessment. In M. A. Bray & T. J. Kehle (Eds.), *Oxford Press handbook of school psychology* (pp. 224–259). Oxford University Press.

Tharinger, D. J., & Pilgrim, S. (2011). *Child Experience of Assessment Scale (CEAS)*. Unpublished manuscript. University of Texas at Austin.

Tharinger, D. & Roberts, M. (2014). Human figure drawings in Therapeutic Assessment with children: Process, product, life context, and systemic impact. In L. Handler & A. D. Thomas (Eds.), *Drawings in assessment and psychotherapy: Research and application* (pp. 17–41). New York: Routledge.

Trevarthen, C. (1993). The self-born in intersubjectivity: The psychology of an infant communicating. In U. Neisser (Ed.), *The perceived self: Ecological and interpersonal sources of self-knowledge* (pp. 121–173). New York: Cambridge University Press.

Tronick, E. Z. (1989). Emotions and emotional communication in infants. *American Psychologist, 44*, 112–119.

Weiss, J. (1993). *How psychotherapy works.* New York: Guilford.

White, M., & Epston, D. (1990). *Narrative means to therapeutic ends.* New York, NY: Norton.

Williams, C. L. (1986). MMPI profiles from adolescents: Interpretive strategies and treatment considerations. *Journal of Child and Adolescent Psychotherapy, 3*(2), 179–193.

Winnicott, D. W. (1958). *Collected papers: Through paediatrics to psychoanalysis.* London: Tavistock.

Zaretiski, W. K. (2009). The zone of proximal development: What Vygotsky did not have time to write. *Journal of Russian and East European Psychology, 47*, 70–93.

Ziffer, R. L. (1985). The utilization of psychological testing in the context of family

3 Phase I: Initial Sessions: Phone Contact, Parent Session, and Parent-Child Session

We turn to the practice of Therapeutic Assessment with Children (TA-C), starting with the first phase of TA-C, the Initial Sessions. This phase has three steps: initial phone contact(s) with parents, first session with parents, and first session with parents and child together. We discuss each step, in detail, and present the corresponding case study material after each of the three steps.

Initial Phone Contact with Parents

Our first contact with a family that is exploring the possibility of contracting for a TA-C is usually over the phone. This first conversation allows parents to tell us about the concerns they have about their child and their family at that time. We listen carefully and compassionately to their concerns and their "story." We begin to formulate tentative hypotheses about the family that we will revisit and reformulate across our time with them. We inform parents about TA-C and how it differs from a traditional assessment. We also introduce and explore the idea of parents developing Assessment Questions to guide the assessment. While we are conversing, we use a collaborative tone, not an "expert" tone. We seek enough information to determine if a TA-C seems like a good fit. If it is, we discuss who might be involved. Finally, we discuss the structure and format of the assessment, including scope, timeline, scheduling, written documentation, and estimated cost. The goals of this initial parent contact can be seen in Box 3.1.

Educate Parents About TA-C, Using a Collaborative Tone

As assessors, we are curious about why parents are seeking an assessment of their child at this time. It could be that they were encouraged to do a TA-C by a friend, family member, mental health provider, school personnel, or other informed party. We have found that when parents contact us, they may: (1) be well informed about TA (perhaps through a friend who has experience with TA) and ready to commit; (2) have some awareness of TA (perhaps because a health provider talked with them about it) and need more

DOI: 10.4324/9781003000174-3

Box 3.1   Goals of Initial Phone Contact

- Educate the parents about TA-C.
- Set a collaborative tone.
- Hear the parents' concerns and collect enough information to see if a TA-C is a good fit.
- Explore whom to involve in the TA-C.
- Introduce the idea of Assessment Questions and begin to develop them.
- Introduce the prospect of a family session.
- Inform the parents about the comprehensive feedback provided.
- Discuss the assessment agreement.

---

information about the process and pragmatics; or (3) may have no or little information and need an in-depth introduction to TA-C. One of our initial goals is to provide parents with the knowledge they need to understand TA-C and decide if a TA or traditional assessment would best address their needs.

To provide ample information, in addition to speaking with parents directly, we have each developed our own "parent information sheets" to describe TA-C (based on a general template we share). Typically, we each address common questions (FAQs) parents have about the process. We offer to mail or email this information sheet and to further discuss parents' questions after they have read it. In our experience, parents find the information sheets to be useful themselves and can easily share them with others (relatives, therapists, and friends) who may become involved. The information sheets we use are geared toward clients in an outpatient independent practice setting. We encourage you to create your own information sheet that works for your setting, population, and style. If you like the format of answering FAQs, you might address the following questions:

- What is a Therapeutic Assessment?
- How is a Therapeutic Assessment different from a traditional assessment?
- What will happen during a Therapeutic Assessment of my child?
- What are the benefits of Therapeutic Assessment?
- What kind of questions can a Therapeutic Assessment answer?
- What are some examples of questions?
- Will you really tell me the results of the Therapeutic Assessment?
- Who else will have access to the results of my child's Therapeutic Assessment?
- Is there possible distress that can occur during a Therapeutic Assessment?

- How can I support my child throughout the assessment?
- What is the time frame and cost of a Therapeutic Assessment of my child?

Below is Finn's response to the question, "What will happen during a Therapeutic Assessment of my child?"

> *During the assessment, I will meet with you to discuss any concerns and worries you have about your child. I will help you form questions to be addressed by the assessment and then will talk with you about these questions. I may also ask your permission to talk with others (e.g., teachers, health providers) who have information about your child's situation, and we will discuss if it would be useful for me to observe your child in school or at home. Next, your child and I will spend several sessions doing psychological tests. I will meet with you during or in between these sessions to discuss them, collect background information, and get your thoughts on themes that are emerging from the testing. In the latter part of the assessment, I typically schedule a session with everyone in the family present, so I can see how your child acts in the family environment. At the end of the assessment, I will meet with you to discuss the results of your child's testing and how they relate to your questions. I will provide you with a letter or a written report summarizing your child's assessment results. I will also meet with your child to let her/him know the assessment findings. Last, if you wish, I will meet with personnel at your child's school or health providers to discuss the findings and recommendations.*

Collect Enough Information to Determine If a TA-C Is a Good Fit

We have found that we can usually determine, during the initial phone conversation, if a TA-C is likely to be helpful to a child and family at this time. We listen to the kind of concerns the parents are voicing and how complex their concerns are. We consider TA-C to be very useful for families with complicated issues that involve not just the child but the family. We are not surprised if the parents are feeling very stuck with their child and at their wits end, having tried many things they consider to have failed. For example, a mother relays that her child has been very sad and is starting to fail at school. She also lets you know that her side of the family has a history of bipolar disorder. Further, she tells you that things are so hard that she and her husband are considering a separation. This example would likely be very appropriate for at TA-C, as would the following scenario: parents report that their child seems angry all the time, won't follow family rules, and is especially mean to his sister—who is described as being "just about perfect."

We also have found that we can usually determine when a TA-C is *not* a good fit. In the first type of scenario, the needs the parents voice are very straightforward and a more limited assessment or parent consultation would likely be sufficient. For example, a parent reports that her six-year-old son's teacher says he seems bored at school and thinks he may be gifted. An assessment is needed to determine if he meets the criteria to be considered for the gifted and talented program. Or, parents new to the community want recommendations on where to send their child with severe learning disabilities to school. Unless more extensive concerns were revealed, neither of these examples seems to warrant a TA-C.

There are other situations when a TA-C may not be advisable, not because the concerns or needs are mild and singularly focused. If the child/family is in an acute crisis, such as the child being actively suicidal or homicidal; or if an intense forensic process is ongoing (e.g., determination of child custody arrangements with antagonistic parents), we usually encourage the parent to contact us at a later time when things have resolved sufficiently, as a TA is likely to be more beneficial then.

Explore Whom to Involve in the Assessment

While exploring the parents' request for an assessment, we also listen carefully for who the key players are in the child's life and if it might be useful to involve them in the assessment. Typically, if the child is in treatment, we want to include the referring professional and other professionals already involved in the treatment (e.g., psychotherapists and psychiatrists). Also, we want to include the adults who have major parenting responsibilities for the child, unless there is some clear reason why parents want to exclude such individuals. Determining who are the main caregivers can be more complicated than it sounds, as families and caregiving structures are often complex. In a family with two in-house parents, we stress the importance of involving both parents throughout the TA-C. Although stereotypic, not infrequently a mother will call to discuss the assessment and will initially insist that the father has no time to be directly involved. In such instances, we do everything we can to involve both parents, including appealing directly to the father. In a single-parent household, we seek to understand if an aunt or grandparent or older sibling has major responsibilities for the child and possibly should be invited. When families have experienced divorce, separation, or re-partnering, we listen carefully to figure out who has legal rights and caregiving responsibilities. We seek to determine if two parents can work together or if separate sessions are needed. We may also ask about the roles that stepparents or live-in partners play in childrearing and, in some instances, it may be very helpful to invite such people to an initial session.

In general, we stress the importance of parents and other involved caregivers participating as a team, although we assure them that we will make adjustments as needed. Some parents find they can work with a former spouse/partner with the support of the assessor; others cannot. Our guiding principle is that, if possible, adults who are committed to the child and actively engaged in a parenting relationship should be invited and encouraged to participate. It is not always clear in the initial phone contact who the important players are, but sometimes it is clear. Here is a typical discussion.

Assessor: Thanks for that background. So, right now Mathew lives with …?

Father: Mostly with his mother, Susan, and his little brother Max. I see him one night during the week and he spends every other weekend with me and my wife, Denise. And he is close to my mother, who lives in Dallas, but he doesn't get to see her much.

Assessor: Who were you thinking would be involved in the assessment?

Father: Well, I was assuming it would be Susan and me. We communicate pretty well and work together when it comes to the children.

Assessor: And Denise?

Father: I don't think that would work so well. It's a new marriage, and Denise and Mathew are just starting to find their way—he's very loyal to his mother. I think for now it would be best to include just Susan and me.

Assessor: OK. Let's start there. If anything comes up where I think involving Denise in some small way could be useful to Mathew, you and Susan and I can talk and see where that goes.

Father: OK—but that makes me a little nervous. Seems like a big step.

Assessor: Let me assure you that I won't ask you to do anything that would make you or Susan uncomfortable.

Introduce the Idea of Assessment Questions and Begin to Develop Them

In the initial phone conversation, we ask parents to start thinking about what they wish to learn about their child and family via the assessment. At first, we may ask this naturally and informally (e.g., "What is it you want to figure out through the assessment?"), but often before the phone call is ended, we explain that a TA-C starts by parents (with some assistance from assessors) posing specific questions that will then form the basis for the assessment. This explanation lets the parents know, from the beginning, that TA-C is a collaborative process, they have the opportunity to direct where the assessment will go, and it will focus on their concerns about their child and family. In our experience, some parents are a bit surprised by the idea of "coming up with questions to be answered," as they may be accustomed to being asked only about their child's "problems," or they may not have yet taken a step back from their situation to think about what they want to know. Sometimes it can be helpful for the assessor to reflect a possible question based on what has already been said (illustrated later). Also, if parents seem at all anxious about the questions, we assure them that we will work *with* them to construct and refine questions for the assessment at the first parent session. Last, if you develop an informational brochure to give parents after the phone call, you may want to include some example assessment questions to give parents a sense of what others have come up with. Here is a typical discussion.

Assessor: So, the first step will be for us to develop questions about what you want to learn about Mateo through the assessment.

Parent: I'm not sure about coming up with questions. Can't I just tell you what isn't working?

Assessor: Certainly. But I want to make sure that you get what you want out of the assessment and knowing the specific questions you have will help. From what you said, it sounds like one question might be, "Why is Mateo so angry all the time?" Is that right?

Parent: Yes, and what we can do about it.

Assessor: Those are both great questions. If you can, think about other problem areas and what questions you have, jot any of those down and bring them with you to our first meeting. We'll work together on your questions when you come.

Parent: Suppose something is important but I don't know enough to ask about it?

Assessor: I certainly will tell you important things that will be helpful, even if you haven't asked a specific question.

Parent: OK. I'll start thinking about my questions and what I want to learn.

Mention Having a Family Intervention Session

As these sessions are rare in traditional models of child psychological assessment, we mention the opportunity for a family session at the very beginning of explaining how a TA-C works. Usually, we say something in passing like, "Oh, and I should tell you—later in the process we will want to have a session with you and your child together so we can see how she acts with you." We do this so that families are not caught off guard when the time arrives, and we believe that just this brief mention of a family session will get parents thinking systemically about their child's problems. Often, we make it clear that family sessions are a routine part of our child assessments, which helps families not take the request just personally. We also mention family sessions in our brochures that we send to parents when they are first considering a TA-C. It is worth noting that when speaking to parents we don't use the term "Family Intervention Session," but rather speak about a "family session" or "session with you and your child together."

Inform the Parents About the Comprehensive Feedback Provided

We let parents know from the very beginning that they will receive comprehensive feedback, both orally and in writing at the completion of the TA-C (Tharinger et al., 2008). For written feedback, we mention and explain the possibility of a parent letter and a psychological report as options at the end of the assessment. In addition to fulfilling an ethical requirement, when parents know they will receive a comprehensive, user-friendly explanation of test results and their relevance to their family's life, parental anxiety decreases, and cooperation and collaboration with the assessment increases. As explained previously, feedback can also offer a therapeutic intervention for the family, promoting better child-parent relationships, improved understanding of the child, and an increase in a child's self-esteem. To be sure, we provide parents with selected results along the way to keep them informed, share what we are learning, and listen to what they are understanding. We strive to determine how readily parents can take in new information, when it might be beyond their emotional capacity, and how we might help them develop more capacity so they can adopt a coherent, systemic, and more compassionate view of their child.

Discuss a Tentative Assessment Agreement

It is important to begin discussing the assessment agreement with parents during the initial phone call. This way parents can discuss the time commitment, schedule, and cost with each other and other involved adults before deciding to go forward. Also, this timing eliminates surprises, creates safety, and invites collaboration. Here is a typical discussion.

Parent: So how long will all this take?

Assessor: Good question. TA-C typically involves 6–8 sessions that take place over a two to three-month period, although the sessions can be condensed into a shorter time period if that is something you need.

Parent: Why so spread out?

Assessor: I find I get a better sense of a child when I see him or her over time. That way, if there's a good day or bad day, I don't get a wrong impression. Also, the testing can be hard on kids, and this way they can give their best effort without getting tired or overwhelmed.

Parent: Sounds like how therapy works.

Assessor: Exactly. The pacing of TA-C is more like a therapy or counseling schedule than a traditional assessment, which often takes place over a few days, with feedback a week later.

Parent: Yeah. We had that kind of testing before—so rushed and so little time to really understand it all. I'm starting to get how this is different. So how much will this cost?

Assessor: Good question. It depends on how many sessions and tests we need to answer the questions you have, and what kind of written summaries you want at the end. We almost always include a fable for the child as feedback. In addition, we typically provide a parent letter, summarizing the major findings and answering parents'

Assessment Questions. Many parents also request a formal psychological report that can be used with other providers immediately or in the future. So, the cost will vary depending on the comprehensiveness of the assessment and the number of written documents requested. From what you told me so far, my guess is that the entire cost would be between $X and $Y.

Parent: Wow. That's a lot more than I expected. Does insurance cover any of it?

Assessor: It depends on your insurance, and I can give you the billing codes if you want to call and ask them. Generally, families get at least some of the cost reimbursed. And I understand that it's a lot. The cost is because I am likely to spend around X hours on the assessment.

Parent: I also talked to Dr. Jones, and her fee was a lot less, around $X.

Assessor: Sure. I know Dr. Jones, and she is really good. You may want to go with her, but I'm pretty sure she would be doing a traditional assessment. Therapeutic Assessment costs more because it combines assessment and therapy and involves the parents in almost every step. Our research shows it can help the whole family. But if that's more than you would want to take on at the moment, I completely understand.

Parent: I'll have to think about that.

Assessor: Of course. Let me know if there are other questions you have that will help you decide. Also, sometimes it helps just to have an initial meeting, and then decide. Those meetings are 2 hours long and cost $X. If you decide to proceed, that cost is applied to the full cost of the assessment. And I usually ask for half of the entire fee up front. Why don't you think it over and let me know if you want to come in that one time and see if the assessment feels right at this point in time? Also, at the end of that session, I can give you a set price, as it will be clear what questions we'll be hoping to answer.

This example demonstrates one way of charging for an assessment, i.e., quoting a flat fee once the major Assessment Questions have been specified and collecting half of the amount up front. Some TA-C practitioners opt to charge by the hour instead, and to bill regularly throughout the assessment. Again, what is important is that assessors discuss in the initial phone call how the assessment will be billed. We now introduce you to the case we will be following.

Case: Initial Phone Contact with Henry's Father

We now follow a comprehensive TA-C from this point through Chapter 10, the Follow-up Session. We tell the story of Henry, a ten-year-old boy in fifth grade, and his parents as they experience a TA-C. We detail the case at the end of each chapter, with the exception of this chapter, where the case is discussed after each of the three components: Initial Phone Call, Parent Session, and Child and Parent Session. This TA-C was conducted by one of the co-authors of this book, Dale Rudin, and we chose it as our main illustration for a number of reasons. We thought it was a very good teaching case and complex enough to be interesting but not overwhelming. Most of the client and family sessions were taped, which allowed us access to verbatim transcripts. The parents were very involved in the assessment and agreed to be tested themselves. The parents provided oral and written permission for their case to be presented in this book, and Henry assented. All the family members' names and other details have been changed to protect their identities. Each of the case illustration sections is written in first-person by Dale Rudin.

Dale's Account of the Initial Phone Contact

I had originally received a call from Henry's therapist, Dr. Jagger, who said that she thought the situation was difficult and she really wanted a Therapeutic Assessment for Henry. I then received a call from the dad and the initial conversation went something like this:

David: Hello, this is David Taylor. I was referred to you by Dr. Jagger who has been seeing my son for about three years—beginning when Henry was in the second grade. He doesn't like himself very much and says he wants to die. He's been struggling for a while. He has been bullied and seems to have a lot of repressed anger and is quite depressed.

Dale: Oh, that must be very difficult for both of you.

David: Yes, for all of us—his mother and brother as well. Dr. Jagger said you might be able to help us with an assessment.

Dale: We do assessment a little differently here. Did she mention that to you?

David: No, not really.

Dale: Has Henry ever been tested before?

David: No.

Dale: Ok, let me explain the process. I meet with clients over time. So, it's different than a lot of assessments where a child comes just 1 or 2 times to be tested. So, the process itself could take 2–3 months. I like to get to know the child and family over a number of sessions. This gives me a better opportunity to figure out what to do to address the difficulties.

David: Family?

Dale: Yes, in my child assessments I include parents and sometimes siblings, if that is also a concern. The first thing we do is develop questions that guide the assessment. In fact, if you decide to do the assessment, I will ask you to think about questions you might have about Henry, yourselves, or the family. You can do that before you come in, or I can help you do that in our first session. What we do in the assessment is guided by your questions.

David: Well, there are a lot of things we are wondering about.

Dale: Like what?

David: His IQ? His emotional functioning. I wonder if there is a discrepancy between his IQ and imagination.

Dale: It sounds like you've been thinking about all of this for a long time and will have a lot of important questions. I'm happy to set up an appointment, and we can go from there. You can see if this type of assessment is something you'd like to do. We have a website that you can look at for additional information, and I can email my information sheets about the process. If you just look up Therapeutic Assessment, you'll find it.

David: OK. What is the cost of the assessment?

We then spent a few minutes talking about the cost and whether or not insurance would cover it. I explained that insurance would cover different parts of the assessment, and it would be wise for David to check with his insurance company to see how psychological assessments are covered. I added that there are some sessions that could be coded as psychotherapy, so it would also be important to know how mental health benefits are covered.

Dale: Would you like to schedule a time for an appointment?

David: Yes, do we bring Henry to this appointment?

Dale: No, our first appointment will just be with you and your wife. Let me ask one more thing—are there any other adults in the household who have major responsibility for taking care of Henry?

David: No.

Dale: Then I'm ready to schedule if you are.

David: Yes.

Reflection After the Conversation

I remember thinking that this dad was rather sophisticated and had been dealing with such a difficult situation for a long time—at least three years, from what he had said. He sounded tired and his voice conveyed little affect. It was interesting to me that the father called since often my initial conversation is with the mother. This led me to think that he might be very involved with his child. I experienced him as open, direct, and informative, but not necessarily warm or emotional.

Contact with the Referring Therapist

After speaking with David and obtaining his permission, I decided to call Dr. Jagger, the referring therapist, and speak with her again. We were acquainted, and as mentioned earlier, she already had information about Therapeutic Assessment and had checked if I were open to a referral. I told her the father had contacted me, thanked her for the referral, and asked her how she thought a TA-C would be helpful. She said she had worked with Henry for three years and was feeling less effective lately because he was resisting therapy and was again feeling suicidal and depressed. We talked further and developed her Assessment Questions. They were:

1. What are the dynamics underlying Henry's depression and suicidal statements?
2. What needs is he trying to meet and how can we, Henry's parents and therapist, do that in a more positive way?
3. Are there signs that Henry is developing a personality disorder?

Initial Session with Parents

When the parents feel well informed about what is involved in a TA-C and elect to go forward, it is time to schedule the first meeting with them and any other caretakers who will be involved. The major goal is to construct and contextualize Assessment Questions that will guide the TA-C. Another overreaching objective is for parents to have the experience of being empathized with, which we hope will help them increase their empathy for their child. We see this parallel process of empathy-building as essential for changing the family story and helping the system take positive steps. As shown in Box 3.2, there are many goals for this initial session. We discuss and illustrate each in depth.

Set the "Frame"

As you recall, TA-C is a semi-structured approach, and this means we seek a balance in each session between pursuing an assessment "agenda" and listening intently and responding empathically so as to build a "holding environment" for the clients. Finding this balance in the initial parent session is sometimes difficult; if we don't structure the session enough and direct the pacing, we may find that it goes very long without any Assessment Questions being framed, and parents may leave without any clarity as to how the TA-C may help them. On the other hand, if we are too directive, parents may not feel listened to and understood. One way to strike a balance is in how we open the session. Typically, after introductions and settling in, we avoid general openings such as "Tell me what brings you here today." Instead, we

---

Box 3.2   Goals of Initial Parent Session

- Set the "frame."
- Enlist parents as collaborators.
- Establish a "holding environment" through active listening, mirroring, joining, and attending to shame.
- Inquire about past assessments.
- Invite the parents to ask questions of you.
- Foster parents' curiosity about the child, themselves, and the assessment process.
- Work with parents to frame and contextualize questions that will guide the assessment.
- Coach parents on how to introduce the assessment to their child.
- Determine if an anonymous observation of the child would be useful before testing sessions begin.
- Enlist parents in collecting historical information or systematic data about a problem behavior.
- Conduct a Parent Check-out (reactions and pragmatics, finalize agreement, collect initial fee).
- Analyze and reflect on the Parent Session and start to plan the next phase.

---

set a frame that is both relational and focused on the tasks of the initial session. For example:

> My goal today is for us to get to know each other and to answer any questions you have about the Therapeutic Assessment process or about me. Then I want to learn about the challenges and concerns you are having with your child and discuss what you want to learn through the assessment. By the end of our meeting, I hope we can come up with specific questions about your child or your relationship with him/her that you would like us to answer through the assessment.

It is good to refer to information you already learned during the initial phone contact and check-in about the parents' understanding of information in the brochure. For example:

Assessor: First, I wanted to see if you have any general questions since we talked on the phone.

Mother: Well, we're not really sure how long this assessment will take and how we will figure out all the scheduling, especially if you want both of us here some of the time.

Assessor: That's a good question. By the end of today's session, I should be able to give you a good idea on how long it will take because we'll know how many questions we decide to tackle. Then we can work together to come up with a workable schedule. Please know I'll be as flexible as I can to make the session times work for you.

Using this semi-structured approach in the Parent Session (and beyond) helps keep the session within the agreed-upon time limit and allows you to explore and "contextualize" some of the developing Assessment Questions (discussed later). Finding a "gentle, but firm" balance—where parents are invited to talk but are not allowed to ramble or go off on tangents for long periods of time—helps them feel heard and listened to, contains their anxiety or disorganization, gives them an experience of "getting down to business," and often leads to their feeling clearer and calmer by the end of the session.

Again, holding to the semi-structured frame can be challenging, as we are striving to develop trust and safety with the parents, model being collaborative, construct and explore Assessment Questions, and offer clarity and hope. Balancing these multiple aims can tax even an experienced assessor. Typically, as this is the first meeting with parents, if they are highly distressed, have a strong need to speak without interruption and be listened to, are clearly on different pages about the child, and have difficulties focusing on Assessment Questions, we lean toward building alliance and trust even if it means few Assessment Questions have been clarified before we run out of time. In such instances, the assessor may even model "slowing down" the session, so as to tend more to the emotional needs that are apparent. For example:

Father: I really don't see how we're going to agree on any questions about Ali since we see him so differently!
Assessor: Thank you. I see what you are saying. I really get a sense of how hard it has been to parent Ali. The issues have been there for a long time and now they seem to be getting worse. Ali's behavior is swinging from acting out to being sad and inconsolable. I also hear that you each view what is going on with him differently, as well as how you respond to him. I'm getting a general sense of what you are dealing with and how hard it has been on the whole family. Let's slow down a little before we try to firm up any Assessment Questions. I really want to hear what you each have been through, and we can meet again if we need to and finish up the questions.

In such instances, we typically schedule an additional parent session and/or have email or phone contact with the parents about a list of possible Assessment Questions before we next meet. It is helpful to remember that although adding another session takes time and adds to the cost, attending to the parents' needs may help them engage more fully in the process and, by the end of the assessment, attend more empathically to their child's needs.

Enlist Parents as Collaborators

From the initial phone contact through the follow-up session, we want the parents to feel that we welcome them as collaborators and value and respect their input without judgment. We want them to know that we see them as the experts on their child and their family. We want them to share our curiosity about their child and know that without their shared investment positive change cannot occur. We want them to feel they are not alone and experience that in working together, there is hope.

Even so, we have experienced that some parents are not comfortable when asked to be in a collaborative role with a professional such as ourselves. This may be influenced by their cultural value of respect and deference to "experts." They may view professionals as all-knowing authorities who provide the answers that parents are to accept and not question. In these situations, we strive to honor their cultural orientation and values. However, at the same time we want to show them that from a Therapeutic Assessment approach, we are all experts and share our knowledge and wisdom with each other. Although this may be a big cultural accommodation for some parents, we have found that most parents accept that they already know a great deal about their children and feel empowered when we recognize this fact.

Additional cultural and societal barriers to collaboration between parents and ourselves can include age differences (e.g., a young mother and a senior assessor), gender differences (e.g., a deferential woman with a formal male assessor), educational differences (e.g., a father with a high school degree and blue-collar job with a doctoral-level assessor), racial/ethnic differences (e.g., a Black father and a White assessor), etc. In all these cases, we have found that recognizing and addressing the differences between parents and ourselves, valuing and respecting their input, welcoming their knowledge and insights, and providing a strong holding environment goes a long way in promoting equality and collaboration. Here is an example from an initial session with a single mother.

Assessor: Maria, I am really looking forward to working with you to understand Sophia and figure out what will help.

Maria: That sounds good, but you are the expert here. I'm not sure I will be of much help.

Assessor: Well, I agree that I am the expert on tests and pulling together what we learn through the testing to help us see what is going on. But tests are not perfect and you know more about your child and your family than I will ever know. I need your help to understand your story and how you see things. By working together this way we can best make sense of what is going on.

Maria: OK. It will be good to not feel so alone with all this.

Establish a "Holding Environment"

As has been introduced and illustrated in previous examples, establishing a trusting and safe relationship with the parents, a "holding environment," is foundational in TA-C. It is similar to establishing a safe and secure base for a child in attachment theory (as discussed in Chapter 2) and developing a therapeutic alliance in psychotherapy and counseling. In our experience, building trust and providing safety with all parties involved in the assessment enhances both the depth and richness of the experience and is predictive of its success. Note that providing a holding environment is a very different experience than "establishing rapport" in traditional assessment, which has the primary aim of creating enough trust to gain the cooperation of the parents and the child.

We now describe certain skills and techniques we have found useful in establishing a holding environment with parents, children, and family systems. These include active listening, mirroring, joining, and attending to shame (discussed in Chapter 2). These methods are not unique to TA-C; they are common to many counseling and therapy traditions. However, when combined with the core ingredients of TA-C, they seem particularly effective. In addition, we will discuss how to inquire about previous assessment experiences and listen for past hurts or disappointments. Such discussions also can be essential to the current assessment succeeding.

Active Listening

This is one of the essential skills of TA-C, as it is with many forms of psychotherapy and family therapy. As discussed in Chapter 2, human beings have a basic inborn longing to be seen and understood—including the good, the bad, and the ugly. We all want to be known. We all want to be *really* listened to and heard. We all want to be accepted. Parents crave the feeling that someone understands what they are going through with their child.

However, parents may not share themselves easily, as they may have been shamed or blamed in the past and no longer feel they can trust anyone to know them without judging them. Active listening helps create the holding environment, offers repair, and allows parents to build or rebuild trust. To listen actively we need to put away any judgments, preconceptions, and theoretical biases and listen with "fresh ears." This is not easy, as we all have the tendency to jump to initial impressions and premature conclusions. This tendency is even stronger when we feel pressed to quickly arrive at conclusions and help clients—either because of our own needs to feel helpful or competent or because of pressures from clients or work settings. However, for parents to be heard and "held," they need us to enter into their existing story with openness, curiosity, and lack of judgment.

Our ability to actively listen without bias also serves another purpose. We are hoping that by the end of the assessment, the parents can actively listen to their own children. Children also want someone to *really* understand them—especially their parent—and, in our experience, they hope the assessor can help their parents to "get" them. Here is an example of an assessor really listening to the parents and then (see later), *joining* with them.

Assessor: So much has happened. I really feel for what you all have gone through trying to figure out Jonathan's disabilities and what he needs. I also hear that you have not felt supported by your own families and have actually felt judged by them. They have not accepted Jonathan's disabilities and have just pulled away. If I were you, I might be feeling very alone and overwhelmed. Is that right?

Parent: That feels so true. We do feel lost and alone. And judged.

Assessor: Well, I want to work together with you to understand what Jonathan and you need and then find those things. I think we will make a good team.

Mirroring

This is another technique commonly used in counseling and therapy to convey to clients that they are seen and understood. In mirroring, we reflect back what is heard, often in slightly different words, to demonstrate or check what we have understood. Here are some examples.

"Seems like you're really scared about Tom's future"

"It sounds like you have tried a lot of things already to help Jean, and now you are starting to lose hope"

"Am I hearing correctly that the two of you see the problem differently? Dad, you think Marie is being manipulative with her anxiety and it's important not to coddle her. Mom, you think she is really scared and needs more reassurance."

Joining

When practicing *joining*, the assessor explicitly shows that she agrees with or identifies with the parents' situation and with the very real restraining forces that make change difficult. For example:

"Given all that has happened, I don't know how you couldn't feel frightened of what will happen next."

"What you've been saying makes a lot of sense to me. A lot of parents of twins I have seen feel that they don't have enough support."

Being Attentive to Shame

We pay special attention to shame in our interactions with parents, as reducing clients' shame is one of the major ways that TA-C is therapeutic, as discussed in Chapter 2. In the initial parent session, we are humbly aware that often even the most confident parents fear being judged, criticized, or shown to be incompetent when they reveal the struggles they and their child are experiencing. At this stage, our focus is on two general principles, "shame avoidance" and "shame repair" (Kamphuis & Finn, 2019). Shame avoidance means that we work hard not to use language, ask questions, or push for information that will bring up overwhelming shame for parents. For example, see the following discussion, drawn from early in an initial parent session:

Parent: And then, after weeks of his refusing to go to bed alone, I resorted to some things that were probably a mistake in retrospect.
Assessor: Sure. That can happen.
Parent: That's part of what got me to call you. I realized that I really need some outside help.
Assessor: I'm glad you did. And I hear that you want us to figure out other ways to handle the issues around going to bed.

Notice here, the assessor could have asked for more information about the strategies the parent alluded to that were "probably a mistake," but did not. Instead, the assessor gave a simple matter-of-fact sign of not being shocked, "That can happen." The parent's comment was not ignored, and might be returned to at a later time when the assessor judges there is more alliance. For example, later in the interview, the assessor might pose a general question, "And what have you already tried to deal with the sleeping problem?" This would give the parent leeway to disclose the uncomfortable information or not.

One caveat to shame avoidance in the initial session is that assessors must be careful *not to avoid* topics because of their own discomfort that parents are clearly signaling they want to discuss. Some years ago, Finn and Tharinger watched an initial parent session done by a trainee. The mother kept trying to say something (that seemed relevant) about her own sexual abuse and how she felt it might be impacting her daughter. Without realizing it, the trainee kept steering the mother away from this topic again and again, and only later admitted that she felt very uncomfortable discussing sexual material because of her own conservative upbringing.

The second technique, *shame repair*, means that the assessor shows a willingness to help regulate parents' shame when it emerges. Let's imagine that the previous conversation continued at a later point in the session:

Assessor: And what have you already tried to help Sammy go to bed on his own?

Parent: Well, at first, I was really patient, you know, rubbing his back and staying in his room talking for a long time. But it didn't really work. He needed more and more time to go to sleep, and I had other things to do.

Assessor: Uh huh.

Parent: Finally, I got so frustrated that I would give him 5 minutes, and then I would leave and lock the door. I thought that no matter how hard he screamed and pounded on the door, he would eventually wear himself out and go to sleep. But he got so frantic and out of control that I think I traumatized him. I feel terrible about it.

Assessor: I see that. You think that you made a mistake trying that, and that it might have hurt Sammy. That's one thing we can explore in the assessment if you want. But I also hear that you were at your wit's end, and were trying to figure out how to balance his needs with your own.

Parent: Yes. I don't have hours to spend putting him to bed every night!

Assessor: I bet you don't. As a single parent you need time to yourself too. Again, I'm really glad you came here to see what we can figure out about this together.

Here you can see how the assessor's empathic comments (e.g., "you were at your wit's end") potentially help reduce the parent's shame, while at the same time the assessor doesn't dismiss or "whitewash" the parent's concerns. By taking the parent's concern seriously about possibly having hurt the child, and introducing this as a possible question in the TA-C, the assessor also sets the stage for further self-disclosures by the parent.

Inquire About Past Assessments

We have found that asking parents about their experiences with previous psychological assessment or testing (of their child, themselves, or another family member) can be particularly informative. We listen for what they took away from the experience and especially for any past hurts or disappointments that might affect parents' ability to trust psychological methods and mental health practitioners. If they relate such an experience, we show genuine interest and demonstrate empathy for their experience. We then stress that is it our commitment that this assessment will be a different experience for them. We also ask the parents to let us know if they feel hurt, angry, or frustrated during this TA-C so we can talk adapt how we work. Here is an example:

Assessor: I remember on the phone you mentioned that Trevor had been tested before. Can you tell me a little about that?

Parent: That was back in 2nd grade. His teacher referred him for special education testing at school because he was having a hard time learning to read. We had a big meeting with lots of people, and they explained that he had a learning disability in reading. After that they tried different things, and there was a little improvement. But he still struggles a lot and now he has a lot of emotional and self-esteem issues that I think are connected with his struggles reading. So, I guess it was helpful—sort of the beginning of really seeing that he had special needs. And now here we are.

Assessor: Well, that's good to know. With this assessment we'll look at the bigger picture and try to figure out what Trevor needs now.

Parent: That's good. You know, thinking back to that time, I was embarrassed that it was all so public and we weren't really ready to hear that he had a disability in that "big meeting." And it was hard to explain it to him afterward.

Assessor: I'm sorry things happened that way. It sounds like you didn't know what was going to come out, and then there were a lot of people watching when you heard the assessment findings for the first time.

Parents: Yes. We were caught off-guard and everyone saw our reaction.

Assessor: That would have been hard for me too! Well, let me guarantee you that no information will be shared with anyone else before you yourselves have heard it and we've talked about your reactions. Also, I'll help you talk to Trevor at the end about the assessment results.

Parents: Great. That feels good.

Invite the Parents to Ask Questions of You

Part of being collaborative is to invite the parents (and later the child) to ask questions of you. This action signals that you are sincere in treating the clients with respect, which can have a profound impact on their experience of the assessment. In our experience, the most common questions from parents are, "Do you think you can help us?" and "Have you seen other families with difficulties like ours?" Both of these questions demonstrate the vulnerability many parents feel and are best met with honest reassurance. Not infrequently, clients will ask about our education and experience, and why we have chosen to provide Therapeutic Assessments instead of traditional ones. Such questions are usually easy to address and again help reassure the parent and provide some equal footing.

Very rarely, parents ask more personal questions, and we make a distinction in our minds about these. Some questions are clear requests for the parent to learn more about our "context," for example, "Do you have children?" "Were you born in this country?" "Are you religious?" "Are you married?", or for gay and lesbian parents, "Are you gay?" Each assessor will need to decide how to respond to such questions, but we believe parents have a right to understand where we are coming from and how our contexts might influence our impressions and recommendations. Thus, in general, we tend to respond briefly and directly to such questions, and to follow-up by inquiring about how the parents have reacted to our responses:

Assessor: I've been asking you a lot of questions. Let me see if you have any questions about me before we wrap up today.

Mother: Do you have children?

Assessor: No, I don't, although I originally hoped to. I do have a goddaughter with whom I am very involved, and that has given me a taste of how hard it is to be a parent. And I have worked with parents and children for over 30 years.

Mother: OK.

Assessor: What is that like to hear that I don't have children myself?

Mother: It's OK. It sounds like you know that it's not always easy.

Assessor: Yes, I know. Sometimes I think it is one of the hardest jobs that exist. But fortunately, it can also be rewarding.

Mother: Yes, thank goodness!

Rarely, parents or children will ask a personal question that seems to have no relevance to the assessor's context or the work of the assessment. In such instances, it seems natural and respectful to ask why they are asking that question before responding, and to inquire about their reactions to our answer or decision not to answer.

Foster Curiosity

A major goal across all the phases of TA-C is to help parents gain new awareness and empathy for their child and thus to begin to change their narrative about their child and family. We further discuss this goal shortly. First, we want to introduce the potential power of fostering curiosity in parents to help them reach that goal. Curiosity involves a type of inquisitiveness that reflects a strong desire to know or learn something. Also, it is a positive emotion that is part of the seeking system (Panskepp, 1998) (often called the exploratory system in attachment theory) and it has strong motivational properties. When our seeking systems are engaged, we are calmer emotionally and more able to explore new ways of thinking and behaving. In TA-C, we aim to grow parents' curiosity about their child, themselves, and their family and be open to new perspectives.

However, fostering curiosity can be an uphill climb. When parents come to us seeking an assessment of their child, they are often stuck, anxious, fearful, exhausted, and not able to move beyond their current view of their child and family. They are often emotionally distressed, less able to step back and take new perspectives, and as a result often "stuck" with their story, as it would take substantial energy and possibly experiencing significant distress to change it. In these cases, the families seem determined to hold tight and not address their dilemma of change, as the restraining forces are overpowering the driving forces, as discussed in Chapter 2. Fortunately, we have discussed and illustrated the importance of providing a holding environment where parents can build safety with us and come to trust us with their concerns and questions. Fortunately, we know that providing a safe base lessens anxiety and fear and builds hope. In addition, similar to the development of the securely attached infant, a safe base allows for exploration. In TA-C, we are encouraging parents to explore, to be inquisitive, to be co-investigators with us, and to discover new possibilities about their child and their family.

One way to enhance curiosity in parents is for us to be curious ourselves. Curiosity is infectious, and therefore our curiosity helps parents get curious. We foster curiosity by helping parents focus on "puzzles," quandaries, or incomplete aspects of their current understanding of their child and family and join us in a spirit of inquiry. Some parents, once their fear and anxiety has lessened, readily begin to explore and question their own earlier assumptions. In our experience, this type of parent, with our support, will start *rewriting* their old story early on in the assessment process. In contrast, other parents, whose fear and anxiety are not easily alleviated, are likely to be more guarded, less curious, and less able to question the status quo. Their capacity to explore openly with keen interest may progress slowly, or may wax and wane as they confront difficult feelings. Each family, in our experience, lets us know what they are ready for at any point in time. We further illustrate fostering curiosity later when discussing exploring the context of assessment questions.

Work with Parents to Frame and Contextualize Questions That Will Guide the Assessment

Assessment Questions are the organizing framework for TA-C. They influence what background information we seek, what tests and Extended Inquiries we use, what interventions we try, and how we present our results. We work together with parents to formulate questions that can reflect a broad range of topics, such as what the child thinks and feels about X; diagnoses; triggers or contributing factors to the child's challenges; parental or family influences on the child's problem; how parents/family can help; how to handle difficult feelings related to the child; and what to expect next.

An additional benefit of gathering specific Assessment Questions is the opportunity for us to learn parents' expectations for the assessment and to provide information about what the assessment may or may not realistically be able to address. Well-formulated Assessment Questions serve as a "contract" of what parents can expect from the assessment. The content and phrasing of Assessment Questions also provide illuminating information about (1) parents' existing "story" about their child, (2) the parent-child relationship, (3) parents' openness to certain kinds of feedback or recommendations, and (4) parents' fears and hopes for their child (Finn, 2007). This information can later be used to inform our decision-making about how to organize and frame feedback to parents in the Summary/Discussion Session. For example, note the contrast between the following Assessment Questions from two sets of grandparents facing similar situations. Think about what we learn about each set of grandparents, their existing story, and what they may be expecting from the assessment from how they framed their question:

- *What are we going to do with our grandson David, who is now living with us? He's a bad seed like his father, who exhausted us when he was growing up. So, I guess our question is, "How can we protect ourselves from being exhausted again and feeling like failures?"*
- *Our grandson David is living with us now. We're afraid that he could turn out to be like his father—who has been in and out of trouble and exhausted us when we were raising him. We want to find better ways of parenting David and setting boundaries so he doesn't turn out the same way. So—I guess our question is "How can we parent and support our grandson David in ways that he can grow to be a healthy happy child?"*

It is quite apparent that the two different sets of grandparents and the ensuing assessments will differ from each other in many ways. The first grandparents seem to fit caregivers in the "scapegoated child" prototype discussed in Chapter 2, and will almost surely need a lot of empathy for their discouragement and desire to protect themselves in order to consider new ways of viewing their grandson. The second set of grandparents seem less scapegoating, more optimistic about the potential outcome, and more aware of potential systemic issues (i.e., that they have personal challenges in setting boundaries) and thus like are more open to input from the assessment. Clearly, both sets of grandparents need and deserve our support, but in different ways.

Process of Constructing Assessment Questions

As described earlier, we ask parents to start thinking about Assessment Questions during the initial conversation over the phone. In our experience, some parents run with the idea of coming up with Assessment Questions and arrive at the first session with a long list. In these instances, we work with parents to prioritize their questions as to which are most important at that moment. Other parents arrive with concerns, but without focused questions. This is not unusual. If parents are struggling with framing questions, inquiring about the events or circumstances that led up to their contacting us often leads to one or more useful Assessment Questions. As they provide a more complete account of their concerns and situation, we listen with our "Third Ear," remaining alert to any implicit questions, confusions, or concerns in the parents' narrative. We then ask if these might be areas they would like the assessment to focus on. We may inquire directly if they may have a question concerning what they are talking about, such as, "Might that be a question for the assessment?" Or we may even propose a possible question, "Might a useful question be…?", signaling with our language or tone of voice that we welcome parents to change or even reject our proposal.

Occasionally, parents are unable to come up with or consent to specific Assessment Questions, even after we use the methods described earlier. There seem to be various reasons why this might occur. One possibility is that the parents aren't fully engaged in the assessment because there are restraining forces that have not yet been addressed and they need more alliance with us before they can fully buy in. Thus, a general strategy if there are difficulties developing Assessment Questions is to slow things down, pay attention to building a strong holding environment (through empathic listening, joining, modeling, etc.), and then try again. It can also be helpful to ask directly about any reservations and/or to inquire about past assessment experiences and listen for past hurts. If reservations emerge, we try to address those directly and see if the parents' engagement improves. Another possibility is that one parent, likely the one who called about getting an assessment, may be interested in the TA but is holding back because the other parent is not convinced about doing a TA. This is not uncommon in families fitting the Solomon's Child prototype (Chapter 2). If this appears to be true, we work to get both parents on the same page if possible—possibly by allowing them to form separate Assessment Questions or Assessment Questions that reflect their differences (e.g., Does the testing suggest that Johnny needs more structure or more unconditional acceptance?). We also make it clear that we value both of their perspectives, welcome skepticism, and don't expect blind trust—but don't recommend that we proceed with the TA-C until both agree. We work slowly and at their pace.

Still another possibility is that the parents are overwhelmed and need help stepping back and getting curious about their child and family. They may be so exhausted and so focused on everything that isn't working, that they can't begin to think *about* their situation. In our experience, such parents need extensive support from us to feel accepted and not blamed or judged. Mirroring their intense emotions typically assists such parents in becoming less emotionally flooded. Only then can they open up and slowly begin to become curious and ask helpful Assessment Questions.

Last, even though they are not acutely overwhelmed, some parents are not capable of stepping back and taking a "big picture view" of their child and family because they do not seem to have a strong capacity to "mentalize." Mentalizing is the ability to understand the mental state of oneself or others that underlies overt behavior and to recognize that individuals have different mental states (Allen et al., 2008). Assessment Questions both facilitate and are enriched by parents' ability to mentalize about what might be motivating their child's acting out or withdrawn behavior or even their own reactions to the child. If parents have little ability to mentalize, we anticipate very basic Assessment Questions and work with the parents within their current level of understanding. As mentioned earlier, if the parents' capacity for mentalizing is temporarily compromised due to their intense emotional overwhelm, we provide them with extensive support to lessen their feelings of overwhelm and then proceed. Or we might suggest the parents receive therapeutic support of their own and return later for a TA-C.

We want to stress that in all of these situations we accept what the parents bring to the task of constructing Assessment Questions. What they contribute informs us about their readiness for the assessment and for change, as well as what they may need from us to proceed.

Collect Background Information

In addition to constructing Assessment Questions, it is important to collect background information to "flesh out" the questions. One method we use is Circular Questioning (Cecchin, 1987), an interview technique from family therapy that helps identify temporal, contextual, and relational variables related to problem behaviors or relationships. Circular questions provide the family with an opportunity to view itself systemically instead of linearly. Developing an awareness of the reciprocal interrelatedness of behaviors may, in and of itself, promote significant spontaneous change. The following example illustrates using circular questioning and promoting curiosity to flush out Assessment Questions.

Parents: Robert doesn't seem to have a conscience. He is never sorry when he does something wrong.

Assessor: Can you give me an example?

Parents: The other day he broke a window while playing ball, and when we yelled at him, he shrugged his shoulders and just walked away.

Assessor: Wow! What did you do then?

Parent: We made him go to his room and spend 3 hours there alone.

Assessor: Did he show any remorse once he was there?

Parent: No, not at all.

Assessor: And is that the same even with more serious things he has done?

Parent: Yes, last year he punched a girl in the face at school and she fell down. He got suspended. When we talked to him about it he said she "deserved it."

Assessor: Did he ever show any guilt or discomfort about that at all?

Parent: Not to us.

Assessor: To anyone else?

Parent: Well, his teacher said that he cried when it first happened.

Assessor: Did that surprise you?
Parent: Not really. Sometimes he fakes feeling guilty.
Assessor: Have you ever seen him cry when he has done something wrong?
Parent: Well, the other day he accidentally knocked over his little sister, and when she cried, he cried too.
Assessor: Did it seem genuine?
Parent: Yes...it did.
Assessor: That's interesting, isn't it?
Parent: It is. We hadn't put that together with what the teacher told us. Is it possible that he feels bad when he hurts someone else, but not us?
Assessor: I'm not sure. Is that a question we might pose for the assessment?
Parent: Maybe...
Assessor: Let's see if we can put it into words...

Another method we use to further develop and contextualize possible Assessment Questions, borrowing from Fischer (1985/1994), is by listening for a behavior of concern and exploring its context. We have found the following questions to be helpful and illustrate their use with an example.

- When did the behavior begin?
- What was going on the child's/family life at that time?
- When/where/with whom is the problem worse?
- When/where/with whom is the problem behavior better?
- Are there any contexts when the problem behavior disappears?
- How do different people react to the child's behavior?
- What has the family already tried to address the problem behavior? Did it work? If so, is the family still using that approach?
- How was this type of behavior handled in the caregivers' families when they were growing up?

Here is an example.

Mother: John is always angry, no matter what I do.
Assessor: When did the behavior begin—John always being angry?
Mother: Well, John has always been a little grumpy, but it just seemed like part of his personality. But I guess about a year ago it got really bad.
Assessor: What was going on at that time?
Mother: Let me think. How could I forget? I was starting to get depressed—I had lost a very good friend. I just wasn't myself. I wasn't very available. I'm better now.
Assessor: So, John is mostly angry with you?
Mother: Yes, with me. Especially when I ask him to help with things at home.

Assessor:	Does it ever seem better—John being not so angry?
Mother:	Good question. I guess when he's with his dad and they do stuff outside.
Assessor:	Are there any times when the anger just isn't there at all?
Mother:	Now that you mention it—when John plays video games with his friends. He never seems angry then.
Assessor:	How do different people react to John's anger?
Mother:	I get exhausted and hurt. His dad gets upset when he sees me upset.
Assessor:	What have you already tried to address his anger? Did it work?
Mother:	I tried talking to him about it and so did his dad. That seemed to help a bit but didn't last.
Assessor:	How was anger handled in your family growing up?
Mother:	That's easy. We weren't allowed to express anger toward our parents. If we did, we got in serious trouble.
Assessor:	I think we might be coming up with an Assessment Question. What do you think?
Mother:	I see. Something like—"How come John gets angry when I ask him to help—and it seems to happen when he sees that I'm sad?" And I guess I also want to ask—"Why is that so hard for me?"
Assessor:	I think those are great questions to explore and that we'll be able to get some answers.

At times when we are contextualizing a problem or question with a parent, we may ask for information that seems intrusive to parents. For example, continuing with the above scenario:

Mother:	That's easy. We weren't allowed to express anger toward our parents. If we did, we got in serious trouble.
Assessor:	What do you think that was about for your parents?
Mother:	Do we really need to go there?
Assessor:	No, not if you don't want to. I asked because I thought it might help understand more about why it is so hard for you when John expresses anger.
Mother:	OK. Let me think about that and we can come back to it.

Another method we use to explore assessment questions is to ask: *If you had to answer this Assessment Question today, what would be your best answer?* To stay with the aforementioned example:

Mother:	If I had to answer my question, I'd say that John is afraid when I'm sad and doesn't know how to handle it, so he gets angry instead of telling me he's afraid.
Assessor:	That seems like a real possibility. Let me think about how we might check that out.

Continuing with this example, there is another method we often use to allow parents to express their fears:

Assessor: Before we stop, let me ask—what is the worst thing I could tell you at the end of the assessment?

Mother: You could tell me that I can't handle anger and John can't handle sadness—so our relationship will always be hard. Or you could tell me that John thinks I'm weak.

Assessor: We'll certainly check those things out, and I'll want your opinion too as we move ahead.

Here are additional examples of parents' worst fears.

> You could tell us that you think Marian isn't just depressed but is developing bipolar disorder, like my sister has. Her condition almost destroyed our family.

> You could tell us that Daniel will never be able to live independently.

> You could tell me her problems are totally my fault because of my alcohol use when she was young.

> You could tell me that Mark hates me for divorcing his father and doesn't ever want to live with me.

> You could tell us that we made a mistake adopting Mari and that she'll never be OK.

We find that these various methods of fleshing out Assessment Questions help us promote curiosity, introduce context as an influence on behavior, invite parents' fears into the room, and potentially enhance parental empathy.

Finalizing Assessment Questions

When the potential Assessment Questions have been explored, it is a good idea to restate them as a set and invite parents to modify them further. It is possible that some can be combined and others now seem less important and can be dropped. There also may be a question that creates a natural opening to introduce the idea of parents being tested themselves to understand systemic aspects of the child's problems (discussed in Chapter 4). For example, if parents agree on the question "*Why is Jonathan so responsive to his father and not to me?*" there may be an opportunity to propose testing the parents.

After any additional modifications, it is useful to send the parents home with a copy of the Assessment Questions to think about (or email them soon after). We let them know we are open to making changes before or during the next session. We also invite the parents to pose further questions as they arise during the assessment even if this happens during the very last session.

Coach the Parents on How to Introduce the Assessment to the Child

Toward the end of the initial session with the parents, as suggested by Finn (2007), we talk with them about how to introduce the assessment to their child (assuming they have not already discussed it). We ask that parents do this before they bring the child with them for the next session, typically the Parent-Child Session. We suggest that they be open and direct and tell their child what some of their concerns are and why they think an assessment would be helpful. We want them to communicate that there is nothing that is too bad to talk about. We also coach the parents on sharing one or two of their Assessment Questions with their child, particularly ones that are systemic in nature (if they posed such a question). For example, if parents have asked, "Why is Billy so angry all the time?" we might work with them to rephrase that question as "How can we change things so Billy isn't so angry?" This could then be shared with the child and is much less scapegoating.

Determine if an Anonymous Observation of the Child Would Be Useful Before Testing Sessions Begin

In some cases, it can be useful for us to observe the child before meeting the child. If parents agree, we arrange to do an anonymous observation, most often at the child's school. This can be a unique opportunity to learn how the child functions in academic and peer settings and may be especially useful if Assessment Questions touch on those areas. If the parents are in agreement, we usually ask them to contact school professionals first, and we follow-up to arrange the final details. Parents sometimes give input on what part of the child's day they think it would be most useful for us to observe.

Enlist Parents in Collecting Historical Information or Systematic Data About a Problem Behavior

During the initial Parent Session or when discussing the parents' observations of their child's testing sessions, we often find that we need additional information to further explore an Assessment Question, such as about the child's behavior at home. In such an instance, we may ask parents to systematically observe the behavior at home. For example, the parents may have reported that their child goes into rages that are of great concern. We might ask the parents to track the rages, in particular what happens right before they occur, how the parents respond, and what happens afterward. When parents are enlisted as "co-investigators" in such ways, we find they become more curious, are less reactive to their child's behavior, and often have insights that they can already put to use in addressing their own presenting concerns.

At other times, we find we would like additional background information to inform an Assessment Question. When this is the case, as addressed by Finn (2007), we might ask the parents to contact a family member (e.g., a grandmother) who may be able to fill in the details. For example, parents tell you that they have heard that Aunt Mary had some real problems that started in childhood that no one talked about much. They fear that their daughter, due to biological connections, may be starting to develop similar serious problems. Getting clarification from the grandmother as well as exploring the parents' fear may alleviate their anxiety and help them be curious about the complexity of their daughter's development. We have also found that suggesting parents reach out to extended family members can provide them with additional support as they go through this process.

Address Remaining Pragmatics

Near the end of the Parent Session, we address any remaining pragmatics. These often include (1) finalizing the assessment agreement (we generally do this verbally, but some practitioners do it in writing); (2) asking the parents to take home and complete a broadband child behavior checklist and possibly a version for someone else to fill out (e.g., grandparent); (3) getting releases to contact agreed-upon collateral professionals; (4) setting the next session time (and possibly subsequent sessions); and (5) discussing financial aspects of the assessment. Finally, we check to see if the parents have any additional reactions or questions and address these before ending the session.

Reflect on the Session

As soon as possible, we take time to reflect on the session. We think about what we have learned and experienced and begin to develop further hypotheses about factors related to the child/families' challenges. We also check ourselves to see if we are having strong emotional reactions, perhaps related to our own history or issues. We seek to find a curious, compassionate stance in which to hold these parents and their current story. We now proceed to the case of Henry and the first session with his parents.

Case: Initial Session with Henry's Parents

Dale:　　Nice to meet you both. Please have a seat. I sit in that chair (*pointing*), feel free to sit wherever you like. (*Parents sit next to each other on the couch.*) I had several referrals at the same time. So, I think David said your son was seeing Connie Jagga. Whoops, I mean Jagger. Every now and then my New York accent slips out.

Barbara:	I heard that accent. We lived in New York for a while. I have a client who can't say "drawer."
Dale:	Nor can I. *(Everyone laughs.)*

I often use self-effacing humor with clients, which I think is my unconscious way to set them at ease and help them not feel one-down.

Dale:	Well, let's talk about Henry a little bit. As you know, David and I already talked on the phone. But tell me, what made you call me at this time?
Barbara:	Right! Just take a deep breath before that story.

It was interesting to me that the mother spoke up right away since I had made the first connection with the father. I wondered if she tended to take the lead and he let that happen when the two of them were together.

Barbara:	Well so I'll give you the short version, when Henry was seven and in the second grade, one night he became morose.
David:	Yes!
Barbara:	He's always been, like he's always been, not moody, but deep. Like an old soul. Kind of quiet and very contemplative, and very cautious. A rule follower.
David:	Very cautious.
Barbara:	Very cautious. Very in-tune to everyone and everything around him. Never gonna move first or make a mistake or miss an instruction. So, not light-hearted. Not a lot of levity with Henry. I feel like that was apparent from Day 1. But, you know, normal, and then by the time he was 7 all of a sudden one night, it felt all of a sudden, he said, and I can't remember his exact words, I wish I had written them down but he said something that alluded to that he had been considering or thought of the idea of killing himself. Suicide. He didn't use the word suicide.
Dale:	Oh, that's so difficult for a parent to hear. *(Notice the joining here.)*
Barbara:	Yeah.
David:	Did he say, "I want to die," or did he say, "I want to erase myself?"
Barbara:	I think it was, "I want to die. I want to erase myself."
David:	Yeah, "I want to erase myself. I want to disappear."
Dale:	Oh, that's hard. I can't imagine….
Barbara:	That's right, that was his language. It was very pointed.
David:	Oh also, it was, "I want to kill myself."
Barbara:	That came later, that wasn't the first night.
David:	Oh, right, that came later. And it seemed that at first, we dismissed it because it seemed like an expression some people were saying: "Oh, I want to kill myself, oh I want to die." So, I thought, "He's a little New Yorker." He may have been picking up

> on the language from me. But then he used it in the proper
> context, like an embarrassing moment, but then he used it
> separately as a statement.

I wondered about David having such a dismissive reaction to Henry saying he
wanted to die. I thought, "Perhaps it's just too much for a father to bear or to
feel." I decided to move ahead to get information about the context of the
problem behavior.

Dale: And he just came to you one night and said that? (*Notice the*
circular questioning.)

Barbara: I was tucking him in, every night I always tuck him in and he,
actually at that time he sometimes cried himself to sleep. But there
didn't seem to be any reason. It didn't seem like there was
anything triggering this. It just seemed that he was a deep thinker,
and you know he doesn't get this from strangers. It's not like I'm
light-hearted either, so it didn't seem that odd. But then when he
said those words, we took action immediately and went to see his
school counselor the next day. It ended up she was unhelpful,
really. (*I felt relieved they had taken this seriously.*)

Dale: Not helpful?

Barbara: She told me to take him to Shoal Creek (*a local psychiatric hospital*)
that day. I mean it was just over the top, her response, and that's
been consistent from her. I've mostly stayed away from her during
this because it was not helpful. We found a therapist for him, and
he's been seeing Dr. Jagger for the last few years. But recently
we've been leaning on the counselor at school a little more,
because Henry has been asking to see someone during the day, if
he's feeling anxious.

Dale: Well, it sounds like you have a question there.

David: Oh, yeah, I did write down a number of questions.

Dale: Great. Shall we start with the one that relates to what we've been
talking about?

David: Yeah, what I wrote is, "Is he clinically depressed or is it
situational? What can we do to get him the help he needs?
What can we do to intervene with him?"

Dale: Those are all good questions. Why don't we start with, "Is he
clinically depressed or is it situational?" What do you mean by
situational?

Here I wanted to make sure I understood what he meant by situational and
not assume our definitions were the same.

Barbara: Situational as in lots of things going on. One important thing I
want to just kind of mention, since he's pre-puberty, is that he's

got a little bit of a Peter Pan thing going on. All summer he refused to wear shorts that fit him. He was always wearing shorts that were too small—insisting that they were big on him. He doesn't like the idea that his size is getting bigger. He's very body conscious now. That's new. He doesn't like it when you say he's getting taller or bigger.

Dale: What else you might think of as situational?

David: Well, he'll be going into middle school and we need to figure out which middle school to go to. He's tracked through to RBG Middle School, but he may want to go to Kennedy. We'd have to apply. I think a lot of his friends want to go there.

Barbara: I'm not pro Kennedy because he already has anxiety and there's a lot of homework. But he wants to go there because that's where his heavy hitter friends are supposedly going. But it's a real competitive school. All of this starts now.

There was more discussion about other possible schools. After a little bit of time, I reoriented us to the Assessment Question.

Dale: So, let's talk a little about if he's clinically depressed and it's not situational, what would that mean?

Barbara: We started keeping a notebook right before school started. One day he woke up around 4 in the morning and came to bed with me. And then around 6:30, he was trying to get me out of bed talking about being sad and about no one ever being in the kitchen with him in the morning. There was also a note around this time that said he never wants to go to anything. He'll say, "I don't want friends, I don't want to be happy. I don't want to go to a birthday party." Then he goes and seems to have a good time. He has a very tight group of friends he's been friends with since kindergarten. He says he wants to be sad.

David: Yeah, he doesn't want to get better. He wants to be sad.

Dale: What have you done to try and address it?

Barbara: You know, you get frustrated and you're just like, "If you don't stop talking this way—we've got to start talking about something else; we've got to try to get out of this mode, you know." I try to give him tasks to look around to become connected, "Let's go for a walk." "If you don't stop talking this way, I'm going to take video games away from you." And he'll say, "I want to never have video games again." And, he wins. He wins. Um, he's unbribable. You know you bribe your kids to do stuff, you're like, "Here's some chocolate." If he thinks you're going to get something over on him then he's just not interested in video games or anything. He'll always take it further than you. Um, does that make sense?

Dale:	Yes, it sounds very frustrating. Have you ever just sat with him with the feelings and the sadness?
Barbara:	Yes. Yes. So, every night now we have sad talk time. Which I've tried to turn into just talk time, but it's hard to change it. That's how we've tried to limit it from being all day to only at night. We did it (sad talk time) last night, and I really did just stay with him. Sometimes it's hard when you've done it for this long, but he cried and cried last night. He's just genuinely sad. It's heartbreaking. His eyes have circles under them. He's worried and he's like twisting his hair and flipping his ear and he says he's terrible at everything, everybody's better at school than him. He's a straight-A student. He's been made fun of. He had a bullying situation earlier in the year. So, you asked why did we come now? Just to let you know why we came, he asked, he's asked me on the 22nd of August, "Why am I sad all the time?" He's also said on the same day, "I should've chosen never to be born."
Dale:	Oh, this is hard to just listen to. This must be so difficult.
Barbara:	It's awful.
Dale:	Yes, it's terrible. What are you able to do for yourselves so you can keep dealing with this?
Barbara:	I mostly don't do any self-care at all. David goes to therapy.
David:	I go to therapy every other week.
Barbara:	He exercises.
David:	I also go to a spiritual director once a month.
Barbara:	I drink wine. I go walking with my friends. I go out twice a month with friends and I try to keep it in perspective because I realize I have to be strong for him and that guilt, me feeling guilty will not help him. Me feeling these things will not help him. So, I try to think of solutions and try new things and try to get him help. Yesterday I was on the American Association of Suicidology website just to find out about suicide.
Dale:	So, you try to educate yourself.
Barbara:	Educate myself, and I've, we've tried early on when we started going to the therapist, I felt a little bit accused because I work a lot, and especially then, it's true I was working a lot then. I was trying to get my business up and running. I work less now, but that was a critical time. I got to be a stay-at-home mom with him for a long time. I got to be a stay-at-home mom for most of three years. That's pretty good. I mean we orchestrated our lives so I could be at home so anyway not to get too into that. That's how I've tried not to focus too much on what we may have done. (*Notice Barbara struggling with shame here.*)
Dale:	Yes, it's so difficult when you feel like you must have done something wrong to have your child be so sad. But sometimes we really don't know what causes such sadness. It can be multiple

factors. It sounds like you've tried to address this for a long time. (*Notice the shame-reduction intervention.*)

Barbara: Yes. We try not over-schedule our family, because our children are both introverts. They need a lot of down time and free play. I try to, Dr. Jagger's helped me, to remember to try to provide some levity and some fun and try to change the conversation where possible, but still taking it seriously.

I began to feel like Barbara was reciting a narrative that she had shared before without any affect, so I decided to focus on feelings to try to deepen the conversation.

Dale: There must be a lot of feelings that come up for you both.
Barbara: Yes. I feel angry.
David: I feel frustrated with him many times.
Barbara: Oh yeah.
David: When he's being stubborn or being provocative.
Barbara: Oh, he's very provocative.
David: That can be very frustrating. You know sometimes it feels like you can't reach him. I feel like I have all my emotional energy drained. Sometimes it's very difficult to find my grounding. When Henry seems very depressed, it's hard for any of us to feel good.
Dale: Yeah, I imagine it's awful.
David: It throws me off balance.
Barbara: I feel bullied by him.
David: I feel bullied by him as well.
Barbara: I was going down a dark path recently where I had stopped worrying about him being suicidal a little bit because Dr. Jagger and I had talked about it and she didn't think he was really suicidal. She thought he was just saying that because he was provocative, and I'm careful with that because I think that if I think he's provocative it's potentially a problem. I think maybe he is, I don't you know. I almost feel like she's more scared of it than I am in a way.
Dale: More scared of?
Barbara: Of him being truly suicidal more than I am.
Dale: Oh, because she backs away from it?
Barbara: She does a little bit. I was going down a dark path where I was feeling very bullied by him so now, we have even gotten to a point where we are like we're just not going to have these conversations anymore, this is absolutely ridiculous. We have another child. He's very happy. This cannot be his life. He's being defined by it. We are all being defined by it.
David: That's how the sad talk time came up.
Barbara: Yeah.

David: He like spent almost half a day on the couch and he wants to talk about being sad. And I said, "No we're not going to do that anymore. For 5 minutes at bedtime, we can have sad talk time. We need to get up and do something else." And it worked.

Dale: So, you set a limit on it and it seemed to be helpful.

Barbara: Yeah, but it, it goes throughout the day. It's just now we've kind of stopped it from being verbal. And then, so what he does is he self-medicates. He uses technology. We've always been very limited with technology, but you know you loosen the reigns a little; it's self-medicating for him. It's how he keeps himself distracted from his own thoughts and um so he's often asking for more and more time on the phone or with other technology.

Dale: I can understand that if his thoughts are so difficult.

Barbara: Yeah, he's trying to escape.

Dale: Is he on medication?

Barbara: No.

Dale: And tell me about your feelings about medication.

Barbara: Well…

David: I'm quite hesitant about it. We've gone this long without approaching that subject because I'm hesitant, and I think Barbara may be as well. Many of the things I've read about medication, actually, I'm fearful that it can actually exacerbate suicidal ideation.

Dale: Yes.

David: Yeah so, I'm concerned about introducing drugs that affect the brain to a small, like young child. His brain is still developing.

Dale: What about supplements or that or that sort of thing? Have you thought about those?

Barbara: Well, I just brought those up in the car on the way here. I was thinking maybe something to help him sleep. Like melatonin or I don't know if that's safe to give to kids because maybe he's tired a lot because of his anxiety keeping him up. Cause I think, I don't know if he's depressed, he's definitely anxious.

Dale: I'm wondering, are there times when he doesn't do the sad talk and seem depressed?

Barbara: You know if you observe him in the world like he'll be the kid at the birthday party jumping straight up and down with a smile ear to ear. Running with his friends. I mean he doesn't want to leave.

David: We had a great time camping the other weekend. He was really enjoying himself and when I remind him of that he just says he was miserable. We've started taking videos to show him when he's happy.

Dale: This is very complicated. Before I asked you the last question, about when is Henry not sad, we were talking about medication.

Maybe you have another question there? Something about medication or what can help if he is depressed?

David: I wrote one down that may be related to that. "How do we prevent him from becoming further anxious and depressed?"

This session lasted for 1.5 hours. As you saw, I tried to follow the parents' lead but also to generate Assessment Questions and get background information on each question. Also, I tried to share my emotional reactions and offer support as the session went on.

Here are the Assessment Questions generated during this session:

1. Is Henry clinically depressed or is it situational?
2. Has he experienced an unknown trauma that has adversely affected his self-image and how he engages with the world?
3. How do we prevent him from becoming further anxious and depressed?
4. What are Henry's intellectual strengths and weaknesses? Is there a disharmony among them? What kind of learning environment is best for him?
5. How can we help Henry feel confident and loved?
6. Why does Henry make provocative statements to us?

The parents understood that they could ask additional questions if something came up during the assessment. I also spent a few minutes coaching them about how to explain the assessment to Henry. I suggested they let Henry know why they contacted me and how they hoped working with me would help them understand why he was so sad, how they could help, and what middle school would be best for him to attend. I also asked them to share one of their questions to give him an idea that he too could ask questions about himself. We decided that their question about the learning environment would be best, because of Henry's interest in where he would go to school next year.

Reflections After the Session

After the session, I sat for a few minutes and wrote down my thoughts. I liked the parents. They were bright and easy to engage. Both were self-reflective and wondered how they might have contributed to Henry's difficulties. I thought this would make it easier to introduce systemic ideas, but also sensed I had to be very attentive to shame, as they seemed prone to blaming themselves. I noticed that David spoke very quietly and let his wife have center stage, but he did speak up as needed. I felt sad for the parents and sympathized with how difficult it would be to have a young child so sad. While I could feel their sadness, I could also feel their frustration and un-derlying anger as well. They were concerned about their other child and how Henry was affecting him. They felt they had tried many things already to help Henry, and nothing had worked. From a systemic perspective, I thought their presentation of Henry best fit that of a "sick child" (Chapter 2). But I also sensed some elements of a scapegoated child because of their frustration and anger. I looked forward to meeting Henry and was intrigued by how much power he had in the family. We now move to how to conduct a Parent-Child Session.

Parent-Child Session

Having settled on the assessment agreement for the TA-C in the initial session with the parents—including the main questions they want to explore through the assessment—we are now ready to meet the child and begin to observe the family system in action. Thus, typically the next TA-C session includes a substantial period of time (e.g., 30–40 minutes) with the caregivers and child in the same room together, followed by the assessor introducing an assessment activity that parents either observe or in which they and their child participate together. Again, this contrasts with the way most traditional child assessments are conducted, where after an initial parent session, children are typically led to another room for "testing," while parents sit in a nearby waiting room or go out to do errands. We now detail the goals for the Parent-Child session (Box 3.3).

Goals of the Initial Session with Parents and Child

Check-In with Parents to Address New Reactions/Questions Since Last Session

We find that check-ins at the beginning of sessions with parents are key to maintaining continuity and connection. We track their questions and insights since the last meeting and share our thoughts with them. It is also good to check in about significant events that may have occurred during the week that might be affecting the child or the family system. If the child can tolerate waiting out of hearing range, it is easy to touch base with parents alone before starting the current session. For children who are not able to tolerate being on their own, either one member of the assessment team stays with them while the other talks to parents (in the two-assessor model) or we touch base with parents by phone or email prior to the session at hand.

Parents Introduce Child to the Assessor

At this first Parent-Child Session, we ask to meet the child with the help of parents. This is an important moment as it begins our relationship with the child. We appreciate that all children are unique, and we are excited to start to know this child. Our experience may confirm or extend what we have learned from the parents' perspectives shared at the previous meeting. One

---

Box 3.3   Goals of Initial Parent-Child Session

- Check-in with parents to address new reactions/questions since the Parent Session.
- Ask parents to introduce their child to the assessor.
- Observe family interactions.
- Begin to develop a connection with the child while also staying connected to parents.
- Collaborate with parents to review process of the assessment with child.
- Ask parents to share one or two Assessment Questions with child, as coached in advance.
- Possibly ask the child about previous assessment experiences.
- Invite the child to contribute Assessment Questions about self/ family.
- Invite the child to engage in an activity while parents observe directly or indirectly, or invite the parents and child to engage in an activity together.
- End the session by addressing any questions the child may have, explaining the next session, and sharing something genuine and positive.
- Spend time with parents to address and discuss any questions from their observations, share something genuine and positive, and confirm the next session.
- Reflect on the session and refine hypotheses.

---

child may be hesitant or shy with us initially, hiding behind a parent. Another may be energetic and need to be on center stage, engaging us from the get go. We adjust our approach to fit the individual child, and begin to form a connection that we hope will grow and be a change agent during the entire assessment process.

Observe the Family Interactions

Throughout this session, we keenly observe the interactions between the parents, between parents and the child, and between parents and child with us. Proximity, body language, tone of voice, who takes the lead, and who the child defers to are just some of the things we take in as we strive to know this family. We also pay close attention to our own feelings and reactions as the session progresses, believing that these are an important source of information about the family system. Our focus goes between two perspectives: First, we try to get in the child's shoes, as we are curious about what it might be like to be this child in this family. Also, our observations inform our curiosity about what it is like to parent this child. These beginning hypotheses contribute to an emerging, tentative case conceptualization and to our developing sense of interventions that could be useful.

Begin to Develop a Connection with the Child,
While also Staying Connected to Parents

When the child joins, we want to extend a "holding environment" to the child to begin our relationship of trust and safety. We also want the parents to continue to feel "held" by us and supportive of us "holding" their child. This dual alliance is essential for the success of TA-C, and requires a kind of differentiation on the part of assessors via which they form a connection to the child, form a connection to each parent, and form a connection to the entire family system. The more conflict there is in the relationship between parents and child, the more difficult this may be to do. Also, some families accept the assessor's differentiated stance with ease (usually healthier family systems), some make us feel they want us to take their child home and keep the child, and still others appear guarded and act as if they do not really want to share their child, at least not yet. We strive to be alert to these varied dynamics and make adjustments for each family. At this early point in the assessment, we prioritize our connection to parents, while also building a connection to the child. We continue to use active listening, mirroring, joining, and attending to shame with parents, and we find ways to use these techniques in age-appropriate ways with the child. Often, being playful, creative, and humorous with the child goes a long way and also models a more positive relationship for parents.

Collaborate with Parents to Review the Assessment with the Child

We continue our conversation with the child and possibly ask what they know about the purpose of our meetings. Since we have previously coached the parents on how to introduce the assessment to the child, this is a chance to learn what they said and how it was heard and understood. If the child seems confused, we typically ask the parents to explain the process at that point of the session. We join the conversation as needed to add to the child's understanding and to show the child that we are working closely with their parents. We find that the more we facilitate the parents and child communicating with each other, and not through us, the more we reinforce that the purpose of the assessment is to help the family work together.

We help clarify any other concerns or questions and then inquire if the child is willing and ready to go forward and be part of the assessment. The conversation continues, and we encourage the parents to share one or two of their Assessments Questions with the child. As coached in advance, we hope they will share a question that is systemic in nature (e.g., "How can we all learn to control our anger and talk together about what bothers us?"), rather than one that singles out the child (e.g., "How can Susie learn to better control her anger?"). But again, how the parents handle this invitation and how the child responds tells us a lot about where the family is at the moment and what will be needed to help it shift.

If Relevant, Ask the Child About Previous Assessment Experiences

Although not warranted in every TA-C, if parents indicated that the child was assessed before, and especially if the previous assessment was noteworthy in some way, we may ask the child what they remember to gauge how that experience may color the current assessment. If the child describes a negative memory, we state that we are sorry they had that experience and that we will do our best to have this assessment be quite different. We invite children to let us know if they feel uncomfortable at any time. If children share positive memories, we build on those with our work.

Invite the Child to Contribute Assessment Questions About Self/Family

We also invite the child to contribute their own Assessment Questions at this time while parents are present, or at any time during the assessment. In our experience, it is hard for most young children to generate their own questions at this time. They may feel overly self-conscious during this first meeting with the assessor, or again they may not be at the developmental level to step back and be curious about their situation. However, we have found that more outspoken or "advanced" children are sometimes able to construct questions. If the child does come up with questions, we may decide to explore and even contextualize the question(s) during this initial session to see what parents might add. Another possibility is to do this is when we will be working just with the child a bit later in the session. Further, in our experience some children pose questions later in the assessment process (as is the case for Henry), when they feel more comfortable with the process and the assessor. Exploring and contextualizing their questions then becomes a possibility and an opportunity to understand their concerns and needs.

Invite the Child to Engage in an Activity

In TA-C, we have been influenced and informed by the use of play, playfulness, and creative methods from play therapy, filial therapy, and family therapy. We have been inspired by the work of Handler (2007), who encouraged assessors who use therapeutic approaches in assessment to set aside some of their traditional training and focus on being more playful and imaginative with children. In his experience, engaging playfully would greatly facilitate the success of the assessment. That has been our experience as well. Handler described some of his favorite playful approaches with children, including the squiggle game (Winnicott, 1958) and the Fantasy Animal Drawing Game (described in Chapter 4). As discussed in Chapter 2 and as will be apparent in our illustrations and the case of Henry, we have integrated many of Handler's techniques into TA-C, including his call for the assessor to be playful and creative in working with the child and the parents.

At this point in the Parent-Child Session, typically we invite the child to talk with us and engage in an activity (e.g., drawing or free play) with us while the parents go to an area to observe (introduced below and discussed fully in Chapter 4). If the child is ready to separate, we follow the procedures we are about to discuss. However, if the child is reticent or the parents seem anxious about separating, or if we simply want more time to observe the family system together, we slow the process down a bit. We may build on the Assessment Questions and ask the family members to each share: (1) "something they would change in the family if they could" and (2) "something they wouldn't want to change in the family." Or, we may invite the whole family to draw (e.g., a picture of their house and neighborhood or of the whole family doing something together), or to play a game together. We may ask questions or make comments related to the Assessment Questions (e.g., "I see what you mean about Rico wanting to move around a lot"). And we certainly begin to look for family interactions that are relevant to the presenting issues. But even if this time is rather low key, in our experience it pays off in that the child becomes more comfortable with the setting and the assessor, the parents become less anxious, and we have set a positive tone for the assessment.

With children who are ready to separate, once we are alone with them, we typically talk more about the process of the assessment, discuss any Assessment Questions they may have, and try to learn more about the context of their questions, if applicable. Depending upon the child, this discussion may be lengthy or short. We sometimes invite the child to do a series of drawings (Tharinger & Roberts, 2014). Standard instructions are used, and questions follow each drawing (part of the "Extended Inquiry" discussed fully in Chapter 4) that may include asking the child to tell a story about one of the drawings (Finn, 2007; Handler, 2008). This initial child session often ends with 10–15 minutes of free play (in which the child chooses from a variety of toys and games), to provide the child with the opportunity to engage in unstructured activity that can be fun. Free play is also an opportunity for the child to reveal aspects of their personality and life themes (Tharinger et al., 2011), as well as express reactions to the experience of the session.

Parents Observe Child and Assessor, Either Directly or Indirectly

As will be discussed in detail in Chapter 4, while we prepare for our time with the child, and with the child's knowledge, the parents are situated for observation. The parents either settle in the back of the assessor's office, or leave to go to an observation room, either behind a one-way mirror or connected to a live video feed. The parents are encouraged to jot down their thoughts, reactions, and questions, as well as to pay attention to any surprising emotions they experience while observing. We discuss these reactions with parents, either immediately after our time with the child (again if the child is able to be alone for a brief period) or later, perhaps by phone or email.

Wrap Up with the Child

Following our activities with the child, we move to end the session. We check in with the child about any questions that have arisen, explain when we will meet again, and what we are likely to do, and provide the child with some positive and specific feedback. For example, "*I really enjoyed our time together. I especially liked how you used the animal toys and gave them each their own voice. That was very creative, and I had fun!*"

Wrap Up with the Parents

At this point, we ask the parents to join us. If the child is able to spend time alone or supervised by office staff, perhaps reading or playing with toys in a waiting area, then we can process the parents' reactions and offer our input. If the child cannot tolerate being separated from parents any longer, this conversation will need to take place later, perhaps by phone. When parting, we confirm the next appointment and share something positive about the parents, with the child present or not. For example, "*I really appreciated how closely you watched Janie play with the animal figures and what they all were saying.*" If expressed with the child present, such comments confirm to the child that her parents were listening and that the assessor can be a good bridge between the parents and child.

Assessor Reflects and Refines Hypotheses

Following this session, we reflect on our reactions to the child, parents, and family. We review our earlier impressions and hypotheses and think about what has been confirmed and what has changed in our thinking since the Parent Session. We check in with ourselves about any emotions or reactions that have surfaced and how they are similar or different than those we experienced following the Parent Session.

Now we return to Dale's account of her session with Henry and his parents.

Case: Initial Session with Henry and Parents

I greeted Barbara and David in the waiting room and then they introduced me to Henry. I asked if he was ok if I checked in with his parents first and he nodded OK. The parents came into my office, and I asked how the week had gone and if they had any thoughts after our last session. They indicated they were looking forward to the assessment and were feeling somewhat hopeful. I also asked if they had other Assessment Questions to add to those we had previously generated. They did not. After a few minutes, I went out to the waiting room to invite Henry back to my office. As soon as Henry walked into the room, he noticed a very big blue ball, sat on it, and began to bounce.

The parents had already talked to Henry about the assessment process, and I asked what he thought about it. He seemed rather blasé, showing little affect or curiosity. I explained that first we would just get to know each other and then we'd try and figure out together why he was so sad and what might be a good middle school for him to go to. I asked if it would be all right with him if I videotaped our sessions. He said he didn't know, and I said, "OK, well do you want to try and see what it would feel like?" He said, "Yes" and the session continued.

Dale: (*Turning on the camera.*) OK, do you want to keep bouncing and see what you look like?
Henry: (Nods, yes.)

Henry bounced for a few minutes, looking directly into the camera. I felt a playful energy in the room. He continued to bounce, and I asked if he wanted to see what he looked like on the video.

Dale: Do you want to come and see? It's not just you that we'll be taping.

I wanted him to know I wouldn't just be focusing on him so that he would feel less like an identified patient, but rather I'd be working with him and his parents—taking a systemic perspective.

Dale: You have to come around this way. See your mom and your dad. Do you see them both sitting on the couch? And then, if you're in the middle, we get to see you too. (*I was trying to get him off the ball in a non-confrontational way.*) Would that be ok? Let's try it, and we can see it at the end. How's that?
Henry: Ok. Can I get the ball back?
Dale: Sure. You can play with it later. For now, let's talk about what will happen for the next month or so. Our goal together is to answer the questions your parents asked. Did they share any of their questions with you?
Henry: Yeah, which middle school I should go to.
Dale: Great. Is that a good question?
Henry: (*Shrugged his shoulders.*)
Dale: Well, you'll get a chance to ask any questions you might have. We'll hang out together here and do different things; some will have to do

with reading and writing, some might have to do with numbers and how you see the world, and at times we might focus on feelings. I might ask you to tell stories or draw. Do you like to draw?

Henry: No.

Dale: Do you like to tell stories?

Henry: No.

Dale: Do you like school?

Henry: No.

Dale: Do you like to play games?

Henry: Not really.

Dale: Do you like to stand on your head? (*I felt the need to break what already felt like relentless nay saying.*)

Henry: I can't.

Dale: Are you sure?

Henry: I'm sure.

Dale: Did you ever try?

Henry: Yes, I've tried a lot.

Dale: You have?

Henry: Yes, I just fall down

Dale: You know how I used to do it when I was your age?

Henry: How?

Dale: I had this bed, so the bed I had, here's the wall here's the corner, right? And so, I think my bed was like this in the corner. So, I would stand on my head in the corner and then the wall would support me. Did you ever try it that way?

Henry: I normally try the couch sometimes.

Dale: Yeah, see how it works on your bed, if it's near the wall, because the wall may help even more than the couch...So, I have one more question before we just play a game or do something else. Would that be nice? No? OK. So, I have one more question, OK?

Henry: (*No response.*)

Dale: I wonder if you have any questions that you'd like to ask about yourself?

Henry: No.

Dale: OK. So, what kinds of games do you like? Because at the end of the session, I'd like us to do something fun. Do you all play games at home? Ever?

Henry: Sometimes.

Dale: What do you play?

Henry: Life. (*This is a child's board game sold in the USA.*)

The dialogue about games continued, and I noticed that the mother began to take over for Henry, suggesting a number of games. Then, the father talked about a game they play that included their dog Ginger. The dad seemed to be trying hard to engage Henry. We talked about competition and what happened when Ginger wins. I decide to share a little information about myself to see if that would be helpful in engaging Henry.

Dale: I love games. I'm very competitive. I like to win. Are you competitive?
Henry: (*Shakes his head no.*)
Dale: No? You don't care if you win?
Henry: I hate competition.
Dale: Do you? What do you hate the most about it?
Henry: I don't know.
Dale: Maybe the pressure?
Henry: Probably.
Dale: Yeah, if you feel like you need to win, it's pressure, isn't it? Ok, so we need to think about games that are enjoyable and not competitive. So, in finishing up, we won't play a game. I think we'll do a little activity with everybody and then maybe we'll ask your parents to leave, if that's ok with you. But for now, I would like for each of you to take a minute to draw your family doing something together. I'll give each of you a piece of paper, and here are some pens and markers. Ok? (*Everyone agreed.*) Great.

As they were drawing, Henry sat and played with his ear, which I suspected was a sign of anxiety, and seemed to be thinking about what to draw. I tried to support him by lessening the pressure he might be experiencing in having to draw something specific. So, I suggested that if he wanted, he could just use different colors to represent the family. He didn't draw and refused by quietly not complying. I then asked each family member to show their drawing. Without consulting each other, both parents had drawn a recent campout that they had gone on. Both emphasized how much fun it was and how everyone had had a really good time. We then turned to Henry, who hadn't drawn at all. He didn't appear angry or forceful. But his refusal added weight to the room. The parents didn't say anything to encourage him or shame him. I again thought, "Henry seems to hold a lot of power in the family."

Dale: Great job you guys! Thank you. I can see how much you enjoyed that camping trip. (*Talking directly to Henry*) OK, so I'm going to give you a choice, all right? Can we let your parents go out in the waiting room so we can talk?
Henry: (*Shakes head no*)
Dale: You want them to stay?
Henry: (*Nods yes*)
Dale: Ok. Well, let me explain a little bit about what will happen next. Henry, you and I will do a number of different things together. Different activities. If you want to come over here, I'll show you some of the type of things we'll do. (*I showed him different materials*

and he seemed engaged in hearing about what will happen.) We'll try not to do any drawing or any writing. Is that good? Ok. I'll ask you some different questions and you can answer them, like, "Can you name an ocean?"

Henry: The Atlantic Ocean.

Dale: Yup, perfect. Just like that. I'd also like to know if you have any questions about yourself that you might like to have answered?

Henry: No.

Dale: Henry, what grade are you in?

Henry: 5th

Dale: So, you have to pick a school next year. Where do you want to go?

Henry: I really don't know where I want to go.

Dale: So, this might help you to decide where you want to go. Do you know that? Sometimes we do this with kids when they're transitioning from preschool to elementary school or elementary school to middle school, and it helps decide where you want to go. We can talk about that too. Ok? We can talk about anything you want to talk about. Alright?

Henry: Alright.

We ended the session by talking about the family dog, Ginger. This was the first time Henry was actively engaged in the conversation. He laughed at how funny he thought Ginger was. This interchange demonstrates a number of things. The assessor must be flexible and follow the child's lead. Henry didn't seem excited about a game, so I changed the activity. Although he didn't participate in the family drawing, he was attentive and curious about his parents' drawings. I tried to share how the process could be useful in helping him make a decision about middle school.

Reflections on the Session

By the end of the session, I was tired. Henry's negative mood was heavy, and it was draining to deal with his lack of engagement. I was surprised that following his lead didn't seem to help him be more engaged. My natural tendency is to be playful with children, and it's usually pretty easy for me to engage a child, but this situation felt different. Henry seemed intent on not having fun, except when he was jumping on the ball. I wondered if he was trying to make a statement about how miserable he was and, possibly trying to provoke his parents or me. I also wondered about how anger was handled in the family and if Henry had another safe way to express anger.

For the most part, as I talked directly to Henry, his parents did not interrupt or try and cajole him into being more engaged or positive. At various points in the session, I found it hard to read the parents. At the end when

Henry refused to draw, his mother looked frustrated but didn't say anything. His dad did not show much response to Henry's lack of participation. Again, I wondered about anger and how feelings were shared in the family. Were the parents not responding typical or were they inhibited with me in the room? Perhaps they didn't want me to see them get irritated at Henry. Even though he didn't participate in the family drawing activity, Henry was curious about what his parents drew and what they had to say about their drawings; I took this as a positive sign.

In thinking about the next session, I was curious if Henry's demeanor would change when his parents weren't in the room. Therefore, I looked forward to our next session. I was also aware of some anxiety, thinking that if Henry's demeanor did not change, this would be a very difficult assessment.

References

Allen, J. G., Fonagy, P., & Bateman, A. W. (2008). *Mentalizing in clinical practice*. Arlington, VA: American Psychiatric Publishing.

Cecchin, G. C. (1987). Hypothesizing, circularity, and neutrality revisited: An invitation to curiosity. *Family Process, 26*, 405–413.

Finn, S. E. (2007). *In our client's shoes: Theory and techniques of Therapeutic Assessment*. Mahwah, NJ: Erlbaum.

Fischer, C. T. (1985/1994). *Individualizing psychological assessment* (2nd ed.). New York, NY: Routledge.

Handler, L. (2007). The use of therapeutic assessment with children and adolescents. In S. Smith & L. Handler (Eds.), *Clinical assessment of children and adolescents: A practitioner's guide* (pp. 53–72). Mawah, NJ: Erlbaum & Associates.

Handler, L. (2008). Supervision in therapeutic and collaborative assessment. In A. Hess, K. Hess, & T. Hess (Eds.), *Psychotherapy supervision: Theory, research, and practice* (2nd ed.; pp. 200–222). New York, NY: John Wiley & Sons.

Kamphuis, J. H., & Finn, S. E. (2019). Therapeutic Assessment in personality disorders: Toward the restoration of epistemic trust. *Journal of Personality Assessment, 101*(6), 662–674.

Panskepp, J. (1998). *Affective neuroscience*. New York: Oxford University Press.

Tharinger, D. J., Christopher, G., & Matson, M. (2011). Play, playfulness, and creative expression in Therapeutic Assessment with children. In S. W. Russ & L. N. Niec (Eds.), *An evidence-based approach to play in intervention and prevention: Integrating developmental and clinical science* (pp. 109–148). New York: Guilford Press.

Tharinger, D. J., Finn, S. E., Hersh, B., Wilkinson, A., Chistopher, G., & Tran, A. (2008). Assessment feedback with parents and children: A collaborative approach. *Professional Psychology: Research and Practice, 39*, 600–609.

Tharinger, D. & Roberts, M. (2014). Human figure drawings in Therapeutic Assessment with children: Process, product, life context, and systemic impact. In L. Handler & A. D. Thomas (Eds.), *Drawings in assessment and psychotherapy: Research and application* (pp. 17–41). New York: Routledge.

Winnicott, D. W. (1958). *Collected papers: Through paediatrics to psychoanalysis*. London: Tavistock.

4   Phase II: Data Gathering/Testing

Having developed collaborative alliances and agreed upon Assessment Questions, we move on from Phase I, the Initial Sessions, to Phase II, Data Gathering/Testing. The Assessment Questions put forth by the parents and the child strongly influence the information we pursue, what tests and methods we choose, and what theoretical perspectives we consider in coming to understand and integrate the findings. Our primary goal for Phase II is to help parents understand their child in a new light, build empathy for their child, and be open to future interventions and potential systemic change. We use tests and other methods and activities with the child and parents to understand the child and the family system. We also gather information from collateral sources, such as referring professionals, teachers, and health care providers. We may also do school and/or home observations if they seem pertinent to the Assessment Questions.

The number of actual sessions in this phase varies by case, and is determined by the nature and extent of the questions guiding the assessment and the length of time the child can tolerate testing. In our experience, five to six testing sessions with the child are typical. In addition, we usually meet with the parents alone for three sessions and with the parents and child together two or three times. The number of sessions can vary greatly and the plan is negotiated with each family. We individualize test selection for each case, and tests are added along the way as needed.

To gain further information from the parents beyond that provided in the initial phone call and the initial session, we almost always schedule an additional parents-only session or two in the time frame in which the child is being tested. Our goal is to obtain more in-depth information from the parents about the child's and the family's developmental history, past and current life changes and stressors (using the *Timeline of Major Child/Family Life Events*), information about previous generations (a genogram), resources available to the family from extended family and friends, and any other topic that may extend our understanding and inform the Assessment Questions. For example, we have sometimes asked parents to bring in photo albums, scrapbooks, samples of schoolwork, etc. to assist us to more deeply understand the family and their journey to this point.

DOI: 10.4324/9781003000174-4

We use Extended Inquiry (EI) methods (not unique to Therapeutic Assessment with Children [TA-C]), but not commonly used in most child assessment models) to explore selective test responses a child gives. There are several ways to use EIs. They can assist in getting below the surface of responses the child has provided, especially having to do with emotional content and perceptions of family functioning. For example, if a child has responded on a self-report test that she feels sad often, it would likely be a good idea to explore that response after the administration of the entire test is completed. EIs are also used to try out new strategies with a cognitive or academic task, such as trying out a new way to enhance short-term memory after completing the Digit Span subtest of the WISC-V. Overall, EIs help us go beyond the test responses themselves to gain more insight into the child and what he/she is experiencing emotionally or interpersonally and what he/she is capable of cognitively when provided with new strategies. Although EIs are used to explore the child's test responses and, to some extent, expand the child's awareness, their primary purpose is to offer observing parents the opportunity to understand what their child is feeling and thinking.

Somewhat unique to TA-C, we typically invite parents to observe all or part of their child's testing sessions and discuss their observations with us. We describe options for parental observation below. Following the session (or during the session if a two-assessor method is being used), we actively discuss what parents have observed. We collaborate with parents and strive to stimulate their curiosity and promote new ways to think about their child.

When we have completed the testing sessions in the Data Gathering/Testing Phase, we may have another parents-only session, depending on the timing of the earlier one and what additional information we would like to gather. This session will likely be designed to check in about the parents' observations of their child's testing sessions, extend the mini discussions/consultations we have had along the way, explore questions the parents have, and share some of their child's test results to see how the parents react (which informs us about what might be Levels 1, 2, and 3 Information). This session is an opportunity to further strengthen our collaborative relationship with the parents by working together to make sense of the information we are gathering. And, if applicable, the parents-only session provides an opportunity to share with the parents the results from any test(s) they have completed about themselves. Parents' test results often go a long way in supporting a systemic view of the child's challenges and help the parents consider their role in the family system and their child's challenges.

We have organized the remainder of this chapter into six parts. In Part 1, we clarify how testing and test responses are viewed from a TA-C approach. We also discuss how and why we chose specific tests and activities. In addition, we provide a rationale of when and why we might invite parents to be tested to learn about their own personality and parenting style in relation to their child. In Part 2, we thoroughly cover EI methods, introduced earlier. In Part 3, we fully explain the rationale, methods, and benefits of inviting parents to observe and process their child's test responses and behavior with the assessor. We also discuss when this method would not be indicated or might raise concerns. In Part 4, we propose steps for conducting testing sessions. And finally, in Part 5, we review the need for assessors to organize their materials well and examine the results of each individual test. This process prepares the assessor for the next steps (described in Chapter 5). In Part 6, we return to Henry's case and illustrate his experience and findings from the testing sessions, as well as additional input and reactions from his parents.

Part 1: Testing and Test Responses

We have structured Part 1 as a series of questions and answers.

- How is testing viewed from a TA-C approach?
- How are test responses viewed from a TA-C approach?
- How are tests chosen and why?
- When/why do we invite parents to be tested?

How Is Testing Viewed from a TA-C Approach?

We view testing as a process that occurs between the child and assessor in the present moment and in a particular context, rather than as a procedure that will yield some "Absolute Truth" about a child or family. For example, we remember that the child's responses may be influenced by what the child thinks the parents need to hear or what the child wants them to hear. Also, test responses are inevitably influenced by the collaborative alliance between the child, assessor, and family system. If the child and/or parent have developed trust in the assessor, the child's responses will be different than if they have not. And if parents are observing a testing session or the child knows they will review a video later, that can also influence how the child reacts.

In TA-C, we keep in mind that standard psychological testing can be an uncomfortable and confusing process for many children (and parents). The standardized administration procedures for many tests (e.g., cognitive, achievement, neuropsychological) inherently involve "failure experiences," as the assessor is required to continue administering a subtest until the child has answered a string of questions incorrectly, in order to establish a ceiling (a stopping point) (Handler, 2007). Generally, the assessor cannot provide immediate feedback about the child's performance, and this, as well as the traditional assessor's typical detached, impersonal stance, may arouse anxiety for children (and observing parents). For example, a child who has struggled with basic academics in school may be asked to take a comprehensive achievement test or cognitive test. As mentioned earlier, these tests usually require that the child fail several sequential items before the assessor ends a subtest and goes on to the next. Many children are frustrated or demoralized by this experience, and it can bring back painful memories of previous failures and perhaps teasing or shaming. The observing parents may also have this experience, as they likely had many feelings about their child's past academic struggles.

In addition to this possible sense of failure responding to academic and cognitive tasks, a similar experience can occur with self-report tests when, for example, children are asked to complete a long list of test items about their behavioral, emotional, and social functioning. If they hit close to home, some of these items may be painful for the child to acknowledge. In reaction, a child may tune out, answer falsely, not respond, or start acting out in order to end the testing. And again, parents can have strong reactions to their children's test responses. Similarly, performance-based personality tests, such as the Rorschach or various "picture story tests" such as the Children's Apperception Test (CAT; Bellak & Bellak, 1976); the Roberts Apperception Test for Children (RATC; McArthur & Roberts, 1982); and Thematic Apperception Test (TAT; Murray, 1943) can also be stressful, as they can elicit painful feelings in both children and in parents who are observing. Any and all of these experiences could create ruptures in the relationship between the assessor and the child or the assessor and parents that, if not addressed, could render the overall assessment a failure.

These potentially difficult experiences also offer opportunities for increased understanding, alliance, and relationship building between all the parties involved (child, parents, assessor). In TA-C, we have developed methods that greatly lessen the chance of a rupture and subsequent assessment failure. Although generally we follow standard procedures so that test responses can be properly scored and norm-referenced, we put a lot of attention into supporting clients emotionally so they are not overwhelmed or traumatized by the testing experience. We ask about clients' experience of the test once standardized administration is complete (Finn, 2007), and we use EI methods. Thus, in TA-C, standard administration of tests is adhered to, but within an interpersonal context. This difference from traditional assessment has a huge impact, as we find that the child and parents are more trusting and more open to change when their experiences are recognized and explored. We also find that the collaboration and alliances we build allow for the repair of a rupture, should one occur. Thus, in TA-C, testing is utilized in a way that children and parents feel respected, understood, listened to, and more capable.

How Are Test Responses Viewed from a TA-C Approach?

Test responses are viewed as communications (both conscious and implicit) from clients to the assessor to help answer the questions for the assessment. In the case of children, test responses are also considered to be communications to the parents, with the possibility of the assessor helping parents to accurately "decode" the child's communication. Test responses also are seen as representative of present functioning, embedded in the context and relationship with the assessor and parents.

As mentioned earlier, test responses in TA-C represent a "snapshot" of the child's current behavior, state of mind, and subjective experience within the current context and relationship with assessor and parents. Responses are not seen as "Absolute Truth" since testing at another time in a different context with a different assessor is likely to result in different findings. As in all the TA models, tests are viewed as empathy magnifiers, that is, tools that allow assessors (and observing parents) access to the child's subjective experience and feelings, letting the adults walk in the child's shoes and deeply feel what the child has experienced. And finally, test responses allow for further exploration through methods of EI. Responses to EI prompts often generate a deeper understanding of the child and enhance parental understanding and empathy.

How Are Tests Chosen and Why?

In TA-C, we select tests in similar ways to traditional assessment models of child assessment, but yet somewhat differently. As in most models, tests are chosen from multiple categories of interest that stem from the reason for referral or from Assessment Questions. These areas may include cognitive functioning, academic achievement, personality, behavior, trauma, diagnostic labels (e.g., Autism Spectrum, Depression, etc.), family functioning, resiliency, adaptive behavior, social functioning, etc. Within these categories, it is typical for assessors to choose specific tests in part because of their expertise and experience with those tests. It is also important to seek out other tests that may be useful to inform the questions, and when possible, to use tests with different types of response formats (e.g., self-report, observer report, performance-based) that measure the same construct (Meyer et al., 2001). Consultation with experienced colleagues is useful in exploring tests to use and prevents falling into using a fixed battery for all cases. It is also best practice to choose more than one test to measure an area of functioning that is central to the aim of the assessment.

Similar to traditional models of child assessment, both nomothetic and idiographic tests/methods are chosen to capture normative comparisons and individual differences. Tests are chosen to sample both narrow and broad domains of functioning. Tests with multiple informant versions (child, parents, perhaps teachers) are valuable for comparison purposes. Also, we may schedule a home visit, a method not incorporated into most traditional assessment models, and consider a school visit, which is more typical in a child assessment.

We are also guided by other principles in choosing tests for an individual case. We do not use a standard battery, but gear our choice of tests to each unique case, the Assessment Questions, and how the case progresses. We almost always use both objective and performance-based tests (historically called "projective" tests). We use well-developed scoring systems for performance-based tests and supplement them with EI methods to give richness to their interpretation. We give understandable explanations to the child and parents of why each test has been chosen in relation to the Assessment Questions they posed and other aims of the TA-C. And we usually chose the first test administered according to its face validity for one or more major Assessment Questions that the parents proposed. We want them to experience from the start that the assessment is guided by their concerns.

We also use play and other creative methods with our child clients to enhance the relationship and explore underlying themes and existing stories they may express in this modality. Although other models also do this, it is usually with pre-school-aged children. We find it applicable with elementary school-aged children as well. Tharinger et al. (2011) have well described the benefits of utilizing play, unstructured and structured, in testing sessions in TA-C. Invitations to play when taking a break from testing can enhance the assessor-child relationship and serve to increase the child's comfort and co-operation with testing, which may enhance the quality and depth of test responses. Children's play at breaks or the end of a session also may give the assessor insights into the child's world in general and in relation to what is going on in a testing session. Themes and characters in the child's play may also be food for thought for the development of a fable when planning how to give feedback to the child at the end of the assessment. And lastly, play is often fun for the child and may simply provide an opportunity to leave the rigor and demand of testing behind for a short time and refresh.

Other creative assessment methods we use include Individualized Sentence Completions constructed for each child client as opposed to using standard sets of incomplete sentences (Box 4.1). The items are written to reflect the Assessment Questions and other aims of the assessment for this child. Select responses are chosen for follow-up EIs. We do not score this measure, but use it to access individual information, similar to an interview.

We also are very fond of the Fantasy Animal Drawing Game developed by Handler (2007, 2014), in which the child is asked to draw a "make-believe animal that no one has ever seen or heard of before" and then engage in a mutual story-telling task with the assessor (Box 4.2). The fantasy animal has become the main character in the fables for some children (e.g., in the fable for Sarah in Chapter 1).

Or we may ask the child to produce a series of drawings (e.g., a house, tree, person, family, or something more individualized, such as how the child is feeling) and invite the child to elaborate on what they have drawn or perhaps tell stories about the drawings. This method is well described in Tharinger and Roberts (2014). We find that these methods also provide rich material for developing fables for children.

When/Why Do We Invite Parents to Be Tested?

This decision is guided by a close look at the parents' Assessment Questions (Finn, 2007). If they are completely child focused or scapegoating, parents

Box 4.1   Writing and Using Individualized Sentence Completions

Instead of using standard sentence completion sets, consider writing targeted sentence completions that are tailored to a particular child. In this way, you explore the Assessment Questions and show parents that you are keeping their assessment goals in mind. Here are some tips:

1. Depending on the age of the child, write about 15–25 incomplete sentences and print them on a sheet of paper with room for the child to write in the end of each phrase. At the top of the page write "Sentence Completions for (child's name)" to illustrate the personalized nature of the activity and signal to the child the importance of their individual responses.

2. Start with 3–5 general prompts that "break the ice" and which the child will not find emotionally arousing, e.g., "My favorite color is…." "The game I most like to play is…"

3. Then write 10–15 prompts that are related to the presenting issues and Assessment Questions. For example, if the parents have asked, "Why is our child so angry all the time?", you might construct incomplete phrases like "I get angry when…." "When I'm really mad I…." or "The most frustrating thing in my life is…." If the parents have asked, "How is our child adjusting to our divorce?", your sentence completion items might read "Divorce is….", "Since my parents divorced….", or "What grown-ups don't understand about divorce is…." You can also follow clinical hunches you have about the family system, even if they are not directly related to the Assessment Questions, e.g., "Since my younger sister got sick…."

4. Finish with 3–5 prompts that are soothing or positive, such as "Something I look forward to is…." Or "I can't wait until…."

5. Read over the prompts you have written to make sure they are appropriate for the child's age, reading level, etc.

6. Consider showing the prompts to the parents before you present them to the child, so they can add, make modifications, or ask questions.

7. Depending on the child, you may present the incomplete sentences and ask the child to write in her/his answers or you may read them aloud to the child and take dictation. Either way, ask the child to answer with "the first thing that comes to mind."

8. Generally, it is good to complete the entire set of items, and then to discuss those that stand out to you or that the child wishes to say more about.

Box 4.2   Handler's Fantasy Animal Drawing Game

This technique is often a good ice-breaker with children, but it can be used also with adolescents and even adults. Detailed guidelines are presented in a chapter by Handler (2007) and there are several published case examples of Handler's skillful use of this technique (Handler, 2012, 2014; Mutchnick & Handler, 2002). Here are the basic instructions:

1. Ask the child if they are interested in playing a make-believe animal game. If the child says Yes, or asks for more explanation, give her/him a blank piece of paper and some drawing instruments (e.g., colored pencils, markers, crayons, etc.).
2. Tell the child, "I want you to draw me a picture of a make-believe animal, one that no one has ever seen or heard of before." Let the child draw at her own pace, and if you are unsure, say: "Let me know when you are finished."
3. Show interest or pleasure in the drawing (e.g., "Oh that's an interesting creature!") and then ask the child to tell you about the drawing. You may help by asking about noteworthy characteristics (e.g., "Are those spikes?" and "Are they all that color?"). Also, if the child doesn't spontaneously tell you, ask "What is this creature called?"
4. Then say, "Now please tell me a story about your <animal's name>." If the child is reluctant, offer assistance, e.g., "I'll help you get started … . Once upon a time, a long long time ago….," and then motion for the child to continue. If this doesn't help, suggest that you and the child tell the story together. Then ask the child to start and to point to you when they want you to take over, or to say "Your turn."
5. On your first turn, stick fairly close to the child's story, but extend it a little and then give the child a turn. For example, the child says, "This is a drago-lion, a fierce animal that breathes fire and roars loud," then points to you. You might say, "The drago-lion was incredibly strong and fierce, which meant that no one could attack it. But it had one problem that it didn't know how to handle," then point to the child and see if the child follows your lead.
6. If the back-and-forth storytelling is going well, on subsequent turns you can test out therapeutic messages to see how the child responds. For example, if the child says the drago-lion is fierce but also lonely because everyone is scared of it, on your turn you might say, "One day the drago-lion realized that it didn't have to growl and scare other creatures all the time, if only it could tell who was dangerous and who was friendly and could be a friend. And so, the drago-lion … ." and point back to the child.

7. Sometimes children will ask to continue the same fantasy animal story in subsequent sessions, and doing so can give information about how the child is responding to the TA-C.

are unlikely to be open to being part of the assessment in such a direct way; they are not looking for input on how their personalities or behaviors impact their child at this time. However, if parents include questions about their own influence on their child's challenges or what more they can do to help, we interpret this as openness to learn more about themselves.

If parents agree to be tested, we usually use a self-report test such as the Minnesota Multiphasic Personality Inventory (MMPI-2; Butcher et al., 1989), the MMPI-3 (Ben-Porath, et al., 2020), the Personality Assessment Inventory (PAI; Morey, 2007), or the Millon Clinical Multiaxial Inventory-IV (MCMI-IV; Millon et al., 2015) and focus on what the results tell us about how their personality profiles affect their parenting and co-parenting, stress levels, coping mechanisms, and overall psychological well-being. Parents who are very interested in their part in the child-family system may even be invited to engage in additional testing, such as cognitive testing or performance-based tests, for example, the Rorschach Performance Assessment System (R-PAS; Meyer et al., 2011) or the Adult Attachment Projective Picture System (AAP; George & West, 2012). In some situations, when parents are not interested in being tested to learn about their personality, the administration of family rating scales or parenting stress scales may be acceptable, without seeming too threatening. Inviting parents to take an interest in understanding their level of stress as related to their family functioning and/or parenting may be welcomed. Sharing the results can serve to build the alliance with the parents and offer empathy for what they have been going through raising their child. When parents are tested, the child is not informed or privileged to the results. The test findings and their implications are discussed with the parents privately and typically described in a separate written document at the end of the assessment. In Henry's case, his parents both agreed to take the MMPI-2 (Butcher et al., 1989) and those results are shared when we return to the case study at the end of this chapter.

Part 2: Extended Inquiry Methods

We have also structured Part 2 as a series of questions and answers.

- What is the history of EIs in psychological assessment?
- What is an EI in TA-C?
- What are the goals of EIs for the child and the parents?
- Why do we use different types of EIs with different kinds of tests?
- What do we keep in mind when conducting EIs in TA-C?

What Is the History of Extended Inquiry Methods in Assessment?

EIs have a long and notable history. They were used by Klopfer et al. (1954), Piotrowski (1957), and Harrower (1956) to explore Rorschach responses with adults. Luria (Ardila, 1992) and Vygotsky (Lidz, 1995) always used EIs when using cognitive tests, and their methods had a great influence on the field of Dynamic Assessment (Lidz, 1997) and on the Boston neuropsychological approach (Milberg et al., 2009). Handler (2007, 2012) and Fischer (1994, 2001) routinely used EIs in their collaborative assessments, and Handler was the first to coin the phrase "extended inquiry." As described earlier, Handler (2007) further developed innovative methods of doing an EI with children, often asking children to tell a story or draw a picture to expand on a test response. Finn (2007) incorporated EI techniques from Vygotsky, Fischer, and Handler into Therapeutic Assessment, and recommended that EIs of standardized tests be used only after completion of standardized test administration. In this way, standardized tests could be scored and interpreted using established norms, followed by further exploring individual test items.

In recent writings, Finn has emphasized how the EI provides an opportunity for clients to build trust in the assessor because they feel "held in mind" (Kamphuis & Finn, 2019). It is our experience that through the use of EIs, children feel you really want to understand them and their worlds, and they understand that you will be "translating" what they say so their parents can hear them more accurately. We have also found that parents, through observing and discussing EIs, feel you are creating opportunities for their child to tell them things that have been hard to express in the past and feel emotionally supported by you as they take in new, sometimes difficult information. Thus, both the child and the parents feel "held in mind."

What Is an EI in TA-C?

Most simply, an EI is a collaborative exploration by the assessor and child of a response given to a test question. For example, after completing a self-report test with a child, we ask the child to expand on selective responses: (Assessor:) *"You answered 'True' to 'I feel sad a lot of the time.' Can you tell me more about that?"* (Child:) *"Well, I'm sad when I feel I don't do something as good as I should. I think some people, like my parents, get mad at me a lot."* As this example shows, an EI is a chance to foster self-exploration in the child. The child is asked to expand on a response and the assessor provides different, more supportive interpersonal interactions with the child following an EI response. For example, (Assessor:) *"That sounds hard! I would feel sad too. I hope we can talk with your parents about this and learn more about what's going on."*

This type of exchange provides a chance to deepen our relationship with the child, become more attuned to the child's experience, and grow in our empathy for the child. With parents observing, they too have the opportunity to become more curious about their child, grow their empathy, and begin to change their core narrative and beliefs about their child. It is important to note that sometimes the child's response to an EI is very emotionally arousing, especially for parents. Fortunately, the holding environment we have provided from the beginning of the TA-C supports parents as they try to integrate the new information. Overall, we want to help parents develop a core narrative that is more coherent, compassionate, accurate, and useful. In our experience, as the parents begin to shift, the child is freed up to integrate previously unspoken aspects of the self.

Another type of EI involves testing the limits of a response. Typically used with academic and cognitive tests, we may want to see if a child can achieve more typical or better-quality responses, and figure out what help is necessary for them to do so. This method is similar to that used in Dynamic Assessment (Lidz, 1997), briefly summarized as "test-teach-retest." For example, after completing a math achievement test where the child has rushed through it and made many errors, the following exchange might occur:

Assessor: How was that test for you? How do you think you did?"
Child: Well, I didn't like it much. I probably didn't do very well.
Assessor: What do you think kept you from doing well?
Child: Well, I went fast and couldn't remember all the multiplication. I guess I didn't pay much attention after a while.
Assessor: So, can you think of another way that might help you do better?
Child: Maybe going slower?
Assessor: Good idea! How about doing two or three more problems with me? I have a multiplication table here you can use. Just take your time.

This type of exploration allows us to learn under what conditions the child can succeed. The observing parents also may learn new strategies. And if we provide the right conditions for the child, the child can feel successful and hopeful. In contrast, if the child is unable to do better under the new circumstances, this helps us know what kind of help is unlikely to lead to better performance.

What Are the Goals of EIs for the Child and Parents?

As illustrated earlier, the major goal of EIs is to explore the personal meaning of selected test responses, thus helping the child and, most importantly, the parents arrive at new understanding. In many ways, we are training the parents to think more psychologically—about their child, themselves, and their family system. EIs are also an opportunity to obtain new words and metaphors from the child that can be used later to talk about issues. For example, the child may give the response "A big angry bear" to a Rorschach card. During an EI following completion of the test, the child tells a story about a "big angry bear" who is upset because their parents are on their phones all the time. This metaphor may be useful when planning how the parents can "tame the angry bear" by increasing positive time with their child. Also, "angry bear" might end up in the fable for the child, in which the bear family learns to listen to each other and not rage so much.

The responses to EIs also are useful in getting a sense of which information is Level 1, 2, or 3 for the child and for the parents. For example, a child who indicates a strong level of sadness on a self-report measure and during the EI tells you all the ways they are sad would not be surprised if the fable written for them is about a very sad unicorn, as this is clearly Level 1 Information for her. However, the observing parents who dismiss their child's sadness—perhaps claiming that the child is being manipulative—would likely be surprised if the assessor strongly underlined the child's sadness in feedback, as this is likely Level 2 and maybe even Level 3 Information for the parents.

Thus, EIs with children are extremely useful for gauging what changes in narrative parents are ready to adopt, and in showing us where to begin in scaffolding new narratives. For example, with the parent we just described the assessor might explore the idea that the child is being manipulative—without at first directly challenging it. At some point, the assessor might then respectfully offer a different view, e.g., "Of course, you know your child best, but that didn't seem manipulative to me because ... ." The assessor might then discuss with the mother what it would mean if her child truly is so sad. We may find out that the mother herself has been experiencing significant depression that she tries to hide and that she would experience intolerable guilt if her daughter also is sad. Through these types of discussions, we hope to move the mother closer to a more accurate, useful, and compassionate narrative, which we call shifting Level 3 Information into Level 2. When these kinds of shifts are accomplished, the family can move onto addressing the child's (and mother's) depression and getting healthier.

The previous example also illustrates that parents often need emotional support from a caring professional in order to suspend their usual ways of perceiving and understanding their child, as the existing narrative may serve many important psychological functions (Chapter 2). By helping parents slowly revise their "story" about the child during the EI, the assessor helps parents to take in the new perspective little by little, avoiding overwhelming emotional reactions.

Yet another way that EIs can be helpful is by providing opportunities for parents and assessors to discuss information that hasn't yet been come into the assessment, but which may be very relevant to the Assessment Questions. For example, Finn and Chudzik (2013) reported on the TA-C of seven-year-old boy who had developed enuresis two years prior that had not responded to medical or behavioral interventions. Finn asked the boy to participate in an activity that involved him taking photos of important things in his life, and the boy repeatedly photographed a photo of his uncle. When queried, the boy responded that his uncle had died two years earlier. The parents had failed to mention this event earlier in the assessment or connect it to the boy's bedwetting. Discussing this loss led to a breakthrough in the TA-C and in the parents seeing shortcomings in the ways they themselves dealt with grief.

Why Do We Use Different Types of EIs with Different Kinds of Tests?

For cognitive and academic tests, we suggest the following procedures after the standard administration is completed. First, discuss strengths and other interesting or surprising elements of the test responses. Then consider doing some experiments. Consider "testing the limits." Suggest other ways the child might approach a task. Perhaps modify the instructions, for example, give more time or provide more guidance. Possibly provide scaffolding (little steps) to explore the minimum amount of help the child needs to be successful. Collaboratively with the child, review the results of these experiments to see what new strategies have been learned. You might ask the child if there are parallels in their daily life, such as problem-solving tasks at school. If so, you may want to invite the child to export the new successful strategies outside the testing room and to report back on how it went.

For self-report tests, we recommend starting in an open-ended fashion, asking about the child's general experience of the test. Follow-up on any comments that are particularly relevant to the Assessment Questions. For example, parents have asked about the child's difficulties making choices, and the child says how hard it was to choose between "True" and "False" when responding. You can explore what was so difficult and whether certain items were easier than others. Then, the EI usually consists of interviewing the child about certain "critical items":

- *"You said* True *to this one.* (Read item.) *Can you tell me more about that?"*
- *"Let's look at some of your answers together.* (Read responses.) *What would you think if someone answered like you did?"*
- *"If a friend of yours answered this way, what would you think?"*

To explore Rorschach responses (after completing the formal response clarification of the standard administration), again we usually start in an open-ended fashion, asking about the child's general experience of the test. As before, listen carefully and follow up on any comments the child makes about the process. For example:

Child: It was really hard to see two things on each card. I wanted to just see one thing.
Assessor: I saw that. What made it hard?
Child: After I saw one, my brain kind of locked, and it was hard to see something else.

Assessor: I see. That can be hard. Does your brain lock other times too?

Child: Yes, at school. That's why sometimes I don't talk at all in class. I can't think of what to say that is different than what other people already said.

Assessor: Thanks for telling me. Your teachers did ask about why you are so quiet sometimes. And do you know anything that helps with the brain lock?

Child: No.

Assessors: Well, maybe we can think of something together and try it out with the inkblots.

With the Rorschach another common EI technique is to choose specific responses (e.g., MOR or AGG) to read and discuss with the child:

Assessor: I was really interested in some of the things you saw (read responses). Do you notice anything about them?

And depending on the age of the child, we often use indirect, more developmentally appropriate methods of EI, following the spirit of Handler (2007). For example:

- *"Can you tell me a story* about (read response)?" Assessor can ask for further elements of the story (e.g., beginning, ending, feeling, thinking, etc.) or use an interactive story-telling method to expand the content, such as that used for the Fantasy Animal Drawing Game. *"If this (e.g., 'big angry bear') could talk, what would it say?"*

- Ask the child to put herself in the physical position of a figure depicted in one of her drawings and ask her how she feels.

- Invite the child "play out" a dynamic percept in action with you and discuss it (e.g., two people pulling apart a basket (Rorschach card III)).

What Do We Keep in Mind When Conducting EIs in TA-C?

- Hold the Assessment Questions in mind.
- Be present! Carefully pay attention to the child's behavior and responses during the test administration. Monitor your own feelings and thoughts. If you feel sad, notice when that started.
- Conduct the EI in a way that is attuned to the child's level of cognitive and emotional development, e.g., instead of asking interpretive questions, you might ask the child to tell a story, or act out a response through play.
- Hold the parents in mind. If you see a pattern or believe the child is "sending a message" relevant to the Assessment Questions, are the

parents likely to see or get it? If you're not sure, what can you do with the child to make the pattern or message even clearer to them?

- Ask yourself:

   What aspects of the responses to the EIs might be related to the Assessment Questions?

   What is surprising or noteworthy about the child's way of doing the test? What would be a more adaptive way for the child to respond? Do you want to try out other ways the child might be able to provide an adaptive response?

- Connect your discussions with the child to the child's life outside the testing room and to different contexts.

- Move the discussion gradually toward certain important concepts or behaviors using half steps to try to support the child's being the first one to notice important things.

- Don't go too fast!

- Pay attention to signs that the child is not following you or is overwhelmed. If so, pause, back up, or readjust. If the child becomes highly emotional, pause and offer support.

Part 3: Parent Observation and Processing Child's Testing with the Assessor

Finn (2007) described the development, method, and benefits of inviting parents to observe some or all of their child's testing sessions and processing their reactions and questions with the assessor immediately (if a two-assessor method is being used) or afterward. Finn adopted this method from Fischer (1985/1994) and other professionals who work with high-risk parents (Holigrocki et al., 2009). In TA, the parental observation piece is unique to TA-C; parents do not observe their child's testing sessions in Therapeutic Assessment with Adolescents (TA-A), as it is not developmentally appropriate (Tharinger et al., 2013). The one exception is during assessments of older, impaired adults and their families, where the adult child or children are functioning in the "caregiver" role and are invited to observe the older adult's testing sessions.

In working with the observing parents, we maintain a collaborative stance by adopting the terms the parents use, actively and empathically listening to their concerns, and encouraging their questions and comments about the process as they learn first-hand what their child is thinking, feeling, and experiencing. In most cases, we can assist parents to develop renewed empathy for what their child is experiencing. We emotionally support them as they reach new understandings about their child. This process also provides insight into parental readiness and resources for change, which will inform the family intervention session and feedback sessions.

In our experience. parents usually find observing their child's standardized testing and EIs to be extremely useful. For example, parents participating in the Therapeutic Assessment Project at the University of Texas (Tharinger et al., 2009) reported that watching their child's assessment sessions was one of the most valuable parts of the TA-C. Parents rarely get to see their child respond to a cognitive, achievement, or social-emotional test or activity, and in general do not get to see how their child interacts with other people when they are not present. Many parents seem glued to the one-way mirror or video screen, listening to every word their child says, often while also following along with the protocol of the test their child is taking. We find that we often learn a lot by asking parents what they noticed about their child in the standardized testing situation and through EIs.

There are a variety of ways to set up the observation experience for parents, depending on the set-up of the assessor's office, available equipment, and if the one-or two-assessor method is being used. We encourage you to choose the option that best fits your practice situation and particular clients. In all cases, the child understands that parents are observing, either in the moment or, with videotapes, at a later time. We have developed the following options: (1) Parents can observe unobtrusively through a one-way mirror, with or without a second assessor. This method is most likely to be available in a training clinic. (2) Parents can watch over a video hook-up in another room, again with or without a second assessor. This method works well in a clinic or practice with ample space and video equipment. (3) Parents can observe off to the side of the testing room, behind the child's back (with very young or unregulated children, we have occasionally administered tests while the child sat on the parent's lap or even squirmed under the chair). (4) Sessions with the child can be videotaped and excerpts can be shown to parents at a later time.

In our experience, all of these options can be fruitful. It is ideal to have a second assessor with parents behind a one-way mirror or watching the video in real time with a second assessor. With these methods, everything observed can be discussed, not just selected interactions and responses. However, this method is costly and may only be possible in a training setting (where a trainee can test the child while a supervisor sits with the observing parents). Some of us find having the parents in the room allows for discussion at breaks or at the end of a session, whereas others of us find this difficult to manage with some children and parents. Perhaps the video method where the assessor chooses clips to review with the parents is the most universally applicable.

When working with the video method, we have found it useful for the assessor to select clips of standardized test administration and EIs that contain new or puzzling information for parents, or where there seems to be a "message" from the child to the parents. We ask the parents to look at the clip carefully (maybe even several times), put their "psychologist hats on," and ask them to describe what they see, how they understand it, how it is similar or different to what happens at home, and to try to put themselves in his/her child's shoes emotionally. When parents are stuck, we use "half-steps" to help them along. We might say, "I am not sure but ..." "Could it be ...?" "What do you see?" "I can see that and I was also thinking ..."

Whatever observation method is used, when parents report perceptions or conclusions that seem inaccurate or distorted, we don't counter these perceptions directly, but explore and offer alternative narratives without insisting that we are right. For example, see the following dialogue that occurred after parents observed their ten-year-old son decline the assessor's request to draw a person.

Assessor: What did you think about the way Doug responded when the assessor asked him to draw a person?

Mother: I'm glad you saw that. This is an example of how lazy he is. He reacts the same way when we ask him to do anything at home.

Father: Yes, everything is too hard. He just wants to get out of things so he can play his video games all day long.

Assessor: I see. So, this is what you meant by your question, "How can we get him to stop being so lazy?"

Both: Exactly!

Assessor: That's very interesting that you saw him being lazy there. Did you hear what he said, "Oh, I'm not good at drawing. I don't want to do that"? I thought he looked insecure about his drawing abilities.

Father: That's what I mean. Everything is too hard. But it's just an excuse. He really just doesn't want to do anything.

Assessor: Well, you know him best. I guess I was just responding to his shame posture—you know, how he slumped his shoulders and looked at the ground when he said that.

Mother: Oh, he knows how to be manipulative alright!

Assessor: OK. So that's how you see it. And what do you think about his doing the drawing after all when the assessor said it didn't matter if it was good, just to try his best.

Father: He did, didn't he? I forgot about that. That surprised me!

Mother: Could it be he was just trying to please her?

Assessor: That may be. Let's keep watching for other times you see him being lazy and manipulative, or times when you're surprised that he's not.

Benefits of Parent Observation

We now describe the extensive benefits we have found in using this method. We illustrate how these benefits were apparent when presenting Henry's case at the end of this chapter. We also encourage you to review an article by Tharinger et al. (2012), where each benefit is illustrated in depth with excerpts of dialogue between the observing parents and a second assessor who watched the testing sessions together through a video feed in an adjacent room.

1. We educate parents about psychological tests and other assessment procedures. Psychological testing becomes "de-mystified" and parents understand how and why certain conclusions have been reached. We usually have copies of the test materials for parents to view and follow along with as their child is being administered a given test.

2. We foster parents' curiosity about their child and the assessment process, and help them "step back" and look with new eyes. Many parents have never before had the chance to watch their child privately while the child interacted with another adult. This creates an opportunity for parents to notice and reflect on many things.

3. We help parents notice similarities and differences in their child's behavior in the problem situation (e.g., at home) and in the assessment situation (contextualizing). This can help parents take experienced difficulties less personally, e.g., "Even this trained professional doesn't know what to do when my child has temper tantrums!"

4. We help parents think about contextual influences on behavior (perhaps using circular questioning or behavioral analysis questions discussed in Chapter 3). This helps break up "global" attributions (e.g., "My child is lazy to the core.") and fosters more refined attributions (e.g., "When my child has intense attention and focus from a supportive adult, he can work really hard.").

5. We model psychological mindedness and "looking below the surface" for the parents, fostering their curiosity as discussed in Chapter 3. Helping parents step back and think, "What might my child be communicating through his behavior?" is one way to promote "mentalization" (i.e., reflective functioning) in parents, and this has been linked to secure caregiving and attachment (Fonagy, 1998).

6. We gather information about how parents perceive their child across the course of the assessment. For example, if a child begins to show new ways of approaching problem situations, we assess whether parents are open to seeing this.

7. We consensually validate certain perceptions the parents have about their child. All parents want affirmation that they are not totally off base in how they see their child, or as some say, that they "are not crazy." Typically, in every assessment, there is much that can be consensually validated.

8. We gently confront other perceptions the parents express by asking them to note data that conflicts with the existing story and/or we can respectfully offer different interpretations of events, potential helping to create a new story. Because parents' narratives inevitably shape what they perceive and how they interpret what they perceive, assessors may need to help them pay attention to information that might contradict those narratives. And assessors can "scaffold" new narratives that are emotionally acceptable to the parent.

9. We provide parents with opportunities to reintegrate split-off emotions and experiences that the child might be "holding" for the family, thus creating a potential new balance in the family system. Through their test responses, some children express grief, anger, or fear that parents and other family members may not be in touch with. Gently drawing attention to the child's emotional states and fostering empathy for them can help parents find their own versions of the feelings.

10. We observe parents' reactions and, if applicable, their interactions with each other to see what they are ready to absorb and if they are on the same page or significantly apart. We have found that for a TA-C to be therapeutic, the assessor needs to be aware whether parents have a common narrative or discrepant one. This often becomes very apparent as we ask parents to say what they see when they observe the child during testing.

11. We continue to gather relevant background information about the child/family that will inform our hypotheses and provide deeper historic and intergenerational background. Sometimes, during the testing, the child refers to some event that was previously not discussed, or parents mention some important piece of information they had "forgotten" to bring in. Again, when the testing environment fosters curiosity and is safe, a kind of non-linear "emergence" can occur that helps set the stage for therapeutic transformations.

12. We emotionally support parents as they reach new understandings, achieve new emotional awareness, or are confirmed in their existing understandings. As mentioned earlier, often parents cannot interpret their child's behavior accurately because it would lead to overwhelming emotions, "My child is not learning disabled, he is just lazy! If he is learning disabled, he might not be able to take over our family business!" With the assessor showing empathy and support, parents can face things they otherwise would never be able to realize.

13. We assess parental readiness for change. It also becomes clear at times, over the course of an assessment, that parents cannot shift their perspective on their child. We then think of what kind of support they might need when we are making recommendations at the end of the TA-C. We have found in such cases that parents may be stuck in their Dilemma of Change, as introduced in Chapter 2. They may be weighing, consciously or unconsciously, the costs and benefits of changing versus remaining the same. This process is not to be taken lightly, as choosing change is likely to permeate through the system and require much restructuring (but to potentially great benefit). Lack of change maintains the homeostasis in the family, but often at great cost.

14. We continue to foster trust between parents and ourselves. By our "showing our cards" and being transparent about where and how we see things, while also being humble about our perceptions and emerging understandings, parents come to see us as expert, helpful "consultants"

rather than as potentially shaming or overwhelming professionals who may insist on new perspectives that may be traumatizing.

Possible Concerns About Parent Observations

Even with the extensive benefits just discussed, inviting parents to observe all or some of their child's testing sessions may raise concerns for some assessment professionals. One concern is that test security may be compromised to some extent. However, parents only view the testing materials (child versions) briefly and do not take the tests themselves. Inviting the parents to observe is done in the spirit of collaborative empiricism as practiced in cognitive-behavioral therapy (Beck, 2021). We have found that the opportunity for parents to observe their child and discuss their reactions affects the process and outcome of the TA-C in significant, positive ways (Tharinger et al., 2007). As mentioned earlier, many parents have shared with us that the observation experience was one of the most impactful aspects of the assessment.

In addition, some assessors may be concerned about the willingness of children to disclose while their parents are observing. However, we have found that most pre-adolescent children not only willingly accept their parents observing assessment sessions, but use this set-up as an opportunity to communicate to their parents. For example, a girl may finally be able to let her parents know, through a test response given to the assessor, that she is very sad but has not wanted to upset her parents by letting them know this. Another child might finally be able to share how hard it is to move back and forth between separate households so often, despite their loyalty to both parents. For parents, observing their child communicate difficult thoughts and feelings is almost always more powerful than our later revealing what the child has said. In our experience, this process can enhance parents' empathy for their child and help move the new story along.

A third concern is one we have called "germs in the test tube"—that is, that introducing parental observation alters standardized procedures such that test data are "ruined" and nomothetic norms can no longer be used to validly interpret test results. We don't mean to dismiss such concerns as frivolous, but we tend not to give them that much weight for several reasons: (1) We believe test scores must always be interpreted holding contextual factors in mind—even in traditional testing—for example, whether the child was hungry or rested at the time of the testing. Responsible assessors always consider such factors and think about how they may have bearing on the test results. (2) Our many years of clinical experience have made us confident that standardized norms are still extremely useful in interpreting test scores derived from child testing observed by parents. (3) If we or the parents suspect that the child's test responses are highly influenced by the child's awareness that parents are watching, it is always possible to administer or re-administer a test without this variable. This type of collaborative empiricism can greatly help identify systemic variables that result in the child or family's problems in living.

Having said all this, we want to acknowledge that there are cases and circumstances when parental observation of their child's testing sessions clearly is not advisable, and can even be overwhelming and possibly detrimental. We are aware of families where parents with backgrounds of severe trauma have been overwhelmed and traumatized while watching their children describe traumas that they also witnessed, even with good support from the assessor. Also, some parents or guardians without trauma histories have been overwhelmed hearing their child speak of their own trauma. Rarely, parents are also so stirred up emotionally watching their child's testing that they cannot refrain from interrupting (if present in the corner of the room), or making unhelpful or shaming comments to the child after the session. In all these instances, it might be best to choose the video option and show excerpts to the parents later, carefully choosing what might be useful for the parents to view.

Part 4: Steps in the Data Gathering/Testing Phase

You have now become familiar with how testing and test responses are viewed from a TA-C approach; EIs; and methods, benefits, and concerns about parent observation of their child's testing. With this knowledge in mind, it is timely to review the steps for conducting the testing sessions in the Data Gathering/Testing Phase. Illustrations of these steps are provided when we discuss Henry's case at the end of this chapter.

Steps for Conducting the Testing Sessions

- Before the first testing session, review the Assessment Questions again with the parents and make any adjustments. It can be helpful to have the printed questions clearly in view throughout the testing sessions so that you and the parents can easily refer to them.
- At the beginning of each testing session, check in with the parents and child and inquire about what has happened since the last contact. Be particularly attentive to any signs that parents or child were overwhelmed by the previous session or have questions.
- If not done earlier in Phase I, introduce the idea of parental observation of the child testing to the parents and the child, choose the method to be used, and demonstrate how it would work.
- Collect formal rating forms you provided to the parents to complete at the end of the initial parent session, such as the Behavior Assessment System for Children 3rd ed. (BASC-3; Reynolds & Kamphaus, 2015) or the Child Behavior Checklist (CBCL-2; Achenbach & Rescorla, 2001). This could be done anytime during the testing sessions, but we find that the earlier the better. The results are useful in illuminating the parents'

current narrative about their child. After reviewing their responses, inquire about those that you want to understand more fully. If rating forms were given to involved professionals such as teachers, therapists, or the referring professional, do the same.

- Discuss setting up a meeting to obtain additional background information from the parents beyond what was obtained in the initial Parent Interview in Phase I. This can be an opportunity to more formally gather information to fill in a *Timeline of Major Child/Family Life Events*. We typically begin with the mother's pregnancy and the child's birth, although sometimes we list incidents in the parents' lives that occurred before that. On the timeline, we not only record single discrete events (e.g., births, deaths, separations and divorces, hospitalizations, family moves) but also our sense of the family's situation at regular intervals in the child's life. We also indicate when problem behaviors began, got better, and got worse. For example, for an eight-year-old girl, Greta, here is a portion of the timeline: "age 4 years, 3 months—younger brother, Tim, is born 3 months premature; parents spend lots of time in NICU, Greta cared for by maternal grandmother; age 6 to 7—mother at home with Greta and Tim, dad traveling a lot for work, but maternal grandmother helping out a lot; age 7 years 2 months—maternal grandmother passes away suddenly, mother depressed, Greta begins to have sleep problems and troubles eating … ." We pay special attention to events that may have some connection to the Assessment Questions the parents have asked, as history can be extremely informative as we strive to understand how challenges and problems may have developed. We demonstrate one possible way to depict a timeline when we get to Henry's case.

- This same meeting may be an opportunity to further query about multigenerational family history and prepare a genogram. We construct the genogram (family tree) based on information gained through interviews and consultations with parents, sessions with the child, and any family-history questionnaires that were given as part of the TA-C. There are many excellent texts available on how to construct and interpret genograms (McGoldrick et al., 2020), so we will not go into detail here about the mechanics of making genograms. But let us mention that genograms are very helpful in summarizing information relevant to several major theories we use in case conceptualization, particularly Family Systems Theory and Object Relations Theory. We usually strive for a three-generation genogram and typically, we work together with parents in drawing it. Although much of the information will be gathered through interviews and consultations along the way, you may find you need a more formalized method to gather remaining details. The intent is to further inform the answers to the Assessment Questions. For example, if one of the questions is about the child's struggle with reading, asking whether others in the family had similar challenges may shed light on biological underpinnings of the child's struggles, such as dyslexia. In addition, parents may share important information about how the family handled academic challenges, which may help explain their own emotional reactions to their child's struggles with reading. If one of the questions is about the child's possible depression, understanding the existence of depression in the extended family may raise awareness about biological influences on the child's development, and about the personal meaning "depression" has for each parent.

- If agreed to earlier, arrange for the parents to be tested to gain insight into how their personality affects their parenting and co-parenting. Collect the completed measures, score them, and arrange for a time to meet with the parents for feedback. Results are often discussed mid-assessment or after testing sessions with the child are completed. During the discussion of the findings, note the parents' reactions, including what feedback was: (1) easily accepted, hesitantly agreed with, and strongly resisted. We think of this as Levels 1, 2, and 3 Information. Did the parents make any connection between their own test results and their child's challenges? Between their results and the family's functioning? Are they starting to think more systemically?

- Begin testing the child. Explain to the parents and possibly the child what test/activity you have chosen to begin with and explain how it (and subsequent tests/methods) contributes to exploring the Assessment Questions. Use standardized administration for tests and follow-up with selective EIs with the child. Score the tests completed prior to the subsequent testing session so you are able to follow up with the child and parents as needed. In addition, the test results may reveal an unexpected finding that needs further exploration and possibly additional testing. In addition, keeping in mind the scored findings as you progress to the next testing session helps you integrate what you are learning and be prepared for the parent consultations along the way.

- Look for the endorsement of critical items on tests the child completed (e.g., on the BASC-3). Responses to these items may alert you to serious concerns that need immediate attention. These are essential items to follow up with an Extended Inquiry to gain a fuller understanding.

- Pause and offer the child support between tests (or even subtests if needed) or at signs of overwhelm. As discussed earlier, consider offering the child a play break if child appears overwhelmed or shut down. Consider giving a time for free play at the end of a testing session, as children will often show important reactions to the testing through their play (Box 4.3).

- At the completion of each testing session, check out with the child and parents by addressing any questions they have, planning for time to process the session with the parents, and discussing the pragmatics for the next session.

Box 4.3 Instructions for Free Play at the End of Assessment Sessions

Before saying goodbye to children at the end of their assessment sessions, we encourage assessors to spend 10–15 minutes on free play. Not only does it reward the children for their focus during the assessment session, but it is also a powerful way to build an ongoing relationship, while helping them process the work they did during the assessment tasks. Here are some general guidelines to keep in mind:

1. Depending on the age of the child, you might want to let them know that play time will follow completion of the assessment tasks. Sometimes children benefit from quick reminders during the session if they need some extra motivation to keep going or staying focused. This strategy can be especially helpful with younger children and can offer additional information about a child's ability to utilize structure and capacity to delay gratification.

2. Consistently plan the assessment sessions to allow enough time to play. Don't skip this part, especially if the child knows it's coming.

3. Let children choose from the activities, toys, and games available in the office (e.g., it is a good idea to have a variety of options and show children where they are located). Allow children to explore and engage in unstructured play to let their personalities and ideas emerge. Pay close attention to the emotional tone of the play or selection of toys as these might relate to the activities in the assessment session or to the Assessment Questions posed at the beginning of the assessment.

4. Follow the child's lead as to whether you should just observe and comment during the play or whether you should actively engage or play along. Imagine, the child sets up a classroom with stuffed animals and "teaches" them in a strict and shaming way shortly after being administered attention or cognitive measures. You can give voice to the feelings you suspect the child is expressing in the play: "These math problems must be really hard for the bear and the fox" or "Oh, no! Math again for the little bear and the fox. They must be so unhappy about it." When you comment, watch the child's reaction, which will help inform you whether you are on track.

5. Since parents might be watching (or you might want to show them a segment of the video later), model for parents a child-centered, playful interaction. This can be an opportunity to model emotional attunement, mirroring of feelings, and using creativity and fun to enter into the child's world. Discussing aspects of a child's play with parents can also offer very important information about the parents and how they are reacting to the assessment. Imagine a

parent who is very uncomfortable with aggressive play, or one who is anxious that the play is not being used as a "learning tool." Parents' reactions and attitudes regarding unstructured play can offer significant insights into children's experience at home and in their families.

6. Before ending the session, give children a five-minute warning (or longer depending on the child) to prepare them for the transition out of the office. Invite the child to clean up together, and offer to safely store new items or creations (e.g., new Lego structure, drawing, etc.) to welcome children the next time they come in. It is nice for children to see their work displayed (if the assessor has the space to do so and if the child agrees to it), but it also might be sufficient to take a photo of the creation or ask children to keep their art in your file.

7. Thank children for their participation in the session and invite them back for the next one.

Part 5: Organize and Examine Findings Test by Test

The following steps are designed to help you organize and analyze the test-by-test findings and other pertinent information. In this way, the pieces of the puzzle are closely examined before putting them together, as covered in Chapter 5.

- Emerge yourself totally in the case by reviewing your entire case file (possibly also select video recordings), including the Assessment Questions, personal notes on your subjective and interpersonal experiences, all individual test results, the genogram, and the *Timeline of Major Child/Family Life Events*. Again, these are the individual pieces of the puzzle. This step is intended to bring the entire case back alive and prepare you for the tasks required in Chapter 5 (integrating all materials, arriving at the major findings, applying theoretical models to the findings, deriving an initial case conceptualization, and drafting answers to the Assessment Questions).

- Keep your eye on informing the Assessment Questions. At the same time, never ignore an important finding that is not related to any of the Assessment Questions posed. For example, the child may have indices on the Rorschach suggestive of a thought disorder. No one asked about this area through an Assessment Question. Nevertheless, this finding needs to be explored thoroughly, understood, and possibly, eventually, discussed with the parents.

- Be attuned to the child's test-taking behaviors across tests and sessions. What was notable? How stable or variable were the behaviors? What might that tell you?

Take into account your impressions of the child during unstructured and semi-structured play activities with you, if applicable. Consider what you learned about the child through play. If the parents observed, what were their reactions?

- Moving to the child's test findings, examine and interpret each source of information independently, that is, test-by-test. What do the findings on each test tell you? What does the normative comparison say about this child in relation to their same age peers? In examining each test, take into account your observations and subjective experience during the testing, including information gained through Extended Inquiries. For example, if a child seemed to "give up" during a cognitive test, you may interpret the score differently than if the child made a strong effort throughout. If you tested the limits by changing the instructions to a test and this led to higher performance, take into account what this experiment tells you about the child's struggles in this area. Also, importantly, this step ensures that you consider each piece of information (and not cherry pick) before moving into looking for patterns across and within the data.

Having completed an initial analysis of each test and behavior during testing, you will be ready for the next steps covered in Chapter 5 about Case Conceptualization. We now return to the case study.

Case: Henry's Testing, Parent Contact, and Collateral Contacts

After our initial meetings (Phase I), I (Dale) thought about how to proceed. Because of Henry's demeanor and intense need to share how sad he was, I was concerned that if I began with a test or activity that allowed open responding, he might reject it or use it as a vehicle to share only his sadness. Therefore, I decided to begin the data collection phase of the assessment with cognitive testing, as these types of tests involve more objective responses to specific tasks. I hoped that Henry would want to participate because one of the Assessment Questions concerned the following year's school placement. I knew Henry was interested in this topic because he wanted to go to the same school as several of his friends.

I began the first testing session by briefly checking in with Barbara to see how the week had gone and if she had any concerns or information to share. I did this without Henry present because I wanted Barbara to speak freely. She indicated that things were status quo at home, but that Henry seemed a little more energized since our previous meeting. I felt relieved by this information. I explained that we were going to begin with cognitive testing, and I reminded her of the specific Assessment Questions such tests would address. I also shared with Barbara that I wanted to begin with an activity that was structured and required responses that Henry might be more apt to engage with, rather than open-ended questions or unstructured activities. I asked if this made sense to her, and she agreed with the approach.

I then got Henry from the waiting room, while his mom stayed in my office. I explained that I had talked to his mom first because I wanted to hear her impressions of how the week went. I asked Henry how he felt about the past week, and he said, "All right, I guess." I explained to him that we were doing this first activity because it would give us information about "your strengths and challenges when it comes to school and learning." I also said it would help answer one of his parents' questions about where he should go to school next year. He nodded and seemed interested in this. I asked Barbara to leave because I wanted Henry to focus on the activity. Sometimes I invite parents to observe the testing, but in this case, I thought his mom's presence might lead to Henry's focusing on his sadness as it had occurred in the previous session. I knew that Henry did well in school and wanted to see if he were able to engage with me in a different way than during our first meeting. Since neither parent was present, I videotaped the testing session planning to choose excerpts that I would show them later.

I began with the WISC-V (Wechsler, 2014), and Henry seemed to fully engage in the testing. He was attentive, serious, and focused on each task at hand. I also began to notice a pattern: Henry didn't appear anxious or negative about himself or how he was doing until he began reaching the limits of his ability on each subtest. As each test grew more difficult, he got anxious, began to play with his ear (which I already had recognized as an anxious tic) and stopped answering the test questions.

At the end of the WISC-V, I asked Henry how he thought he did, and he said, "Horrible!" I was surprised to hear him go back to being so negative. I decided to do a brief Extended Inquiry. The conversation continued:

Dale:	Really? That's too bad. I'm so sorry you felt that way. Was there something that really bothered you about it?
Henry:	Yes, the whole thing.
Dale:	The whole thing? That's awful! Maybe this testing feels horrible, huh? Should we stop doing this? That would be OK with me if it feels too horrible to continue.
Henry:	No.
Dale:	No? You want to keep coming to see your strengths and challenges?
Henry:	I guess.
Dale:	Well, you know you actually did really well on a number of the parts.
Henry:	(No response)
Dale:	Do you know which parts you did the best on?
Henry:	No.
Dale:	Would you like to know?
Henry:	Yes.

I quickly computed Henry's scores on the subtests I thought he did best on (Information SS = 15, Visual Puzzles SS = 14) and shared the results. I shared them both verbally and visually, by graphically showing him how far above the average line his scores fell. He did not respond overtly but seemed pleased, as evidenced by a half smile. We then continued the conversation.

Dale: Are you surprised at how well you did?

Henry: Well, I did OK.

Dale: Actually, the scores say you did better than just OK. You are certainly above average, Henry. That really is better than just OK.

Henry: I guess, but I could have done a lot better. I didn't get as high as I should have.

Dale: Oh, you mean if you don't get them all right you didn't do well?

Henry: I guess.

Dale: That must make being in school really, really hard. When I was in school no one hardly ever got things all right. You know what's interesting? According to how you did on this test I would think you could do well in school. Is there a subject you feel you're pretty good at?

H: Um…I don't think I'm good at anything.

Again, I was somewhat surprised that Henry showed no pleasure or even relief when I shared the positive results of the testing. I felt an urge to respond to his negativity by emphasizing how well he had done but caught myself and realized that I ought to switch gears because I didn't want to respond positively while he was feeling negatively. I immediately got in touch with how this must be similar to how Henry's parents felt—rather helpless and wanting to flee or contradict his all-encompassing negativity. After recognizing this I knew I needed to mirror his dysphoric affect rather than counter it:

Dale: Not feeling like you're good at anything? I feel sad that such a bright, capable boy like you would feel like he's not very good at anything. You don't feel like you're good at anything, and I bet that makes you feel even worse, sadder. Remember, when we met with your parents I asked if you have any questions about yourself? I wonder if perhaps you might have a question about this.

Henry: Yeah, "Why am I so sad all the time?"

Dale: Should we add this to the assessment questions?

Henry: Yeah.

At this point, my heart went out to Henry. He seemed so profoundly sad. I noted that he had such high standards and expectations of himself that he might never be satisfied. I remembered his mother telling me that she had videos of Henry having a great time camping, but when they got home all he could do was to say how miserable the whole camping trip was. I wondered why this boy couldn't acknowledge joy or satisfaction. I also noticed that when I stopped contradicting his pessimism and mirrored it ("I bet that makes you feel even worse ..."). Henry was able to be curious and ask a question about his sadness. This was an important moment in teaching me the best way to respond to Henry's dark perspective.

After my initial sessions with Henry, his parents, and the completion of the WISC-V, I reviewed my experiences with and thoughts about him. I synthesized what I presently knew or thought about Henry. This is summarized in the statements below and can be viewed as early hypotheses.

1. Henry was bright but very anxious and insecure about his cognitive ability (Table 4.1). He had three composite scores that were in the above average

Table 4.1 Wechsler Intelligence Scale for Children—Fifth Edition (WISC-V)

Composite Scores	Score	Percentile	95th % Confidence Interval
Verbal Comprehension	113	81	104–120
Visual Spatial	119	90	110–125
Fluid Reasoning	112	79	104–118
Working Memory	97	42	90–105
Processing Speed	98	45	89–107
Full Scale	110	75	104–115
Verbal Comprehension Subtests			
Subtest Scaled Scores			
Similarities		13	
Vocabulary		12	
Information		. 15	
Visual Spatial Subtests			
Block Design		13	
Visual Puzzles		14	
Fluid Reasoning Subtests			
Matrix Reasoning		11	
Figure Weights		13	
Picture Concepts		8	
Working Memory Subtests			
Digit Span		7	
Picture Span		12	
Processing Speed Subtests			
Coding		11	
Symbol Search		8	
Cancellation		4	

range (VCI = 113, VSI = 119, and FRI = 112) and his other two scores were in the average range (WMI = 97, PSI = 98). Given his emotional state, I believed the WMI and PSI likely were a lower estimate of his intelligence because these tasks are most affected by depression.

2. Henry seemed determined to let everyone know how miserable and sad he was.

3. There was a quality to his sadness that felt aggressive and punishing.

4. His parents were very unemotional when sharing information about how difficult it was to parent Henry.

5. I wondered about Henry's thinking because it seemed distorted when he talked about the teachers at school and what was required regarding homework assignments. There were times when he was so insistent on being the worst in his class, or his teacher hating him, or not being good at anything at all that I thought I needed to check how intact his reality testing was. His mother had also said that he would be having a wonderful time at a family event and when he came home, he would say how miserable he was. Were these exaggerations really more of a need to make sure I knew he was so very depressed or was his thinking really distorted?

6. The family system definitely seemed to match the "sick child" prototype described in Chapter 2.

7. I could see why Henry's parents felt like he was exaggerating his symptoms. His sadness was so black and white and all encompassing that it just didn't feel real.

8. I wondered if the energy Henry put into his negative feelings was in response to not feeling that anyone could join with him and help him "hold" them. Perhaps the more he felt contradicted, the more intensely he felt the need to push back.

After this review, I wanted to get more information from his current therapist. Some of my questions had to do with how she saw the family system. What were her impressions of their parenting style? Did she think there might have been some sort of trauma that Henry experienced? In addition, when thinking about upcoming testing sessions I knew I needed to do performance-based tests to see what was going on with Henry at a less conscious level. My plan was to do the Rorschach next. I wanted to see if Henry's responses would be consistent with his highly negative view of his life—knowing that the Rorschach is less easily influenced by the respondent's desired presentation. I also wanted teachers, parents, and Henry to complete BASC-3s to see how they viewed Henry. I felt it would be important to see if teachers and parents were consistent in their view of Henry, giving me more information as to his status as the "sick" child in the family.

Henry and I also completed other, less structured activities that would provide me with more information about his emotional state, thinking, and place in the family. These are discussed as follows.

1. *Periodic mood ratings.* From the start of our sessions together I decided to have Henry periodically evaluate his emotional state as "very sad," "sad," "neutral," "happy," or "very happy." We did these during different activities in the session (Figure 4.1).

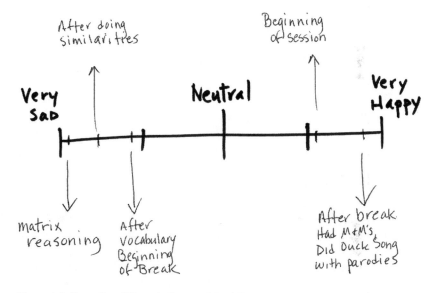

Figure 4.1 Example of Henry's Session Mood Ratings.

He consistently came into the session feeling either neutral or OK and became sad after most tasks. He also said he was happiest when we played a video game at the end of the session and when he ate some of the candy that was available in my office.

2. *Ratings of family members.* I wanted to assess how Henry saw himself in the family system, so we used a horizontal line to depict how he rated each family member on different emotions, including anger, guilt, stress, and loneliness (Figure 4.2). He usually placed himself in direct opposition to where he placed other family members. For example, when asked about who was most angry, his family members were at the "most angry" line on the continuum, while he was in the middle. He was consistently most guilty, most lonely, most stressed, and of course most sad.

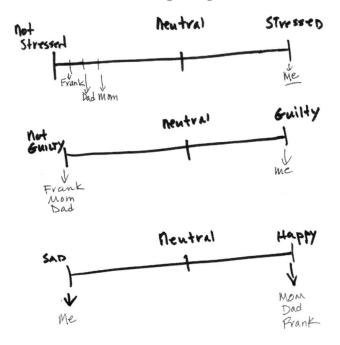

Figure 4.2 Henry's Ratings of Family Affect.

3. *The Fantasy Animal Drawing Game.* When asked to draw a fantasy animal that no one has ever seen or heard of (as described earlier), Henry drew an irregular rectangular shape shaded in pencil. When I asked him to tell me about the animal, he said it was "a giant void of nothingness." I said, "Maybe we can tell a story about it." So, I started, "Once upon a time there was a giant void of nothingness...." Henry continued, "It's existed since the beginning of time and doesn't have a name because it is nothing and you really can't name nothing." As hard as I tried to engage with him about the story, Henry stuck with the theme that it was nothing and would say no more. About a week later we tried the activity again and Henry drew a tiny, tiny dot. Again, as hard as I tried to encourage Henry to tell me about the dot, he was not very forthcoming:

Dale: And this fantasy creature was just a dot. And does the dot do anything? Could we name the fantasy creature? Could we name the dot?
Henry: Dot.
Dale: Ok.
Henry: Dot the dot.
Dale: Dot the dot?
Henry: Uh huh.
Dale: Ok. And what does Dot the Dot like to do?
Henry: Be a dot.

Dale: Oh, be a dot. What does she…is it a she or a he?
Henry: It doesn't have a gender.
Dale: Does it have friends?
Henry: Nope.
Dale: No friends? Um, tell me something about it.
Henry: Um, it lives on a, um a wide stretch of white plain.
Dale: If it would talk, what would it say?
Henry: Just wouldn't have much to say. Probably just say hello.
Dale: Ok. Who does it live with?
Henry: It doesn't live with anybody.
Dale: Must be very lonely.
Henry: Yeah, very lonely.

By the end of this interaction, I began to feel exhausted and irritated. It did not feel like Henry was constricted or scared to take a risk but rather that he was being oppositional. Again, this gave me empathy for how Henry's parents might feel, and I also noted how good Henry was at making others feel anger.

4. *Individualized Sentence Completions.* Using the technique discussed previously in the chapter, I wrote individualized sentence stems (Table 4.2) to see if I could elicit more information about Henry's emotional and family life. My hope was to get more information about his place in the family and to see how and if he felt supported.

Table 4.2 Individualized Sentence Completions for Henry

1. My favorite activity/hobby is *sitting around playing video games like Minecraft.*
2. I really, really like *my dog Ginger.*
3. I wish my teachers were *nicer.*
4. When a teacher tells me what to do, I *follow their directions.*
5. I feel like a nervous wreck when *I answer wrong on any kind of test.*
6. When I am at school I feel *dread in my stomach.*
7. When I don't have enough time *I start to panic and I have a meltdown.*
8. I wish my dad *would not pick me up by the back of my neck and throw me into the bathroom.*
9. I wish my mom *would listen to the negative things I say.*
10. When I have my feelings, I talk to *my parents but they don't listen.*
11. When I am alone *I think about killing myself.*
12. I worry that my parents *will stop listening to me completely whenever I'm feeling sad.*
13. When I am with my dad *if I make one mistake he'll get super angry at me and start yelling.*
14. When I am with my mom *she doesn't want to hear my sad talk and will leave the room or get super frustrated.*
15. People like it when *I insult myself.*
16. The best thing about me is *there is nothing good about me.*

The items indicated that Henry: (1) felt his parents were unable to listen to him about being sad, (2) saw his father as being angry, and (3) comforted himself with screen time. I took note of Item 11, which showed some suicidal thinking that had already been reported by his parents. Because one of the Assessment Questions concerned which school Henry should attend the following year, other sentence stems focused on school. His responses demonstrated: (1) how much pressure Henry felt at school, (2) how cooperative he was, and (3) that he wished his teachers were nicer. It seemed that he was stressed out at school and did not necessarily see the teachers as supportive.

5.   *Self-Report Measures.* Henry's scores on The Personality Inventory for Youth (PIY; Lachar & Gruber, 1995) indicated that he answered the items consistently. However, he clearly endorsed items that reflected how miserable he was to such a degree that the Dissimulation Scale (the scale that measures exaggerated responding) is elevated. This was not surprising to me because Henry's general presentation of his sadness and depression are constant.

His scores indicated that he sees himself as being cognitively challenged, with poor achievement, learning problems, and inadequate abilities. He reported a lot of parent-child conflict, had some distortion of reality, experiences a lot of somatic complaints, a severe amount of psychological discomfort expressed as fear and worry, sleep disturbances and depression. The only areas that were not significantly elevated were Impulsivity and Distractibility, and Delinquency (Table 4.3).

Table 4.3 Personality Inventory for Youth (PIY)

Scale	Standard Score	Scale	Standard Score
VAL	69	COG	86[*]
INC	08	Cog1	72[*]
FB	90+[*]	Cog2	82[*]
DEF	47	Cog3	75[*]
ADH	52	DLQ	45
Adh1	49	Dlq1	48
Adh2	57	Dlq2	42
Adh3	49	Dlq3	50
FAM	66	RLT	68[*]
Fam1	77[*]	Rlt1	60
Fam2	57	Rlt2	76[*]
Fam3	53		
SOM	82[*]	DIS	88[*]
Som1	82[*]	Dis1	75[*]
Som2	77[*]	Dis2	90[*]
Som3	66[*]	Dis3	76
WDL	83[*]	SSK	82[*]
Wdl1	68[*]	Ssk1	75[*]
Wdl2	90[*]	Ssk2	82[*]

Note
[*]   Clinically significant.

Henry's self-report scores on the BASC-3 were consistent with the PIY as I expected. The validity pattern was interesting. The F-Index, an infrequency scale, indicated that Henry rated himself in an extremely negative fashion (Raw Score = 15) and the results should be interpreted "with extreme caution." This, of course, was consistent with Henry's presentation throughout the assessment. The other validity scores were in the "Acceptable" range, indicating that Henry did not choose to present himself in a socially desirable way (L Index Raw Score = 85), responded to the items in a consistent manner (Consistency Index Raw Score = 11) and there wasn't a clear pattern to his responses (Response Pattern Raw Score = 85). The V-Index (Raw Score = 2) again indicated that the results should be interpreted with caution. As we might have been expected, all of the clinical scales were in the "Clinically Significant" range with the exception of three that were in the "At-Risk" range and one (Hyperactivity) that was in the "Average" range . I interpreted these scores as Henry communicating, "I am really miserable. Please take me seriously!!" (Table 4.4).

Table 4.4 Behavior Assessment Scales for Children—Third Edition (BASC-3): Self-Report

	T-Score	*Percentile*
Attitude to School	80	99[**]
Attitude to Teachers	90	99[**]
School Problems	89	99[**]
Atypicality	66	82[*]
Locus of Control	93	99[**]
Social Stress	91	99[**]
Anxiety	96	99[**]
Depression	111	99[**]
Sense of Inadequacy	103	99[**]
Internalizing Problems	104	99[**]
Attention Problems	67	94[*]
Hyperactivity	58	80
Inattention/Hyperactivity	64	90[*]
Emotional Symptoms Index	111	99[**]
Relations with Parents	14	1[**]
Interpersonal Relations	10	1[**]
Self-Esteem	12	1[**]
Self-Reliance	15	1[**]
Personal Adjustment	10	1[**]

Notes
* At-risk.
** Clinically significant.

6. *Teacher and Parent Report Measures.* Two of Henry's teachers completed the BASC-3 (Table 4.5). The pattern of scores was remarkably consistent. Both teachers rated Henry as being depressed and anxious but not at the level he had rated himself. They did not see him as having any Externalizing Problems, such as Hyperactivity, Aggression, or Conduct Problems. Barbara's and David's BASC-3s (Table 4.6) were

Table 4.5 Behavior Assessment Scales for Children—Third Edition (BASC-3): Teacher Report

Subtests	T-score (Cortez)	T-score (Smoot)
Aggression	43	43
Conduct Problems	43	48
Externalizing Problems	42	44
Anxiety	72**	80**
Depression	77**	87**
Somatization	50	78**
Internalizing Problems	71**	−91**
Learning Problems	39	45
School Problems	39	49
Atypicality	67*	55
Withdrawal	51	77**
Attention Problems	40	53
Behavioral Symptoms Index	54	62*
Adaptability	51	40*
Social Skills	55	41*
Leadership	57	38*
Study Skills	61	52
Functional Communication	49	47
Adaptive Skills	55	43

Notes
* At-risk.
** Clinically significant.

Table 4.6 Behavior Assessment Scales for Children—Third Edition (BASC-3): Parent Report

Subtests	T(Mom)	T(Dad)
Hyperactivity	47	53
Aggression	69*	61*
Conduct Problems	42	48
Externalizing Problems	53	55
Anxiety	73**	80**
Depression	88**	98**
Somatization	68*	86*
Internalizing Problems	81**	87**
Learning Problems	n/a	n/a
School Problems	n/a	n/a
Atypicality	60*	62*
Withdrawal	58	65*
Attention Problems	35	40
Behavioral Symptoms Index	63*	68*
Adaptability	29**	25**
Social Skills	38*	35*
Leadership	33*	38*
Functional Communication	45	39*
Activities of Daily Living	57	48
Adaptive Skills	39*	35*

Notes
* At-risk.
** Clinically significant.

consistent with the teachers' reports and consistent with each other's. In addition, the parents did not see Henry as being very adaptable, and their responses placed him in the "At-Risk" range on the Aggression scale, suggesting that Henry had problems managing anger.

7. *Performance-Based Measures.* Interestingly, Henry's Rorschach (Table 4.7) did show significant distress and disturbance, but again, much less than he had

Table 4.7 Rorschach Inkblots (R-PAS Scoring)

Scores are in Standard Score Format (mean of 100, standard deviation of 15)

Engagement and Cognitive Processing	Perception and Thinking Problems
Complexity = 107	EII-3 = 112
R = 95	TP-Comp = 100
F% = 92	WSumCog = 112
Bln = 109	SevCog = 106
Sy = 101	FQ-% = 96
MC = 94	WD-% = 100
MC-PPD = 79	FQo% = 90
M- = 97	FQu% = 117
M/MC = 104	P = 107
(CF+C)/Sum C = NA	
W% = 126	
Dd% = 87	
SI (Space Integration) = 115	
IntCont = 90	
V = 94	
FD = 117	
R8910% = 71	
WSumC = 92	
Mp/(Ma+Mp) = NA	

Self and Other Representation	Stress and Distress
ODL% = 133	YTVC' = 117
SR (space reversal) = 90	m = 117
MAP/MAHP = NA	Y = 118
PHR/GHR = 118	MOR = 119
M- = 91	SC-Comp = NA
AGC = 119	PPD = 116
H = 84	CBlend = 118
COP = 90	C' = 108
MAH = 90	V = 94
SumH = 92	CritCont% = 115
NPH/SumH = 122	
V-Comp = 109	
r =134	
p/(a+p) = 99	
AGM = 106	
T = 119	
Per = 92	
An = 88	

reported on the BASC. There were indications that his psychological resources were overwhelmed (MC-PPD = 79). His scores suggested that he was under a moderate amount of stress and was feeling helpless (m = 117, Y = 118), and that he had a damaged and negative self-view (MOR = 119), perhaps related to some traumatic experiences (CritCont% = 115). Overall, his thinking scores were in the average range indicating that generally he saw the world similarly to other ten-year-old boys and did not distort reality or have significantly disordered thinking (EII = 112, TP-Comp = 100, WSumCog = 112, SevCog = 106, FQ- = 96, P = 107, FQo = 90, WD% = 100). However, there was an indication that Henry did perceive the world somewhat idiosyncratically (FQu% = 117). What stood out most in Henry's responses was his overall need for and dependency on others for support and nurturance. He appeared to be longing for attention and wanting to be taken care of (ODL% = 133). But, while he longed for nurturance, he did not necessarily see others as being able to support him (PHR/GHR = 118, H = 84, V-C = 109) and tended to be more self-centered than most children his age (r = 134). What a conflict! Also, one score (AGC = 119) suggested that Henry was preoccupied with aggressive feelings and behavior—either within himself or in others.

Because the Rorschach gave a somewhat different impression of Henry's internal state as compared to the severity of his self-presentation, I wanted to do another performance-based test that might help explain this discrepancy. I thought the Wartegg Drawing Completion Test (WDCT; Crisi, 2018) would be a very good measure to use, as it is research-based, normed for children, and often overlaps with both self-report tests and the Rorschach. The WDCT consists of a paper form that is divided into two rows of four boxes. In each box, there is a mark. The client is asked to make a complete drawing that incorporates the mark that is in each box. After drawing, the client is asked to say what was drawn. The test is rigorously scored and has proven validity (Crisi, 2018). When presented with this task, Henry immediately drew tears and sad faces in each of the boxes. This was consistent with how he presented himself throughout our time together, but I didn't feel that it was an accurate measure of what was going on inside of Henry, except that it did convey his urgency at presenting the sadness.

On another day we did the test again, and I said, "Why don't you try and draw something that isn't all tears?" In that retest he either didn't draw in the boxes or connected the marks that were in each box. Again, I did not think this revealed much apart from Henry's resistance to being controlled and his intent on doing things his own way. Finally, I asked Henry to try and do the task again, in the best way he could, without drawing tears and sad faces. I also framed the task more collaboratively, explaining that it might tell us different things about what's going on inside of him and that it could be very helpful in answering his question about why he is so sad.

This third attempt was more fruitful, again reminding me how important it was to remind Henry that I was trying to address his goals for the assessment. The scoring and qualitative analyses of the WDCT were generally consistent with the Rorschach but indicated a more severe level of disturbance (Global Assessment = Pathological, I.I.T.-2 adj = 0.7/57.3, W.I.P. = D/Beta). Even when the disturbing drawings of tears and sad faces were eliminated, Henry's Wartegg responses suggested that he was severely depressed (I.S.T. = 5+2), had limited energy for daily activities (Box 3-D), was under severe stress (MI = 3), and had a lot of social anxiety and disconnection from others (Box 8 = NC, H% = 0, HS% = 25, SIG% = 25). As with the Rorschach, there were indications of unresolved dependency needs (Oral Impulse Response = 1). Also, in line with the Rorschach were signs of idiosyncratic thinking (AP = 3, P% = 0). One suggested potential strength was that Henry could be aggressive in overcoming an obstacle (Box 5 = C), as was experienced by his parents and me when Henry resolutely presented his sadness and depression (Table 4.8).

Table 4.8 Wartegg Drawing Completion Test—Crisi Wartegg System (CWS)

BOX 1 = C	BOX 2 = C	BOX 3 = D
BOX 4 = AD	BOX 5 = C	BOX 6 = AD
BOX 7 = D	BOX 8 = NC	M/m = 0/3
E.C.+% = 50	IIT-1 = 0.625	SIG% = 25
AQ+% = 44	IM = 0.13	ARC% = 13
FQ+% = 88	AI = 0.50	AS% = 13
A/F = 1.5/3.5	IIT-2 = 3.0 : 5.0	ICE% = 13
P% = 0	WIP = D, Beta	I.I.T.-2 = 3/5
P+% = N.D.	M/m = 0/3	AP = 3
O% = 13	H% = 0	m = 1
O+% = 50	OBJ% = 38	MI = 3

Contact With the Parents

In order to best understand Henry's behavior in the context of the family, I scheduled several meetings with the parents during this portion of the assessment. In the first of these sessions, I explained that I wanted to understand the context of Henry's difficulties and so was curious about each parent's family of origin. Both Barbara and David were very willing to talk about their families. I organized our conversation by constructing a genogram (Figure 4.3) This gave us a concrete way to focus on the relationships, values, and mental health issues in each of their families.

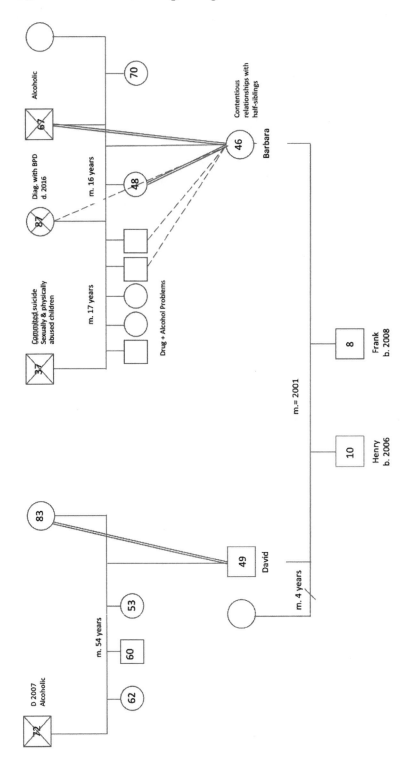

Figure 4.3 Genogram of Henry's Family.

This session also allowed us to fill in more details about Henry's development and important life events in the family (Table 4.9).

Table 4.9 Major Child/Family Life Events Timeline

Date	Life Event
4/2006	Birth complicated by very long delivery 55 hours. Henry not in distress. Family narrative "Didn't want to be born."
14 months	Walked
19 months	Weaned
20 months	Brother born, nursed until he was 4+ years old
22 months	Delayed expressive language- speech therapist
42 months	Toilet trained
10/2008	Family moved back to Texas
09/2012	Mother went back to work when Henry was in 1st grade. Started her own business. Dad became primary caregiver.
12/2012	Some difficulty making friends in 1st grade. No problems with schoolwork.
08/2013	Second grade first said, "I want to die."
09/2013-3/2015	Saw therapist. Individual therapy, with some parent coaching, "sad talk" behavior improved 2nd and 3rd grade.
05/2014	Father finished his schooling. Unable to look for full-time employment because of childcare responsibilities.
11/2014	Henry struggles in school around writing, other than that does well in 4th grade and therapy is discontinued after spring break.
08/2016	Right before 5th grade started, "Sad talk" behavior increased again. "Mistake to be born." Returned to therapy.
10/2016	Assessment begins.

Barbara had a very traumatic background. She described her mother, Donna, as very "difficult, narcissistic, and borderline." Barbara had a number of half-siblings who were raised by Donna and her first husband, Max, prior to Barbara's being born. Donna was physically and sexually abused by Max, who also sexually abused their children for a number of years. Max committed suicide shortly after Donna found out about the children's abuse. Five years after Max died, Donna married Byron. The couple had two children, one of whom was Barbara. Although she acknowledged her father was an alcoholic, Barbara described him as a "great dad." She described her interactions with her half-siblings as "totally crazy." Several of them were drug-addicted and others did not talk to their mother, Donna, at all. Barbara joked, "I wouldn't know what a normal family looks like. I just put my head down, went to college, and have a job I love. I didn't want to be part of my mother's craziness. So, our nuclear family looks pretty good to me." I thought, "Here is a woman who can tolerate a lot of distress while still moving forward!" I also had the impression that although Barbara had been able to distance herself from her family, she had not fully worked through her early trauma.

David said he came from an all-American blue-collar family in which feelings were not acknowledged and hard work was admired. David had four other siblings. His mom, Connie, was a stay-at-home mom until the youngest child was about 12, when she went to work part-time. David said there was alcoholism on both sides of the family in the previous generation. He described his mother as very controlling and intrusive and not very warm. Emotions were rarely expressed in the family, but when they were, the feelings were easily dismissed.

By this time in the assessment, I was thinking that Henry's parents were united in seeing him as the "sick child" as discussed in Chapter 2. Both parents were at their wit's ends as to how to help their son. They experienced Henry as very draining and demanding. They felt like he was provocative and said things that really stirred up the family system. They wanted help figuring out what was going on with their son and admitted to how frustrated they were. As described in Chapter 2, often when there is a "sick child" constellation, there are major difficulties integrating and expressing anger in the family. This seemed quite likely to me. In addition, it seemed that all the emotional energy was going toward Henry and I became curious about whether Henry's issues were distracting the parents from issues in their own relationship. I also wondered how much time and energy, if any, the parents had to take care of each other.

I scheduled another parent session to show a videotape of one of my testing sessions with Henry. As discussed previously, this method serves many purposes. In this case, I felt that watching the video together would: (1) strengthen the collaborative process, (2) provide me with information about the parents' perspectives as they spontaneously reacted to the video, and (3) help me understand if the parents viewed Henry's behavior similarly or if there was disagreement between them.

After greeting Barbara and David, I explained that I wanted their help understanding some of what I was experiencing with Henry. I then showed them the Extended Inquiry of the WISC-V (captured in the transcript earlier). As we sat down to watch the video, before the image even came up, Barbara immediately said that she wondered if Henry was really depressed. I was surprised by her question and wondered why she asked it, since to me it was so clear that Henry was depressed. The following conversation ensued:

Dale: Do you have any doubts that he's depressed?

Mom: Yeah, I have doubts.

Dale: Can you tell me about the doubts? (I was surprised by her comment, given that she had rated Henry as depressed on the BASC-3.)

Mom: I live in the world as a high functioning anxiety person. So, it's normal to me for people to have fatalistic thoughts. I thought everybody walked around like that all the time. So, it just feels like, "Oh, that's just life." I think that I have a different perspective. I think I may have a skewed view of the world. Maybe that's part of it. Henry just doesn't act depressed so much of the time. And I realized that maybe I just don't understand depression, or depression and children. But it's hard because you go pick him up at school, like I did yesterday, and he's wearing a Santa hat. I gave him his little cards to give to his teachers. He ran up to the teachers really confidently. Hugs his teachers. Hanging out with his friends. So, I don't really … it's hard for me to understand because I think of depression as the way I saw my sister, which was literally curled in the fetal position.

Dale: You mean when she was little?

Mom: Well, all her life—off and on, all her life. She had a severe breakdown, when she lost 30 pounds, and I was up with her every night all through high school. She was in a transition from high school to college while I was still in high school. (This was the first time I heard this information.)

Dale: Wow, she sounds really depressed.

Mom: Yeah, so I don't really have a good view of how things are supposed to normally be.

As we talked more, it became clear that both parents doubted the severity of Henry's depression. They felt like he was comfortable with it, as his mother said, "Like putting on your favorite outfit, because its comfortable, and 'I'm going back to what's comfortable.'" I validated how difficult it must be to see Henry so happy one day and then so sad the next:

Dale: Yeah, he's very confusing. That's why I'm taking my time getting to know him and collaborating with you. Somehow, what we are talking about seems to relate to your assessment question: "How do we stop the cycle of manipulation, anxiety, suicidal talk, and anger that is so familiar in Barbara's family?" Did you think your sister was manipulative? When we talked about your family of origin, I thought you were talking about your half-siblings, that family. I didn't realize things were as difficult when you were growing up.

Barbara then explained that her mother had continuously threatened to kill herself or to kill Barbara and her sister. Barbara said that the police had often been called to her home because her mother was so "out of control." She physically attacked Barbara and threatened her with guns and knives. We also talked more about David's family and how emotionally constricted they were. He said that his mom was always trying to control the environment in the house so as not to get David's father upset because he could be quick to anger. David said his mom would withhold important information from his dad. Barbara chimed in, saying that she thought some of these patterns were repeating themselves because she withheld information from David a lot because he could get really upset and angry.

Barbara: He (David) scares me with his anger because he's very quick to anger. And it's hard for me to predict when that's going to happen. Um, he's just very in his head, and then something will happen, and he just gets very angry very fast. It's usually gone really quickly, but there's a low level of kind of grumpiness that's just part of the way that he's constructed. So, it's like it's a dual nature of incredibly nurturing and giving, and pretty grumpy and quick to anger. Henry describes being scared of it. He'll describe you (to David) as just monstrously scary, and Frank (Henry's brother) will say, "Henry, it's not that bad." So yes, I do tip toe around David. I definitely do. And now I feel like I am tiptoeing around Henry. I won't ask him questions about his day because I don't want the conversation to turn negative. I won't ask him about his homework just in case it's going to be a trigger point. If we're having a pleasant conversation, I don't want to screw that up. So, I just don't engage.

Our conversation about anger and manipulation continued. This was so important because I had been wondering about anger in the family. Was Henry acting out someone else's unexpressed anger when he seemed provocative? Did he need to be the "sick child" in the family because of how expressing and experiencing anger was not allowed? In the typical "sick child" family, everyone is afraid of anger and needs to express it in an indirect way (such as being rigidly negative) or people alternately constrict and then lose control of their anger. I knew that this conversation would be instrumental in formulating a case conceptualization. The session allowed me to introduce the idea of both parents completing MMPI's, as well as discussing a systemic understanding of Henry's behavior.

Dale: I'm sorry we didn't get a chance to view the video, but this session has been so important in my understanding of Henry and each of you.

(I was happy I didn't stick to my original plan because if I had, I wouldn't have gotten as much rich and essential information. Flexibility is important throughout the assessment. In this case, we wouldn't have the new information if I felt I HAD to stay with the plan.)

I've been thinking that several of your assessment questions relate to how you can best support Henry, such as "How can we help Henry feel confidence and loved?" I think it would be helpful to get more information about your own strengths and challenges. I was wondering if you would be willing to take the MMPI. This is a self-report test that would help me understand each of you a little better.

I explained a little bit about the test and how it would benefit our work together. Both parents were more than happy to complete the MMPI-2. I was interested in seeing what the parents' MMPI's said about anger and sadness. In closing this session, we planned another time to view the video.

The parents gave me their completed MMPI-2s the next time I saw Henry. There were no signs on Barbara's validity scales of inconsistent reporting, generalized over-reporting, or underreporting. The Higher-Order and Restructured Clinical (RC) Scales were remarkable in that none were that far from the average. This result fit my sense that Barbara was able to function adequately and didn't have a major mental disorder. Her score on RC4 (Antisocial Behavior) was slightly elevated (62T) and another elevated scale, Substance Abuse (SUB-77T), revealed that Barbara had endorsed a number of items related to drug or alcohol concerns. For example, she answered True to items 192 ("After a bad day I usually need a few drinks to relax"), 266 ("I have a drug or alcohol problem"), and 297 ("Once a week or more I get high or drunk") among others. This was the first time Barbara had disclosed any information about her drinking to me, and I was glad that she had felt safe enough to do this.

Given significant elevations on several Internalizing Scales (Anxiety [ANX] = 90T; Stress/Worry [STW] = 73), I suspected Barbara was using substances to numb her feelings, and I decided to ask her about that at a subsequent meeting. Barbara also had the highest possible score on Self-Doubt (SFD = 76T), accompanied by the lowest possible scores on Helplessness/Hopelessness (HLP = 40T), Shyness (SHY = 37T), and Disaffiliativeness (DSF = 44T). These scores told me that she saw herself as extremely outgoing and relational and tried to maintain a determined, optimistic attitude even if she was full of anxiety and self-doubt. Given Henry's presentation, I also took note of Barbara's low scores on RC3 (Cynicism [CYN] = 38T), Aggression (AGG = 37T—the lowest possible score), and PSY-5 Aggressiveness (AGGR-r = 45). All of these scales suggested that she had difficulties expressing anger and would have trouble being assertive, setting limits, and protecting herself. Overall, the MMPI-2 made me wonder if Barbara might have some degree of PTSD from living as a child with a mother she had described as erratic and unpredictable. Her profile also suggested that as a mother, she would have difficulties being empathic to a child who felt hopeless and helpless, and she would have difficulty setting limits in a firm but modulated way.

David's MMPI-2 Validity Scales showed that he too had answered the items carefully and not tried to make himself look good or look bad. Even more than Barbara, David's profile was almost devoid of emotional distress (EID = 49T; RCd = 53T; RC7 = 46T; NEGE-r = 45T), and in fact his score on RC2 (Low Positive Emotions = 38T) was well below average for men his age. This lack of emotional pain really struck me, given how disturbing Henry's behavior had been for so long, and I wondered if David was not connected to his feelings and/or was particularly blocked against feeling sadness and depression. I remembered him saying that his mother had dismissed tender emotions; perhaps as a result, he had learned to cut them off. There was a slight elevation on the Helplessness scale (HLP = 60T), which I thought might be how David felt in relationship to Henry. Also, very surprisingly David had marked True to item #93: "I have recently considered killed myself." I resolved to bring this item up with him at a future meeting and wondered if it was an error or a possible sign that David was in more pain than he let himself know. Similar to Barbara, David presented himself as interested in people (DSF = 44T) and as socially engaged and not shy (SAV = 50T; SHY = 52T). My perception of him was that he was shy and reserved, and I resolved to make sure he was given enough space relative to Barbara in our sessions. Also, like Barbara, David scored low on PSY-5 Aggressiveness (AGGR-r = 45T) suggesting he too would have trouble setting limits and being assertive. Overall, the MMPI-2 suggested that as a father, David would have trouble being empathic to depressive feelings and would have trouble setting limits and expressing anger in a modulated way.

Taken together, Henry's parents' test results provided some support for viewing the family as fitting elements of both the "scapegoated child" and "sick child" prototypes. As discussed in Chapter 2, parents with a scapegoated child generally struggle with integrating grief, sadness, shame, and depression in themselves, and therefore "invite" their children to help hold these feelings for the family. Parents of "sick" children have not integrated their anger; hence their children feel uncontained and may act out the unexpressed family anger in direct or indirect ways, sometimes by "torturing" the whole family with their "fragility."

I briefly shared some of the MMPI-2 results with David and Barbara when I met with them next. I emphasized that they had both taken the tests in a reliable and valid way. I suggested that David's results suggested that he was emotionally constricted, meaning that he didn't easily share his feelings. He said he had a lot of feelings but just didn't express them. I gently asked about the item that indicated he had thought about suicide. He said that was in the past and he was presently on antidepressant medications. I asked Barbara if she might cope with stress by drinking. She agreed this was true. I shared that her test results indicated that she was anxious, outgoing, and dealt with her insecurities by being active. She agreed with this and said something about "getting busy" to avoid negative feelings.

Overall, both Barbara and David agreed with what I shared about their MMPI results. I thanked them again and said the results would help me think about how they could best support Henry.

Then, I continued the session by showing the video from when Henry said he did "horrible" after completing the WISC-V. I explained the Information subtest and what it measures, and how Henry had done really well on it. I showed an excerpt where I told Henry his score was way above average, he smiled, and then continued:

Henry: I wish I did do horrible because I feel like that. (He began to cry.) I deserve to do horrible.

At that moment I felt really connected to Henry's grief and sadness—very different than the way I felt in the face of his relentless, provocative negativity at other times during the assessment.

Dale: What have you done to make you feel that you deserve to do horrible?

Henry: Nothing.

Dale: That is so sad Henry. That must be so painful. But I can't imagine that you deserve to do or feel horrible.

Henry's parents confirmed that Henry's extreme negativity was very typical of how he was with them. As we watched the video, David noticed that there had been a slight change in Henry's facial expression. The parents agreed that Henry had seemed very proud of his score and of the fact that he was above average, and that he then had "corrected" his face to looking sad. We watched the video again, and I saw what the parents had focused on, but I wasn't sure that this meant Henry was consciously choosing not to feel pride. Barbara and David discussed how frustrating this was for them because Henry seemed to have to stick with feeling sad.

Dale: Yes, I can see what you're talking about. I noticed the smile as well, but his tears and his sadness seem quite genuine. I wonder if you notice the smile because his sadness is unbearable for you. It must be hard for you to stay with his sadness, which is so striking when he cries. Do you feel sad when you see this? Or do you feel irritated or some other way?

Barbara: It depends on the mood I'm in. This here is heartbreaking. I think it's heartbreaking.

Dale: Yes, heartbreaking!

Barbara: Sometimes I'm just irritated because it feels like he can control it and he doesn't. But then, once I sit with him for a while with it, and I see real tears, and I really see that he's struggling with something. Or I'll have just a real clear moment where we're having a normal day and he'll ask, "Why am I so sad all the time?" That's when I realize there is something going on.

We then watched another portion of the video where Henry and I were doing the BASC-3 self-report together. He answered every question in the most negative way. As the parents watched his responses, they seemed to be irritated. It was easy to understand why, but I also saw it as an opportunity to help them have more empathy for his provocative negativity. I selected a section of the video I thought would help with this.

Henry: Do you think I answered these questions accurately?

Dale: Well, you're being very black and white, and you don't strike me as a black and white kind of person, but I think you feel really bad and want me to know it.

Henry: (Nods) I am actually really miserable, and I want you to know how miserable I am. If I answered more accurately you won't know how miserable I am.

Dale: Yes, I can see how miserable you are, but I wonder if you can circle the parts of the form that aren't quite accurate?

Henry then took the pencil and circled three items that he seemed to have actually answered accurately and changed them to make them inaccurate. For example, Henry changed his response from "False" to "True" on the item "I have never been to sleep." Both parents were clearly disturbed as they watched this part of the video. They explained how provocative Henry's behavior felt to them, saying Henry knew what pushed their buttons about his sadness and said or did things that feel so intentionally aggravating. I wondered if they had heard Henry's explanation about why he needed to exaggerate—that otherwise he wouldn't be heard. I asked about this.

Barbara then talked about how her frustration contributed to Henry's maintaining his sadness. When she tried to apologize for getting angry or yelling at Henry and tried to change the direction of what has been happening, Henry resisted. Barbara said it felt like Henry didn't want to stop feeling badly or respond positively to her attempts at listening to him and doing something different. She said it just felt like he must be so angry. "Why is he so angry at me that he wants to make sure that I do not feel happy or relieved to see that my efforts have made a difference in his life?" Dad then talked about how, "Anger is fiercely toned down and controlled in our house." I was thankful that through our meetings and observation of Henry we had gotten the topic of anger—so evident in their MMPI-2 results—into the room and were beginning to discuss it. I could see how the parents might be inadvertently contributing to Henry's negativity. It seemed that they were so uncomfortable with direct anger that they had created an environment where Henry needed to express his anger indirectly, by being a victim. This was so similar to how Barbara's mother handled anger that it was impossible for her not to take this personally and be furious at Henry. And David's inability to relate to any feelings of depression—again adaptive to his childhood with a "tough minded" mother, seemed to me a perfect set-up for Henry to hold depression. I felt that I was beginning to understand how the parents' and Henry's emotional issues interfaced to create a system that was painful for all of them.

Contact with the School

At the beginning of the assessment, with Barbara and David's permission, I contacted the school counselor to let her know that I was doing a

Therapeutic Assessment and to explain how it might be different than other outside evaluations. I shared how important it was to collaborate with the school and get their perspective on Henry. We spoke a number of times throughout the assessment because Henry was often upset at school. It became clear that there were several issues that were problematic. First, there was a teacher, Mr. Hanson, with whom Henry felt extremely uncomfortable. Henry said that this teacher picked on him, had crazy expectations, and that when Henry was anxious Mr. Hanson wouldn't let Henry leave the room as other teachers had done to accommodate Henry's anxiety. In addition, Henry was very uncomfortable with changing his clothes for gym and this caused a lot of anxiety and fear. Henry insisted that being in school caused him a great deal of stress even though he was making good grades, had friends, and most of his teachers really liked him. The school counselor allowed Henry to visit her in her office when needed. She said she was concerned that Mr. Hanson did not allow Henry to leave the classroom when it was needed.

I shared that my testing results indicated that Henry might meet the criteria for Special Education services under the Emotional Disturbance criteria. He did well in school, but he often left classes because of his anxiety. Whether or not he met the criteria would be a decision that would be made by an Admission Review and Dismissal (ARD) Committee meeting if Henry was referred for Special Education. I shared my surprise at how this hadn't come up before, given how often Henry was leaving class. The counselor and I wondered if it would be in Henry's best interest to call an ARD meeting for Special Education or to develop a 504 Plan to meet Henry's emotional needs. We decided that I would discuss these alternatives with the parents and see what they wanted to do.

The parents and I met that following week. I explained the possibilities for more support at school and they decided that it would be best to pursue 504 Accommodations. We agreed that I would prepare a letter for the school documenting that Henry has a "mental impairment that substantially limits one or more major life activities." Specifically, I would document that Henry had undergone a psychological assessment with me and met the criteria for depression and anxiety. Furthermore, I would add that, in my professional opinion, these conditions interfered with his ability to remain in class at times when his feelings overwhelmed his resources.

The parents contacted the school counselor who quickly arranged for an in-school meeting that included Henry's teachers, the 504 facilitator, Assistant Principal, Henry's parents, and me. Dr. Jagger was unable to come due to a scheduling conflict. At the meeting, we discussed a number of possible accommodations that included extra time on projects, the ability for Henry to leave class as needed, and daily check-ins with the counselor, if necessary. The meeting attendees agreed that these three accommodations would help Henry to benefit more fully from his educational program and we drew up a formal 504 Plan.

Contact with Dr. Jagger

After our initial discussion, I spoke with Dr. Jagger at least two other times during the assessment to get more information about her perspective of Henry and the family dynamics. She indicated that Henry made most of his suicidal and provocative statements to his mother. Dr. Jagger thought that Henry was more passive-aggressive and oppositional with his father. She had never recommended family therapy because she didn't feel like Frank, Henry's brother, could handle it. Frank was very distressed by Henry's negativity. She did, however, do some parent coaching. I shared that I noticed that it was hard for both parents to empathize with Henry's negativity. I wondered if his parents were able to validate his feelings. Dr. Jagger indicated that this is what she worked on with Henry's parents, but she felt that it was still difficult for both of them to get into Henry's shoes for different reasons. She felt that Barbara minimized the severity of Henry's depression while David intellectualized the sadness. Dr. Jagger felt that anger was not directly expressed or discussed, and she wondered if Henry's behavior was an expression of difficulties in the marriage.

Final Thoughts

In this part of Henry's case, I have tried to illustrate the process and details of (1) data gathering from specific tests as well as getting information from Henry's individual therapist and school personnel; (2) building a relationship with both the child and parents; and (3) beginning to frame Henry's behavior in the context of the family system. While we all can't have parents in the room observing or watching behind a mirror, we can still make them part of the process by observing videotaped sessions. In the next chapter, you will see how I think about integrating results across tests to arrive at major findings, begin to formulate a case conceptualization, and sketch my answers to the Assessment Questions.

References

Achenbach T. M., & Rescorla L. A. (2001). *Manual for the ASEBA School-Age Forms & Profiles*. Burlington, VT: University of Vermont.

Ardila, A. (1992). Luria's approach to neuropsychological assessment. *International Journal of Neuroscience*, 66, 35–43.

Beck, J. S. (2021). *Cognitive therapy third edition: Basics and beyond*. New York: Guilford.

Bellak, L., & Bellak, S. S. (1976). *The Children's Apperception Test (CAT)*. Larchmont, NY: C.P.S.

Ben-Porath, Y. S., & Tellegen, A. (2020). *Minnesota Multiphasic Personality Inventory-3 (MMPI-3): Manual for administration, scoring, and interpretation*. Minneapolis: University of Minnesota Press.

Butcher, J., Dahlstrom, W. G., Graham, J., Tellegen, A., & Kaemmer, B. (1989). *MMPI-2 manual*. Minneapolis: University of Minnesota Press.

Crisi, A. 2018. *The Crisi Wartegg System (CWS) manual*. New York: Routledge.

Finn, S. E. (2007). *In our client's shoes: Theory and techniques of Therapeutic Assessment*. Mahwah, NJ: Erlbaum.

Finn, S. E., & Chudzik, L. (2013). L'Evaluation Thérapeutique pour enfant?: Théorie, procédures et illustration [Therapeutic Assessment with children: Theory, techniques, and case example]. *Neuropsychiatrie de l'Enfance et de l'Adolescence, 61*(3), 166–175.

Fischer, C. T. (1985/1994). *Individualizing psychological assessment*. Mawah, NJ: Routledge.

Fischer, C. T. (1994). Rorschach scoring questions as access to dynamics. *Journal of Personality Assessment, 62*, 515–525.

Fischer, C. T. (2001). Collaborative exploration as an approach to personality assessment. In K. J. Schneider, J. F. T. Bugenthal, & J. F. Pierson (Eds.), *The handbook of humanistic psychology: Leading edges in theory, research, and practice* (pp. 525–538). Thousand Oaks, CA: Sage.

Fonagy, P. (1998). An attachment theory approach to the treatment of the difficult patient. *Bulletin of the Menninger Clinic, 62*(2), 147–169.

George, C., & West, M. (2012). *The Adult Attachment Projective Picture System: Attachment theory and assessment in adults*. Guilford Press: New York.

Handler, L. (2007). The use of therapeutic assessment with children and adolescents. In S. Smith & L. Handler (Eds.), *Clinical assessment of children and adolescents: A practitioner's guide* (pp. 53–72). Mawah, NJ: Erlbaum & Associates.

Handler, L. (2012). Collaborative storytelling with children: An unruly six-year-old boy. In S. E. Finn, C. T. Fischer, & L. Handler (Eds.), *Collaborative/Therapeutic Assessment: A case book and guide* (pp. 243–266). Hoboken, NJ: Wiley.

Handler, L. (2014). The fantasy animal and story-telling game. In L. Handler & A. D. Thomas (Eds.), *Drawings in assessment and psychotherapy: Research and application* (pp. 117–130). New York, NY: Routledge.

Harrower, M. (1956). Projective counseling—A psychotherapeutic technique. *American Journal of Psychotherapy, 10*, 74–86.

Holigrocki, R., Crain, R., Bohr, Y., Young, K., & Bensman, H. (2009). Interventional use of the Parent-Child Interaction Assessment-II enactments: Modifying an abused mother's attributions to her son. *Journal of Personality Assessment, 91*(5), 397–408.

Kamphuis, J. H., & Finn, S. E. (2019). Therapeutic Assessment in personality disorders: Toward the restoration of epistemic trust. *Journal of Personality Assessment, 101*(6), 662–674.

Klopfer, B., Ainsworth, M., Klopfer, W., & Holt, R. (1954). *Developments in the Rorschach technique (vol. 1)*. New York: Harcourt Brace.

Lachar, D., & Gruber, C. P. (1995). *Personality Inventory for Youth (PIY) manual*. Los Angeles: Western Psychological Services.

Lidz, C. S. (1995). Dynamic assessment and the legacy of L. S. Vygotsgy. *School Psychology International, 16*(2), 143–153.

Lidz, C. S. (1997). Dynamic assessment approaches. In D. P. Flanagan, J. L. Genshaft, & J. L. Harrison (Eds.), *Contemporary intellectual assessment: Theories, tests, and issues* (1st ed.; pp. 281–296). New York, NY: The Guilford Press.

McArthur, D., & Roberts, G. (1982). *Roberts apperception test for children—manual.* Los Angeles: Western Psychological Services.

Meyer, G. J., Finn, S. E., Eyde, L. D., Kay, G. G., Moreland, K. L., Dies, R. R., Eisman, E. J., Kubiszyn, T. W., & Reed, G. M. (2001). Psychological testing and psychological assessment: A review of evidence and issues. *American Psychologist,* 56, 128–165.

Meyer, G. J., Viglione, D. J., Mihura, J. L., Erard, R. E., & Erdberg, P. (2011). *Rorschach Performance Assessment System: Administration, coding, interpretation, and technical manual.* Toledo: Rorschach Performance Assessment System.

McGoldrick, M., Gerson, R., & Petry, S. (2020). *Genograms: Assessment and treatment* (4th ed.). New York: W. W. Norton.

Milberg, W. P., Hebben, N., & Kaplan, E. (1996). The Boston process approach to neuropsychological assessment. In I. Grant & K. M. Adams (Eds.), *Neuropsychological assessment of neuropsychiatric disorders* (pp. 58–80). New York, NY: Oxford University Press.

Milberg, W. P., Hebben, N., Kaplan, E., Grant, I., & Adams, K. (2009). The Boston process approach to neuropsychological assessment. *Neuropsychological Assessment of Neuropsychiatric and Neuromedical Disorders,* 3, 42–65.

Millon, T., Grossman, S., & Millon, C. (2015). *Manual for the MCMI-IV.* Bloomington, MN: Pearson Assessments.

Morey, L. C. (2007). *The PAI professional manual.* Lutz, FL: Psychological Assessment Resources.

Murray, H. A. (1943). *Thematic Apperception Test manual.* Cambridge, MA: Harvard University Press.

Mutchnick, M. G., & Handler, L. (2002). Once upon a time…: Therapeutic interactive stories. *The Humanistic Psychologist,* 30, 75–84.

Piotrowski, Z. A. (1957). *Perceptanalysis: A fundamentally reworked, expanded, and systematized Rorschach method.* New York: Macmillan.

Reynolds, C. R., & Kamphaus, R. W. (2015). *Behavior Assessment System for children* (3rd ed.). Bloomington, MN: Pearson.

Tharinger, D. J., Christopher, G., & Matson, M. (2011). Play, playfulness, and creative expression in Therapeutic Assessment with Children. In S. W. Russ & L. N. Niec (Eds.), *An evidence-based approach to play in intervention and prevention: Integrating developmental and clinical science* (pp. 109–148). New York: Guilford Press.

Tharinger, D. J., Finn, S. E., Arora, P., Judd-Glossy, L., Ihorn, S. M., & Wan, J. T. (2012). Therapeutic Assessment with children: Intervening with parents "behind the mirror." *Journal of Personality Assessment,* 94, 111–123.

Tharinger, D. J., Finn, S. E., Gentry, L., Hamilton, A., Fowler, J., Matson, M., Krumholz, L., & Walkowiak, J. (2009). Therapeutic Assessment with children: A pilot study of treatment acceptability and outcome. *Journal of Personality Assessment,* 91, 238–244.

Tharinger, D. J., Finn, S. E., Wilkinson, A. D., & Schaber, P. M. (2007). Therapeutic Assessment with a child as a family intervention: Clinical protocol and a research case study. *Psychology in the Schools,* 44, 293–309.

Tharinger, D. J., Gentry, L. B., & Finn, S. E. (2013). Therapeutic Assessment with adolescents and their parents: A comprehensive model. In D. H. Saklofske, C. R.

Reynolds, & V. L. Schwean (Eds.), *Oxford handbook of child psychological assessment* (pp. 385–420). New York, NY: Oxford University Press.

Tharinger, D., & Roberts, M. (2014). Human figure drawings in Therapeutic Assessment with Children: Process, product, life context, and systemic impact. In L. Handler & A. D. Thomas (Eds.), *Drawings in assessment and psychotherapy: Research and application* (pp. 17–41). New York: Routledge.

Wechsler, D. (2014). *Wechsler intelligence Scale for Children* (5th ed.). Bloomington, MN: Pearson.

5 Phase III: Case Conceptualization

At this point, we have completed the Data Gathering/Testing Phase. We have attended to individual test findings, behavior during testing, and noted possible historic events and intergenerational patterns that we want to keep in mind going forward. We are now prepared to enter Phase III and construct a tentative case conceptualization. (The Family Intervention Session (FIS) is also part of Phase III and is addressed in Chapter 6.) To begin, we briefly discuss how case conceptualizations are typically conceived of in psychological and psychiatric assessment. Following, we highlight unique influences on the scope and uses of case conceptualizations in Therapeutic Assessment with Children (TA-C). We then provide a process to arrive at forming a comprehensive, theoretically integrated, and useful case conceptualization. Following, we discuss drafting initial answers to Assessment Questions, being sensitive to the Levels of Information contained in our responses in light of what we think parents are likely to be able to hear. Finally, we return to the case of Henry and offer an in-depth look at case conceptualization in process.

Case Conceptualization in General

There are many and varied definitions/descriptions of case conceptualization (sometimes called case formulation) in the literature and reflected in assessment practice. A case conceptualization reflects the clinician's integrated understanding of a client's problems and challenges as seen from a particular theoretical orientation and within the contexts and culture of the individual (John & Segal, 2015). A theoretical orientation, supported by research findings and well-accepted practice methods, provides a framework for the clinician from which to condense and synthesize multiple pieces of information into a coherent and well-developed narrative about the client. This narrative aims to identify not only the precipitating cause(s) of the client's problems (etiology) but also the forces at work, both internal and external to the client, which serve to maintain the problems (John & Segal, 2015). The case conceptualization culminates in a diagnosis and a treatment plan reflecting the uniqueness of the client and their context.

DOI: 10.4324/9781003000174-5

The common elements in case conceptualizations across theoretical orientations are diagnosis, theoretically informed hypotheses about etiology and problem maintenance, and recommendations for treatment. Most psychological assessments and resulting case conceptualizations are focused on an individual and are driven by a single theoretical approach. The assessor's theoretical orientation is a strong and guiding influence on the development of a case conceptualization. The task is for the assessor to: (1) match the client's history, problems, and symptoms with an established diagnosis, usually using DSM-5 (American Psychiatric Association, 2013) or ICD-10 (World Health Organization, 1992); (2) hypothesize from a theoretical frame what led up to the client developing the disorder and maintaining current problems; and (3) propose a theoretically grounded or empirically-based treatment plan to reduce the symptoms and promote improved life functioning.

Case Conceptualization in the TA-C Model

Case conceptualizations in TA-C share the features of the definition above, but tend to be more individualized and idiographic. In TA-C, diagnosis is seldom *the* focus, but sometimes *a* focus. If the parents pose an Assessment Question about their child's possible diagnosis, either at the beginning or along the way, we carefully examine the findings for differential diagnoses. Coming to understand how a problem developed (etiology) and what sustains it (problem maintenance) are central goals in TA-C. We consider multiple theoretical frameworks (often those introduced in Chapter 2), to interpret the findings and offer: (1) an understanding of how the family arrived at where they are (etiology and old narrative); (2) what is going on now in the family that keeps the family stuck (problem maintenance and continued old narrative); and (3) what would need to change for the family to overcome their current struggles (new narrative). Before addressing the process involved, let us address principles that impact how we construct a case conceptualization in TA-C.

Core Features of Case Conceptualization in TA-C

Child/Family Assessment Is Undertaken in a Particular Socio-Cultural Context at a Specific Point in Time; the Case Conceptualization Reflects These Realities

We seek to understand the child in the context of his or her family; thus, a TA-C case conceptualization is incomplete if it does take into account the reciprocal relationships between the child and other family members and the overall family system. Children and families are also inevitably influenced by the socio-cultural context in which they live, and an adequate case conceptualization takes account of racial, economic, religious, cultural, and other relevant factors (such as sexual orientation and gender identity). Finally, a

TA-C case conceptualization is not a picture of who the child/family "are" in some immutable sense, but rather a "snapshot" of a complex system at a certain moment of time. A good case conceptualization in TA-C captures a sense of "movement" of where the child and family have been, and where they could potentially head next.

The importance of contextual conceptualizations is further stressed by Wright (2021), who argued that deliberately considering clients' environmental context (e.g., the dominant culture's expectations regarding normative behavior), and clients' personal historical context (e.g., their history of trauma or adverse life events) is an important way to mitigate at least some of biases psychologists may unconsciously bring when looking at a set of assessment findings. When we take clients' contexts into account when constructing our case conceptualizations, we reach more complex understandings of their difficulties and take at least some of the burden off the client for why they struggle as they do.

TA-C Involves Assessment, Intervention, and Response to Intervention,
Thus Greatly Expanding the Parameters and Richness of
the Case Conceptualization

Some professionals in the field refer to Therapeutic Assessment (TA) as a short-term intervention informed by test findings, while others describe it as an assessment that has therapeutic impact. We would say it is both, and that at times assessment is in the foreground and intervention in the background, while at other times the reverse is true. A good case conceptualization includes both of these practices and is influenced by the findings from the testing, the ongoing discussions between the parents and the assessor (mini-interventions), and the family's response to a planned intervention.

The Interpersonal, Subjective Experience of the Assessor Is a Valued Way
of Knowing and Is a Central Contributor to Case Conceptualization

We view our experience as giving important cues to the systemic and intrapsychic forces operating in a child's and family's life, and as providing important information about potential interventions. When multiple assessors/teams are involved in an assessment, we also pay special attention to co-assessor/team dynamics, as these parallel processes are often extremely helpful in conceptualizing dilemmas of change in a family system.

The Total Experience Is Often an Intervention in Itself and Increases
the Likelihood of Acceptance of the Case Conceptualization and
New Family Narrative

In the 35 years since the model was developed, it has become clear to us that participation in a TA-C benefits the family directly. This occurs through the respect, compassion, and safety provided by the assessor, the clients' experience of really being heard and seen, and the collaborative relationships and trust that develops between the family members and the assessor. We well remember one set of grandparent caregivers who told us that what had impacted them the most in the TA-C of their granddaughter was the respect they received from us and our integration of their cultural background into our understanding of the granddaughter and the family. They had never felt that way with other health or educational professionals. The grandparents said that our respect was what motived them to be open to participating fully in the assessment and to be willing to make changes. In our experience, this type of openness positively impacts the case conceptualization and new narrative, as the child and parents are much less likely to hold back and keep us from knowing them. The family also has the opportunity to guide the assessment and help interpret the findings, which can empower them. In addition, the family is protected from feedback that could be overwhelming and perhaps lead to disintegration.

The Assessor Holds a Multi-theoretical Framework and Tries Out Different Theories and Combinations of Theories to Understand the Findings

This is in contrast to being grounded in one major theoretical orientation, as is true in many traditional assessment models. TA-C's trans-theoretical stance greatly influences the process of case conceptualization in that assessors are encouraged to consider and integrate a number of existing psychological theories when making sense of test data, observations, and child/family history. The theoretical models and concepts relied upon by many TA-C assessors and the authors of this book were described in Chapter 2. They include Attachment Theory, Trauma and Adverse Childhood Experiences, Systems Theory, Family Systems Theory, Diversity and a Multicultural Perspective, Complexity Theory (includes driving forces, restraining forces, and dilemma of change), Developmental Psychology, Narrative Identity, Phenomenological Psychology, Self-verification Theory (including Levels of Information), Zone of Proximal Development, Shame, and Object Relations Theory including Projective Identification. For most of our TA-C cases, we integrate a variety of these theories/models, depending on which best captures the assessment findings, gels into our tentative case conceptualization, and leads to a useful, practical new narrative for the particular family at hand.

Developing a Case Conceptualization Is an Iterative and Organic Process

The case conceptualization begins to take form during the initial phone contact with parents, becomes more substantial as we gather test findings and observe the family's responses to interventions, and is elaborated and revised even at the last contact (typically the Follow-up Session). The case conceptualization is a "lightly held," living, changing formulation that is expected to develop, be revised, and become more complete as an assessment proceeds.

The Developing Case Conceptualization Provides a Guide on How to Interact with the Parents and Child Throughout the Assessment

For example, if parents do not accept hypotheses we tentatively present as the assessment unfolds, we do not dismiss their reactions. Novice assessors might jump to the conclusion that the parents are rejecting Level 3 information, but that might not be the case at all. When parents do not resonate with a theoretical integration we are starting to develop, we pay close attention and see this as an opportunity to understand the family better. Perhaps the parents hold a different opinion based on different experiences with their child that we don't understand yet. Perhaps there are family secrets being protected. Or perhaps the set of lenses that parents use to view themselves, their family, and the world are vastly different than ours, possibly due to cultural differences we have failed to consider. When parents and assessors have apparently incompatible understandings of the family's struggles, we strive to be open and curious and to seek common ground. We strive to let ourselves be influenced by parents' thinking, and believe this increases the possibility that they will be open to being influenced by ours. We strongly believe assessors are more likely to make errors in conceptualizing a child and family if they attempt to work in isolation, without input from the parents.

The Measure of the Adequacy and Success of a Case Conceptualization Is the Extent to Which It Is Useful to the Family

We believe that a case conceptualization should be a helpful way of thinking about the child's and family's current development and challenges in a way that makes sense to the family, reduces shame, brings empathy from others, and highlights viable next steps.

Arriving at a Tentative Case Conceptualization

Keeping these distinct features of TA-C case conceptualization in mind, we delineate a series of steps we find useful in arriving at a case conceptualization. There is a lengthy discussion of how to organize and analyze assessment results, followed by shorter discussions of the other steps. Henry's case at the end of the chapter will richly illustrate the process through these steps.

- Organize and analyze across assessment results to explore major findings.
- Determine the major assessment findings.
- Work with a variety of theories to interpret the major findings.

- Select a theoretical integration that fits well and is useful.
- Draft a tentative case conceptualization.

Organize and Analyze Assessment Results to Explore Major Findings

At this point in the assessment, there is a vast amount of material to keep in mind, and the first step is to further organize this material. We need a framework to organize across all the results that will assist in selecting the major findings. To facilitate looking across all findings, we have found it invaluable to create a table that (1) lists all tests given along the top of the page; (2) records the constructs of interest going down the left side of the page; and (3) summarizes the findings in the grid created. We also add two columns for child comportment and parent comportment during the course of the assessment.

The constructs of interest reflect what the tests, selected based on the Assessment Questions, measure. Other constructs are included that arise from the data, but that may not be immediately relevant to the Assessment Questions. For example, if no one mentioned a concern or question about the quality of the child's thinking, but results from the Rorschach suggest the child's thinking is impaired under certain circumstances, we would include it as a construct. Or, if no one mentioned concerns about self-harm, but the child endorsed multiple items that indicate self-destructive impulses, self-harm is included as a construct. This test-by-construct layout creates a grid within which test findings and our observations can be organized, recorded in a succinct way, and easily examined. It allows one to see similarities and differences across tests and observations and will be very helpful in identifying major findings. There are many ways to work with a table like this, and we encourage you to develop a method that works well for you. Here is a structured approach we have found useful.

Examine Cognitive Test Results

We compare the results of multiple tests that are in the same category. For example, we often first review findings across the intellectual, cognitive, achievement, and neuropsychological tests. An understanding of the child's functioning in these areas is foundational to understanding how the child operates in the world and at school and may shed light on the interpretation of findings. It is important to remember that tests that were not solely designed to measure cognition and achievement can offer important information on these areas. (As you will see in the case of Henry, findings from performance-based tests helped us understand what gets in the way of Henry using his full cognitive capacities.) Then we ask ourselves a series of questions. From this analysis of the cognitive test results, does a major finding emerge, i.e., do we reach a tentative understanding of the child/family that addresses some of the main challenges/questions that brought them for assessment? Does the child appear to have processing challenges or dyslexia? Is the child functioning at a lower-than-expected level of achievement? Does the child have higher intellectual functioning than was expected? Keep these possibilities in mind.

Examine Results from Observer and Self-ratings

Next, we review and compare the findings across self-report measures completed by the child and observer-report measures completed by parents, teachers, and other significant people in the child's life. These measures are typically used to evaluate social, emotional, and behavioral functioning, and because they are normed, allow us to compare the child's scores with same-age peers. Some self-report and observer-report scales measure a single construct, such as depression or anxiety, while others, often called broadband tests, cover 10–20 constructs or more. The Behavior Assessment System for Children (BASC-3; Reynolds & Kamphaus, 2015) is a good example of a broadband measure. It includes a self-report form for the child to complete, as well as parent and teacher rating forms. One approach is to first look at the ratings from different informants to see if they generally converge and support each other. If they do not converge, or converge in some areas but not others, we look for patterns in the differences among respondents. For example, you may find that the father's scores were much lower (i.e., in the "healthier" direction) on the BASC-3 Clinical Scales than the mother's, suggesting he sees the child as less problematic than the mother does. Does this pattern support earlier impressions or does it surprise you? Is this an important finding? Also, for example, does the child report significant depressive symptoms across several measures, while the parents endorse an overall pattern of anger and acting out? Could this be central to understanding the presenting issues? Could depression be a major finding?

Parent ratings can also provide information about whether the family fits one of the prototypes presented in Chapter 2. If so, keeping the prototype in mind may help you understand other major findings and what kinds of interventions are needed. In the example just mentioned (where the parent ratings of the child are highly discrepant), the results bring to mind the "Solomon's Child" pattern, where parents are in open disagreement about the child. Recognizing this possibility early on helps you keep important considerations in mind, e.g., the possibility that the parents are triangulating the child as a way to manage their underlying marital conflict. If this seems true, it can underline the need to validate the parents' different perspectives and work toward an integrated narrative in order for the assessment to succeed.

Parents who rate the child as angry and disobedient and whose ratings are highly similar might fit the Scapegoated Child pattern. Parents who agree in rating the child as anxious and depressed may be in a Sick Child pattern.

And parents who agree in rating the child as having considerable strengths and no problems, in spite of some dramatic signal from the child that all is not right, may be in the Orphan Child pattern. These are all important findings.

Contrasting parent and school ratings can also be useful, and can give information about how the child behaves in different contexts. When teachers rate the child as normative in all respects, but parents rate the child as highly problematic, this may be a sign that there is something in the family context that elicits and/or maintains the child's difficulties. This gives direction for further exploration and may be the basis for a major finding. Similarly, when one teacher's ratings are more positive than those from the other teachers, this can prompt the assessor to speak to that teacher to see if they have a unique way of managing the child's challenges, or if the particular class context (e.g., gym class) provides an environment where the child is at her/his best. This can be a major finding that suggests the need for school interventions.

We also pay special attention to whether the child's self-reports are similar to or different than the parents' ratings of the child. This type of comparison can be useful in developing a case conceptualization. For example, as mentioned earlier, in the Orphan Child prototype, parents typically see the child as having no problems, but the child's self-reports may show much emotional distress.

We next turn to the parent self-ratings, which again can be focused on a specific construct (such as the Beck Depression Inventory) or include a number of constructs (such as the MMPI). You may want to start by comparing the parents' findings. Are there similarities between the parents? For example, do one or both parents report depression? What might that mean for their parenting availability and capacities? And do the parents appear to have vastly different personalities/emotional styles? How might the child experience that kind of split? It is also useful to compare the child's findings with the parents' self-ratings on the measure(s) they completed, if they measure similar constructs. Does the child report depression? Anger? Acting out behavior? Do the parents? What might these comparisons between the parents' and the child's findings suggest about the family system? Might this be a major finding; again, does it help to tentatively explain some of the main puzzles that led to the assessment?

Examine Results from Performance-Based Tests

Next, we review, compare, and interpret the results of performance-based tests completed by the child. These tests are also used to examine social, emotional, and behavioral functioning, as well as the quality of thinking, and several would be considered broadband measures (e.g., the Rorschach; the Wartegg, Crisi, 2018). In addition to looking at the child's test scores and comparing them to normative data, we read the performance-based tests with an eye to possible metaphors or images that might be useful in the case conceptualization. For example, a child who is depressed might have many images in their Rorschach of things that are "run over" or "smashed." We might choose to use this language in describing or expanding a major finding of depression in the Summary/Discussion Session with the parents, by saying, "The testing suggests Marie feels 'run over' by the many stresses in her life."

We then compare the findings from self-report measures and performance-based tests that the child completed. Because children (especially young children) often have limited ability to name and report their inner emotions, it is not unusual to see discrepancies between child self-reports and performance test findings. A child may effectively say, "I am fine" on a self-report measure, but show evidence of great emotional distress on a performance-based test. Similarly, a child who appears angry in their behavior may appear very depressed on performance tests. Do these results suggest major findings? Similarly, we compare the parents' ratings of their child with the results of the child's performance-based tests. These comparisons may tell us how aware the parents are of their child's underlying states of mind and emotions, help us identify split-off affect states in the family, and prompt us to consider what information is Level 1, 2, or 3 for the parents. This information could certainly inform other major findings and the developing case conceptualization.

Compare Test Results and Comportment/Observations During the Sessions

By including columns for child and parent comportment on the table, we can compare test results to our clinical observations and notes. Does the child look depressed on the Rorschach, but appear angry and combative in sessions with the parents, who have rated the child as highly aggressive? This might suggest a "masked depression," possibly a major finding that will help address many of the Assessment Questions. Does one parent appear charming and compliant in sessions with the assessor, but the MMPI raises the possibility of narcissistic and psychopathic features? This might lead to a very different case conceptualization, or to other lines of inquiry (e.g., a home visit) before one draws any final conclusions.

Integrate Test Results with Comportment, Child and Family History of Major Life Events, and Inter-generational Patterns

As you are considering possible major findings using the methods of analyses described above, it is useful to get curious about how the challenges being uncovered or validated came to be and continue to remain. It's time to put on your archeology hat. Do you see any connections between the family's major life events and the onset of the child's challenges? For example, could the struggling in school that started in 4th grade be related to the parental divorce and changes that occurred at that time? Have the struggles subsided? Gotten worse? What else may be in play? Did the loss of a grandparent immediately precede the child's initial anxiety symptoms? Did a traumatic event that impacted the mother seem connected to the child's further obsession with playing video games? Did the loss of a parent's job begin a downward spiral for the child, including acting out at school? We believe it is essential to "try on"—via discussions with parents—possible connections between life events, intergenerational patterns, and the development or maintenance of a child's and family's challenges. These new understandings, if accepted by the family, can be very influential in suggesting interventions.

Select the Major Assessment Findings

Once you have analyzed the findings across all tests, integrated with comportment, life events, and intergenerational patterns, you begin to elucidate major assessment findings. In general, we look at which findings are consistent and frequent across tests that measure similar constructs. We attend to any unexpected findings of interest or concern. We also pay special attention to findings that don't appear to fit with other results. For example, we may begin to put together that a child's acting out behaviors at home (visible in parents' BASC ratings) seem related to a "masked depression" that is apparent in the child's Rorschach responses and absent from the child's self-ratings. But we notice that teachers' BASC ratings show no externalizing behaviors at school. Since depression generally affects children across multiple contexts, we have to question whether "masked depression" is the best way to conceptualize the child's difficulties. Perhaps the Rorschach scores generally interpreted as signs of depression are better captured by another construct, such as shame or low self-esteem. If so, we might expect the child to do better in supportive, non-critical environments (which our school observation affirms is true of the child's classroom environment) and worse in interpersonal situations that are critical and shaming.

Through this iterative process, we gradually "hone" and articulate the major findings from the assessment that best capture the child, parents, and family system. Although the Assessment Questions are involved to the extent that they influenced which tests were used and constructs sampled, the major findings are not "answers" to the Assessment Questions. Responses to Assessment Questions will come later after the tentative case conceptualization is completed.

Work with a Variety of Theories to Interpret the Major Findings

Next, consider different theories and how they would explain the major test findings, taking into account what you know about the child and family history and significant life events. Of course, you may wish to start with theories you know best, but it is also good to consider other theories you know less well or that you have moved away from since your initial training.

One thought experiment is to think back to professors in graduate school or other colleagues you know who are experts on different theories and ask, "How would my cognitive-behavioral professor explain these test results? What would my family systems supervisor say? How about my psychodynamic office mate?" Another option is to actually speak to or seek consultation from colleagues who are more expert with theories outside your usual ones.

Select a Theoretical Integration

Having considered diverse theoretical perspectives, consider whether certain theories do a better job at explaining the sum of the findings, whether there are findings that contradict certain theories, and whether the various theories are incompatible or seem to complement and build on each other. It may be helpful to review the theories we summarized in Chapter 2, as we have found them helpful in thinking about many families and children. In our experience, after having worked with a child and family for many hours with many different assessment instruments, you may find that a few theories "rise to the top" and provide the most coherent overview, while providing slightly different emphases and perspectives. One family situation and assessment materials may fall neatly into a conceptualization based on attachment theory, while another may stand out as a perfect representation of the effects of Adverse Childhood Events, while yet a third family may seem to fit elements of both.

Draft a Tentative Case Conceptualization

Write down or sketch a unified, tentative case conceptualization. We say "tentative" because we know it will continue to develop as we learn more in the upcoming Family Intervention Session (FIS) and see how well it informs the Assessment Questions. The developing case conceptualization aims to capture the family's old narrative and introduce a new narrative that is gradually evolving over the assessment. The old narrative reflects the story the parents began the assessment with and captures their "stuckness" with their child. The new narrative contains a fresh, compassionate view of history and challenges in the family, and gives parents a new lens from which to view their "stuckness."

The developing case conceptualization seeks to inform (1) how the family arrived at where they are (etiology and old narrative); (2) what is going on now in the family that keeps the family stuck (problem maintenance and old narrative); and (3) what would need to change for the family to overcome their current struggles (new narrative). We suggest you don't "censor" your tentative case conceptualization at this stage because of what you think the family can easily "hear" at this point in time. You can hold the family closely in mind after the FIS when you are considering what will be useful and therapeutic to say to the family.

Draft Answers to the Assessment Questions

You are now in a position to use your tentative case conceptualization to sketch out your initial answers to the Assessment Questions. Again, we suggest you do this without holding in mind how the family would react to what you say. Another thing we advise is to *directly* answer the Assessment Questions, not beat around the bush, although you can still qualify what you write at this point if necessary. For example, parents may have asked, "Does Alex have ADD?" A direct answer might be, "No. The testing isn't consistent with that. Rather it appears that Alex's problems concentrating are related to the anger, sadness, and guilt he feels about the conflicts you are having in the family lately." The following answer is similarly direct, but more qualified:

> At this point it is impossible to tell. Alex does have attention problems, but it's possible they are caused by all the emotions he has about the current conflict in the family. If you can reduce that conflict, or protect Alex from it more, we could retest him to see if he still has problems concentrating.

Consider Level of Information

Finally, look over your "uncensored" answers to the Assessment Questions and consider which information is likely Level 1, 2, or 3 for the parents. Again, it can be useful to look back at the test results, as they can provide direct evidence of what findings/information are consistent with the family's current narrative. Answers/findings that are consistent with parent-child or self-ratings are more likely to be Level 1 or 2 Information. Findings that appear primarily on performance-based tests, and that are inconsistent with parent-child or self-ratings, are more likely Level 2 or 3 Information. Also, levels often change over the course of an assessment, due to the scaffolding and collaboration assessors do with parents. The assessor's job is to gauge to what extent the "blunt" answers to the Assessment Questions would provoke shock, distress, or shame in the parents/family at that point in the assessment. Often, we notice that parents have greatly shifted how they view the child from when they first filled out the BASC or CBCL, and what was previously Level 3 Information is now Level 2. Therefore, besides testing, we also consider our ongoing discussions with parents about their Assessment Questions, as we often repeatedly ask, "Now that we have discussed X (a particular test), do you have any new thoughts about how to answer your question Y?"

Final Thoughts

Developing a case conceptualization is an iterative and complex process, with multiple applications. At this point in the assessment, the tentative case conceptualization is used to understand the family's dilemma of change and to determine what the focus of the FIS will be. As you may remember from Chapter 2, the FIS is an important component of the TA-C process and it can be crucial for promoting lasting change. The goals and steps in planning the FIS are explained in Chapter 6. We now turn to Dale's account of Henry's assessment and illustrate the processes described earlier.

Case: Henry's Case Conceptualization

In order to synthesize and better understand the major test findings, I (Dale) made a table to document and organize the findings and reveal consistencies and inconsistencies in results across the tests I administered. First, I looked at individual tests and listed what the major test and assessment findings were in the first column of the table (Table 5.1). I worded the findings broadly, not paying attention to minor differences in how each test defined a construct, so I could see similarities across tests. Of course, this required me to tolerate some ambiguity.

I then listed all the measures used throughout the assessment in the top row. Next, I added a column to include Henry's behavior throughout the testing (comportment), as well as a column for the results of his parents' MMPI-2s. As assessors we tend to focus on pathology, so I wanted to be sure to include Henry's strengths as well. Therefore, I spent some time looking at the results from this perspective of strength.

As shown in Table 5.1, the "Y" indicates that the test in question measures the relevant construct and it was found on the test. "NF" indicates that the test in question measures the relevant construct but, it was NOT found in the results. A "?" indicates that the test measures the relevant construct but there is a reasonable question about what was found. The "NM" notation indicates that the test in question did not measure the relevant construct.

In looking at Table 5.1, the test findings that are most consistently and frequently reported are those that have to do with depression, anxiety, and anger. It is interesting to note that Henry is suffering with anxiety and depression, while each of his parents suffers with either anxiety or an underlying depression. In other words, Henry is not the only one in the family who has these difficulties. Anger is underlying or indirectly expressed in each member of the family. It is noteworthy that the teachers do not see Henry as aggressive. His anger is more directly expressed at home with his brother and indirectly expressed through his unwavering, aggressive reporting of his sadness. While the WISC-V (Wechsler, 2014) indicates above average intelligence, the results of the Rorschach and Wartegg (Crisi, 2018) are more consistent with average intelligence (although clearly, these are not direct measures of intelligence). Because of the emotional constriction, depression, and anxiety, I think the performance-based testing actually underestimates Henry's cognitive ability. Or said another way, the Rorschach and Wartegg

Table 5.1 Assessment Findings by Test

	Child Findings								Parent Findings	
Major Test and Assessment Findings	Henry's Overall Comportment	BASC-3 Self-Report	WISC-V Scores and Behavior	BASC-3 Teacher Report	BASC-3 Parent Report	Rorschach	Wartegg		Mother's MMPI-2 RF	Father's MMPI-2 RF
Depression/ Damaged View of Self	Y	Y	Y Gave up	Y	Y	Y	Y		NF	Y Underlying?
High Anxiety/Stress Worry	Y	Y	Y Worried about perfor-mance	Y	Y	Y	Y		Y	NF
Cognitive Strength	Y	NM	Y	Y Comments	NM	NF	NF Most likely due to psychological inhibition		NM	NM
Anger/ Oppositionality	Y	NM	NM	NF	Y	Y	Y		NF Split-off?	NF
Emotional Constriction	Y	NM	NM	NM	NM	Y	Y		NF	Y Split-off?

(Continued)

Table 5.1 (Continued)

Major Test and Assessment Findings	Henry's Overall Comportment	BASC-3 Self-Report	WISC-V Scores and Behavior	BASC-3 Teacher Report	BASC-3 Parent Report	Rorschach	Wartegg	Mother's MMPI-2 RF	Father's MMPI-2 RF
	Child Findings							**Parent Findings**	
Low Adaptability	Y	Y	NM	Y	Y	Y	Y	Y	Y
Formal Thought Disorder	NF	NF	NM	NF	NF	NF	NF	NF	NF
Idiosyncratic Thinking/Behavior	Y	Y	NM	Y	NF	Y	Y	NF	NF
Unresolved Dependency Needs	Y	NM	NM	Y Somatization 1 of 2 teachers	Y Somatization	Y	Y	NF	NF
Persistence	Y about expressing his distress	Y about expressing his distress	Y until he got anxious	NM	NM	NF	Y Perseverated on dysphoric content	NM	NM
Good Attention	Y	Y	Y until he got anxious	Y	Y	Y	Y	NM	NM

show how much emotional factors influence Henry's ability to utilize his cognitive strengths.

After completing Table 5.1, it was now time for me to integrate all that I knew about Henry using the major test findings, my notes on all sessions, early hypotheses, and several videos of our sessions together. I then came up with a number of major assessment findings that would inform the case conceptualization.

Major Assessment Findings

1. Henry is suffering from a major depressive disorder and a damaged view of himself.
2. Henry experiences high levels of anxiety and distress.
3. Henry has underlying anger.
4. Henry has cognitive strengths that are mitigated by his anxiety and depression
5. Henry has longings to be taken care of but doesn't rely on or feel connected to others.
6. Henry's coping mechanisms are overwhelmed; he has low energy, poor emotional regulation, and constricts his feelings. He self-regulates with videogames and eating.
7. Henry has some idiosyncratic thinking but there is no evidence of a major thought disorder.
8. Both parents are constricted around anger.
9. Henry's father does not endorse any distress, while his mother experiences low self-esteem, anxiety, and stress but optimistically keeps on going.

Theoretical Models

My next step in formulating the case conceptualization was to see how different theories would integrate and explain the assessment findings.

Attachment Theory

The assessment findings are consistent with Henry having an insecure attachment status. He doesn't appear to feel safe in the world and hasn't developed an age-appropriate ability to comfort himself. Also, he doesn't feel confident that his parents see his emotions and needs accurately and will respond in an attuned and timely manner. Although both parents make attempts to respond empathically to Henry's depression and anxiety, it is difficult for them to "hang in there" because: (1) most likely they have insecure attachments, (2) they have trouble tolerating intense emotions themselves, and (3) they become overwhelmed with helplessness when they see Henry's distress. In the face of his parents' struggles, Henry then becomes needier and escalates his bids for attention.

Trauma and Adverse Childhood Experiences

As best I knew Henry had not experienced any major traumatic event nor been exposed to noteworthy Adverse Childhood Experiences (ACEs). Barbara had a number of ACEs (alcoholic father, mother and sister with mental illness, half-siblings with trauma and drug/alcohol problems, chaotic family environment) and had experienced emotional abuse from her mother (Figure 4.3 and Table 4.9). David did not report any ACEs, but I wondered if he might have experienced some because he was so emotionally constricted. I recalled the research that shows trauma experienced in previous generations can be transmitted to children through epigenetics and unconscious psychological processes (Yehuda & Lehrner, 2018).

Family Systems Theory

Henry and his parents were clearly mutually influencing each other. As Henry felt "missed" emotionally, he expressed his depression and sadness more intensely, which then made it more difficult for his parents to respond in an attuned way. As they grew frustrated and took Henry's bids for attention personally, he felt their reactions and grew despondent and angry. There also seemed to be a split between Henry and his brother, Frank. The parents described Frank as sturdy, happy, flexible, and easy to comfort, while Henry was seen as overly needy, negative, rigid, provocative, and very difficult to soothe. Also, Henry's symptoms likely served a systemic purpose. He distracted the parents from unresolved issues regarding their families of origin, marriage, and individual growth paths. By uniting in their concern for Henry, Barbara and David experienced a degree of closeness that they might not have felt otherwise.

Object Relations Theory

In terms of Object Relations theory, Henry seemed to be containing and expressing sadness and depression that the parents had split off. Also, his stubborn rigidity was eliciting anger in his parents that they felt was justified. Even I felt irritated and exasperated in the face of Henry's unrelenting dysphoria, which gave me empathy for the parents and the pull to counter Henry's negative stance. I noted the parents' frustration often evolved into their feeling helpless and inadequate. Object relations theory would see this as Henry successfully getting them to feel what he felt via projective identification. Lastly, Henry's demanding "neediness" was likely a sign that he was holding intense dependency needs that everyone else in the family dissociated.

Looking at the family prototypes in Figure 2.2 that are based on Object Relations Theory, you may notice that this family has characteristics of several of the patterns. At the start of the assessment, the parents seemed united in their concern and worry about Henry, and I thought the family best fit the "Sick Child" prototype. As discussed in Chapter 2, the parents in the Sick Child System often do not set adequate limits because anger isn't well-integrated. At an early session, when Henry and his father were leaving the office, Henry stayed in the bathroom for over 15 minutes. David waited without saying a word or trying to speed up Henry. At first, I was impressed by David's patience, but then it seemed too much. I wondered if, in general, David was out of touch with the typical irritation a parent would feel in similar situations. Similarly, Barbara was irritated and overwhelmed that Henry talked constantly about his sadness but seemed unaware that she could set limits. Eventually, Henry's therapist suggested the family create a limited, special time for "sad talk" (20 minutes at bedtime), and that Henry be re-directed if he brought up his dysphoria at other times. Initially, Henry responded well to this limit. Could this be seen as Henry's longing for containment as well as attention?

As the assessment continued, I began also to see features of the sca-pegoated and orphan child. As the parents grew more comfortable with me, in part because I mirrored their frustration, they became more in touch with the level of anger they felt toward Henry. In particular, I remember his mother's exasperation at Henry's insistence on being sad, especially when she saw him having a good time. If she commented on any positive feelings she perceived, he would immediately deny them. Both parents seemed confused by Henry's neediness and also a little disdainful of it. This is typical of parents in the orphan child constellation who themselves did not have their healthy dependency needs met as children. In fact, as I collected more background information it seemed that there were times when Henry might have been expressing his needs appropriately, but his parents had a lot on their plates and may not have attended to him adequately.

Dilemma of Change

Henry and his family seemed "stuck," which indicated that restraining forces in the system were greater than driving forces (Chapter 2). The major restraining forces I saw were the parents' avoidance of many different emotions, Barbara's minimization of Henry's distress in light of her unresolved family traumas, and both parents' shame, which got in the way of their acknowledging and repairing understandable past parenting errors. One way of expressing the parents' Dilemma of Change is:

> To respond more appropriately to Henry we have to get in touch with our own painful feelings and past trauma, and that could be overwhelming given how little support we have. If we don't do this Henry

will continue to hold all the negative affect, continue to be symptomatic, and won't reach his potential.

My sense of the best potential tipping point, which might produce a "butterfly effect" in Henry's family, would be for the parents to have an interpersonal experience of facing their own and others' emotions—particularly anger, sadness, and longing—with support, to find out that they could become comfortable with these feelings.

Developmental Perspective

Henry achieved major developmental motor milestones (sitting, crawling, walking) at the appropriate ages. Interestingly, the parents said he didn't practice walking with assistance, instead just started walking on his own one day while at a play date. At 22 months, Henry's parents were concerned that his speech was delayed and had him assessed at a regional early learning center. The Speech/Language Pathologist found that Henry's expressive language was delayed by six months, but that he was not frustrated and communicated adequately and did not qualify for services. Henry was toilet trained at 3.5 years of age, apparently with some difficulty. When Barbara or David wanted Henry to use the potty he would often refuse. I had a sense that a power struggle probably ensued.

As far as I knew there were no major disruptions in Henry's attachment in his first year of life. His parents described him as appropriately attached and able to soothe and entertain himself when he was very young, with the exception of him becoming agitated for about 10 minutes when he was put to bed. The agitation got worse when Henry was almost 2 and his brother was born. I imagined his mother's attention was diverted to her newborn, and his dad was busy with school and unable to provide the emotional attunement Henry continued to need. I wondered if Henry was experiencing some separation anxiety at that time.

When Henry was about 6, Barbara went back to work, although she had very mixed feelings about this. She was starting her own business and was extremely busy and often away from home. This was a big change in the family, and David began to do more of the daily childrearing activities. Since this is also the time in development when children expand their world outside of the home and learn more prosocial behaviors, I wondered if this change in the family might have influenced Henry's interactions and security with his peers. About a year later when going into second grade, Henry began to vocalize his sadness and suicidal ideation. As soon as Henry began to talk about dying, his parents immediately found him an individual therapist. When I saw him in our sessions, he had difficulty regulating his emotions and would roll around on the floor and couch as if he were a much younger child.

Biological Perspective and Diathesis-Stress Model

In my view, Henry met the criteria for a Major Depressive Disorder. Although it was impossible for me to track or measure the biological and genetic factors that might have influenced Henry's depression, I knew that Barbara's family had a history of depression and anxiety and suspected that Henry (and she) may have inherited a genetic vulnerability for depression (Figure 4.3). In addition, there were a number of stressors that occurred in Henry's early childhood, as discussed above, that could have impacted and activated this predisposition (Table 4.9). Given existing biologic hypotheses about depression (Cowen, 2008), I considered that Henry would benefit from a referral to a psychiatrist for evaluation for pharmacological intervention.

Behavioral Perspective

I also thought about how Henry's behavior was being reinforced. Did he get more attention when he voiced his sadness? I imagined that was initially the case. However, as the parents felt overwhelmed by his persistently reporting his dysphoria, I imagined the parents might have gotten impatient and at times ignored or withdrew the positive attention. This intermittent reinforcement may have served to strengthen the behavior. What was the function of the behavior? Certainly, there seemed to be a need for attention, but the behavior was also very punishing of the parents. Was Henry angry at his parents and this was his way of expressing it? Henry's parents ended up feeling inadequate, angry, and as sad as Henry felt.

Control-Mastery Theory

I wondered if Henry harbored several pathogenic beliefs about himself and his parents: (1) I'm too needy and others will reject me if I show my needs directly; (2) no one will contain or accept me if I show my anger directly; and (3) my sadness is too overwhelming for others. From this perspective, Henry's "provocative" behaviors can be seen as tests he is unconsciously presenting to his parents in hopes they will "pass" them, thereby discrediting his pathogenic beliefs. To "pass," Henry's parents would need to be able to sit with his deep sadness without being overwhelmed and getting lost in it, handle his anger non-punitively or defensively if he were able to express it directly, and never shame or reject him, while still setting appropriate limits.

Cultural Perspective

I wanted to make sure I was not missing any possible cultural components that might have influenced the case. I remembered some of Putnam's (2000) work on the influences of being part of the contemporary dominant, white, higher SES, American culture. Putman concluded that American families, over the last half-century, have been less connected and more isolated than at any other time in history. This differs from other cultures in which extended family and the community are more involved and supportive. I wondered if Barbara's going back to work would have affected Henry as much if the family lived in a close-knit community where families shared childcare responsibilities. I was also aware of American "optimism" and discomfort with negative affect states (Henrich et al., 2010). Thus, I wondered how things might have unfolded differently in the family if there was not a stigma associated with childhood depression. I began to see how the struggles in this family might be exacerbated in our current American culture, and this gave me increased compassion.

Tentative Case Conceptualization

Having considered the various theoretical perspectives, I found them to complement each other and provide an incremental understanding of the family. Each of the theories added a specific explanation of Henry's and the family's circumstances. I even thought of the metaphor about the blind men touching different parts of an elephant and each contributing his own truth. Only when putting all the parts together can one really understand it's an elephant. The following is my attempt to describe the whole "elephant."

How Family Arrived at Where They Are

Henry currently is experiencing a Major Depressive Disorder. He may have been born with a genetic predisposition to depression, which was then activated by attachment disruptions in early childhood. These effects were exacerbated by financial and family stress and limited extended family and community support. From their own backgrounds, Barbara and David were not well equipped to respond to Henry's depression. Barbara was concerned, but having survived her own chaotic family of origin, she also tended to minimize Henry's dysphoria and to be frustrated when he couldn't appreciate or remember positive experiences. Likewise, David was concerned about Henry, but his own affective constriction kept him from being able to validate Henry's feelings. Each parent was sympathetic but lost patience and was inconsistent, creating an intermittent reinforcement schedule that strengthened Henry's negativity. Both parents also had trouble setting limits, which left them feeling victimized and frustrated with Henry's moods. Henry also had difficulty being aware of and expressing anger, which led to his using his depression as a weapon.

Family Narratives

At this point in the assessment the predominant family narrative held by the parents was:

Henry is depressed and overly needy. He stubbornly refuses to acknowledge the positive things in his life and incessantly stresses his negative
mood in order to manipulate us, get more of our attention, and punish
us. Nothing we have tried makes a difference.

The new narrative I wanted to create through the assessment was:

Henry's problems are partly the result of a biological predisposition to
depression inherited from both our families. In spite of our best efforts
when Henry was little, we weren't able to give him the extra attention
and care that he needed because we were stressed economically and
emotionally. Then, when Henry began to get depressed, we tried to
respond in an attuned way, but this was difficult because we never
learned to handle our own negative emotions. We emphasized the
positive and tried to be patient and not set harsh limits, but at times, our
approach made him feel out of control and ashamed for feeling sad.
Henry can get better, but we're going to have to learn to deal with his/
our anger, depression, and needs for care and support. To do this we will
need more help from others.

I was aware that parts of this new narrative might be very difficult for Barbara
and David to accept and that even if they could accept the entire narrative, it
might bring up shame.

What the Family Needs to Change

What I thought was most needed to shift the family system was for Barbara
and David to be able to mirror Henry's emotions, set appropriate limits,
repair attachment disruptions, and help Henry develop an age-appropriate
capacity to regulate his emotions. I also felt if Barbara and David could give
Henry more positive attention and be less triggered by his dramatic bids for
connection, Henry might become less provocative. It was clear to me that
both Barbara and David needed to become more comfortable with their own
emotions. I was unclear as to how much they would need to confront unresolved issues from their own families of origin.

If Barbara and David couldn't accept the entire new narrative, what I
thought would be enough was if they could think more systemically, i.e., not
see Henry as the sole problem in the family and realize that changing their
own behavior could help everyone get unstuck.

I did not want to emphasize that Barbara and David may have done things
in the past that contributed to Henry's problems. Rather, I wanted to decrease their feelings of helplessness and underline that with the right interventions, they would be an essential part of the solution.

Assessor's Initial Reflections on Assessment Questions

After formulating my tentative case conceptualization, it was time for me to see what my initial reflections were on the Assessment Questions. This first pass at answering the questions is just for me and is usually blunter than anything I would say to a family. Allowing myself this kind of spontaneity frees me up, engages my unconscious, and often highlights: (1) whether I need more information in order to answer a specific question, (2) which answers might be difficult for a family member to hear (i.e., Level 3 Information), and (3) potential foci for the Family Intervention Session (FIS).

1.   *Is he clinically depressed or is it situational?*

Yes, he is clinically depressed, way more depressed than you've allowed yourselves to imagine. And even though the school stress may be exacerbating it, he won't get better without multi-pronged clinical intervention that involves all of you.

   Earlier in the assessment, Barbara was surprised that Henry was depressed but at this point we had already discussed this quite a bit. This would not be new information (Level 1).

2.   *Has he experienced an unknown trauma that has adversely affected his self-image and how he engages with the world?*

As far as I know, there was no big "T" trauma, but there were a lot of small "t" traumas that have contributed to Henry's current struggles. You, Barbara, have had significant Traumas that still affect you and your parenting, and these events have indirectly influenced Henry. David, you don't report any past traumas, but I question this because of your affective constriction. Your neutral facial expression can be frightening and confusing to others, including Henry. Henry has had developmental trauma that has led to insecure attachment and difficulties regulating his emotions.

   I think this will be difficult for both parents to hear. While Barbara knows how dysfunctional her family of origin was, she may not understand how it has influenced her dismissive stance when it comes to Henry. David is unaware that he can be seen as withholding and/or angry because of his constriction (Level 2+).

3.   *How do we prevent him from becoming further anxious and depressed?*

First, you have to realize for Henry to get better, the two of you have to change. If you do your own work so you can be comfortable with a wide range of feelings, you will be able to respond in a more helpful way to Henry and he will learn how to regulate his own emotions better. You will have to learn to validate his feelings, especially those that "push your buttons" and that you were not allowed to express when you were growing up. You will need to model sharing your own feelings appropriately, especially anger, including being able to set limits in a firm but non-reactive way.

This has been alluded to throughout the assessment however I don't think they really understand how much their behavior has influenced Henry and how much they have to process their own feelings in order to be available for Henry's needs (Level 2+).

4. *What are Henry's intellectual strengths and weaknesses? Is there a disharmony among them? What kind of learning environment is best for him?*

Henry is bright enough but not a genius. His weaknesses are more a result of his depression and anxiety. He has trouble persevering when the material gets a little challenging, but I found with gentle encouragement he could do more than he thought. He needs a supportive learning environment, where competition is not emphasized by teachers or students. I think individual tutoring will be helpful. The school you are considering is not a good choice because it is known for being a high-pressure environment.

This will not come as a surprise to either parents. They know Henry is bright and that his emotional state affects his performance (Level 1).

5. *How can we help Henry feel confident and loved?*

It is important to have a balance where he feels cherished and also contained. Be available when he needs you without impatience toward his needs. Validate his wide range of feelings, clearly show him when you enjoy him, help him realistically appraise his schoolwork, reward his persistence in trying rather than focusing on the product, and set appropriate limits.

Barbara and David know that they can be impatient when Henry is too needy. They will think they already validate his feelings but may not understand the level to which Henry needs consistent responses (Level 1+).

6. *Why does Henry make provocative statements to us?*

This is his safe way of expressing anger and getting you to be more responsive to his needs for attention, interaction, soothing, etc. He's dramatic because for the most part you minimize, Barbara, and David, you don't show much reaction and as a result, Henry doesn't feel heard or seen. He'd prefer to see you angry about his being provocative rather than feel left alone with his feelings.

This will be the most difficult information to convey because it can trigger shame in the parents. I would expect they know there is underlying anger in the family but not how it has affected Henry (Level 2+).

Final Thoughts

After briefly focusing on the questions, it was now time for me to think about the FIS. I thought addressing the part of the case conceptualization that highlights how the parents had a difficult time experiencing, expressing, and responding to difficult emotions would also address their question, "How do we prevent him from becoming further anxious and depressed?" Therefore, I wanted to plan an FIS that provided the family with an experience that encouraged interaction and attention to emotions. I believed that if Henry's parents could accurately mirror and validate Henry's negative affect, he would feel more supported and contained, which might allow his anxiety and depression to decrease. Henry was stuck on his sad feelings, and I hoped that this type of intervention session might enable him to shift from this rigid position.

References

American Psychiatric Association. (2013). *Diagnostic and statistical manual of mental disorders* (5th ed.). Arlington, VA: American Psychiatric Publishing.

Cowen, P. J. (2008). Seretonin snd depression: Pathophysiological mechanism or marketing myth? *Trends Pharmacological Sciences, 29*(9), 433–436.

Crisi, A. (2018). *The Crisi Wartegg System (CWS) manual.* New York: Routledge.

Henrich, J., Heine, S. J., & Norenzayan, A. (2010). Most people are not WEIRD. *Nature, 466,* 29.

John, S., & Segal, D. L. (2015). Case conceptualization. In R. L. Cautin & S. O. Lilienfeld (Eds.), *Encyclopedia of clinical psychology, 29.* Chichester West Sussex, Malden, MA: John Wiley and Sons.

Putnam, R. (2000) *Bowling alone: The collapse and revival of American community.* New York: Simon and Schuster.

Reynolds, C. R., & Kamphaus, R. W. (2015). *Behavior Assessment System for Children* (3rd ed.). Bloomington: Pearson.

Wechsler, D. (2014). *Wechsler Intelligence Scale for Children* (5th ed.). Bloomington, MN: Pearson.

World Health Organization. (1992). *The ICD-10 classification of mental and behavioural disorders: Clinical descriptions and diagnostic guidelines.* Geneva, Switzerland: World Health Organization.

Wright, A. J. (2021). Deliberate context-driven conceptualization in psychological assessment. *Journal of Personality Assessment.* doi:10.1080/00223891.2021.1942024

Yehuda, R., & Lehrner, A. (2018). Intergenerational transmission of trauma effects: Putative role of epigenetic mechanisms. *World Psychiatry, 17,* 243–257.

6   Phase III: Family Intervention Session

The Family Intervention Session (FIS) is one of the later additions to the Therapeutic Assessment with Children (TA-C) model (Finn, 2007; Tharinger et al., 2008). It addresses two problems common in many traditional child assessments: 1) children are often seen only individually and never in the context of their families, making it almost impossible to assess systemic contributions to children's problems (Fischer, 1982), and 2) even if systemic aspects of children's problems are recognized by assessors, it is often difficult to help caregivers become aware of these. This phase in TA-C is explicitly designed to address these two limitations. The FIS is the second part of Phase III and is linked to the case conceptualization, the first part of Phase III. Specifically, the FIS usually tests out an aspect of the case conceptualization, often resulting in its revision due to new information obtained about the family. This reconceptualization may, in turn, alter answers to the Assessment Questions.

Typically, there is one family session, although in some circumstances (e.g., with divorced parents) there may be two or even more if needed. In a FIS the parents and child are guided to interact with each other in a structured or semi-structured activity. This session is unique in that –even more than others—it emphasizes the primacy of *experience over explanation* for the whole family (Finn, 2007). Up to this point, there have been many chances for the assessor and the parents to collaborate on alternative *explanations* for what may be going on with their child and family. Adding a FIS creates an opportunity for the family, with a supportive assessor, to have a novel or potent *experience* that may lead to a shift in their understanding of themselves and their family. Research reviewed in Chapter 2 suggests that for some families the FIS serves as a "tipping point" and has an immediate and major impact on decreasing child symptomatology and parental distress (Smith et al., 2011).

We have experienced that many child assessors, especially those without family therapy training, feel quite anxious about having multiple family members present at the same time in the assessment room. Indeed, at first, we felt some anxiety ourselves about asking the child and parents to interact together in one room. But, over time we have become confident in our ability

DOI: 10.4324/9781003000174-6

to conduct successful FISs and are excited to share our knowledge with you. Success rests on matching the intervention with the family's capacity to engage in it and experience something new.

We now discuss the goals of the FIS, how to prepare for the session, and activities we typically use, organized by level of intensity/engagement. We share, in Appendix, examples of FISs from published TA-C case studies. We then offer guidance on how to choose and plan for the level of intervention that is likely to be a good fit for a family. Following, we suggest ways to reflect on what was learned from the FIS and to refine the case conceptualization, as well as further develop answers to Assessment Questions. Finally, we present the FIS Dale did with Henry and his parents, and how what was learned from it significantly advanced everyone's understanding of the family.

Goals and Planning for a Family Intervention Session

FISs serve multiple goals. First, they provide a chance to test out a part of the case conceptualization by observing the family in action. For example, we may have hypothesized that the parents are uncomfortable expressing sadness and grief, leaving their child confused with what to do with their sad feelings. In the FIS, we may see that the parents do indeed struggle with mirroring their child's sadness, but that with support from the assessor, they are able to hear their child's feelings and respond empathically. This confirms both our initial hypothesis and also allows us to refine our case conceptualization: with further intervention, the family can learn to allow sad feelings into their life, changing their experience of how they view what is possible in their family. Thus, an FIS creates an opportunity for parents to revise their narrative, even if just slightly, from one that is more child focused (e.g., "Our child seems confused about how she feels, which is the main problem in our family," to one that is more systemic; "Our child's confusion has to do with our inability to deal with sad feelings. If we change, it will help our daughter and the whole family"). We like to think that we are planting and nurturing a seed for change in the FIS, by helping parents become more empathic to their child.

Another common goal in a FIS is to target an Assessment Question where the desired response would likely be more challenging for the parents (i.e., composed mainly of Level 3 Information), but that would help them make needed changes if they could take it in. In many families, it is the *systemic* aspects of the child's problems that are most challenging for parents to grasp—how they and the child mutually influence each other to yield the problem behavior. This difficulty is very common and natural, as parents rarely get to observe their children in other contexts or to see how their children behave when responded to differently by other adults. The FIS is an exciting opportunity for an assessor to invite parents up on an "observation deck," where they may see things they otherwise have not been able to see.

As mentioned earlier, planning and implementing these sessions may be challenging at first, but they become less anxiety provoking with experience. We have found that the most important predictors of success are: 1) a useful case conceptualization; 2) an assessor who, when needed, can tolerate clients' emotional distress and help family members manage intense emotions in new ways; and 3) strong alliances between the assessor and the parents and the assessor and the child (Tharinger et al., 2008). Interventions are unique and individually developed for each family. In general, we hope that families have a positive experience together, and for some families that alone would be a significant accomplishment. Other families are ready for a moderate or major shift that may involve experiencing some initial distress as new awareness unfolds (such as the example above about the daughter's sad feelings).

In most cases, another goal is to bring the child's "problem" into the room and help the parents observe the resulting family dynamics *in vivo*. However, as we later discuss, whether we pursue this goal depends on the level of engagement or intensity we think the family can handle. We don't want to ask too much of a family or too little. Sometimes, just understanding the systemic variables that elicit the problem behavior is groundbreaking for parents. At other times, with the problem behavior in the room, we try, through active guidance and modeling, to foster a different response, solution or understanding from the parents that potentially creates change. Even if parents do not acknowledge their role in the development or maintenance of the problem, they can come to see themselves as part of the solution.

Questions to Address When Planning for a Family Intervention Session (FIS)

In planning for the FIS, we start by asking ourselves a series of questions. The case conceptualization helps inform our answers to these questions.

What Resources Are Available to the Family at This Time?

Here we think about the parents separately and together, the child, and possibly other children in the family. We consider both psychological and environmental resources and the family's level of stress. Although it is not this simplistic, in general the lower the level of resources and the higher the stress in the family, the lower the demands and expectations we have for the FIS. And if a major caregiver is less ready to shift than another, we tend to gear the session to the first person's level. In such instances, we think about baby steps, such as asking the family to play a simple game together. The exception might be when one of the family members is functioning very well and could join the assessor in helping the family as a whole with a more challenging activity.

What Is the Level of Awareness and Openness to Change in the Parents?

Again, we think about each parent individually and as a unit. Were the parents able to shift their narrative a bit during previous sessions? Were they able to use new information to start to change their strategies? Were they able to think systemically, i.e., see that their child's problems are in part contextual and think about their role in contributing to those problems? Answers in the affirmative suggest the parents have already made significant shifts and are ready for an intervention with a higher level of engagement or intensity. As mentioned earlier, it is important to keep in mind that one parent may be much more ready than the other, impacting the process and the outcome.

What Is the Quality of the Parents' Relationship With the Assessor?

Once again, we think about each parent individually and together. Were the parents able to benefit from collaboration with the assessor? Were the parents able to trust the assessor and respond to new perspectives? Did the parents appreciate and value the child's relationship with the assessor? If so, it is likely that the family has already used the assessor as a resource and is likely to continue to do so. This makes it possible that a higher intensity intervention can be used, depending on other factors. Again, note if the parents are similarly connected to the assessor or not. If not, careful balancing will be needed. Possibly you could make an effort to strengthen your alliance with the less "connected" parent, e.g., by speaking on the phone with a father who has not been able to attend many of the child testing sessions.

What Is the Balance of "Driving Forces" and "Restraining Forces" at This Time?

That is, how ready is the family to make needed changes? How much do they feel the pain of the current situation? How blocked are they? If blocked, do they have any understanding of why they feel blocked? If so, has their shame decreased and self-compassion increased? Are they now open to explore more adaptive solutions to their family's dilemma of change? Are they ready to take a first step, even a baby step? Will they accept support—from the assessor or from others? In our experience, the more motivation there is for the family to change, the more the family is aware of their won distress, and the more they are ready to accept support, the more able they are to make significant shifts during the FIS.

What Likely Remains Level 3 Information for the Parents?

That is, what information from the case conceptualization and other sources do you think is still too discrepant from how the parents perceive themselves, their child and their family that they would not be likely to take it in? You want to ask yourself, "Could the FIS help Level 3 Information become Level 2? If so, how?" If the answer is No, the assessor needs to adjust expectations. If you go ahead when you have serious doubts, it is possible parents may out-right reject the information and experience a rupture with you. Even if you think the parents are ready, you should still be prepared to make adjustments, as Level 3 Information may overwhelm even well-functioning families. Again, one parent may be prepared for new awareness but the other may not be, especially if the information pertains to the latter parent. In such in-stances, it is best to set more modest goals.

We now turn to activities that we have found useful to use in FISs. By attending to the answers to the questions above, you will be guided to the level of intensity/engagement that likely will work best with a given family.

Activities by Level of Intensity/Engagement

There are a wide variety of possible activities and methods available for use in a FIS (Tharinger et al., 2008; see also Appendix A). To meet the needs of the diverse families we work with, our family interventions range from very simple to quite complex, require low to high engagement among family members, and are designed to arouse low to high emotional responses. We group the activities below as low, medium and high in intensity and en-gagement. It is important to note that any activity can be made more or less intense by what the assessor chooses to comment on during the activity. The assessor needs to keep in mind the rationale for the choice of activity for a given family and try to match comments and questions with the intended level of intensity. If it becomes apparent that the family is ready for more intensity, instead of changing activities, the assessor can make the activity underway more emotionally arousing by making more challenging comments. This is also the case when the family seems overwhelmed by the level of intensity in the activity that the assessor chose. Here the assessor could simply comment on positive aspects of the dynamic in the room, thereby helping to regulate the family's level of emotional arousal.

Low Intensity/Engagement Activities

Semi-structured play is a flexible, guided, low-intensity activity that aims to encourage constructive parent–child play. The supported play activities aim to 1) be a fairly basic intervention where most families can be successful, 2) foster positive experiences among family members, and 3) serve to test out systemic hypotheses. Overall, parents are encouraged to follow and support their child's lead in a play activity and attend to their child's desires, rather than to the typical rules of a game or activity. Parents and the assessor ob-serve if and how the child's behavior changes under these conditions. Options include the family playing a game, engaging in free play directed by the child, or participating in a joint creativity task (such as a collage). There are many types of semi-structured play, and it is often a gentle starting place for families who are trying to repair their relationships. This method can help parents learn how to give undivided attention to their child and be truly supportive rather than being competitive or rule-focused.

Family drawings, such as Kinetic Family Drawings (Burns & Kaufman, 1972) usually work well to test out systemic hypotheses; they can facilitate a new, more systemic view of the child's problem on the part of the parents, and help lessen the child's feelings of blame. First, each family member is asked to separately draw the family engaged in some type of activity together (e.g., "Draw your family doing something together;" or "Draw your family when someone is angry or sad"). Then one family member volunteers to go first and shows and explains their drawing, and other family members are encouraged to ask questions about the drawing. It is helpful, but not necessary, for the assessor to ask the first question to demonstrate what kind of questions to ask. Then other family members are invited to share their drawings, and the assessor helps the family notice similarities and differences. For some families, challenging dynamics may be raised with the drawings, and the assessor needs to be ready to work with and possibly temper the intensity. But again, although typically this is a rather low-intensity activity, the assessor can increase the intensity by commenting on patterns the family members may not notice on their own.

Medium Intensity/Engagement Activities

Semi-structured play can also be used as a medium intensity method. If the assessor thinks the parents will be responsive, they might work with the parents before the session and introduce and model parenting skills for them, including labeling emotions, mirroring emotions, "sports-casting" (described below), and empathic listening. The assessor also might serve as an active coach for the parents during the activity. However, with parents who are lacking in emotional resources, even labeling their child's emotions can be difficult. In such families, the assessor might use the activity to model skills the parents could use, reinforcing them in the moment. As this example suggests, the assessor must consistently try and match the intensity of the activity with what the parents are ready to learn and be alert to their emotional reactions.

Parent coaching can be a useful technique to use in semi-structured play activities. It is a fairly low to medium-intensity technique that has the combined goals of testing out how the family responds to a basic intervention and fostering positive experiences between family members. One example of parent coaching is the one we call the "sportscaster technique." This technique method involves the parent narrating, out loud in an excited demeanor, a positive mirroring description of what the child is doing. For example, a young boy plays "nerf" basketball while the parent acts like a sports radio announcer: "Ok folks, now Tommy is coming in for the shot, he weaves past the guard, sends the ball around his back, and throws. AND IT'S IN!! TOMMY SMITH has clinched the game for his team and...." This technique is a way of showing the child that the parent is noticing what the child is doing without instructing or judging the child in the process. It gives the child an intense experience of positive mirroring and of being seen. And, caregivers expressing "intersubjective delight" has been shown to reduce shame and strengthen attachment (Fosha, 2000). This is a particularly useful technique to teach parents who are exerting too much control over their child and are inadvertently preventing the child from developing self-efficacy and independence. It also works well for parents of children with siblings who may not be giving each of the children enough individual attention.

Empathic listening, and responding in kind, is usually a low to medium-intensity technique and works well in semi-structured play activities. The aim is to teach parents how to respond patiently and empathically to their child's emotions about a situation, instead of trying to jump in and solve the problem for the child. Parents are taught reflective statements and how to label their child's feelings, for example when the child loses a turn in a board game, the parent might exclaim "Ohhhhhh...that's so frustrating!" Empathic listening/responding helps parents build a positive relationship with their child so the child feels validated, heard, and seen by the parents.

In *Consensus Storytelling* to Picture Story Cards, family members are asked to craft conjoint stories to picture story cards from the TAT (Murray, 1943), RAT (Roberts & Gruber, 2005), FAT (Sotile et al., 1988), etc. The assessor usually chooses cards that are emotionally arousing based on the case conceptualization and Assessment Questions. Cards are chosen that pull for issues or themes that are present in the family; perhaps in their awareness or perhaps not. One technique is for each family member to first tell their own story to a card and then ask the family to tell a story they all agree on. Another technique is to ask the family to start out co-creating one story together. In either case, the assessor first helps the family notice patterns, e.g., the child always tells sad stories but the parents reject those plots and push for happy endings. Once a pattern is noticed and discussed, the assessor may choose to intervene and ask for a different story or ending than the family created to see how ready they are for altering their pattern. The process is observed and the assessor encourages the family members to discuss what they see going on and what they are experiencing. This task can reveal the emotional arousal patterns and management skills of both parents and the child under the different conditions the cards pull for (e.g., sadness, anger, shame). The procedure has somewhat unpredictable intensity, as it can be hard to anticipate at what level the family members will respond, but is generally thought of as medium. This technique is usually chosen to test out systemic hypotheses about the child's problems, facilitate the adoption of a systemic view of the child's problems, and help children feel less shame. It can be combined with family coaching, for example to teach parents how to "join with" a child's painful emotions, rather than trying to contradict or "fix" them.

The *Consensus Rorschach*, a task in which family members view Rorschach cards together and jointly choose and articulate responses, has a long and illustrious history (see Handler, 1997, or Finn, 2007 for a review). Family members are asked to create joint responses to selected Rorschach cards. This task elicits typical and sometimes problematic communication and interaction patterns (e.g., major power imbalances or struggles) that may affect a child's behavior. These patterns can then be discussed and modified with the family's input. If the family recognizes these patterns, the assessor can then help them try out new, more functional ways of relating during the task, and then to "export" what they learn to life outside the assessment. It also can be instructive to note the quality of responses produced by different groupings of family members. Although the goal is not to produce a scored Rorschach, the assessor may find it helpful to notice how the contributions of each member affect the quality and content of the responses.

The intensity of the Consensus Rorschach is difficult to predict, as the family members may or may not be aware of the structure or interpreted meaning of their responses to the ambiguous stimuli, but we generally see it as medium. Thus, the assessor needs to decide how much to simply observe communication patterns and resulting responses (and weave the information into the subsequent feedback session) or to comment about the potential meaning of what is being observed at the time to and see how family members respond. This decision will be influenced by the assessor's general sense of the family's readiness to profit from more directive intervention at this time.

High Intensity/Engagement Activities

Family Memory of Emotions Task, developed by Finn (Smith, Finn, Swain, & Handler, 2010), is similar to consensus storytelling, but the assessor asks family members to remember and relate situations where "one or more members of the family felt _____ (a certain emotion)." The family must choose the situation together and then all tell what they remember. The assessor tailors the list of emotion prompts to each family, including for example, excitement, happiness, curiosity, disappointment, sadness, anger, shame, and so on.

This task is often high intensity because—depending on the emotions prompted—it can bring up memorable and intense events for the family. It also can reveal which affect states are easy or difficult for various family members to manage, and assessors may make comments such as, "My impression is that this family is really good at dealing with anger together. Many families find that really hard. But am I right that this family has a harder time knowing what to do with sadness?"

Family Sculpting (Constantine, 1978; Papp, 1983) can be quite revealing, as parents may be surprised by the level of insight their child has into family problems. Family sculpting begins by asking each individual to place the various family members into a "sculpture" that represents how they see the family (or people's roles in the family) or feels as a member of the family. Each family member takes a turn, and the sculptures are discussed after each member finishes. Family members are encouraged to ask questions, and the assessor may or may not ask questions or point out patterns that are clear. A second sculpture may then be requested, asking each family member to sculpt how they "would like the family to be." Family sculpting tends to be a moderate- to high-intensity activity, as it can elicit a strong response from family members because they may be placed in positions that may be unflattering. Also, the "body" element can elicit a stronger affective response because people may reveal things of which they are not fully aware, and it is more personal and harder to deny such information than with a discussion or drawing. This activity is often perfect for families that are highly verbal or more "up in their heads," as it can bring to light patterns that are less conscious. This activity is sometimes used following the family drawings (described earlier).

In *Family Reenactments/Role-playing* the assessor asks the family members to reenact a past event, such as an argument or meltdown. The event to be processed with the assessor can be a one-time occurrence, or one that frequently reoccurs, such as putting a child to bed. The assessor then helps the family observe and discuss aspects and emotions they may not have noticed, and perhaps find ways in which they could have reacted differently. Sometimes it is helpful to ask family members to switch roles (i.e., children play parents and parents play the child), which can help with perspective taking and allow family members to communicate their interpretation of the actions, and even intentions, of others. The family is often asked to redo the scene until they feel some success implementing new strategies.

This method has high-intensity potential because family members can get caught up in their past negative thoughts and emotions during the reenactment. Be especially careful about letting families re-enact past traumatic events, as this can lead to trauma "flashbacks" and/or emotional overwhelm. The assessor needs to be prepared to intervene and redirect as needed. The use of puppets, where family members choose a puppet to represent themselves, often serves to decrease intensity, as the family members can somewhat distance themselves if needed. This modification is also very useful when dealing with young children.

Examples of Family Intervention Sessions

Having shared in-depth descriptions of the various methods/activities we typically use in family sessions, brief examples of FISs from the published literature on TA-C are provided (see Appendix A). The cases will give you a sense of goals that can be addressed, various methods/activities that are often used, and the impact.

Brief Examples of Family Intervention Sessions

We know turn to two case examples of FISs that incorporate the guidelines provided.

Case Example #1

Consider a family (a single mother and daughter) where the parent's Assessment Questions included concerns about the daughter's disengagement and anger at home. There was evidence of resources available, openness to systemic thinking (e.g., the mother was curious about her contribution to the daughter's problems), and a strong relationship with the assessor. The tentative case conceptualization involved the girl "giving a cold shoulder" to the mother because the mother had not been sufficiently available in the past. This scenario was not completely out of the mother's awareness, but we could sense how painful this way of looking at her world was for her. Although we could sense some openness in the mother to acknowledge her previous lack of availability, we were doubtful that she could connect the dots without experiencing significant shame. We knew we would need to be ready to provide the mother with extensive support and, if need be, pull back.

We chose the consensus TAT, a medium intensity/engagement activity. We asked both mother and daughter to tell separate stories to three cards that pulled for connections between the people in the cards. The mother experienced that her daughter (through the role of the girl in the pictures) did not seek support or care from the mother figures in her stories, in contrast to the stories the mother told about mothers nurturing the girl in the pictures. The two could not agree on a consensus story, and the daughter insisted that the girls in the pictures could take care of themselves. The mother had a heightened awareness that in their everyday world, her daughter almost never sought nurturance or support from her. She had always valued her daughter's self-sufficiency, but now started to wonder if it was premature and connected to problems at home.

The mother began to be aware that she may have contributed to her child's detachment and started to feel a pain in the pit of her stomach during the session. Although she usually pushed these thoughts away, she began to feel guilty about not having been emotionally available to her daughter in her earlier childhood due to her own depression. The assessor noticed the mother's distraught expression and provided extra support and the promise that they would explore this topic more fully at a later time. In fact, the assessor and mother processed the FIS and the mother's new awareness later that evening in an extensive phone call. The assessor helped allay the mother's guilt by assuring her she had done the best she could for her daughter and that no parents are perfect: the best parents learn how to repair mistakes or times they "missed" the child. After the FIS and the phone call, the family narrative now included an early rupture in the mother-daughter relationship. This defined the mother's next step and was a tipping point. The work would involve the mother exploring her own emotional availability in order to begin to repair her relationship with her daughter, likely through working with a therapist of her own and in parent-child sessions. This is a good example of where the assessor was aware that the planned intervention (chosen to raise attachment issues based on the case conceptualization) would create emotional distress for the mother and was prepared to help her manage and later explore her intense emotions. Again, the assessor "dared" risk this activity because she felt she had a strong relationship with the mother and the mother was opening up to thinking systemically at that point in the assessment.

Case Example #2

Consider a family who brought their extremely precocious son for a TA-C because of his unregulated anger at home. Our tentative case conceptualization included that the boy was "holding anger" for his parents, and that the parents were frightened by anger because of experiences in their families of origin. As a result, they avoided conflict and acted like "everything is fine." The parents gave the appearance of having adequate resources, growing systemic curiosity, and good connections with the assessor. We felt that they were open to change and that it was likely that the right intervention would help certain Level 3 Information become Level 2. We chose a drawing activity. Each family member was asked to draw the family doing something together and then to share their drawings. Although this task is usually considered to be low intensity/low engagement, we felt we could enhance the intensity based on how they responded to the task.

The parents were asked to describe their drawings first, which were happy depictions of the family playing at the beach (father) and making dinner together (mother). The son then described his drawing, which featured family members in the same room with angry faces but not interacting. The assessor asked him, "Will you help me understand your anger at home?" The boy answered, "My anger is big. Somebody has to be mad in this family. You just heard my parents tell you about their pictures and that they're happy and never angry, except when they are angry with me for being angry. They're angels." The assessor asked the boy what he thought was really going on and he said, ever so clearly, "I think that they're angry at each other and should give me a break."

The parents acted (and likely were) shocked, but slowly, with the support of the assessor, acknowledged that maybe their son was right (another tipping point). The boy looked relieved and yet acted cautious. The parents, with a nudge from the assessor, reached out to hug and console their son, which he accepted. This acknowledgement and beginning repair set the stage for a family shift that included the parents no longer projecting their anger onto their son and instead looking at their anger at each other. Again, the assessor had hypothesized that the session might go this way based on the case conceptualization and other information, and was ready to be available to each family member should anyone of them become overwhelmed.

Steps for Preparing and Conducting Family Intervention Sessions

We now present steps to help you prepare and conduct successful FISs (see Box 6.1). Because these sessions vary greatly in their goals and activities, you may find that all the steps are not relevant to every family. Still, we hope these guidelines provide a useful road map to help you keep your bearings during these frequently eventful sessions.

Decide Whom to Invite to the Session

In addition to the parents and child who have participated in the TA-C, at times we ask other family members (siblings, grandparents, aunts, and so forth) to take part in the FIS, even if they have not been included in earlier parts of the assessment. This decision rests partially on whether the assessor

---

Box 6.1 Steps for Preparing and Conducting a Family Intervention Session

- Decide whom to invite to the session.
- Choose your goal for the session and the level of engagement/ intensity of the activity you think is reasonable for the family.
- Decide how to introduce the session and activity and address any reluctance.
- Consider the family's culture when planning the FIS.
- Decide if you need a preliminary meeting with parents right before the FIS to prepare them for the session.
- Ask the family to do the activity together.
- Observe the family interaction.
- Promote family members sharing their reactions before jumping in.
- Possibly repeat the activity after the discussion.
- Be prepared that things may not go as planned.
- Meta-process with the family what happened in the session and discuss how things learned can be exported into daily life.
- Review the next steps in the assessment and have a check out.
- Reflect on the session and how the experience informs what comes next.

---

senses that other family members play major roles in the family's struggles and/or could be useful in helping the family to see and handle the child differently. For example, the assessor may have learned that an aunt who helps care for the child is triangulating the child in her conflict with the parents, or that a jealous sibling is tormenting the child at home. Alternatively, inviting an older sibling whom you have learned is a supportive person in the child's life or a grandmother who the child has mentioned as being loving and caring may prove useful. At other times, an assessor may wish to strengthen the alliance between a particular child and their parent(s), so the assessor may choose not to involve siblings and others in the family session. This latter decision seems particularly applicable when the assessor senses that the child is longing for individual time with the parent(s) and that such unmet needs play a role in the family's struggles. Another common scenario is a single parent who is struggling to differentiate from her own parent and become confident that she can figure out what is best for her child. In such scenarios we might intentionally omit the grandparent from the FIS.

Choose Your Goal for the Session and the Level of Engagement/ Intensity of the Activity You Think Is Reasonable for the Family

In general, the goal is for family members to have an experience that helps them be open to a revised family narrative, even if just slightly. As discussed throughout this chapter, families are at different levels of readiness to change their "stories," in particular whether to shift from focusing on the child as the main problem or to see the child's difficulties as coming from interactions in the larger family. It is our task to think carefully, using all we have learned up to that point in the assessment, about what the family is ready for and to choose an activity that matches their readiness and perhaps tries to stretch them a bit. Is the goal for the family to engage in a low intensity activity, have a positive experience, and regain some hope? Is the goal for the family to engage in a moderate intensity activity that brings the problem behavior into the room, and with the assessor's guidance, respond more effectively? Is the goal for the family to engage in a high intensity activity and experience systemic patterns that are impacting the child's behavior (e.g., realize that the child acts out whenever her parents are in conflict) and make changes in the moment? The guidelines presented earlier in the chapter should help you choose your goal, activity and level of intensity.

In making these decisions, it is also helpful for assessors to be aware of their feelings at this point of the assessment. Assessors who are afraid they are not doing enough may set their goals too high and risk overwhelming a family. Assessors who identify with the family's pain may be protective and choose a task that is too easy. The test findings can be very helpful in making these decisions, so we urge you to study them in considering what level of inter-vention to choose: pay close attention to the balance of emotional pain vs. coping resources revealed in the child's and parents' (if obtained) test pro-tocols. It also helps to remember that you can moderate the intensity of any activity you choose by the kinds of comments you make during the FIS.

Decide How to Introduce the Session and Activity and Address any Reluctance

How one introduces the FIS depends a great deal on the family's existing "story" at the time of the session about why the child is having problems. If parents have asked any Assessment Questions at the beginning of the as-sessment that show an awareness of possible systemic influences (e.g., "Why is our son so good with his teachers and baby sitters, but so terrible with us?"), then the assessor can easily explain the need for a family session to help answer such questions. Also, if parents have begun to shift to a more systemic view during the early assessment sessions, then the FIS is fairly easy to justify. So, in most cases we explain that the family session will help us better answer one or more of their specific Assessment Questions.

If, however, it is clear that the parents are focused on the child as the sole problem—even after the previous meetings, the assessor must find another way to explain the purpose of the session. We want the parents to know that we are not "putting them on the spot" to test or shame them or to observe them in a dispassionate way. Instead we explain that the FIS is part of our effort to consult with them about issues that are important to them and help find new "open doors." For example, the assessor might explain that it appears from the test results that the child might respond to some special parenting techniques developed for children with special needs. The parents are then asked if they would be willing to come to a session in which they are shown and get to practice these techniques to see if they work with their child.

Consider the Family's Culture When Planning the FIS

Different cultures have different degrees of openness to the idea that family members influence each other's behavior and psychological well-being. Thus, a family's willingness to take part or wholeheartedly engage in a family ses-sion can vary greatly according to the family's cultural background. Family therapists have learned that it is imperative to consider culturally grounded values and attitudes (e.g., Canino & Inclan, 2001; McGoldrich, 1998) and current ethical guidelines enjoin psychologists to do so (American Psychological Association, 2017). To give one example, in our experience, many Latino, Asian, and Native American families immediately grasp why a family session is advisable when a child is having problems, and the family may even question the validity of an assessment unless such a session is held.

We have also experienced that many European American families value individualism and privacy, and may be reluctant to a family session. We have found that framing the session as offering special parent training, or as a way to see the strengths of the family, can be good ways to help reach these latter families.

Decide If You Need a Preliminary Meeting With Parents Right Before the Family Intervention Session to Prepare Them for the Session

We find a mid-assessment parent session to be essential when a goal of the FIS is helping parents use new techniques, such as labeling and mirroring their child's emotions, "sports-casting," and empathic listening. In the meeting with the parents we introduce the skills, model them, and practice with the parents prior to the child joining. During the FIS, we may continue to coach the parents and even take a "teaching break" with the parents outside the room to review and refine the new skills if necessary. Also, parent meetings right before an FIS can be an occasion to tentatively "drop in" information related to the current case conceptualization, to see how parents react.

Ask the Family to Do the Activity Together

Here we simply introduce the chosen activity, mentioning one or more Assessment Questions it is related to, and help the family get started. If the family members give their consent, we typically videotape the family activity so we can show it to the parents afterwards and get their additional thoughts.

Observe the Family Interaction

Here we are attuned to each member of the family and may alternate between being a passive and an active observer, depending on how the session is going and what guidance is useful for the family. We watch especially to see if the child shows their targeted problem behaviors and how the parents respond. We see if parents can see the connection between what is happening in the room and what happens at home, and we ask questions that may help the family see the pattern in a new way, e.g., "Did anybody notice what was happening right before Susie withdrew?" "How did each person respond when Tommy started to melt down?" (Notice the circular questioning discussed in Chapter 3). We offer, out loud or by whispering to the parents, other ways to respond that might be more useful. We track how the parents are able to respond differently and how the child then responds. We pay attention to strengths that we hadn't anticipated in the family system. We are open to being surprised and are ready to take the activity to the next level if the family seems ready--just as we would be ready to take it down a level if the family was really struggling or unduly distressed.

Promote Family Members Sharing Their Reactions Before Jumping In

As practiced in general in TA-C, we suggest you contain any observations or insights you might have about what is going on and first ask how the family members see things. Listen carefully and build upon the family members' thoughts and observations when at all possible. Ask questions of the family members that might "scaffold" the family into different ways of seeing things, using small "half steps." Help the family members connect what is happening in the session to life at home and to the Assessment Question you are trying to inform.

Possibly Repeat the Activity After the Discussion

While not always necessary, the parents may have arrived at new ways of seeing their interactions with their child and may benefit from redoing the activity in a new way after the initial discussion. If so, repeat the activity and help the family observe if and how things changed. Also help them put words on what they have experienced. Be sure to hear from multiple family members.

Be Prepared That Things May Not Go as Planned

Although a well thought through intervention is often quite successful, sometimes things don't go as initially planned and it is important for assessors to be flexible and "think on their feet." The family may not react in the way that was anticipated, or other information connected to the presenting issues may emerge that was not previously "in the room." Being aware that things may go differently than planned can help you not be caught off-guard, and can even raise your excitement and curiosity about the family. The most frequent mistake we have made is to be too ambitious and to overwhelm either parents or children by trying to accomplish too much. If this is this case, we have likely chosen the wrong level of intensity/engagement of the intervention and will need to back it up. It is our recommendation that, if possible, in addition to the prepared intervention, the assessor be ready with a less ambitious intervention that, after some explanation, can be fairly seamlessly put into place.

Another misstep we have made is miscalculating the impact the intervention may have on parents' emotional state. Parents may have an important realization during the FIS of how they contribute to their children's problems, but this insight may cause them intense emotional distress. Should this happen, the best repair is typically to stop the activity, help regulate whatever distress has emerged, and if appropriate, acknowledge that the activity was more intense than anticipated. With appropriate repair, most families in this situation come to see the FIS as a "happy accident" that led to more insight and growth than they thought possible.

Also, there is an important assessor countertransference issue that often leads to empathic breaks with parents at this stage of a TA-C. In our experience it is fairly common for assessors to identify easily with the child in a family system and to have more difficulty empathizing with parents. There are many reasons why this happens, but one may be that we frequently have a great deal of information from engaging in activities and testing of children, which helps us get "in their shoes," while we have less information about parents. If assessors feel more empathy for the child, they may push parents to "get" how they contribute to their child's problems—which is generally a recipe for an empathic disruption. Our goal is for each family to take the next step within its capacity as the members work toward becoming a healthier family. This means being able to hold each person in mind and find compassion for the individual dilemmas of change. For example, in the case we discussed earlier, we could have emotionally overwhelmed the mother when she considered that she wasn't available to her daughter early in their life together due to her own depression. However, we anticipated the mother's guilt and shame and felt protective and nonjudgmental of her. Thus, although that mother was emotionally stirred up, the quick supportive response from the assessor during the session and availability afterwards served to help the mother manage her emotions at the time and then commit to working to repair her relationship with her daughter.

Another possible common "error" we have made is underestimating the positive changes that the family has already made during the earlier parts of the assessment and being surprised when the family handles the tasks presented in the FIS in a healthy and adaptive way. This error appears to happen because we are not always aware of shifts that are happening in the family between sessions and we have not fully been in touch with family members' resilience. Alternatively, sometimes families are able to act in healthier ways because of the supportive presence of the assessor, who helps contain and regulate emotions. A good strategy is to mirror the family's healthy behavior, ask family members how they feel, and discuss what combination of factors made it possible for things to go so well in the session. Then one can ask the family members whether they will be able to act in similar ways outside the assessment room. If family members are doubtful that they can maintain this level of adaptive functioning, this is an opening to introduce the idea of family therapy or other interventions after the assessment is completed.

We also have experienced that once in a while things do really go wrong. If we are not able to balance our connection and support of each family member, we may get "recruited" by one of the members and "act out." If we are unaware of our biases and countertransference, we could project anger or shame onto a member of the family and damage our alliance with that person. Seeking consultation from colleagues mid-assessment—especially for families that stir us up emotionally—can greatly forestall such enactments.

Fortunately, even such "mistakes" can result in steps forward for a family (and assessor) if assessors can avoid going into shame, use what happened to learn more about the family dilemma of change and themselves, and make repairs with the family.

Meta-Process With the Family What Happened in the Session and Discuss How Things Learned Can Be Exported Into Daily Life

Some meta-processing may be useful with the whole family, while some may need to take place later, without the child present. If the family found new ways of handling typical problem situations, it can be useful to discuss how these might work in daily life and any impediments that might exist. Help the family imagine ways to reduce these impediments. See if the family is willing to try out their new awareness and skills at home before the next meeting and report back. If so, you might begin the Summary/Discussion Session by asking how things went.

Review the Next Steps in the Assessment and Check Out

Typically, the next step in the TA-C is the parents' Summary/Discussion Session. If this fits your plan, and the child is used to coming weekly, you might inform the child that there will be a longer than usual interval between sessions. We suggest you assure the child that the whole family will be coming back soon for a joint session (typically for the presentation of the therapeutic fable.) Then typically we initiate a "check out" process by asking how the family members are feeling as they prepare to leave. We answer any questions and offer to be available to the parents before the next session. Some parents request an almost immediate subsequent session to discuss the FIS. If that happens, it is very useful if the session was videotaped, as you may review sections of the video together and further discuss what transpired.

Reflect on the Session and How the Experience Informs What Comes Next

After the family has left, it is useful to ask yourself certain questions as a way to learn and incorporate all you can from the FIS:

- What new information did I learn from the FIS?
- How did the parents respond to my interventions or attempts to change the family's current "story" about the child's problem behaviors?
- Do I have a different sense now of what information is Level 1, 2, or 3 for the parents?
- Do I need to change my case conceptualization based on what occurred?
- Did information emerge that makes me want to revise my answers to one or more of the Assessment Questions?

- Did anything emerge that I might want to incorporate in the fable for the child?

Case: Family Intervention Session With Henry and his Parents

As long as I (Dale) have been practicing TA-C and no matter what happens throughout the assessment, I find the FIS to be one of the most challenging and creative parts of the process. I had numerous thoughts and questions about the upcoming FIS session. What did I really want to focus on? What would be the most useful in assisting the parents in getting a new or expanded narrative? While I had a very good working alliance with all members of the family, could I count on Henry to cooperate and participate in the session? If he didn't, what would my back-up plan be? Without Henry's active participation how could I still use the meeting as a positive, information gathering and sharing session? Last, for me, one of the most important things I needed to remember was how to keep a systemic perspective.

After reviewing the case conceptualization and my tentative answers to the Assessment Questions, my hope was to address the difficulty the parents had in experiencing, expressing, and responding to difficult emotions. I planned an activity that would allow us to get feelings into the room, attend to how each member shared and responded to the others' feelings, and perhaps coach the parents on how to respond in a positive, affirming way to Henry's feelings. There was ample evidence that it was difficult for all the family members to spontaneously express a wide range of feelings and be supported by the other family members. I did not think that Henry's parents recognized how much difficulty they had validating each other's and Henry's feelings. Henry was stuck on his sad feelings, and I wondered if an intervention session focusing on everyone's feelings might enable him to shift from this rigid position.

As is often the case before an FIS, I felt a little anxious, as well as energized and excited about the upcoming session. For me the anxiety exists because I never know how the session will unfold. As mentioned above, the FIS requires a great deal of flexibility on the assessor's part and a need to stay in the moment with the family. I can plan the activity, have specific objectives, think through possible family responses, and try to be prepared for whatever may come up, but there is always a possibility that something unexpected may be shared or exposed. It is incumbent upon me to maintain a safe environment for all family members. At this point in the assessment, I felt I had established good relationships with each person in the family. Barbara was easy for me to connect with because she was fairly unguarded, spontaneous, and aware that she had a very difficult family of origin. I was less sure about David and what his reactions might be. He was quiet in comparison to Barbara, and I had to be sure not to let Barbara do all the talking. Henry was still preoccupied with his sadness but had built a more positive relationship with me through the course of our sessions together. I could joke with him a little bit, and he would share a bit more about why he felt so sad and anxious.

I scheduled the FIS and explained that it would involve: 1) checking in with everyone to see how things felt so far in the assessment, 2) doing an activity that would help me understand the family interaction better, and 3) providing more information on several Assessment Questions that concerned Henry's depression, feeling loved, and being provocative. I thought Henry's depression and behavior might shift if we could better understand how the family processed or didn't process feelings. The parents were amenable, and I scheduled a 2-hour session. My plan was to do consensus storytelling to picture story cards, as described earlier. I decided to use cards from the Robert's Apperception Test with which Henry was already familiar.

It seemed to me, as discussed earlier in the chapter, that a medium intensity/engagement would be a good choice. In addition to forming a positive working relationship with me, the family members had demonstrated aspects of healthy family functioning, a moderate level of awareness and motivation to get "unstuck," and a degree of openness to taking in Level 3 Information. Also given the strong therapeutic alliance I felt, I was certain we could handle a moderate level of emotions, should they arise. I was excited to get started.

I began the session with all three family members. We made small talk about what was happening in the family and ended up talking about some of Henry's favorite Girl Scout cookies while he was bouncing on the large ball I keep in my office. He seemed more energetic and comfortable than in past sessions. The general ambience in the office was one of congeniality and fun, and generally more relaxed. As we talked, I explained that we had a lot to do today. Because I hadn't seen the parents in a few weeks I wanted to check in with them to see how the past month had been before we began what might be a difficult session.

In addition, I also let Henry know that I would be talking with him individually as well, after chatting with his parents. I then asked Henry to leave so I could talk with his parents alone for a few minutes. I did this in a playful way because I did not want Henry to worry about being excluded. In retrospect, I think connecting with Henry and his parents separately was my way of cementing the alliances I had with each of them before the FIS.

The following brief conversation with the parents ensued:

Dale: He seems like he's in a great mood.
Barbara: He's been that way for a while.
David: Like 2 or 3 weeks.
Dale: Really? Interesting. What do you attribute this to?
David: The Zodiac.
Dale: (Laughing) No, you're supposed to say, "from coming here."
Barbara: Well it has to be.
Dale: No, really, I'm serious. I'm not kidding now.

Barbara:	I'm not kidding, either. I have no idea. I mean I don't feel like we've changed, but he's really enjoyed coming here. He never resists and goes in easily and comes out in a good mood.
David:	He's also been really cooperative in writing an essay for one of the Middle School applications. When I first asked him to go and look at the application ...
Barbara:	... he came back ten minutes later saying, "I looked at it and it's just like the benchmark tests. It's going to be easy."
Dale:	This is totally different?
Barbara:	Yeah.
David:	Way less resistant. Yeah. The piano teacher came last Friday, and Henry picked a difficult piece to play. He's been working on it all week.
Barbara:	He's been practicing on his own. Nobody ever asks him to...he just goes and practices.
Dale:	That's great.
Barbara:	He hasn't been fighting with his brother.
David:	As much.
Barbara:	As much. He would really get angry, like growl and get mad at him. It's not happening.
Dale:	That sounds great. Well, I just wanted to check in and see if what I was perceiving was consistent with what you were feeling. Why don't I let him come in here so he and I can have a minute to talk?

I invited Henry into the office and his parents left. I commented that he seemed to be doing well, and he said it was because he was going to have an overnight visit with a friend. We made more small talk about his middle school applications and friends. I explained to him what we were going to do today and showed him Card Number 13B of the Robert's Apperception Test (RAT). I asked him to tell me a story before his parents come in. He refused and said he didn't want to do it. My heart sank and I thought, "Uh oh, here we go again with the resistance." We talked a little bit about whether we should do this activity or not, and then we negotiated a plan in which he didn't have to participate if he didn't want to. He was a little curious as to what his parents might say.

The parents came back in and I explained the task. I asked that they tell a story together and to focus on what's happening in the picture and how people are feeling and what they might be thinking. Barbara asked for some clarification, and then I showed the family the first picture that was RAT Card Number 3B. It is a picture of a boy looking clearly unhappy, holding a pencil, sitting at a table with books and papers, and apparently doing some schoolwork. Barbara took the card and asked Henry to start. He refused and Barbara continued to hold the card in front of Henry; the following dialogue occurred:

Dale:	That's OK if Henry would rather listen to your story. (*I added this to affirm the agreement Henry and I made about him not having to tell a story.*)
Dad:	The kid is busy doing his homework. Concentrating.
Mom:	Yeah, he seems to be concentrating on something on the page. And he looks tired. (*They pause.*)
Dale:	Ok, so the kid is busy doing his homework. Concentrating. Looks tired. What might have happened that led up to this?
Henry:	Nothing. (*My first thought was, there goes Henry, trying to thwart the process and then I wondered if he was doing this because his parents had just ignored the negative affect of the card.*)
Dale:	Nothing? (*I paused to see if Henry would add anything.*) Ok, so nothing happened that led up to it.
Dad:	He mysteriously found himself sitting at the table with a pile of books and homework.
Mom:	I think that somebody told him to go do his homework. But it seems like that was a long time ago because he's getting tired now.
Dad:	He might be feeling a sense of accomplishment. (*I noticed David making the scene positive.*)
Dale:	That's great, just like that. Let's try another one.

I chose not to pick up on anything in this story. I wanted to wait to see the pattern. It seemed that the parents ignored or minimized the dysphoric emotions and Henry reacted by being obstructive. I also worried that if I commented on Henry's consistent passive opposition he could be sca-pegoated.

I showed the family the next card (RAT 1B) and a similar pattern ensued. This is a picture of a father, mother and son standing while the father has a hand on the son's shoulder. The father's facial expression is somber while the mother looks concerned, and the son looks attentive. Barbara initiated the response by asking Henry to say what's happening in the picture, and Henry said, "Nothing." Then the parents continued to tell a story:

Mom:	I think the dad is telling the family a story. A sad story. Something that has happened.
Dad:	(*Not continuing with Barbara's sad story.*) I think the dad is telling the son that he really likes it when the son plays Legos on the floor in his bedroom and makes up all kinds of interesting great stories with the Lego characters. And the mom is looking lovingly at the dad for his deep insight. (*I wondered if David was exhibiting his dry sense of humor, or if this is truly what he longed for in the family.*)
Dale:	The mom is looking lovingly at the dad for his deep insight?
Mom:	I think she wants him to finish telling the story so she can go finish making dinner. (*She lets the sadness drop when David doesn't pick up on it, and doesn't go along with David's more self-serving story.*)

Dale:	Ok, what might they be thinking or feeling?
Henry:	Nothing.
Dale:	Nothing.
Mom:	I think the boy feels kind of interested in his dad and looks a little proud at his dad. I think the mom is feeling slightly impatient. The dad seems like he's very serious. I don't think it's sad. They all feel different things.
Dale:	So, the mom is feeling slightly impatient. The dad seems serious. And the boy is feeling proud.
Mom:	Proud of his dad.

At this point I thought, "OK this is interesting. Here's Barbara sharing some negative affect initially and then taking it back after David shares a more positive perspective like he did in the previous dialogue—without mentioning a whole lot of feelings." There are so many choice points in these sessions. I could have commented on the process and the content at that point, but again I chose not to because I wanted to see patterns and the response to the next, more emotionally arousing card. I then showed them RAT Card 13B, which has a boy lifting a chair over his head as if in the next minute he would throw it or hit someone with it. I thought it would be difficult for the parents to tell a positive story to this card.

Dale:	Alright. Here you go. Now this one Henry's already seen.
Mom:	Henry, any ideas?
Henry:	They seem extremely happy. (*Henry did not sound sarcastic, but I wondered if he was mimicking his parents' denial of negative affect.*)
Mom:	I'm going to go with he's not happy. He's angry and he's gonna break that chair up to get his anger out. He's disappointed about something.
Dad:	(*In direct contrast to what Barbara says.*) I'm thinking someone asked him to grab the chair from the other side of the room and he's carrying it over his head, so he doesn't hit anybody with it. (*David's story surprised me given that it is difficult to deny the anger that seems to be in the picture.*)
Mom:	I think he's going to bust up the chair and feel better. Make a mess and walk away. (*Asserting herself and the anger that is there.*)
Dale:	So, bust up the chair, feel better. Bring over the chair and set it down. And he's very happy. Which of the stories does him being very happy go with?
Henry:	Neither one.

Gradually as the session proceeded, there was more and more affect in the room. It was not directly expressed, but in the moment, I sensed the parents' frustration. I thought it would be a good time for reflection.

Dale:	Ok. So right now, this second, I want you to each think about what you're feeling, after doing this exercise together. Ok? Honestly, what are you feeling. Henry?
Henry:	Sad.
Dale:	Sad.
Mom:	Frustrated.
Dad:	Frustrated.

Then, Henry spontaneously initiated a direct question to his parents. I was surprised!

Henry:	Why are you frustrated?
Mom:	Because it feels like you don't want to participate at taking a chance to tell us what's going on in the stories. You just want to be provocative and say something contrary.

I decided to spend some time here because one of the parents' questions was, "Why does Henry make provocative statements to us?" After defining the word provocative I asked Henry how he thought he might be being provocative.

Henry:	I'm being extremely rude.
Dale:	Your mom said she was frustrated because she felt like you were trying to make her angry and trying to get a big reaction from either of your parents. (*Henry nodded.*)
Dale:	David, why were you frustrated? (*I remembered my intention to make sure that both parents' points of view were explained during this process.*)
Dad:	I'm frustrated because I've seen Henry create really detailed incredible stories with Legos, and there's always a complicated story that goes with the activity. So, I know he does have an active imagination when he wants to engage. But when he's confronted with something that seems to be a test, it feels frightening to Henry because the test doesn't have right or wrong answers, then, he chooses not to not to participate or take the test. It's very frustrating to see that he doesn't even attempt to do it.
Dale:	He just gives up?
Dad:	He just gives up or is just very stubborn.
Dale:	So that's very frustrating for both of you?
Mom:	Yes.
Dale:	And then what happens afterwards? Do you hold on to the frustration? Do you get angry?
Mom:	I mean over time yes, it gets exhausting. It makes you feel like you don't want to try because when there is any kind of attempt to get anything out of Henry he shuts down, so you stop wanting to try to interact, which makes me feel sad.

Dale:	You feel sad?
Mom:	Yes. Because I would like to be able to engage in all different levels with Henry, but I also don't want to feel sad and frustrated, and so I'll sometimes just avoid being with him.
Dale:	Oh, that *is* sad.
Mom:	It is sad. It's sad for me, and I think it's sad for Henry. I'm only human and sometimes it gets tiring being shut down again and again and again.
Dale:	That sounds very hurtful, Barbara. I guess it says that Henry is very powerful.(*After reviewing the tape of this session, I realized that I missed an opportunity here to reframe Henry's behavior as a possible reaction to the parents denying the dysphoric affect in the cards.*)
Mom:	Yes.
Dale:	(*to Henry*) How did you get so powerful in your family? Do you know? Do you want to be that powerful? (*Henry shook his head "No."*)
Dale:	I wouldn't think a kid would want to be that powerful, frankly. You know what I mean?
Henry:	Yes, because it makes me get a lot less attention.
Dale:	When you're powerful?
Henry:	Yes, but I get less attention.
Dale:	I'm not sure I understand that. Can you help me? When you're sad you get less attention? It feels that way?
Henry:	I guess.
Dale:	Alright, so Henry gets less attention when he is sad over time, because he's kind of hard to be with. That's Henry's guess, I think. I don't know if I'm getting it right though.
Dad:	It depends on the amount of sadness in his day; I think he gets a lot of attention. Just because we're trying to help him, we worry about him. I think sometimes when things are going along very nicely, when there's not much sad talk, maybe there is a little less attention because things are ok.
Mom:	Maybe, but I also think that we've had a little less sad talk for a while, then we do more together. We've started reading again—and he's gotten more attention.
Dale:	It's very confusing. Sometimes Henry's sad talk gets him more attention because you're worried about him and sometimes it gets him less attention because it's so hard to be around him when he's so sad. That's very confusing. I bet it's confusing for Henry, too.

I was pleased with this discussion because we were talking about feelings and how Henry's sadness affected his parents. Feelings were in the room, but it felt subdued and intellectualized. I thought we might be able to do a little more with the interactions and maybe have someone claim the anger they might be feeling, rather than the frustration. I decided to see if the family could notice any of the pattern, I thought I saw, when they were telling the stories.

Dale: Let's go back to the storytelling you did. Did you notice any themes in your stories? Any ways that they were similar or how you did the task? Henry, did you notice how your parents did the task? (*Henry shook his head "No."*)

Mom: (laughs and shakes head "No" too)

Dale: You didn't either? You took turns. You listened to each other.

Dad: We took turns. There was some agreement in the stories and there was also some deviation from the story line.

Dale: Disagreement you mean in the story? When you say deviation?

Dad: Well deviation, I took a little different way with the boy and the chair. (*David's use of the word deviation rather than disagreement seemed to accentuate his not wanting to say anything negative or disagreeable.*)

Mom: Yeah.

Dale: Ok so take the boy and the chair and come up with a story you all agree on. And Henry it would be nice if you could participate. And mom and dad, try and include Henry if you can.

The family told the story again and this time they reached agreement that the boy was frustrated and about to smash the chair. Then, a surprising twist happened.

Dad: I can go with that. I can actually tell you about a time I did this.

Dale: Well let's hear it.

David: I got back my tax return. This was after I went through a bad break up and I had to pay an incredible amount of money. The other person was not going to contribute because they didn't live in the same city as me. I did smash a chair.

Dale: You must have been really, really angry. (*I was feeling really pleased that some anger was actually being discussed, since this family usually denied or shied away from anger. And I thought it was remarkable that Dad was the one to admit to anger.*)

David: I did smash it to pieces. It was very cathartic. I felt much better. Of course, then I still had to find the money to pay the taxes.

Dale: Well that's cool. Henry, can you imagine your Dad doing that?

Henry: Yes. Because he's grabbed me by the back of my shirt and carried me while I was choking to the bathroom and dropped me and slammed the door.

David did not respond or acknowledge his son's anxious, tentative tone.

Dale: Really, when did that happen?

Henry: When I was really young. It happened to me.

Dale: That sounds really scary, Henry. *(Looking toward the parents.)* Do you all remember that?

David shook his head and began to say he didn't remember anything about that.

Mom: I have been told that story a number of times by Henry.
Dale: Oh really?
Mom: And I've mentioned it to you. *(Looking at David)*
Dad: You've mentioned it to me, but it's only been in the last year or so.
Dale: David when you hear this story what do you feel? It seems like an important story.
Dad: It does sound important. I feel a bit shocked that he holds on to this story, and I don't remember the circumstances. And I also feel shame that there was a time that I reached a point of being so frustrated that I would grab him by the shirt. And I'm pretty sure there have been times that I have threatened the kids, grabbing them by the shirt, but I have never hauled and deposited them by the shirt. It's very upsetting to me that he would feel like he's being choked. It's also very unsettling that I can't even remember this set of circumstances. How much of it is actually factual?
Dale: So, because you have no way of knowing the facts, you're not sure how to respond to it. But if it were true, what would you want to say to Henry? *(I decided to try and guide David in making a repair with Henry).*
Dad: *(turns to Henry)* I'm sorry.
Dale: Yeah. Can you hear that Henry? I think it might be helpful if you look at your Dad and tell him the story, what you remember.
Henry: I think I knew how to read, so I wasn't too young. I was reading a book and I was about to get up and get into the bath and then Dad had gotten extremely mad at me because I hadn't gotten up and gone into the tub earlier. I was about to get up and then he grabbed me by my shirt, and I literally couldn't breathe. I mean slightly but not very well. And I think I was sitting on that wall that now has the antique quilt of the United States map on it and then he picked me up by the back of my shirt and carried me into the bathroom and dropped me on the rug in there and turned around and slammed the door and told me to get into the bath. And I don't think I got into the bath just then. I was surprised. I think I cried for a little bit and then I got into the bath and I took a really short bath. *(I was struck by Henry's detailed recall of the incident which made me think that this had been a traumatic event.)*
Dale: Sounds like you were kind of shocked.
Henry: Yes.
Dale: It was something your Dad doesn't usually do? That must have been really, really scary.

Henry: It was.

Dale: Did you ever talk about it after that? Do you remember that?

Henry: I think so.

Dale: What do you think happened? What did you talk about?

Henry: Everything.

Dale: With your Dad?

Henry: No. I think it was with my Mom

Dale: You're looking at your Mom.

Henry: I'm trying to make her laugh.

Dale: I think you're trying to take care of your Mom because she looks so concerned. I'm feeling really sad for all of you.

Henry: Why?

Dale: Well because I hear how hard and scary this was for you, and also, I know how hard it is to be a parent, and when you scare or hurt your child you do feel a lot of shame. You feel really bad about it and you don't know what to do about it. (*Trying to support Henry while also trying to de-shame David.*) The most important thing is to try and talk about it and for the parent to make a repair with their child. (*Sharing some psychoeducational information.*) So, I'm feeling sad for your Dad and I'm just feeling, thinking about the shame he must feel, and he said he felt ashamed, right? I also feel sad for you Henry, because you never got to talk directly to your Dad about it and say how you felt and see how sorry he might have been. So, David, tell me how you're feeling.

Dad: I feel ashamed. I felt a great deal of shame after that happened. I also feel defensive because there are many times that both of my children will be so engaged in a book that they will not listen to you, myself or their mother and actually do what they were asked to do.

Henry: I was just about to do it and then I get a punishment.

Dad: It's not just the fact that you were about to do it, it's about the fact that I had probably asked you multiple times, 4 or 5 or 6 times. And I had lost my patience. There's no way I can speak to what other circumstances were driving it at this point. But I also feel very judged and defensive because I know Barbara is probably going to judge me about this and point out how I have these shortcomings in how I relate to the children.

Dale: Yes, it's hard. You didn't see Barbara's face when you said that. You know, would you mind saying that directly to her? The judged part.

Dad: I feel like you're going to judge me for this.

Mom: I don't. We've talked about this. I mean the fact that this is such a big deal is to me a success story in our parenting. I'm not trying to be flip. It's just terrible what happened. I mean for him it must have been a terrible experience obviously. And every kid has different sensitivities and he's not used to being carried around by his shirt. That's scary.

Dale:	Yes! Very scary. And what did you mean by this is a success story?
Mom:	The fact that it has happened one time is a pretty good record I would say. To me the important part and the thing I would be judgmental about is not taking responsibility for it and apologizing face to face in as timely a manner as possible. That is the important thing to me because everybody messes up and that's just fine.
Dale:	Different things happen in different families. And so, Henry was really brave in saying this memory.
Mom:	Yes.
Dale:	Really brave. I appreciate that. So, Henry, did you hear how your Dad responded? What did he say?
Henry:	That he was sorry *(said in a baby voice)*.
Dale:	That he would say he was sorry. He hasn't quite said it directly to you yet actually. But we're getting there, right? Did you hear what your Dad said just now about what he felt?
Henry:	Shame.
Dale:	He felt ashamed and something else.
Henry:	I don't remember.
Mom:	Defensive because he felt judged by me.
Dale:	Yes!

At this point Henry asked to get a glass of water and I realized we were getting into couple's work that might be left for a time when Henry is not present. Another short break ensued as both parents asked Henry to bring them some water, too. Henry again left the room. The parents and I agreed to continue our discussion at another time and then made some small talk. The last part of the session had been intense, and I felt it was time to lower the intensity. However, when Henry came back into the room, I felt it was important to explain why his mother may have sounded like she was minimizing what had happened between Henry and his father.

Dale:	OK, we don't have much time left. I'd like to go back to what you said Barbara, about if this was the only time Henry can remember being scared, it was a success story of sorts.
Dale:	Does that seem weird to you when your Mom says it's a success story?
Henry:	Yeah.
Mom:	(laughs)
Dale:	Ok, so let's explain that before we finish. Your Mom might think it's a success story because of the way she was raised.
Mom:	Yes.
Dale:	Ok so why don't you ask her about that Henry. That could be helpful.
Henry:	How were you raised?
Mom:	Well in my house there was a lot of yelling all the time.

Henry: Is that all?

Dale: Ok hold on just a sec. *(I noticed Barbara looked very sad and seemed to be holding back tears.)* Look at your Mom for a second because she's having some feelings.

Mom: It was very... There was a lot of yelling and a lot of kind of crazy acting. Like my Mom would just be mad for no reason that had to do with anything that was really happening in the world. Just like something was going on in her mind to make her mad. And she would do sometimes really crazy mean things. Like throw shoes at us or lock us in our rooms. And she would be really mean to my Dad and throw his things around and sometimes hit him and sometimes hit us and say really, really, really awful things. Because she wasn't well. And then other people would come to our house and there would be big fights. And so, it was unhappy and unpredictable.

Dale: Yeah, unpredictable is very scary for kids.

Mom: And the worst part was you just never knew what was happening at any part of the day. You had to always be listening for the tone in somebody's voice. So, most of the time I would just try to get away as fast as possible or be really, really good. Very quiet. Or stay out of trouble. So anyways, that's why I say that our house is not like that at all compared to the house I grew up in. It's mostly pretty predictable at our house, right?

Henry: Yeah.

Mom: Daddy's going to be grumpy in the morning. Mommy comes home at a certain time. We have dinner together. Playing happens at a certain time. Homework happens at a certain time. So that's why I say that if you can only remember one time that your Daddy did something like that, really lost his temper... I mean he loses his temper but where he physically did that to you one time, then that's why I consider that a success story.

Dale: However, that makes it really unpredictable. It was really unpredictable for Henry when it happened and really scary.

Mom: Yes, because when that happens it's so incredibly rare. It must be really, really upsetting for you Henry. I'm sorry you experienced that.

Dale: So now I'm going to ask you two to trade seats. Henry, would you mind moving over toward your Dad. *(He complied and moved very close, playfully to Dad and Dad responded affectionately.)*

Dale: Ok. So now is the time to look at each other if you can and say what you're feeling. You can move a little further away. But look at your Dad. Your Dad's looking at you. In terms of that, in terms of that happening, what are you feeling David?

Dad: I feel really bad that I caused you to feel like that. I remember a time I was having an argument with my sister at Christmas time. We were supposed to go to my uncle's house, and my Mom and Dad were in their bedroom and they were having a fight and my Mom came out of the bedroom and slapped me on the side of the face. Hurt my head. She was mad at my Dad and she thought Carol and I were having a big fight when we were actually just being brother and sister. It scared me. I know how it feels to be so scared. I'm sorry. Can you forgive me?

Henry: Maybe.

Dad: Maybe?

It felt as if David was really trying to make a better repair and was a little surprised that Henry was unable to wholeheartedly accept it. I thought perhaps this could be an opening into talking about my concern that David was hard to read emotionally, and that others might feel he was angry when he had a "still-face." I knew this might be Level 3 Information, but I thought I would take a chance and share it since the session had gone so well.

Dale: You know I wonder if there isn't a little piece of information that might be helpful here, David. I don't see you at home when you get angry, so I don't really know what that looks like. I see you here and it's hard to know what you're feeling inside.

Dad: I don't know, or you don't know?

Dale: Maybe both. It's difficult to read you. There are people that are easy to read. It's hard to read you. Henry, is it hard for you to know what your Dad is thinking or feeling?

Henry: Yeah

Dale: I wonder if there isn't some way in which you might be more expressive and show what you're feeling. That might be helpful for those around you.

Dad: I could wear a mood ring.

Dale: That's a good idea. *(Matching his dry humor.)* Or use facial expressions.

Mom: Yeah, or you could try that. The clues are very hard to read. It's almost a temperature in the air you have to learn to take. I'm just figuring it out after 13 years of marriage.

Because of where we were in the session and how much hard work the family had done, I decided to join the humor defense.

Dale: So maybe I should give you all family homework to find your father a mood ring.

Mom: Yeah.

Dad: Let's go back to the wedding pictures.

Mom: Oh yeah, the joke is…

Dad: And it's not that much of a joke, it's actually a reality that she constantly, every time we look at our pictures from our wedding.

She's like, "Why wasn't your family smiling?" And, like they're all smiling, my siblings and parents.

Dale: It sounds like you have some pride in being mysterious, hard to read. We can talk more about this at another point. It's getting late. I think it might be helpful to summarize the session and then talk about what happens next. What was this session like for you? (*Everyone was quiet or hesitant to say.*)

Dale: We talked about a lot of different things that seem really important.

Mom: Yes, the incident with David and Henry that happened a long time ago. I was surprised that David thought I would judge him. (*Because Barbara commented on her husband first, I wanted to make sure that Henry wasn't forgotten.*)

Dale: And I imagine, Henry, how important it was for you to hear your dad apologize.

Henry: Yeah.

Dale: I think it's so important to know when we're angry and the effect on others.

Dad: Yeah, that was really hard to talk about, but important.

Dale: Well, Henry you also got to hear about how your mom was raised and how scary it was in her family. What was that like for you?

Henry: Sad.

Dale: Yeah. (*I decided to proceed with the summary rather than collaboratively engaging the family because I could sense how tired they were.*) We also talked about how hard it is to know what your dad is feeling or thinking because he doesn't show a lot of facial expression. You also got to see how well you all can work together and share feelings and stories. I just want to say how impressed I am with each of you and what we did here today. It takes a lot of courage and trust. So, I really appreciate it. What happens next is that I try and pull the whole assessment together and answer the questions you each had. Once I do that, I will schedule a two-hour session with both of you (*looking at parents*) to go over the results and answer your questions. Then, I'll schedule a time to talk with you, Henry, about what we did together and to answer your question. You remember what your question was?

Henry: Yeah.

Dale: Your parents will probably be with us at that time. Any questions?

Mom: I don't think so. Lots to take in.

Reflections

When the family left the session, I was struck with how much had happened and how much I learned. I noticed that I was very tired and yet energized. My first thought was about the underlying anger in the family and how we were able to access it in the session. I was surprised by Henry's straight forward recounting of a traumatic interaction with his father, and I realized that this was spurred by David's being so open about a time he had lost control of his anger. It felt so positive that both were able to trust in the process and share these things.

While family members did not get overtly angry with each other, past anger was certainly felt in the room in an intense way when Henry recounted the incident. I also got to see firsthand how the parents protected themselves. Barbara could be dismissive, and David might intellectualize and deny or not be aware of his feelings. I thought an additional positive part of the session was when Barbara could explain a bit about her upbringing and why she might be more dismissive of the negative interactions that happened in this family. Henry also got to see how his mother was genuinely affected by her family of origin. We had the beginnings of a positive repair between David and Henry. I could see some of the marital problems that could be worked on in support of Henry's treatment, although I was aware that was not necessarily part of our initial contract. I was also pleased that we could discuss that David's lack of emotional expression was difficult for family members to read. I thought that family therapy would be essential in addressing Henry's recovery.

I felt that the case conceptualization really assisted me in planning the session and was validated by the experience of the FIS. I also knew I would revise my tentative answers to a couple of Assessment Questions given the new information. While I had thought about Henry as suffering from little "t" traumas, I felt the incident he brought up was, for Henry, a big "T" trauma, and that this perspective would be almost level 3 Information for the parents during the Summary/Discussion Session. I also saw how essential it was not to shame David while discussing this event, if he were going to continue the repair that Henry might still need. All in all, this session exceeded my expectations. I was pleased and looked forward to using what I learned from the FIS to enhance the Summary/Discussion Session and the fable I would be writing for Henry.

References

American Psychological Association (2017). *Ethical principles of psychologists and code of conduct, including 2010 and 2016 amendments.* Downloaded from *apa.org* June 1, 2021.

Aschieri, F., Fantini, F., & Bertrando, P. (2012). Therapeutic Assessment with children in family therapy. *Australian and New Zealand Journal of Family Therapy*, 33(04), 285–298.

Burns R. C. & Kaufman S. H. (1972). *Actions, styles, and symbols in Kinetic Family Drawings (KFD).* New York: Brunner/ Mazel.

Canino, I. A., & Inclan, J. E. (2001). Culture and family therapy. *Child and Adolescent Psychiatric Clinics*, 10(3), 601–612.

Chudzik, L., Frackowiak, M., & Finn, S. E. (2019). Évaluation Thérapeutique et dépression de l'enfant: faire du bilan psychologique une intervention familiale brève [Therapeutic Assessment and child depression: Using psychological assessment as a brief family intervention]. *Bulletin de Psychologie, 559*(1), 19–27.

Constantine, L. (1978). Family sculpture and relationship mapping techniques. *Journal of Marital and Family Therapy, 4*(2), 13–23.

Fantini, F., Aschieri, F., & Bertrando, P. (2013). "Is our daughter crazy or bad?": A case study of Therapeutic Assessment with children. *Contemporary Family Therapy, 35*(4), 731–744.

Finn, S. E. (2007). *In our clients' shoes: Theory and techniques of Therapeutic Assessment.* Mawah, NJ: Erlbaum.

Finn, S. E., & Chudzik, L. (2013). L'Evaluation Thérapeutique pour enfant?: Théorie, procédures et illustration [Therapeutic Assessment with children: Theory, techniques, and case example]. *Neuropsychiatrie de l'Enfance et de l'Adolescence, 61*(3), 166–175.

Fisher, L. (1982). Transactional theories but individual assessment: A frequent discrepancy in family research. *Family Process, 21*, 313–330.

Fosha, D. (2000). *The transforming power of affect: A model for accelerated change.* New York, NY: Basic Books.

Guerrero, B., Lipkind, J., & Rosenberg, A. (2011). Why did she put nail polish in my drink? Applying the Therapeutic Assessment model with an African American foster child in a community mental health setting. *Journal of Personality Assessment, 93*(1), 7–15.

Hamilton, A. M., Fowler, J. L., Hersh, B., Austin, C. A., Finn, S. E., Tharinger, D. J., … Arora, P. (2009). "Why won't my parents help me?": Therapeutic Assessment of a child and her family. *Journal of Personality Assessment, 91*(2), 108–120.

Handler, L. (1997). He says, she says, they say: The consensus Rorschach. In J. R. Meloy, M. W. Acklin, C. B. Gacono, J. F. Murray, & C. A. Peterson (Eds.), *Contemporary Rorschach interpretation* (pp. 499–533). Mahwah, NJ: Erlbaum.

Haydel, M. E., Mercer, B. L., & Rosenblatt, E. (2011). Training assessors in Therapeutic Assessment. *Journal of Personality Assessment, 93*(1), 16–22.

McGoldrich. M. (Ed.) (1998). *Re-envisioning family therapy: Race, culture, and gender in clinical practice.* New York: Guilford.

Murray, H. A. (1943). *Thematic Apperception Test manual.* Cambridge, MA: Harvard University Press.

Pagano, C. J., Blattner, M. C. C., & Kaplan-Levy, S. (2019). Therapeutic Assessment with child inpatients. *Journal of Personality Assessment, 101*(5), 556–566.

Papp, P. (1983). *The process of change.* New York: Guilford.

Roberts, G. E., & Gruber, C. (2005). *Roberts-2 manual.* Los Angeles: Western Psychological Services.

Smith, J. D., Nicholas, C. R. N., Handler, L., & Nash, M. R. (2011). Examining the clinical effectiveness of a family intervention session in Therapeutic Assessment: A single-case experiment. *Journal of Personality Assessment, 93*, 149–158.

Smith, J. D., Finn, S. E., Swain, N. F., & Handler, L. (2010). Therapeutic Assessment of families in healthcare settings: A case presentation of the model's application. *Families, Systems, & Health, 28*(4), 369–386.

Smith, J. D., Wolf, N. J., Handler, L., & Nash, M. R. (2009). Testing the effectiveness of family Therapeutic Assessment: A case study using a time-series design. *Journal of Personality Assessment, 91*(6), 518–536.

Sotile, W. M., Henry, S. E., & Sotile, M. O. (1988). *Family Apperception Test: Manual.* Charlotte, NC: Feedback Services.

Tharinger, D. J., Finn, S. E., Austin, C., Gentry, L., Bailey, E., Parton, V., & Fisher, M. (2008). Family sessions in psychological assessment with children: Goals, techniques, and clinical utility. *Journal of Personality Assessment, 90*, 547–558.

Tharinger, D. J., Finn, S. E., Wilkinson, A. D., & Schaber, P. M. (2007). Therapeutic Assessment with a child as a family intervention: A clinical and research case study. *Psychology in the Schools, 44*(3), 293–309.

Tharinger, D. J., Fisher, M., & Gerber, B. (2012). Therapeutic assessment with a 10-year-old boy and his parents: The pain under the disrespect. In S. E. Finn, C. T. Fischer, & L. Handler (Eds.), *Collaborative/Therapeutic Assessment: A casebook and guide* (pp. 311–333). New York: Wiley.

Tharinger, D. J., Matson, M., & Christopher, G. (2011). Play, creative expression, and playfulness in Therapeutic Assessment with children. In S. W. Russ & L. N. Niec (Eds.), *Play in clinical practice: Evidence-based approaches* (pp. 109–145). New York: Guilford.

Wilkinson-Smith, A. (2019). Uncharted waters: A case study of Therapeutic Assessment with a child using tele-health. *The TA Connection, 8*, 6–10.

7 Phase IV: Summary/Discussion Session with Parents

At this point we have completed the Family Intervention Session (FIS) and considered modifications to our initial case conceptualization and answers to the Assessment Questions. We have also arrived at our best sense of what Levels of Information the parents can absorb. We are now ready to proceed to Phase IV and plan and conduct the Summary/Discussion Session(s) with the parents. Typically, we plan one session, but sometimes a second or even third session is needed for the parents to digest the findings and the suggestions at a supported pace that works for them. Divorced parents may require separate sessions, although in cases where the co-parenting is working well, a combined session may be workable and is preferred.

We have been working toward the Summary/Discussion session from the start of the TA-C. In cases where parents have been actively involved and have already made shifts that led to a new family narrative, much of what is discussed in Summary/Discussion Sessions is not new. Rather, the material considered is a consolidation of the major findings and provides an opportunity to collaborate on answers to the Assessment Questions. In these cases, suggestions for next steps are also not likely to be a surprise, as they flow from the new narrative and usually have been discussed along the way. In contrast, if parents have been less engaged and less moved or able to make shifts toward a systemic perspective and new narrative, we tread more lightly and cautiously in response to what they are ready for and can take in. That is reflected in how we present and discuss the findings, our answers, and our suggestions.

Although when we first developed TA-C we used the term "feedback" sessions for these meetings, we came to believe that this term implied that an "expert" provided one-way unilateral conclusions about assessment findings and therefore failed to reflect the collaborative, interactive, bi-directional nature of TA-C. Thus, we adopted the term "Summary/Discussion" to capture what we do. We invite parents to corroborate/disagree with/modify test findings and we ask them how the test findings relate to everyday life in the family.

This chapter is organized into three parts. In the first we discuss how to plan the Summary/Discussion Session and present an outline we have found helpful for organizing our thoughts both before and during these sessions. In the second section, we give guidelines for what to do once you are in the

DOI: 10.4324/9781003000174-7

room with the parents (or together on an online platform). Of course, no one can foresee all that can happen once the session begins, but we share ideas to keep in mind. We conclude the chapter by returning to Henry's case to learn about the process of the Summary/Discussion Session with his parents.

Preparing for the Summary/Discussion Session With the Parents

In general, the task of preparing for the Summary/Discussion Session involves "getting into the shoes" of the parents and then asking ourselves, "If I were these parents, what would be the best way to talk to me about the assessment findings?" We use all our previous interactions and discussions with the parents, as well as their own test results (if they agreed to be tested), to enhance our empathy and get in their shoes. We imagine what language would reach us best if we were these parents, what insights we have already had, and what assessment findings are likely to be most difficult to hear. TA-C attempts to hold all these considerations in mind.

Now let us turn to specific steps that will help you prepare.

Consider What Information Is Level 1, 2, or 3

The Levels of Information schema we first introduced in Chapter 2 is extremely important in planning a successful Summary/Discussion Session. Schroeder et al. (1993) demonstrated that when assessment feedback is ordered with Level 1 Information first, followed by Level 2 Information, and concluding with Level 3 Information, that recipients thought about the feedback more deeply and reported that it had more impact on their lives and future decisions. At this point in a TA-C we have a host of ways to estimate what information parents are most likely to accept and take in: their reactions to viewing their child's testing and to discussing test results as the assessment proceeded, their responses to discussing their own testing (if they did any), and their reactions to the FIS. When planning the Summary/Discussion Session we order the information we will present according to our best sense of what is Level 1, 2, and 3 at that moment in time, knowing that parents sometimes surprise us and that we will pay close attention during the session and be ready to adjust our plan if need be.

Consider How to Present Results When Level 1 and 2 Information for One Parent Is Not Level 1 or 2 for Another

This most often happens when one of the parents has not been able to participate in the assessment process and thus hasn't benefited from small step-by-step narrative shifting. But it can also happen when one parent is more open and able to shift an initial narrative than is the other parent. In families like these, we might plan to organize the outline carefully moving from Level 1 to 2 and ask the parent who is "further along" to share her or his thoughts on the subject, focusing on how her or his point of view changed during the assessment process, providing specific examples of what during the assessment helped them change, and offering a tentative new narrative. In general, we believe it is better to balance the Summary/Discussion and aim to be in attunement with the parent who is less receptive than to overwhelm and go too far, too fast, and risk that parent not being able to integrate the new findings.

Consider the Tone of the Session

Early in our planning we consider the tone we wish to use in presenting the assessment findings and how the family constellation or prototype might inform us. We think about the tone of the Summary/Discussion Session as a balancing act between empathy and confrontation. In other words, it's a dance between validating and supporting parents' current narratives and firmness while at the same time presenting new, conflicting findings with their current viewpoint. Tone influences how direct we are, what types of words and examples we choose, and how hard we work to avoid overwhelming parents or possibly eliciting shame. Much of how we balance the tone is informed by the family's constellation/prototype, presented in Chapter 2. Let's consider how the family prototypes inform our planning for the tone of the session.

Scapegoated Child

Start with empathy for the parents by validating their struggles and efforts to make changes. Join with them about your own struggles with the child, if they occurred. Then move on, in a non-shaming way, to offer a summary of what we know underlies the child's problematic behavior. Hold firm when parents attempt to explain the behavior of the child as being "bad," by referring to the data and showing the evidence that there is a lot going on emotionally with the child, which shows up as "bad behavior" such as oppositionality, rule breaking, lying, etc., or any other example of problematic behavior they offered in their reports about the child. Be ready to support the parents' emotional reactions, typically grief and shame, if they adopt the new story; for example, that their child is sad, not bad.

Solomon's Child

Start by validating each parent's view of the child, focusing on the part of their viewpoint supported by the data. Usually it involves saying something like: "As we would expect and because you both very much care about your daughter, you are both right and you are both a little bit wrong in how you came to understand what's going on with her and what she needs. You each hold a very important and accurate perspective about Lexi, but in trying to do so, you tend to go too far from the other's viewpoint and don't see the value in it. We need to bring the perspectives toward the middle and have a more shared understanding of your daughter." The task for the assessor with the Solomon Child family presentation is to stay balanced and equally supportive and confronting of each parent. It really is as if, one by one, the assessor finds truth on each side of the polarization and presents it going back and forth, validating each parent and asking the other parent to see the opposite perspective. The goal is to bring the parents toward the middle to have one shared perspective. When done well, often at the end of the session, both parents can feel respected and validated, while also gently pushed to see the truth in what the other parent is seeing and experiencing.

Orphan Child

Let's remember that typically these families show up for an assessment usually because someone else directed them to do so. Quite often, these parents don't see many problems or vulnerabilities in their children and instead see them as strong and independent. As usual, we start by validating the parents and outlining all of the ways in which we saw the strengths and abilities of their child during the assessment. Then, equally strongly, we move toward outlining the needs and vulnerabilities of a child—often not seen by the parents—or, when seen, ignored or dismissed as something that the child needs to grow out of or fix on her or his own. Without being too confrontational or un-empathic, the tone here is one of concern for the child presented in a way that allows the parents to also become concerned. Quite often in these cases, we find ourselves saying something along the lines of: "While her coping skills are working adequately right now, the testing results suggest that she might be getting to a point when they might not work as well anymore. What we know from research on kids with underlying, untreated depression is that it can get much worse in their teenage years, and it can also bring on other mental health problems." In some more severe cases of an Orphan Child family constellation, the tone of the discussion session is more concerning and firmer than validating or empathic, but never unkind. In short, sometimes with these heartbreaking cases, we find ourselves kindly, but firmly "shaking up" the parents a little, to help the child be seen more accurately and effectively by the adults in their life.

Sick Child

Let's keep in mind that sometimes in this family constellation there is a true medical or disability concern. If this is the case, then beginning with empathy for both the parents and the child regarding the concern is a good place to start, followed by validating how important it is to understand its impact on the child's life. Talking about how the assessment showed such a direct impact is a good next step, followed by sharing with the parents where the assessment also showed areas of strength, ability, and independence. In the family with the Sick Child presentation, the child's strengths are often overshadowed by the concerns that, just like in the other family constellations, lead to misinterpretation of the child. The tone here is to balance the empathy for the disability or illness with the appreciation of the child's re-silience and ability. In children where there is no diagnosable illness or disability, parents may nonetheless view their child as "weak" or "fragile." Presenting the accurate picture of the child as capable and resilient is very important and the tone is one of empowering the child rather than seeing them as frail and incapable. In families where there is a high level of dis-tortion in the parents' view of the child (e.g., a child who is obviously calling for containment but parents are unable to set limits) we sometimes emphasize that the child is "scared" and needing a "firmer hand" to feel safe.

Write Out Your Plan as a Rich Outline or Script

It might be tempting to show up for the Summary/Discussion Session with findings organized mentally, but we strongly recommend that assessors write down what they want to say to parents and review the flow and organization of the findings beforehand. We have found this process to be very useful for many reasons, most important of all to articulate the findings about the child and the family in friendly, accurate, understandable, and precise terms. In addition, writing the outline or script allows assessors to clarify their understanding of the assessment results and find words, metaphors, and examples to share the information with parents in a meaningful and attuned way. In TA-C we write the outlines or scripts as we plan to speak, that is, in second person "you," as if we are directly addressing the parents. Some of us write out complete sentences or bulleted points, while others of us do better with detailed notes. In either case, as mentioned earlier, the work that goes into this preparation (with re-visions based on parents' reactions and input) will pay off in drafting the feedback letter to the parents (Chapter 9). Box 7.1 shows an outline that we have found useful in preparing for the parent Summary/Discussion Session. Sections I-III of the outline are fairly self-explanatory, so we now jump to Section IV which involves crucial planning decisions.

Choose an Organizational Approach

As shown in point IV of Box 7.1, we have developed three organizational options to choose from when presenting assessment results to parents. When preparing for the Summary/Discussion session, we choose one of these op-tions for the particular parents we are holding in mind, and apply it when we draft our outline. There are two main factors we consider: a) how well the parents' Assessment Questions map onto the assessment results; and b) how discrepant the findings are across tests. Let us explain further.

Option A: (Answering the Assessment Questions Directly)

The first option is to organize the session around the Assessment Questions, ordering the questions based on the Level 1, 2, 3 approach. We use this

Box 7.1   Outline for Summary/Discussion Session(s) With Parent(s)

I Check in
Inquire how the parents feel coming in that day, about any significant events that have happened since the last session, about reactions to the previous family session, and discuss any worries/concerns.

II Review Plan
Remind the parents of the purpose of the session, explain how the session will be organized, and ask for input, examples, and disagreements as you go along. Remind the parents that you will sending a summary letter that captures the session and give a time frame when this will arrive. Possibly review the Assessment Questions that guided the assessment (in the order you will address them in the session).

III Share Appreciations
If appropriate, thank the parents for participating in the assessment and acknowledge the energy, financial commitment, and time involved. Make it clear that you know the parents took a vulnerable risk by bringing their child to you and letting you know the family situation. Make it clear that you understand why there have been puzzles about handling the child, and join the parents by expressing any confusion, challenge, or frustration *you* experienced. Balance these statements by expressing liking for the child (if authentic).

IV Review Assessment Results
There are three ways to organize this section:

Option A. Go directly to the parent's Assessment Questions, reviewing tests and observations as you proceed along.

Option B. Give an-depth review of the various tests, then address the parent's Assessment Questions.

Option C. Give a brief summary of the major findings, then address the parent's Assessment Questions.

Option A is the preferred method if the parents' questions map easily onto the major test findings. If the questions don't easily lead to the main points you wish to review, use either Option B or Option C.

V Review Suggestions for Next Steps

    Some suggestions may already have been addressed in answering the Assessment Questions, but it's useful to collect them and repeat them here.

VI Metaprocess: Ask for Questions, Reactions, Feedback

    Review the plan for giving feedback to the child and confirm upcoming session with the child and parents.

VII Close

    Outline guidelines for future contacts (e.g., possibly schedule a Follow-up Session or make it clear that you are willing to be contacted in the future.)

    Thank the parents again for participating.

    Share something you learned or some way you were touched by the child, parents, or family.

---

option when the test results map onto the Assessment Questions well and the tests hang together fairly well. As discussed above, the question(s) where our answer contains primarily Level 1 Information would be addressed first. Questions that are answered with Level 2 Information would be next, etc. We also consider whether to keep each question separate or to group questions based on similarities. The main goal here is to use the Assessment Questions to guide the organization and the discussion. Depending on the needs of the parents we might also show detailed graphs and point to specific findings to support our answers.

For example, imagine parents seeking a comprehensive TA-C at the advice of their pediatrician to find out if their 5-year-old son meets the diagnostic criteria for an Autism Spectrum Disorder (ASD). In the initial session, the parents posed the following Assessment Questions: 1) Does Chris have autism? 2) If he does have autism, how severe is it?, 3) Why does Chris get so upset if we have to change our family schedule, and how should we handle that?, and 4) Will Chris be able to function as an independent adult? In the assessment process the parents were present in each session, asked many questions afterwards, and talked about their own observations that might fit with the ASD diagnosis. The assessor also showed scores of various tests along the way, and the test results both hung together well and also mapped well onto the parents' Assessment Questions. Thus, the assessor chose Option A in organizing the results and prepared the outline shown in Table 7.1.

As you can see, the assessor reorganized the Assessment Questions from their original order to put more difficult information related to the parents' anxiety later, but otherwise planned to take each question and address it

Table 7.1 Outline for Summary/Discussion Session With Chris's Parents: Option A

I. Check in

How are you today? How were you after our last session?

How are you feeling about today's session?

Is there anything important that has happened since we last met?

II. Review Plan

Our goal for today is to answer your Assessment Questions by reviewing the test results together. You have seen almost all of these before.

Reminder: tests are not perfect, so please feel free to agree, disagree, or ask questions about the results. I need your help to make the best sense of the tests. Also, don't worry about remembering everything as I will send a written summary within two weeks, and we'll meet for a Follow-up Session after that. Any questions or concerns?

III. Appreciations

Before getting to the results, I want to thank you again for your active collaboration during the assessment process. Your observations and questions were extremely useful, and I could not have understood the assessment results fully without your input. I also have a lot of empathy for why you were puzzled by Chris. As we discovered, he is a complex child dealing with multiple challenges. But he also has so many strengths, including wonderful parents, and is so lovable.

IV. Review of Assessment Results

Does Chris have autism? If so, how severe is it?

As we already talked about, Chris does have an Autism Spectrum Disorder. We did a couple of different measures that indicated he meets the criteria for autism. The ADOS is a widely recognized screening tool. That was the one where you observed me interacting and playing with Chris. It indicated that he has difficulty using gestures or language to request needed items, has limited eye contact, enjoys lining toys up in a specific pattern, and has trouble knowing how to order pictures to tell a story that makes sense.

You both completed the SRS, the Social Responsiveness Scale, that indicated that he wasn't particularly socially motivated and didn't seem to understand social communication. In addition he has a number of repetitive motor patterns that he does frequently (e,g., hand flapping, juming on tip toes). I think it's important to know and remember that he falls into the highest functioning category of autism, indicating that he does not have an intelletual impairment and is at Level 1. That means he requires support but does not need substantial report.

Will Chris be able to function as an independent adult?

Most people with high level autism are able to live independently, perhaps with some support. Some of the interventions we have already discussed are likely to help with Chris getting to this point. I'll review these again in a few minutes.

For Chris to function more independently he will also need help with his anxiety. Some of that is due to his autism but I think it comes from more than that and is related to many moves you've had to make as a family due to Dad's job.

Anxiety findings: Parent ratings on BASC

Chris's Individualized Sentence Completions

Chris's Family Drawing

Chris's score on Manifest Anxiety Scale

Why does Chris get so upset if we have to change our family schedule, and how should we handle that?

Difficulties like this are typical of ASD (explain more).

(Continued)

Table 7.1 (Continued)

The family moves have been difficult for Chris and he needs help recovering
from them.

As we saw when we reviewed your MMPI-3 results, both of you have some anxiety as
well, and when Chris gets upset it can make both of you anxious and you tend to
get a bit rigid and insist on your way. I think you need more support about how hard
it is to have a kid with ASD and this will help you remain more calm and empathic
to Chris when he gets upset. How does that sound to you?

V. Suggestions for Next Steps

I think you both can benefit from more support and learning more about high
functioning autism. There are a number of books that I can recommend. I also
think joining a parent support group can be very helpful.

It is natural to grieve the loss of not having a "typically developing" child. I would
hope you can get support for yourselves to manage this grief process.

Right now, Chris' behaviors seem to be the most difficult for you to negotiate and can
cause difficulty in the whole family. I would recommend getting in touch with a
behavior specialist who can help you negotiate transitions in a better way. There
are a number of programs that can address this.

Chris is at a great age for being involved in a social skills training/interaction group. I
would suggest beginning this early to encourage prosocial skills.

I will put specific names of books and resources in the letter you will receive.

VI. Questions? Comments? Reactions?

VII. Closing

As we discussed, I would like to meet with you and Chris to give him a fable. Can we
schedule that? Can I email you the fable later this week and then call to get your
comments/suggestions/reactions? As you know, I'll send the report and a letter
answering your questions and then we'll have a Follow-up Session.

How would you like to share the results with Chris's pediatrician? Shall I contact him,
or would you like to? Or do you want to wait until after the report is done?

Thank you again for your trust and openness during the assessment. I really related to how
hard it is to stay flexible when we are anxious; I struggle with that too and our
discussions helped me find more compassion for myself and for parents of ASD children.

I'll see you when we meet for the session with Chris. Do let me know if any questions
arise before then.

---

using various tests and procedures used in the TA-C. Of course, as we will
discuss later, this outline is only a plan for how to conduct the session, and
the assessor needs to be ready to change the order of information if it seems
best during the actual meeting with the parents.

*Option B: (Start With Test-by-Test Findings, Then Answer the
Assessment Questions)*

This is one of the two options we use when test data do not directly map onto
the Assessment Questions. When making a decision between using Option B
or Option C it is best to ask oneself: "How many discrepancies do we see
between the various measures administered?" For example, do self-report
measures present an entirely different picture of the child than the
performance-based measures? Is the data "confusing" when you first look at it?

Is there significant depression on the Rorschach, but nothing even close is seen on the BASC and Child Behavior Checklist? This scenario would be well served by Option B. With this organizational strategy, the assessor presents the results test-by-test, explaining how each measure works and how it taps into a different aspect of the child's functioning. By addressing the discrepancies and explaining them clearly in terms of the data, the assessor helps parents develop and integrate a comprehensive and accurate new narrative. This strategy can be very useful in helping parents understand their child in a new way, often "organically" offering the answers to their Assessment Questions. It is not unusual in this approach to see parents begin to answer their own questions as they hear the assessor explain the various tests and how the test data might seem contradictory. Also, the assessor uses the contradictions between the tests to help explain how the parents might have been confused by the child.

As an example, let's consider the Summary/Discussion Session outline for the parents of Jaime, a 12-year-old boy referred because of aggressive behavior toward his 8-year-old brother, Sean. The parents' main Assessment Questions were: 1) Why has Jaime started being so mean to his brother Sean? 2) Is there something going on that we don't know about, like bullying, that leads Jaime to explode so much? 3) Why can't Jaime tell us what is going on with him when we ask? and 4) What's the best way to handle Jaime's anger? Table 7.2 shows the outline for Section IV of the Summary/Discussion Session. We also illustrate how one would alter Section II from the outline shown for Option A.

As you can see, in this instance the test results did not map well onto the Assessment Questions, so the assessor chose to present the results test-by-test, using tables, scores, and graphs. Also, the test results might seem to contradict themselves, so for each test the assessor planned to explain what the test assessed and how to understand the results. In this approach, there is a feeling of plotting out a mystery novel that unfolds chapter by chapter. But again, the assessor organized the sequence of the test results according to Levels 1, 2, and 3. Once all the tests were addressed, the assessor planned to shift to the Assessment Questions and so drafted possible answers to them.

Option C: (Start With Major Findings, Then Answer the Assessment Questions)

When the test results seem to fit well together but don't map well on to the Assessment Questions, we turn to Option C. We first talk with the parents about the major findings across the measures and then proceed to their Assessment Questions.

Let us turn to a case example using Option C. Imagine a situation where we have an outwardly resourceful, cheerful child struggling at school, with underlying depression and low self-esteem, whose parents are unaware of the level of distress she might be feeling. They have been actively involved in the assessment process and have demonstrated openness and insight about their

Table 7.2 Partial Outline for Summary/Discussion Session With Jaime's Parents: Option B

II. Review Plan

Our goal for today is to go through each of the major tests we used and review the findings. You have already seen most of these before. Then we'll put the test results together and see if we can answer your Assessment Questions.

Reminder: tests are not perfect....

IV. Review of Assessment Results

Let's start with how you see Jamie: [*Show BASC-3 graphs and teach parents how to read them*]

BASC-3 Parent Ratings

- Both of you rated Jaime very similarly; you are both on the same page
- Lots of strengths: social skills, leadership, daily living skills
- Not surprisingly, both rated him high on Aggression and Acting Out Behaviors
- Neither high on Emotional Distress; very low scores on Anxiety and Depression

Now let's see how Jaime sees himself [*Show graphs*]

BASC-3 Self-report

- Very low on most problem scales; "I am doing just fine, thank you!"
- Slight elevation on Attitude to School suggests some negative feelings about school; you said he is no longer at the top of his class, no?
- Slight elevation on Sense of Inadequacy; perhaps school is affecting his confidence?

R-PAS

The Rorschach is a very different test. It "lifts the lid" on our coping skills and reveals things we can't talk about or may not be fully aware of. We talked about this when you watched the Rorschach and the Extended Inquiry. Now I can show you the scoring where Jaime's results are compared to other kids his age. [*Show R-PAS graphs and teach how to read*]

- These scores [Sy, MC, MC-PPD] show psychological strengths and as you can see, Jaime has good strengths (explain)
- Also, consistent with your BASC ratings, Rorschach suggests Jaime is dealing with a lot of angry feelings [AG, AGC]
- What Rorschach shows that is different is a lot of emotional distress [YTVC'] and signs that Jaime is stressed, and anxious, and feeling badly about himself [m, Y, V]
- I think these emotions come out mainly when he is feeling inadequate and not in control; remember how he told me that he really hated the Rorschach because he wasn't sure whether his responses were good enough?

Answers to Your Assessment Questions

Why has Jaime started being so mean to his brother, Sean?

- My best guess is that Jaime doesn't have a general anger problem. Rather he is likely to explode and get angry when he is feeling insecure and inadequate, and that Sean is an easy target.
- He doesn't see himself as bullying Sean. Remember he said that fighting is "just what brothers do"?

(Continued)

Table 7.2 (Continued)

Why can't Jaime tell us what is going on with him when we ask?

- Jaime is behind in general in his ability to know and talk about his emotions
- Also he seems particularly ashamed of feelings of weakness, self-doubt, insecurity so is even less likely to talk to you about those feelings; I wonder if he fears he would be disappointing you?
- Remember, each of your MMPI-3 results showed that each of you can put on a strong, sturdy front and have trouble showing your vulnerability

Is there something going on that we don't know about, like bullying, that leads Jamie to explode so much?

- I don't think Jaime is being bullied; he told me that he and his basketball friends protect each other from any bullying
- Best guess is he is feeling increased pressure academically, is no longer at top of his class, no longer best basketball player on team, and is feeling insecure
- Not able to talk about these feelings, and is ashamed of feeling weak, so he covers it up with bravado and anger; Sean is an easy target
- Have you had any conflict between the two of you about how to handle Jaime? Research shows conflict between siblings often mirrors conflict between parents...

What's the best way to handle Jaime's anger?

- He needs help knowing how to talk about feelings in general, and especially about feelings of insecurity, self-doubt, weakness
- Let's talk about ways you can work on this at home
- Would you also be open to some family therapy? I thought you all did so well in our family session...
- I really think you'll all be able to address these issues and that Jaime and you will be better than ever. He has such psychological strengths, and you are such concerned and good parents...

---

child, but their main questions are focused on their daughter's academic goals. Parents' questions might be:

- *Can Susie handle going to an advanced middle school and what kind of tutoring would work best for her?*
- *Should she stop some of her activities now that her grades are suffering?*
- *What's causing her mood swings?*
- *Is this pre-teen stuff or should we be worried about her?*

Table 7.3 shows how Section IV of the draft outline might look in this scenario. Again, we also illustrate the change to the beginning of Section II.

Typically, by identifying four to six major findings (highlighted in **bold** in the Table) and describing them using examples that arose during the assessment (e.g., the child saying, "I don't like to look weak.") or describing the way a child might be experiencing themselves in the world based on the test results (e.g., "She might be feeling worn out and tired, and bad about

Table 7.3 Partial Outline for Summary/Discussion Session With Susie's Parents: Option C

II. Review Plan

Our goal for today is to review the major findings of the assessment and show you where these come from in the tests. Then we'll put all this together and see if we can answer your Assessment Questions.

Reminder: tests are not perfect…

IV. Review of Assessment Results

Major Assessment Findings

1 **Susie has many coping strengths**. She comes off as really strong. Therefore, it can be puzzling to understand why she is struggling at school, but the testing shows us that there is more going on with Susie than first meets the eye.

2 **Susie is a bright girl**, who scored across most domains in the high average or superior range on the cognitive testing. This is consistent with her past school performance and how everyone perceives her. She is especially talented in expressing herself verbally as she is articulate, presents with extensive vocabulary, and has the capacities to think in complex ways.

3 **Susie struggles with sustaining her attention** and therefore isn't able to learn and retain as much information as we would like her to. She seems to be inconsistent in her ability to focus, at times being able to do it pretty well, while at other times struggling with it significantly.

4 **Susie's attention is affected by her emotions**. Susie seems to get distracted especially when she becomes aware that she is not doing something as quickly or as perfectly as she would like. She can become quite frustrated with herself, but she still wants to show that she is ok and that everything is fine. Remember her saying, "I don't like to look weak"? She tends to cover up her frustrations by trying even harder to do well.

5 **Susie is feeling badly about herself** and discouraged because her learning has become more effortful in the last year and her grades have declined. She is starting to feel powerless and hopeless about improving her grades. She does not like to be perceived as "weak," so she tends to put a smile on her face and keep trying, rather than ask for help. All of these efforts are wearing her out, making her feel stressed, unhappy, and bad about herself. She might be feeling worn out, tired, and bad about herself.

6 Quite understandably, **you have tried to help Susie with her insecurity by praising her** for being bright and trying to encourage her to not feel insecure. Unfortunately, **this strategy seems to backfire** with Susie and makes her feel like she is disappointing you rather than making you proud.

Answers to Your Assessment Questions

Can Susie handle going to an advanced middle school and what kind of tutoring would work best for her?

• Intellectually could handle a high-level academic environment
• But several supports would need to be in place
• Best case scenario: acadmic accommodations for attentional difficulties + therapeutic support, whose goals are:
  • learn better coping skills
  • develops more accurate and compassionate self-image
• Family therapy could also help
  • Teach you emotion regulation techniques
  • Help finding balance in family's and Susie's life

(Continued)

Table 7.3 (Continued)

Should she stop some of her activities now that her grades are suffering?
- I know you don't want to take opportunities away from Susie
- But she also needs more balance in her life and fun activities outside of school
- I suggest you don't stop any activities until therapeutic supports are in place
- And Susie should have a say in what if any activities are dropped
  - Family therapy could be a place to discuss these things together

What's causing her mood swings?
I think about her mood swings as an external representation of what's going on inside of her. At times she feels competent and happy, other times she doubts herself, feels tense and worries about disappointing you. She is not yet able to express these more vulnerable feelings to you directly so instead she shows them with her moodiness and irritability. It can be confusing because she seems angry in those moments, instead of insecure. But as we have seen in this assessment, it's underlying insecurity about her academics and ability to handle increasingly more difficult school-work that's leading to her mood shifts. I predict that as she learns to express her worries more directly and feels understood and supported, her moodiness will decrease over time. Once she has more emotional tools in her toolbox, she will be able to express herself and cope with her feelings more effectively. Now, let's remember that she is a pre-teen girl, so I can't promise that all of her moodiness will go away.

Is this pre-teen stuff or should we be worried about her?
What an important question. As we discussed most of Suzie's current struggles are due to her underlying emotions and her limited ways of being able to express them. This all can be exacerbated by her being a pre-teen with much going on in her life, developmental changes, etc., but I think it's a smaller influence. Since we are intervening right now and you are so involved in trying to help Suzie, I feel optimistic about things getting better. Without any help, I would worry about her in the future, but since you are intervening while the problem is new, as I said I feel optimistic about her progress.

---

herself"), we can create a framework for the discussion of the parents' Assessment Questions. Again, notice that in this example, the assessor still paid attention to Levels of Information in ordering the central findings presented.

Use Parent-friendly Language, Not Psychological Jargon in Preparing Your Outline

At this point, it can be useful to review your outline again to see if it is written in parent-friendly language and whether it is free of psychological jargon or technical terms. While psychological terminology has become a way to communicate among professionals as a short cut, or a shared "in group" language, it is not useful when we communicate with parents. Translating psychological jargon into words and explanations that are understandable and relevant to non-clinicians is one of the talents we encourage TA assessors to practice. In TA-C we pride ourselves on being able to explain psychological concepts in terms that are immediately useful to parents, to encourage discussion rather than to "talk *at* parents," and to eliminate the power dynamic set up in a traditional clinical model of psychological assessment, where some of the power comes from communicating in psychological jargon, intellectualizing, or using clinical diagnosis to simplify a human being.

Seek Images/Metaphors to Capture or Illustrate Findings

After you have written your outline or script, we suggest you go back through responses to performance-based testing and see if there are images or language that metaphorically capture what you plan to say and consider using these images/metaphors instead of, or in addition to showing test scores or graphs. We have found that doing so can make data come alive and become more personal for parents. Depending on what performance-based tests were administered during the assessment, you can refer back to the Rorschach, Fantasy Animal Drawing Game, other drawings, or stories told to picture cards and remind parents of the child's responses or of what emerged during an Extended Inquiry. For example, in responding to Jaime's parents' Assessment Question about his anger outbursts, imagine not just going over test scores on his BASC-3 self-report and Rorschach scores that suggest he is feeling inadequate lately. You could also use the wording of one of his responses to Card V and plan to say: "He's been working hard, but learning is so effortful for him and now he is more aware that he is behind when compared to his peers. I wonder if at times he feels like a bird with a broken wing trying to fly [just like the image he saw when we did the Rorschach together]." We bracket this last phrase because you can explicitly refer to the Rorschach response, or you can simply adopt it and use the metaphor with the parents. The best strategy probably depends on how memorable the image is for the parents based on previous discussions.

Anticipate the Possibility That the Parents Will Become Overwhelmed or Defensive

Having parents' own test results (e.g., MMPI-3 profiles or parenting stress inventories) can be helpful in priming ourselves to recognize when and how parents might become overwhelmed, when they might take the discussion "just personally," or when their own shame or guilt might enter the picture. For example, we might realize: "Dad tends to become detail-oriented and ask a lot of questions when he is overwhelmed. Mom seems to get "fuzzy" and vague when she is struggling." Having thought about these tendencies beforehand can help us recognize when it is time to stop and process what parents are feeling or even end a session and schedule a second one. We also attempt to maintain a compassionate understanding of parents' individual emotional states, their relationship stress (e.g., marital, partnership, conflict post-divorce, etc.), and their emotional resources and parenting challenges (e.g., head of household, full time working mom who travels a lot and relies on a nanny for much of childcare, a father with a history of major depressive disorder, etc.). Keeping these factors in mind helps us plan what parents can handle in the Summary/Discussion Session.

Don't Plan to Share Everything

This leads to an important skill in preparing your outline: containment. It is very tempting to try to include everything you learned from the assessment. While we empathize with this pull, in TA-C we believe in staying attuned to parents' goals for the assessment as expressed in their Assessment Questions. This does not mean that we recommend not sharing important findings. It simply means assessors must strike a balance between answering the Assessment Questions, staying truthful to the data, and being succinct and not giving more information than parents can handle at this point in time. For example, although one of our goals in many TA-Cs is to present a systemic story to the family, some parents might not be ready for that despite our collaborative work during the assessment process. They may need to continue seeing the child as the major problem and to minimize their role in the child's difficulties. In such instances, we focus on weaving a systemic story where parents can be a part of the *solution*, even though they don't see themselves as part of the *problem*.

Another reason we don't share everything we learn from the assessment is simply to avoid overwhelming the system. Unless there is an ethical dilemma and sharing the information is mandated by ethics or the law, we strongly encourage you to carefully select the information shared and the depth of the explanations provided. One example of this is containing a discussion with parents regarding their child's cognitive or learning profiles. We don't spend an hour explaining the details about the WISC-V scales and results if we don't believe it is of benefit to the family or the child. Instead, we attempt to explain the tests results in an understandable, client-relevant manner; sometimes this might involve a briefer summary, while other times it might it might involve a detailed explanation. We use our professional judgment and experience of the family to guide us in deciding how much to tell and how detailed to be. In general, we encourage assessors to select the most important data points to address parents' Assessment Questions and to help them "walk in the shoes" of their child.

Yes, another reason we avoid discussing some of the assessment findings is because they are clearly Level 3 Information and would be likely to cause disintegration experiences or major defensive reactions in parents. One example is when we have gathered information during the assessment from, for example, an Adult Attachment Projective (AAP; George & West, 2001); an Attachment Doll Play Assessment (George & Solomon, 1990-2016); or the

Strange Situation Procedure (Ainsworth et al., 1978) and found that a child has insecure attachment. In our experience, it is rarely useful to tell parents that their child has an insecure attachment, unless this is already Level 1 or 2 Information or asked about in a parent Assessment Question. We find it is generally more helpful to describe the underlying "attachment map" a child has of close protective relationships rather than making pronouncements about attachment status. For example, instead of saying "Miguel has an insecure, avoidant attachment," we might say, "When Miguel is scared or upset, he more often tries to handle his feelings himself rather than turning to a trusted adult for support").

Finally, it can be comforting to remember that when there is a referring therapist and we can't share certain Level 3 Information with the parents, often that information can be shared with the therapist to help her or him work with the family, and possibly introduce it down the line when and if the parents are ready for it. Do be sure, however, to evaluate whether a referring therapist is able to contain information that has not yet been shared with the parents; some therapists find this task too difficult and will "leak" assessment findings at an inopportune time.

Attend to Your Own Anxiety

Finally, we advise you to be aware of any anxiety you might feel before the Summary/Discussion Session and get support. We find that assessors are less able to maintain an open, collaborative frame if they are very anxious. In addition, anxiety can get in the way of being able to read the parents' cues of overwhelm or confusion, and often results in the clinician either talking too much or too fast or going through the outline without pauses to ask for reactions or examples.

Seasoned, as well as new clinicians, can feel anxious about an upcoming Summary/Discussion Session for many reasons. Pulling all of the results together and presenting a "narrative" about a child and the family to the parents is a very daunting task, and it is easy to feel insecure about how one organized the findings and whether the parents will be able to follow. Also, we may be afraid that we need to share information that parents (both or one) will not agree with or be able to take in. Here it can be helpful to remember that the Summary/Discussion is a collaborative undertaking and we maintain a humble, yet knowledgeable stance. By telling parents that our tests are not perfect and that we don't believe test results are the ultimate Truth, we make room for parents to disagree with us or reject Level 3 Information if it is too difficult to assimilate. Of course, self-doubt, a human quality we all share, can lead to assessor anxiety. Talking to a trusted colleague, perhaps role playing a section of the Summary/Discussion, or anticipating what we would do in a challenging scenario can help us feel calmer and more confident when we go into the session.

Conducting the Summary/Discussion Session with the Parents

Having thought carefully and prepared your script, you are now ready to conduct the Summary/Discussion Session with the parents. Typically, we schedule a 90-minute or 2-hour session at first, knowing that we can schedule additional sessions if need be. Here are goals and principles to keep in mind that will help you when you are in the room with parents.

Be Present and Flexible

Paradoxically, now that you have carefully prepared your outline or script for the Summary/Discussion Session, we urge you to hold it "lightly" and to strive to be present and flexible when you are in the room with the parents. Many assessors find it tempting to read from their outlines, and doing so makes them less attentive to an interactive interpersonal process and leads them to miss important cues about how parents are doing. For example, we may have opted to answer the parents' Assessment Questions in a certain order, but early in the session a parent may suddenly ask about one of the later questions. Rather than saying, "I'll get to that later…" we address that question immediately if possible, showing the parent that we want to follow her or his line of thinking. Also, although we organized our outline according to our best sense of Levels of Information, "the best laid plans often go astray…" It often becomes apparent that something we thought was Level 2 Information is actually Level 3 for one or both parents, or that the parents are close to understanding Level 3 Information we had omitted or put later in our outline. In either scenario, it is important that the assessor adapt to the parents.

Below, you will see how Dale demonstrated flexibility in the Summary/Discussion Session with Henry's parents.

Make the Session a Dialogue, NOT a Monologue

By staying present and flexible, assessors can practice one of the most important principles of giving test feedback: making sure the feedback is delivered interactively rather than as an expert "lecture." Research has shown that interactive feedback is by far more impactful than feedback given without clients being able to ask questions or give examples (Hanson et al., 1997). As you saw in the recommended outline for Summary/Discussion sessions (see Table 7.1), we suggest that early in the session you explicitly invite parents to collaborate by asking questions, agreeing with assessment findings, or disagreeing. Then, as the session unfolds, we encourage you to stop frequently to check in: "I am going to pause here for a moment to see if what I described so far seems right to you or if you have any questions about it," or, "Before I go on to the next part, I wanted to see if you can think of some examples from your everyday life that fit with what I am describing."

This back and forth between the assessor and the parents allows for the relationship to be collaborative instead of one-up/one-down, and for parents to feel that they are valuable partners in helping to understand their children. Still, it can be hard to maintain this collaborative stance, as some parents seem to manifest a kind of "oracular transference" (Schafer, 1954), where they long to be told "the Truth" about their child. Such parents may decline to give their opinions or even explicitly say, "But you certainly know better than we do…" Rather than seeing this as "resistance," we sympathize with how uncertain parents can feel at times, but keep telling them how much we need their participation to know if we are on the right track.

The following example returns to the assessment of Jaime described earlier, showing how the feedback outline shown in Table 7.2 actually played out in the collaborative process of the parent Summary/Discussion Session. Again, we jump ahead to where the assessor is covering section IV:

Assessor: At first glance it seems that Jaime is doing OK, but if we look deeper, we see a lot of emotional distress he is holding in. It comes out at times to produce those confusing moments you've been wondering about when he gets so angry out of the blue. It was confusing to me as well until I saw his test results. It seems that he has very good coping skills overall, as shown here in his own self-report. *[Shows BASC-3 graph and teaches how to read.]* Basically, Jaime said: "I am doing just fine, thank you!" He shows no elevations on any of these scales, which might be how he is actually functioning at school or when his life is pretty structured and expectations are set right there in front of him, kind of like taking the self-report test—when all he had to do was respond to the items in front of him. Does that fit for the two of you?

Mom: Yes, that's what's confusing, when we ask him if there is something troubling him, and why he got mad at his brother, he tells us nothing is bothering him at all except for his brother.

Dad: Yes, but the things he points to with his brother don't really make sense.

Assessor: Exactly, I think things are not as straight forward for Jamie when the structure goes away and when the situation gets more stressful or emotional. It's a bit like what happened when he took the inkblot test and was not given many instructions. He started doubting himself, became very anxious, and told me he didn't like the test. Interestingly, that's what the test showed as well. When Jamie feels out of control and when things get unstructured for him, he starts to feel insecure and anxious, which then leads to frustration and anger. He does not have a general anger problem as you were worried; rather he feels insecure about his abilities when he doesn't feel in control of a situation, and then he "explodes" rather than expresses his vulnerability and worry. Does that seem right to the two of you?

Mom: A lot. For example, the other day I wanted him to go with me to visit a friend who has a son about his same age who Jaime has never met. He got really angry and said he didn't want to go, and the reasons he gave didn't make any sense. Now I think maybe he was feeling insecure or out of control meeting a new kid.

We see here that the mother offered an example without even being asked. This is a good sign that she was feeling involved in the session as a collaborator. To continue:

Assessor: One of your Assessment Questions was: "Is there something going on that we don't know about like bullying, for example, that leads Jamie to explode so much, especially at his younger brother?" That was a big concern for you both, and I wanted to talk about it in light of the results. Do you have a better sense of the answer to this question now that we've discussed the findings?

Mom: I think it's the feeling out of control that you talked about earlier and feeling insecure. He wants to impress us with his grades and basketball, but things have gotten harder this year in school. He is not at the top of his class as he used to be. I am still worried about his being bullied, especially when I see how mean he can be to his younger brother, but it makes sense what you said about his feeling vulnerable instead, just not wanting to say it.

Dad: That is probably my fault, I want him to be tough and strong, but I don't want him to be a bully to his younger brother. Maybe he feels he can't show his vulnerability because he wants my approval.

Assessor: You are both right, and I appreciate your taking into consideration the test results. When he completed his Individualized Sentence Completion, one of the stems read: Being a bully is... *a pathetic sign of weakness.* When I asked him about it in our session, he shared that there are two boys in his class who target younger kids and he and some of his friends are very upset by it. I asked if he has ever been bullied and he said no, because he and his basketball friends hang out together and the bullies target kids who tend to be alone on the playground. He said he thought about talking to the teacher but doesn't want to be "that kind of kid." He doesn't see his own anger as mean, especially toward Sean, because "that's what brothers do" he said, and he is not aware of the more tender, vulnerable feelings he is having. My sense is that as we help him express some of those feelings, his anger could decrease. Right now, it seems to be his "go-to emotion" when he feels anything. Our goal here is to help him label and express a variety of feelings he has and to be more aware of how unexpressed feelings end up coming out as meanness and anger. And, if we can make these feelings more acceptable and welcome in the home, it will help a lot.

Dad: We can do that. He can't continue like this with his brother and I don't want him to stuff his feelings all the time, the way I grew up.

Again, you can see in this example how the assessor invites the parents' collaboration, and how they actively participate in making sense of the test findings.

Make Comments/Notes on Your Outline/Script as You Present and Discuss the Findings

As the session progresses and we follow our plan, we actively make notes in the margins of the outline to add the parents' comments, examples, and modifications when the various findings are presented. These notes help document the parents' participation in the Summary/Discussion Session so that we may incorporate this material in the upcoming written feedback. Again, because the outline or script is seen as the first draft of the feedback letter, we fully expect that important modifications will take place when we discuss our outline with the parents. An example of such side notes might be: "Mom agreed with this finding; dad not convinced that it explained John's anger." Or "Both parents seemed sad. Dad said it reminds him of his own childhood." As you will see in Chapter 9, incorporating this type of information in the final feedback letter will make it more personal, relevant, and alive.

Pause and Support the Parents' Emotional Reactions

Most parents find that discussing their own child's assessment results is a very vulnerable experience. Many come to the Summary/Discussion Session worrying that they will be blamed or told things that will bring up guilt or grief. And as we have said before, if parents do not have enough support for the feelings that arise when they try to shift their narratives, they will typically not take in new narratives, so as to avoid intolerable emotional overwhelm. For these reasons, supporting parental emotional reactions is a crucial part of a Summary/Discussion Sessions in TA-C. We remind you of the emotional support techniques we discussed in Chapter 3: active listening, mirroring, joining, and attending to shame. To illustrate how these might come into play in a Summary/Discussion Session, imagine that as a single mother hears an assessor talk about her daughter's level of depression and loneliness, she starts feeling remorseful for not spending enough time at home. The mother starts to tear up, and the assessor notices and slows down:

Assessor: I can see how hard it is to hear about Jane's depression. I am so sorry that this is so painful. Can we stop for a minute to see what's coming up for you as you hear me describe these results?

Mom: Yeah, it's hard. I can't help but think that it's my fault for working so much. Ever since the divorce I have taken on extra clients to keep up our standard of living, and I always thought it was best for her and to give her a good future- you know, good school, vacations, all the things that other kids have. But, instead she's been more and more withdrawn and sad. And, now these tests show that she is really depressed. I've done it all wrong.

Assessor: I have no doubt that you've tried hard to give Jane the best possible opportunities; it's clear how much you love her. Every time I have seen you two together it's been such a pleasure to witness your relationship. But I think you might be right about her needing you more, and that your working so much and being out of town a lot is affecting her. But you didn't know this before, so I hope you can forgive yourself. I'm a parent too, and I've come to accept that even when I'm doing my best, I often make mistakes. But then I try to just readjust and change things in the future. Do you know what I mean?

Mom: I do, and I think it will be good for me too to be home more. (*crying*) I miss her terribly when I am gone. I leave her these little notes to find when I am away, and it's a game we play before she goes to bed, we read them together on the phone to see how many she found. I cry almost every time after we hang up.

Assessor: You are a wonderful mother, and it's clear you try very hard. I have a feeling that you already have made some changes in how you are with her when you are not traveling, and that's a good start for now. Let's keep talking about how you can make the time you are in town the most attuned and focused on her, and then we can talk about what other possible changes can be made. We can't change your life completely right away, but maybe we start with small adjustments now that you understand better what Jane needs.

In this example, the assessor noticed the mother's tears, and paused to see what she was feeling. The main emotion coming up seemed to be guilt, and the assessor sensitively shared that she was a parent too, who also made mistakes. She then directed the mother to focus more on what she could do in the future rather than focusing on the past. This can be a good tactic to help parents move forward.

Another common emotion that arises in Summary/Discussion Sessions is grief, perhaps about missed opportunities or about not having understood the child's problems before. See this dialogue from two parents who are just understanding that their 8-year-old son has severe learning disabilities:

Father: I can't believe that the school hasn't picked up on this before now. Tom has been struggling for two years, and we've talked to his teachers numerous times. He even had some kind of school assessment earlier this year. And now from what you showed us, this is a not a subtle problem he has; instead, it's pretty glaring!

Assessor: Yes, how frustrating for you that the learning disabilities weren't identified earlier. It could have saved everyone a lot of anguish.

Mother: And there were all those nights when Tom was crying about feeling stupid. I feel sad that he went through that and we didn't know how to help.

Assessor: Yes, you must all have felt pretty powerless.

Father: So, you'll be willing to go with us to talk to the school.

Assessor: In fact, you'll remember I've already had contact with Tom's teachers and the principal. I believe they'll be open to what we've put together in the assessment.

Mother: Well at least we can get things straightened out from now on.

Assessor: I hope so, and I'll support you.

In this example the parents seem mainly to have needed mirroring from the assessor, and the felt sense of not being alone with their emotions or with the next steps in approaching the school. By "accompanying" the parents as they felt their sadness and anger, the assessor helped them think about moving ahead.

Whatever the emotions that come up might be, in TA-C we prioritize supporting the emotional reactions and offering parents a space to process them in the moment, before moving on to the next task or point of the discussion session. On some occasions, we even choose to schedule a second Summary/Discussion Session because parent(s) might not be able to finish after getting emotionally overwhelmed.

Never Argue with Parents

Perhaps it goes without saying, but we never argue with parents about an assessment finding. In our way of thinking, if a client does not agree with a finding we present, we might be wrong, or have used wording that's mis-attuned, or over-estimated what parents are ready to hear. Whatever the reason, in TA-C we never try to convince parents that we are right and they are not. Such a stance would violate the TA core values of collaboration, humility, and respect, and would represent a real failure of the core values of openness and curiosity. If parents disagree, above all we aspire to be curious, and to be open to learning something we have not yet grasped in the assessment process. Most importantly, arguing with parents over a finding has the potential to damage the relationship and the work of the assessment prior to the Summary/Discussion Session.

Rather, if the parents disagree, we suggest that the assessor humbly back off stating: "This doesn't seem to resonate with you or how you experience your daughter; can you tell me what's off in how the testing captured this part of her?" or "It seems that we are describing these behaviors in two different ways. I am going to defer to you, as I believe you know your child better than I do or the testing can describe. Perhaps we can just keep this finding in mind and put it to the side. Would that be ok?" Or finally, if needed, say: "You don't think this finding captures what's going on with John. I respect that, and your perspective is very important to me. Thank you for bringing it in. These tests can sometimes be wrong, and we can miss things. Let's look at some of these other scores to see if they are more useful in helping us understand what's going on with John. And let's see if we can figure out how these tests could have come up with such a different perspective."

Review and Discuss Suggestions

As you can see, Section V of Box 7.1 involves discussing next steps for the child and family based on the results of the TA-C. Again, perhaps because of the pulls toward "oracular" transference and countertransference (Schafer, 1967), many assessors learning TA-C seem to forget the importance of collaboration once they get to the point of discussing next steps. Parents very much want expert help, and there is a set-up to deliver this from a "one-up" perspective. The following dialogue shows an example of maintaining the collaborative stance in compiling next steps.

Assessor:	So, I thought it might be helpful to summarize next steps in dealing with Susie's anxiety based on what we have learned from the assessment.
Mother:	Yes, what do you think we should do?
Assessor:	Well, help me remember what we learned has worked so far.
Father:	Well, we all agreed those breathing exercises we started in the middle of the assessment have been very helpful.
Mother:	Yes, so we should keep on doing those. And the game night once a week has been really fun and seems to have really made her less afraid of the family falling apart.
Assessor:	That's great to hear. And am I right that you both have changed how you respond when she brings up her fears?
Father:	Yes, I stopped trying to just talk her out of them and try to listen and understand her first.
Mother:	I'm having a harder time with that, but I see how it would be helpful.
Assessor:	So, what do you think would help you do that more consistently?
Mother:	So, as we talked about with my MMPI-2 results, I have my own anxiety I need to deal with. I've been thinking I might look into some individual therapy.
Assessor:	I'm glad you've been thinking about that. Please let me know if you'd like me to help find you someone to talk to.
Mother:	I will.

Although the above example illustrates a review of suggestions for next steps that have been collaboratively derived across the assessment, an assessor also needs to think about what Level of Information the suggestion would likely be to the parents and avoid suggestions that could be seen as Level 3, as they are likely to be rejected. For example, suggesting individual therapy for one or both of the parents when it was never part of the conversation across the assessment could easily overwhelm parents and distract from the suggestions that have been developed along the way and have entered the parents' comfort zone. A repair likely would be needed to regain the parents' trust.

Last, we try to explicitly connect any suggestions we offer to the assessment results and make them detailed enough to be helpful. For example, instead of just recommending "family therapy," we try to specify what the goals would be, who might attend, and how long it might take. Also, all suggestions are offered tentatively, respectfully, and with real openness to parents' input about what is feasible and what they are ready and willing to do.

Close the Session

During this last part of the session, the assessor thanks the parents again for their collaboration and work in the assessment process and shares some appreciation for the work done together. The assessor mentions the plans for delivery of the letter and any other written documents contracted for; discusses the plan for the second Summary/Discussion Session where the child is included, including getting parents' input into the fable for their child if one is being developed; and possibly schedules the Follow-up Session with the parents (or agrees to contact the parents to schedule the Follow-up Session after they have received the parent letter/report).

Case: Summary/Discussion Session with Henry's Parents

It was finally time to plan the Summary/Discussion Session. I (Dale) scheduled a 2-hour session with the parents and also included the referring therapist, Dr. Jagger. I began the planning process by completing the Outline for Summary/Discussion Session with Parents (see Appendix B) discussed previously in the chapter (see Box 7.1). This helped me focus on both the process and content of the upcoming session. Also, it allowed me to take time to think through how I wanted to present information in order to be clear and encourage collaboration. After completing the outline, I had a number of thoughts.

1. Since the results of the major findings mapped well onto the questions, I thought I could go directly to answering them (Option A), but I decided I would first briefly review the test results to make sure both parents and therapist were on similar pages as we focused on the Assessment Questions. Throughout the assessment I had "sprinkled in" results to the parents. Therefore, I knew they had heard much of what I was going

to share already. They just hadn't heard it all at once, which I knew could make things overwhelming if I were not sensitive.

2. Because I had not interacted with the parents since the FIS, I wanted to be mindful that they might have thoughts and feelings to share about that session because it was so intense.

3. I felt that the family's difficulty in being able to process anger was a key factor in Henry's depression. I thought this was Level 2+ information and would have to be handled delicately, even though the FIS had brought anger into the room.

4. I thought it might be difficult (Level 2+) to let the parents know that in order for Henry to change they would have to make individual changes and learn more about their own emotional worlds so they could respond more empathically to Henry.

5. I was not sure how committed the parents were in continuing Henry's individual therapy with Dr. Jagger and didn't know if this would come up; but I wanted to be prepared for it in case it did.

6. Because the family decided to suspend Henry's therapy during the assessment due to scheduling difficulties, I had kept Dr. Jagger updated. Shortly before this session I had a telephone conversation with her to: a) review the results of the assessment, b) discuss the answers to her questions, c) share that it is most helpful for therapists to support the parents during the session, and d) encourage her to collaborate throughout the meeting—feeling free to give her perspective on Henry and the findings. During this conversation I also shared what occurred during the FIS. Because the FIS was so powerful and informative, I thought it would come up in the upcoming session, and therefore, it would be important for Dr. Jagger to have some knowledge of it beforehand. Also, Dr. Jagger agreed with how I planned to handle the Level 2+ information mentioned above.

Conducting the Summary/Discussion Session

I felt well prepared for the session. Since I hadn't seen anyone in the family for a couple of weeks, I was looking forward to checking in with the parents at the beginning of the session to see how things were going. Initially, they seemed a little quieter and more reserved than at previous sessions when we had met without Henry. I immediately wondered if their reserve had to do with the FIS or perhaps the introduction of another person into the session. I also wondered if I were behaving differently because Dr. Jagger was there. The parents indicated that things were pretty much status quo, maybe Henry was a "little lighter." I wondered out loud if they thought that might have anything to do with our FIS.

Dale: Do you think Henry seeming a "little lighter" had something to do with our last session?

Barbara: Maybe. I hadn't thought of that.

Dale: It was an important session and I imagine it affected all of you. David, what do you think?

David: I guess so. We really didn't talk much about it afterwards. (*I let the conversation drop because it seemed that they were hesitant to go in that direction. I wondered if they needed a little more time to feel comfortable. I felt that we would be able to talk about the FIS more organically later on.*)

I set the stage by sharing that we were going to proceed just as we did with the assessment—collaboratively. I emphasized that the scores on the tests don't tell the whole story and that it was equally important for them to share their perceptions and feelings about what I was saying because it would help us all understand Henry better. I then explained how I thought we would proceed:

Dale: I know we've gone over a lot of the test results along the way, and I've shared some with Dr. Jagger. But I thought we would start with a very brief overview of the results, so we are all on the same page and then proceed to answering the questions. How does that sound? (*Each person nodded in agreement.*)

Dale: Before getting to some of the results, I want to thank-you, Barbara and David, for your openness and participation in the assessment. I know what a vulnerable process this is. (*I wanted to join with the parents empathically, especially since I thought that the family best fit the Scapegoated and Sick Child family system.*) You provided me with lots of information about yourselves and your families of origin, which allowed me to get to know you and Henry in a deep and authentic way. I think this speaks to how much you love Henry and want to help him in any way you can. This has been a challenging assessment also given how persistent Henry is in sharing his misery. I can only imagine how hard that has been for each of you. I came to understand how difficult it is to have empathy for Henry when it feels like he is punishing you. (*They nodded and seemed like they were able to take in my appreciation.*) I also want to say that Henry can be delightful—funny, quirky and energetic. He came alive when he shared how to play a video game with me. He's a good teacher!

Barbara: Yes, isn't it amazing how engaged he can be? I love that part of him!

Dale: Dr. Jagger, I certainly appreciate you referring Henry for the assessment. I know you've been with Henry and the family for a long time and have helped them through many difficult times. It also takes a lot of trust and openness to refer a client mid-therapy.

Dr. Jagger: Well, it felt like Henry and I were a bit stuck, and I thought another perspective would be helpful.

David and Barbara were quiet and attentive, so I continued with the plan of sharing an overview of the results that would impact the answers to the questions. I highlighted the following:

1. Henry is bright but very anxious and insecure about his cognitive ability. Three of the five composite scores were in the above average range (VCI=113, VSI=119 and FRI=112) and his other 2 scores were in the average range (WMI=97, PSI=98). I defined the WMI and PSI and gave examples of how this might reveal itself in everyday life. Given his emotional state, I believed the WMI and PSI were a lower estimate of Henry's intelligence, because they are most affected by depression.
2. Henry was determined to share how sad and depressed he was, and this came out in all our interactions: his self-report on the BASC, his answers to the Individualized Sentence Completion Task, as well as his responses on the performance-based tests.
3. Both teachers and parents saw Henry as depressed and anxious, as reported on the BASC.

Dale: Any thoughts or comments? (*Both parents and Dr. J. just shook their heads "no."*)
Dale: What's it like to see that you and the teachers were all on the same wave length--both confirming his anxiety and depression?
David: Well, we kind of figured that would be the case. Not surprised at all.

At this point I realized that I was doing most of the talking, and both the parents and Dr. Jagger were not being as responsive as I might have liked. I then decided to ask them if they had any comments or questions. All shook their heads, "no," so I went "off my script" and asked all three what would be the most important or difficult thing to hear. (*I realized that I needed to be flexible and change the direction I was going in if I was going to get more participation and collaboration with parents and therapist.*)

Barbara: I am frightened that you're going to tell us that he is psychotic or something like that—given my family history. (*She looked tearful and a little anxious.*)
David: I'm not clear that you got a good view of what he is capable of. I have seen him be very creative and tell imaginative stories which he refused to do here. I don't think you got to see that part of him.
Dale: Dr. Jagger? (*I purposefully directed the same question to Dr. Jagger. I wanted to encourage her to feel comfortable in collaborating and participating in the session.*)
Dr. Jagger: I guess I'm looking for what would really help in his treatment.
Dale: OK. Great! I think we will be able to address each of those concerns as we continue. (*I decided to address Barbara's concern*

immediately because I was worried that her anxiety might prevent her from being fully engaged.) It seems important to address your concern right now, Barbara, because I don't want you to have to sit with that worry throughout this session. I want you to know that there isn't any indication that Henry is psychotic. (*I pulled out the Rorschach results immediately and showed her the section on Perception and Thinking Problems.*) Remember, how we talked about this chart? Anything that is coded green means that the results are within the normal range of functioning compared to his peers. All of Henry's scores in this area are in the green, indicating that his thinking is not distorted, psychotic, or worrisome.

Barbara: (*Showing tears of relief*) I have been so scared about this. I don't know what I would do if he was psychotic. I've worried about this a lot.

Dale: That is totally understandable given how fixed he can be on being miserable. I'm really glad you brought this up and that we could reduce your anxiety.

Barbara: Yeah, I think I was distracted by my fears.

Dale: Well, shall we continue and answer your questions? Why don't we do the most straightforward one first, "What are Henry's intellectual strengths and weaknesses? Is there a disharmony among them? What kind of learning environment is best for him?"

Because we had already talked about this a lot, I asked them how they would answer the question.

Barbara: He's really smart and maybe even smarter, but his sadness may be making some of his scores lower.

David: I wondered about his creativity. How did that show up?

Dale: Well, the test we used doesn't directly measure creativity. And, he was very intent on not sharing those parts of himself. You remember how he refused to tell stories to those picture cards? It never felt like he really couldn't do that, but rather chose not to.

David: Yeah. That was really frustrating for me. He's so creative and you didn't get to see that.

Dale: Yes, it's disappointing, but I thought he was pretty creative in all the ways he let me know how miserable he was.

Both parents nodded their heads and smiled ruefully.

Dale: Do the results of the cognitive testing influence where you think Henry should go to school next year? Remember that his working

memory and ability to process information were lower than his
other scores. That could make it difficult for him to do extra work
in a timely fashion.

Barbara: Yeah, well I have concerns that a magnet school would be really
hard for him. But if all his friends are going there, would it be fair
to prevent him from going there if he gets in?

Dale: What do you think David?

David: I'd like to give him the opportunity to go where he wants to go.
But I worry about it, too.

Dale: That's totally understandable. I'm not sure there is a right or
wrong. But if you choose for him to go to the magnet school, then
we need to make sure there are enough supports in place.

The session continued and we went through the answers to the Assessment
Questions that are detailed in the Parent Summary/Discussion Outline (see
Appendix B) and the letter sent to the parents (see Chapter 9). For the most
part, because there had been a lot of active parent participation and co-
operation throughout the assessment process, there were not a lot of disagreements or conflicts. I often find that during this session information
comes to light that sheds more understanding on the case in a very natural
way. Also, if we are able to stay in the moment, the session can flow easily.
For example, the following dialogue took place when we focused on the
question, "Is he clinically depressed or is it situational?"

Dale: Do you remember the first time I showed you a video of Henry
during the testing? I think that session started with you, Barbara,
asking if he was depressed. I responded with a bit of surprise and
asked, "Do you have any doubts that he's depressed?"

Barbara: Yes, I did have doubts. I have a bit of a skewed view about the
world because of how I was raised and because I'm fairly anxious
and I think everybody walks around with some anxiety and
depression. You remember I took care of my older sister who was
severely depressed, and she was very different.

Dale: How was she different?

Barbara: Well, my sister was always depressed. I saw Henry as having a lot
of fun and good times, so I didn't get how he could really be that
depressed and still have fun.

Dale: Yes, that's very confusing.

Barbara: Also, David has been depressed, and it's not nearly like when
Henry is depressed.

David: Yes, when I've been depressed, I don't take it out on other people.
It often feels that Henry is trying to get a rise out of us by beating
us up with how depressed he is. It felt as if there was nothing we
could do to assuage that.

As we talked, I realized that the parents were more engaged in the discussion. I think we were all settling into the session and the task at hand. And, I was more comfortable with having another professional in the room.

Dale: Yes! That feeling of being beaten up by his negativity can really be frustrating and it leads right into your next question. "Why does Henry make provocative statements to us?"

The dialogue in this next section hopefully illustrates how a new understanding and additional information can be brought out in the Summary/Discussion Session.

Dale: I think this is an important question because it influences how empathic and present you can be for Henry. During the assessment I experienced how provocative Henry can be and how infuriating. At one point I really felt irritated at him. Do you remember the session where he completed the BASC in such a negative fashion that the results suggested interpretation should be done with extreme caution? During that session he asked me if I thought he answered the questions accurately. And, I said I didn't think so and asked him if he wanted to change any of his answers. So, he said "yes" and then proceeded to answer the question that weren't negative with a more negative response. That was so irritating. I wonder Dr. Jagger did you ever feel that way? Irritated at Henry? (*I was trying to get anger into the room so we could talk about it in a non-shaming way.*)

Dr. Jagger: I think there have been a number of times over the years that I have felt aggravated rather than saddened by Henry's sadness. This isn't usual for me, so I wondered about it. Often, depression in kids comes out as anger. But Henry's not directly angry or aggressive, is he?

Barbara: No, not really. He does antagonize his brother. But it makes me crazy when he pushes and pushes us with his negativity. Like I see him being happy and he denies it. I think some of what he was angry about came out in the last session when we were all together. (*Barbara said this hesitantly.*)

David: That was a really hard session for me. I couldn't believe that Henry remembered that incident. It just didn't feel real to me.

Dr. Jagger: Dr. Rudin told me about that session. I'm surprised the incident never came up in his individual therapy.

Dale: Why do you think it might not have?

Dr. Jagger: I'm not really sure. Perhaps he feels that anger is not supposed to be expressed.

Barbara: It didn't seem possible that Henry could hold on to that for so long. Or, that it would impact him. I felt sad and bad about the whole thing. I wished we had been able to discuss it at the time it happened. I guess I just didn't see it as so awful. I just wanted it to go away.

Dale: Well maybe that's why he was so affected by it. It was never dealt with and fully acknowledged. I wonder, how you both feel like anger is handled in your family.

David: I don't really get angry much. I feel frustrated but I wouldn't call that anger.

Barbara: Well, I get anxious and I feel your anger (*talking to David*) more than you recognize it. I'm sorry I didn't talk to you more about that incident after Henry shared it with me. I guess I was afraid.

David: I find that very shaming! You keep things from me, and I feel a lot of judgment from you but don't really know what it's about.

Dale: That must be frustrating, David.

I was aware that we were getting into some delicate territory that involved marital issues, but I chose not to directly address David's comment about feeling shamed because I wanted to stay focused on Henry and sharing the results. I hoped what I was going to say next would indirectly decrease David's shame.

Dale: You know, feelings are complicated in families. And parents don't always know how their feelings and expression of them affect their kids. Expressing feelings can be a very confusing undertaking. We'll get to this a little later, but this is one of the reasons that I'm going to suggest doing some family therapy. The more each of you is aware of your own feelings, the more you will be able to support Henry in validating and being present for his feelings. Does that make sense?

David: Yes, but I feel like I am aware of my feelings. I'm not sure how that will work.

Dale: You may be aware of them, but maybe there's room for being even more aware and really seeing the impact of your feelings on others. And remember, Henry is very sensitive. If we think back to the FIS, I don't think you fully understood the effect of your feelings and behavior on Henry. What do you think?

David: I guess I have to agree. That was somewhat shocking.

Dale: Yes. It was so beneficial because by having that come out in the open, you were able to begin a lovely repair with Henry. Do you agree?

I wanted to highlight that this was the beginning of a repair because I thought more work needed to be done. And, I also wanted to appreciate David for starting the process.

David: Yes. Maybe that's part of why Henry was a bit lighter these last couple of weeks.

Dale: I agree. He was able to get something off his chest, and you both responded well. You didn't deny what happened or make him think it wasn't a big deal. That's so important.

The session continued with us discussing and answering all the Assessment Questions. There was a nice collaboration, much better than before we had all "warmed up." I sensed some tension between the parents when we discussed anger, but this wasn't surprising since this was an area that I knew would need to be addressed in family therapy. When I thought back to the case conceptualization, I again remembered how the family prototypes of the sick and scapegoated child fit with this family system. As stated previously, in both of those formulations, anger is not well integrated and can be problematic in the life of the family, as was clearly true here.

After the questions were discussed, I asked the parents and Dr. jagger what they thought good next steps might be. These largely fit with suggestions I already had in mind.

These suggestions will be discussed in detail in the letter to parents (see Chapter 9), but let me highlight one of the suggestions to show the collaboration that can occur even during this part of the session.

Dale: I have been starting to think Henry should go to a smaller private school in which he could feel the support of the staff, and you could have the support of the administration. I *would not recommend that he go to the magnet school.*

David: Do you think he couldn't handle the work, or you don't think he's smart enough?

Dale: I don't think it's a question of his intelligence. I think his anxiety about school and his focus on comparing himself to his peers could be detrimental for him.

Barbara: But he has his heart set on being with his friends.

Dr. Jagger: I think it's really important for him to maintain his relationships. If this is something he really wants, don't you think he could rise to the occasion?

Dale: Yes, I also think his friendships are very important, but I think it would be very difficult for him to handle the pressure that comes with the competition at the magnet school. I think this could be difficult for lots of kids, but especially for those, like Henry, with his level of anxiety and depression. But if you all feel like this is important and Henry should go to the magnet school, then what supports do you think would help in him being successful?

David: We can provide him with a tutor to make sure he stays up to date with assignments and has support in the subject areas.

Dale: Great! I think that's a good idea. I know a great group that supplies tutors for all sorts of ages and subjects. They are also

	very sensitive to psychological issues. I'll get you that information.
Barbara:	Access to the school counselor has been very useful. That would be an important resource.
Dr. Jagger:	And if that occurs, I could plan to make sure the person and I stay in contact throughout the year.
Dale:	Because it's a transition year, it's important to have this in place before school starts. Maybe you can set up a 504 Meeting in order to do this in advance.
Barbara:	I think that's a really good idea. It would be nice if this year's school counselor could meet with the counselor at the magnet school.
Dale:	You might request this in the meeting or invite both of them to that meeting.

Toward the end of the session it was time to do some meta-processing and discuss our next steps and how to provide feedback to Henry.

Dale:	Well, I know this was a lot to take in all at once, but you will get a letter spelling all of this out, and I will include a lot of what we discussed today. I'm curious how are you feeling right now? Any reactions? Thoughts?
Barbara:	I'm a little overwhelmed and amazed at the amount of information we got. It was really important for me to hear, right from the start, that he wasn't psychotic. I've been worried about that for a long time.
Dale:	I'm glad we could address that. What else?
Barbara:	I'm still anxious about next year and what we should do. I want him to feel like he has a say in where he's going to school. But I am worried about the magnet school.
Dale:	I think we did a nice job of pointing out the supports that Henry will need if he attends that school. Does that help with the decision?

Barbara nods and I moved on to focus on David, remembering how easy it is for him to be quiet and not take up much space.

Dale:	David, how are you feeling about today?
David:	I think it went well. It feels like there's a lot for us to attend to in moving forward, but I feel positive about it.
Dale:	A lot of times I recommend family therapy, but people are hesitant to do that. What do you think about that?
Barbara:	I think it will be really helpful, especially because Frank, Henry's brother, gets upset when Henry continuously comments on his

sadness. I also know that we could benefit from communicating more directly as a family.

David: I agree. I think the times we were together as a family in here were really helpful.

Dale: Anything in particular?

David: Yes, I keep thinking about feeling frustrated but kind of pleased when Henry refused to cooperate with an activity.

Dale: Pleased?

David: Yes, I was glad someone else witnessed it and got a sense of how frustrating it was. Also, I was surprised that Henry seemed to be interested in what we were saying even if he didn't participate in some of the activities.

Dale: I think parents can feel alone and confused sometimes when their child is struggling. There are so many mixed feelings. That's one reason why I think family therapy will be helpful. It can really support the entire family--not just the child-and make it a little easier to change interactions. I really hope you decide to do this.

Barbara: We haven't talked about it, but I think I'd like to do it. David?

David: I think it seems like a good idea.

Dr. Jagger: I think it would be a really good addition to his treatment. He's complicated and an additional support person will be helpful.

Dale: Great! Right now, I'd like to switch gears and talk a little about how I'd like to share the results of the assessment with Henry. We often write a fable specifically for the child that highlights the assessment process--what we found out and how to understand what has been going on in the life of the child. A new way to look at things is presented that helps the child change his or her own story. I would like to do that with Henry the next time I see him. It would be great if both of you could be in the waiting room so we could all read it together after I share it with Henry.

I shared how I would take specific content from our work together to write a meaningful fable that would help Henry change his personal narrative. I said the fable I would write would empathize with his sadness, make sense of how it might have originated, and provide ideas that might help ameliorate it. Sometimes I invite parents to review and collaborate on the fable I write before I present it to the child, but I didn't in this case because I sensed the parents were already pretty overwhelmed.

I then discussed that I was going to share the fable first with Henry, without them, because I thought he might be more open to hearing it with just the two of us. Then, I would call them into the session so that we could all read it together. I said it would not contain anything we hadn't already discussed. I wanted to first share the fable alone with Henry because I was afraid that Henry might be more inclined to continue his pattern of negativity if his parents were present. I also wanted to give him the opportunity to illustrate the fable in order to make it his own and buy into the new narrative. I thought he might be more inclined to do this if his parents weren't present. I ended the session by sharing my perspective about the process and what I learned.

Dale: Barbara and David I want to again share how much I appreciated your participation in the process. There were times that I thought you really did an amazing job of letting Henry be Henry even when he was really uncooperative. You didn't make excuses for him or try and demand different behavior. You both taught me a bit about love and resilience. It reminded me of a Zelda Fitzgerald quote I love: "Nobody has ever measured, not even poets, how much the heart can hold." Even when things were disheartening and very difficult, you both kept focusing on helping Henry—trying to understand and support him. It was very touching to witness. I hope you are able to appreciate that about yourselves.

Both parents said how difficult it had been to parent Henry and that it was really positive to have the support of a professional who was able to take their perspective. We ended the session with scheduling our next appointment. Dr. Jagger and I lingered a few moments and shared that we were pleased that we were able to get to some of the more difficult information. I was pleased that both Barbara and David were open to the family therapy. I thought this was a direct result of their involvement in the assessment process and the important work that was done during the FIS.

References

Ainsworth, M. D. S., M.C. Blehar, M. C., Waters, E., & Wall, S. (1978). *Patterns of attachment. A psychological study of the Strange Situation.* Hillsdale, NJ: Erlbaum.

George, C., & Solomon, J. (1990–2016). *Attachment Doll Play Assessment and Classification System.* Oakland, CA: Mills College.

George, C., & West, M. (2001). The development and preliminary validation of a new measure of adult attachment: The Adult Attachment Projective. *Attachment and Human Development, 3,* 30–61.

Hanson, W. E., Claiborn, C. D., & Kerr, B. (1997). Differential effects of two test-interpretation styles in counseling: A field study. *Journal of Counseling Psychology, 44,* 400–405.

Schafer, R. (1954). *Psychoanalytic interpretation in Rorschach testing: Theory and application.* New York: Grune & Stratton.

Schroeder, D. G., Hahn, E. D., Finn, S. E., & Swann, W. B., Jr. (1993, June). *Personality feedback has more impact when mildly discrepant from self-views.* Paper presented at the fifth annual convention of the American Psychological Society, Chicago, IL.

8 Phase IV: Summary/Discussion Session with Child

Having engaged in collaborative feedback with the parents, we now plan and conduct the Summary/Discussion Session that follows, which is focused on providing feedback to the child, with parents present. In Therapeutic Assessment of Children (TA-C), we strongly believe that children deserve to be appreciated and treated with respect during the assessment, and therefore, we endeavor to provide them with meaningful results. It has been our experience that other models of child assessment fall short in this regard, often not providing children with feedback at all.

In TA-C we individualize our approach to providing child feedback. We may first briefly talk with the child, in a developmentally appropriate way, about the process of the assessment and some of the findings. If Assessment Questions were posed by the child, we may answer the questions (as you will see in Henry's case, he opted for the fable first, followed by the answer to his Assessment Question). However, in our experience these attempts are seldom very effective, as most children tend to tune out to a direct approach. Therefore, we typically engage in a child-focused, creative activity that is attuned to the child and communicates aspects of her or his "story" while referencing the family. We have come to favor creating individualized therapeutic fables (although we have used other methods, one of which is introduced below). We have found fables to be an effective way of communicating families' old and new narratives in a way that can be easily absorbed by the child. Also, in our experience, fables appeal not only to children but also to parents. And we have been delighted that using fables as a feedback method has been embraced by assessors around the world (e.g., Aschieri et al., 2012; Hansson et al., 2016), and many tell us that writing fables has become a beloved part of their assessments. Thus, we begin this chapter explaining why we write fables, how to write a fable, and how we present the fable. We then turn to the Summary/Discussion Session with Henry and his parents, where Dale shared the therapeutic fable written for him, and we discuss his reaction. Following, we introduce and illustrate another creative method that can be used in place of the fable, Collaborative Therapeutic Collage, developed by one of the co-authors of this book, Marita Frackowiak.

DOI: 10.4324/9781003000174-8

Why We Write Fables

Fables have been used for centuries to educate, communicate important morals and lessons, and entertain children. They are a special aspect of growing up, and are loved by many children into their adult lives. Fables are timeless and powerful because they offer more than a beautiful story; they pass on culturally relevant narratives about humankind. Many authors have written about the educational role of fables and tales (e.g., Booker, 2019). Fables are a wonderful way many cultures have found to warn children about the dangers of the world or, on the contrary, to show them the right path to follow. We can tell children not to talk to strangers, but they might well prefer reading the story of Little Red Riding Hood and having a conversation about it. Fables are powerful because they reflect our fears, fantasies, secrets, and dreams. We feel understood by fables because they have a way to speak to us directly and reach what is hidden deeply inside of us. And they can inspire us by showing a hero's journey through adversity to come to resolution and peace, while learning an important life lesson.

For most of us practicing TA-C, writing a therapeutic fable is worth the additional effort and time it requires because of the impact it can have on children and families. Children and parents often delight in the creativity and power of the fable. And in our experience, children and parents often re-read the fables at home, as a reminder of the new family narrative and the changes they are trying to implement. Furthermore, as discussed in detail in Chapter 2, there is research documenting the therapeutic power of fables. Tharinger and Pilgrim (2011) studied children and families participating in a neuropsychological assessment and found that when children received fables, they said they learned more about themselves, had a more positive relationship with their assessor, felt a greater sense of collaboration in the assessment process, and believed their parents learned more about them than did children who did not receive fables. Also, parents whose children received fables reported a more positive relationship between their child and the assessor, a greater sense of collaboration with the assessment process, and higher satisfaction with the clinic services compared to the comparison group. Although more research is needed on the role fables play in assessment feedback and their therapeutic impact on children, speaking from our clinical observations and experiences, we have found the impact to be very powerful.

What underlies the therapeutic impact of fables? Our discussions with children and parents have provided us with hypotheses. Because the fable is individualized and written for the specific child/family, children and parents often have a sense of feeling "seen" and understood when reading the fable. Also, the fable can reflect both individual as well as cultural values of the family, showing that we respect and celebrate the family's culture and take into account their context when addressing the issues that led to their seeking help. In addition, fables written for children often demonstrate how a child's surface level problems (e.g., behavioral difficulties, learning differences) are connected to deeper, emotional processes that underlie the behavioral presentation (e.g., fears, shame, anger) (Purves, 2016). In this way, fables promote psychological thinking and reflective functioning. Also fables written at the end of a TA-C often depict changes the family is in the process of making during the assessment; thus, fables often provide a roadmap—in metaphor—of suggested next steps, and foster hope that everyone in the family can be part of the solution to persistent difficulties in living.

Last, the fable is a transitional object for many children, reminding them of the special relationship with the assessor and helping them internalize that experience. We believe, and parents consistently report, that the fable plays a very significant role in helping children tolerate the end of the assessment relationship. In addition, the fable helps children process assessment findings and changes resulting from the assessment (e.g., seeing a therapist or receiving tutoring, following up with a neurologist, changing school environment).

Having said all this, we remind you that no one step or method in TA-C is written in stone, and we encourage you to think about each particular child and family when deciding whether to write and present a fable. A child with severe dyslexia might groan at being given something to read at the end of an assessment, and in at least one such situation, several of Deborah Tharinger's students wrote and recorded a rap song feedback for a child who had difficulties reading. Also, some pre-teens or emotionally mature children under 12 might not appreciate a fable, believing they are too old for such "childish" stuff. In contrast, younger children (up to about age 10) typically enjoy fables very much. Others of us have found that children (and adolescents) of all ages appreciate a fable, if they can identify with it and feel understood. One of our colleagues, Diane Engelman, even routinely writes therapeutic stories for adult clients at the end of a TA, with good results (see Engelman et al., 2016).

Constructing the Fable

Writing the fable can take various paths. It can be:

- A shared effort between parents and the assessor, where parents actively participate in drafting the fable. It is a collaboration between parents and the assessor, where parents offer suggestions/ideas/inspiration; the assessor writes the fable; and parents review it and make additional suggestions.
- A solo writing process done by the assessor, but with the fable shared with parents when it is completed for their input.
- A solo writing process by the assessor after the parents have given their verbal support for the main themes of the fable, but the parents do not view the fable in advance of the session with the child.

Bottom line, we want parents prepared for what is in the fable, as they are usually depicted metaphorically as supporting positive change for the child. If we have collaborated successfully with the parents across the assessment, we can be fairly certain that they will be on board and will work well with any of the methods introduced above. For parents who have struggled with embracing a new narrative for their child/family, working on the fable collaboratively provides an additional opportunity for the assessor to help parents get in their child's shoes and think systemically. One can imagine that different families benefit from slightly different approaches, just as different assessors might prefer more or less collaborative methods of fable writing. In addition, some of us let the child know in advance that we will be writing a fable just for them and some of us keep it as a surprise.

A Step-by-Step Guide to Writing Fables

We now present one method for writing fables (see Box 8.1).

1. A slightly different, less detailed method is presented in Tharinger et al. (2008).

Box 8.1   Step-by-Step Guide to Writing Fables

- Select a character and genre.
- Introduce the setting of the fable by including child specific detail.
- Introduce a struggle the character experiences.
- Introduce the helper, e.g., wise owl, wizard, coach, etc.
- Include assessment details, e.g., looking at inkblots or completing magical math.
- Introduce some of what the parents learned from the wizard or owl (the helper/assessor).
- Provide suggestions in an attuned way, with examples.
- Write the fable attuned to the child's developmental level and language ability.

Select a Character and Genre

The main character or protagonist is one of the most important features of the fable, as it personifies the child and allows her or him to identify with the story. For that reason, the main character needs to come from the child's world and to share some of her or his characteristics. There is a bit of art, heart, and soul involved in selecting the "right" character for a child's fable. Sometimes ideas for the main character come to us very early on in the TA-C, e.g., when a child brings a favorite toy into the session or when a response to a particular test gives a window into the child's internal world. For example, not infrequently the child's fantasy animal drawing and story spark the assessor's imagination, and the fable becomes a continuation of the Fantasy Animal Drawing Game (Handler, 2007).

Occasionally, selecting a child specific character is difficult. Certain children are not very expressive, or their age or a specific cognitive/learning difference might have prevented them from elaborating their internal experience. In such cases, the assessor might choose to write a simpler, yet still individualized fable, set in the world of animals. This approach offers attuned reflection of the child's world in an emotionally safe, relatable world of little bears, puppies, or sharks. And parents can be very helpful in choosing an animal that the child particularly likes or is interested in.

By genre, we refer to the context in which the fable will take place and the type of content that will be highlighted; for example, sports, science, car racing, Harry Potter, unicorns, cartoon characters, or video games. Selecting the genre is usually an easy task and is guided by the child's interests. Again, if you are unsure, parents can collaborate in choosing an appropriate genre.

Introduce the Setting of the Fable by Including Child Specific Detail

Once the main character and genre are selected, the assessor is invited to "play." This step involves assessors creatively and kindly "surprising" a child by including specific information they have about the child and family in the fable. This is also an opportunity for assessors to demonstrate their understanding and appreciation of the child's and family's culture, traditions, and/or ethnic background by reflecting these elements in the therapeutic fable. It is because of these well-chosen parallels between children's lives and those of the fables' main characters that children often, while reading or hearing the fable, pause, look up and excitedly say: "This is about me!" For many of us practicing TA-C, this moment is precious, as children often seem to feel delight and increased curiosity when they realize that the fable is about them. For example, a child whose parents are divorced realizes that the family of bears in the fable who live in two separate parts of the forest are similar to her or his family. Or a boy with questions about gender identity relates to the fictional fox who secretly likes to wear sparkly tiaras. We believe the delight children show when reading these types of elements stems from their feeling seen and understood by the assessor.

We offer examples of details to consider including:

- A child's favorite sports/activities (e.g., a child whose family's tradition is Flamenco dancing receives a fable with flamingos who do Flamenco; a fable for a child who loves rap is full of rap terms).

- Foods mentioned in sessions or snacks brought into the sessions (e.g., a depressed bunny gets help from magical dried berries; a dinosaur who can't make friends at school brings homemade Dinosaur-taquitos for his classmates; a Latinx boy's fable includes a scene where a family comes together to make tamales at Christmas, even though the grandmother has died).
- Family constellation and living situation (e.g., a character lives with Grandma Bear and Papa Bear but misses Mama bear; another character lives with two Pappa Wizards; another travels between planets every week and has difficulty adjusting to the different atmospheres; another child, a recent immigrant, moves with her or his family to a new forest where all the other deer speak a foreign language).
- School factors (e.g., a boy at Hogworts can't remember his spells correctly until Dumbledore discovers that he learns differently than the other young wizards; a child who feels different from others is featured as a giraffe in a school of gazelles; a child whose parents don't speak English receives a fable about a puppy who has to learn a whole new dog language at school.
- Special talents/likes or what the child does for fun (e.g., cloud scooter riding, daydreaming, singing in the community/church choir, creating new inventions).

The assessor's creativity and familiarity with the child guides this part of the process. We are not suggesting that a fable needs to include all of these categories of examples. To the contrary, sometimes one or two meaningfully selected detail(s) offer the desired impact we want for the child.

Introduce a Struggle That the Main Character Experiences

Once the character, genre and setting are properly introduced, we suggest moving into the plot or story line. We typically introduce that the main character in the fable has been struggling or "having a hard time" with something specific that is consistent with at least one of the parents' Assessment Questions. Often, we soften the introduction of the "challenge" by suggesting that "Despite trying his best, little bear had a hard time learning how to read. Because of this, he started to think he wasn't as smart as the other little bears in class." Or "Even though it seemed the young Dinosaur told everyone that he was fine, his dads thought that he looked sad much of the time and they didn't know what to do." Once children recognize that the main character is going through struggles and challenges that are similar to their own, they typically feel a connection to the character and can't wait to see what happens. As Purves (2016) notes, fables can differ in how directly they depict the child's and family's difficulties. We strive to be direct enough to address problems that are out in the open, while not naming struggles the child is not fully aware of or that will overwhelm the child emotionally.

Introduce the Helper, e.g., Wise Owl, Wizard, Coach, etc.

By this point when children are reading their fables, they are typically "hooked." They often smile and make a comment when they realize that the fable is about them and are eager to hear more. Back to writing the fable, now it is time to bring yourself, the assessor, into the fable by introducing a "helper" character and describing the assessment process in a relatable way.

Keeping with the characteristics and genre of the fable, we create a wise and friendly helper figure who helps the parents understand the child's struggles and offers possible solutions. For this section it might be interesting or funny to say something specific about the "office" of the helper, e.g., "at the edge of the forest where the pink flowers bloom" in situations where the family had to travel quite far to meet the assessor, or "a clinic up in the trees with the fast magic elevator" if the child enjoyed taking the elevator each time when coming to the assessment sessions. The helper character is *not* meant to have an elaborate presence in the fable, but should offer a feeling of safety and credibility to the child and parents.

It is useful if the helper in the fable, upon meeting the child and the parents, reflects back to them that "indeed it makes sense that they would be puzzled," indicating that their concerns are valid and taken seriously, or that it "makes sense that the parents are worried" validating how painful it is for parents to see their children struggle. Additionally, it helps when the helper expresses initial puzzlement, but offers hope that "together we will work hard to figure it out." While these brief comments might seem insignificant at first, they reflect the values of TA-C, including collaboration, humility of the assessor, and empathy for the child and family, and they contribute to the warmth we are trying to communicate in the fable.

Include Memorable Details From the Assessment Sessions

Regardless of the type of assessment (e.g., cognitive, developmental, neuropsychological, emotional/behavioral, personality, etc.), the process requires a lot of commitment, emotional energy, time, and effort from both the child and parents. The relationship that develops in the process of the assessment can be nicely reflected in the fable by mentioning certain special, particularly difficult, funny, silly, or emotionally moving moments that took place during the assessment sessions. We typically refer to one or two of these to give the child and the family concrete reminders of the work we did together. For example, the helper figure and the child work together on tasks such as filling out long forms, solving tricky riddles, looking at pictures or inkblots, etc. Or, you can mention the meeting when the whole family came together to better understand how to "break the terrible, dark spell" by practicing new ones.

Introduce Insights the Parents Learned From the Wise Helper

We arrive at the core message of the fable, usually a depiction of Level 2 findings that explain and address the challenges facing the main character in a new way. As discussed earlier, in TA-C we are working on changing parents' narratives and understanding of their children to make those views more accurate, systemic, coherent, useful, and compassionate. We capture this understanding in a fable, often by having the helper share new information with the "parents," either by stating it directly or indirectly. For example, "The wise owl told Clarissa's parents, 'The magic mirror showed us that Clarissa feels lonely inside. She doesn't feel like she has any friends at the Wizard Academy. She is missing her friends from the old school but doesn't want to worry you, so she doesn't share her feelings.'" Alternatively, the fable may depict the helper talking with parents without directly indicating what was said, e.g., The wise figure "whispered special spells for parents to use when the dark cloud returns," "showed them lots of graphs and numbers that helped them understand," or "told them a secret about how to help alligators who love to ballet dance." Again, as Purves (2016) has explained, the assessor decides how direct or general to be in the fable depending on many things about the child, such as age, psychological maturity, degree of overwhelm, level of ongoing support. Overall, it is better not to give children more information than they can handle with the supports they have at the time.

Also, since fables are for parents as well as children, the content and tone of this section depends a great deal on how the parents reacted to the Family Intervention Session (FIS) and the Parent Summary/Discussion Session. In instances where parents were open to the new narrative and collaboratively worked on co-creating a new understanding of their child's needs and dilemmas, the direct and clearly articulated approach is often advisable (again if it does not overwhelm the child). This approach offers a concrete reminder of the work parents did and it communicates to the child the parents' understanding and willingness to make changes. However, in cases where one or both parents were less open to the new narrative and suggestions or clearly needed more time to integrate the new information, a simpler, more cautious approach works better, with no information included that comes close to Level 3.

We are also cautious how we end our fables. We don't want to offer the child "false" hope or put too much pressure on parents to go in a direction they might not yet be ready to take. In our minds, it is always better to under-promise than to over-promise and disappoint a child and family by suggesting outcomes that are not likely within their reach. Creating a fable that is attuned to both parents and child is a delicate and challenging task. It requires us as assessors to have a certain "feel" for where the family is and where it might be going therapeutically after the assessment. We want the fable to authentically reflect the positive strivings the family has made, without glossing over or denying the struggles they might still be facing.

Include Viable Next Steps

When we say that fables are written for parents as much as the children, we mean it. This is especially important when we offer examples of what parents can do differently per the Helper's/Wizard's/Wise Owl's suggestions. However, as much as we don't want to give children "false hope" about changes in their lives, we also don't want to shame parents or make them feel inadequate in their parenting. Hence, we don't make suggestions in the fable that we did not discuss and affirm in the Summary/Discussion Session with parents or earlier in the assessment process. We do offer specific examples in the fable of attuned parental responses--based on the new narrative adopted in the assessment process—that we believe are within the parents "reach." These examples provide a concrete reminder of what was discussed in the assessment and provide both parents and children with a new script for their interactions.

For example, the main character in the fable may feel very bad about herself or himself (the main assessment finding being low self-esteem) and the parents in the fable might be determined to help by constantly offering general, but inaccurate, praise and compliments (e.g., "Oh, you are the smartest bird in the forest!). By doing so, parents in the fable inevitably make the main character feel worse. Then, the wise helper instructs the parents how to be "self-esteem builders" using one specific rule: "Make your praise timely, small, and specific," such as: "I really like how you helped your sister bird catch her worm this morning; that was very caring of you," or, "You stayed really focused on your math problems today, I can see how hard you are working." These examples may be included in the fable only after the assessor and parents discussed specific ways they could help their child build self-esteem, and the parents practiced these new ways of interacting during the FIS, with good success. Thus, this example in the fable serves as a re- minder of all these discussions and interactions should the parents need this support down the line.

Review the Fable to Make Sure It Is Appropriate for the Child's Developmental Level and Language Ability

The most elaborate, embellished, fantasy-based fables are not going to im- press children who struggle with reading fluency or decoding, and instead may make them feel badly about themselves. Similarly, a simple, warm fable about little bears or foxes is not going to "speak" to a "cool" ten-year-old boy who wants to be seen as older and covers up his tender emotions with an angry persona. We can't stress enough how important it is to match the style, language level, tone and setting of a fable with the abilities and develop- mental needs of the child who will receive it. In our experience, assessors can become excited and fascinated writing fables, and may make them too long or mis-attuned to the child client. Thus, after we write an initial draft of a fable, we routinely look again at all the test findings, and ask ourselves, "Does this fable match what I know about this child's cognitive abilities and characteristics?" In some instances, it might be advisable not to write a fable at all if there is a possibility that the child would experience it as infantilizing rather than caring. As mentioned earlier, the assessor may consider other forms of collaborative feedback instead, such as making a joint collage, writing a song or a poem, or simply talking about the assessment findings and addressing the child's questions.

Sketch Out a Plan for the Fable

Before writing it can be helpful to draft a rough plan for the fable. Below are two such drafts that follow the above guide and steps. The full-length fable from the rough plan provided below, *Sparky the Unicorn*, is included in Appendix C.

Example 1:
- Character and genre: Sparky the unicorn; Fantasy
- Setting: Enchanted cloud + magical things
- Struggle: School challenges
- Child details: Has a favorite bunny stuffed animal, family speaks different language at home, older sister, good at math
- Helper: Unicorn "Miri Shoma"
- Assessment process: WISC-V + academic and psychological testing
- First major child finding: Dyslexia
- Other major child findings: Low self-esteem, a bit shy, doesn't share insecurity
- Parent findings: Parents did not realize how much the child was struggling, rewarded outcome rather than effort, but now empathic, wanting to mirror and join, concerned, willing to help
- Suggestions: referral to a reading tutor, play therapy, consultation with teacher; parents will reward effort rather than outcome,
- Impressions: Sparky feels understood; parents will help and work with the school, family feels hopeful
- Level: Gear to 4th-grade reading level, include clip art illustrations

Example 2:
- Character and genre: Little Wizard; Fantasy/Magic
- Setting: Two homes in the Magic Kingdom, magic red broom to carry the little wizard between the homes, far distance despite the speed of the magic red broom, very different spells used in each home making it confusing for the little wizard
- Struggle: Sadness and emotional dysregulation
- Child details: Loves animals, drawing
- Helper: Wise owl at the "Caring Clinic for Creatures Big and Small"
- Assessment process: Looking at strange inkblots, telling magical stories, talking to the wise owl who wants to understand the little wizard and is really worried about him
- First major child finding: Sadness, hopelessness /learned helplessness

- Other major child findings: Senses parental conflict post-divorce; attachment security threatened
- Parent findings: Divorce not completely resolved, but parents willing to work to make things more consistent for child
- Suggestions: Referral to parent coaching to learn how to use more similar spells in both homes to help the little Wizard feel less confused and scared; psycho-education about attachment
- Impressions: Little Wizard feels more understood and a little more hopeful about using the same spells in both homes
- Level: 2nd grade reading level; include some clip art but with room for child to illustrate

The structure/steps offered above represent *one* of many ways of writing therapeutic fables. We offer this structure in case you feel unsure and/or intimidated by the idea of writing a fable at the end of your child assessments. But again, we encourage you to deviate from this structure if you want and find your own style. The fable at the beginning of Chapter 1, *Henrietta, The Coo-Coo Chuck*, does not exactly follow the steps we outlined, nor does the fable written for Henry, as you will see in the upcoming case material.

Also, there is one other resource that may be helpful if you find that writing an individualized therapeutic fable is not possible, for example, because you did a brief TA-C (discussed in Chapter 11). One of the authors of this book, Marita Frackowiak, has published a short fable, *Little Bear's Cup and Saucer* (Frackowiak, 2016), that is general enough to fit many child and family situations. The fable describes how Little Bear learns to manage strong emotions through attuned support from his mother. The fable has been useful to both children and parents dealing with various emotional and behavioral challenges, as it offers a child-centered, therapeutic explanation of how emotional attunement from parents helps a child.

Conducting the Summary/Discussion Session With the Child

This Summary/Discussion Session is our last opportunity to meet with the child during the TA-C. (As we will explain in Chapter 10, we do not invite children to the assessment Follow-up Session.) In preparation for this Summary/Discussion Session, we decide on a framework. The therapeutic fable remains the central means of providing feedback with children, especially younger children, and may be the only feedback given to the child. In our experience, children are usually excited about receiving a fable written just for them, and listen attentively as it is read, taking in the therapeutic messages that are embedded within. For older children, and especially children who have posed their own Assessment Questions, we may also take a little time to summarize major assessment findings and answer those Assessment Questions.

Also, as mentioned earlier, we recommend that, if possible, assessors review with parents the fable and what will be said to the child *before* meeting with the child. Clearly, we do not want to give messages to the child that the parent has not approved, and many parents are very helpful in suggesting modifications to the fable to make it "fit" the child better. If we have the fable at the time of the Summary/Discussion with the parent, we may share it and discuss it then. Otherwise, we typically send it to parents to review and discuss with us by phone before we meet with the child. This also gives an opportunity to address reactions or questions that came up after the parent Summary/Discussion Session.

Structure of the Session

When presenting children with age-appropriate feedback, the assessor can structure the session in a similar way to how the parent session was structured. in. Here is a common structure for the child Summary/Discussion Session. Again, feel free to modify this outline to fit your specific family.

1. Welcome the family back and check in, especially with the child if it has been some time since you last met. Give the child a chance to acclimate again to your office.
2. Remind the child that this is the last time you will meet (unless you will be involved in child's ongoing treatment).
3. Share appreciations of the child and reflect on how the child worked during the assessment or what you enjoyed about working together. Don't just present generalities. Instead, refer to specific events that occurred during the TA-C, e.g., "Johnny, I really appreciated how hard you worked on all the tasks we did during the assessment. Do you remember how hard those inkblots were for you? And yet you really hung in there with me and tried hard."
4. If the child posed any Assessment Questions, answer these in a way that is developmentally attuned to the child, perhaps also by briefly summarizing major assessment findings. Here is an example:

Assessor: Mary, today I wanted to tell you what I think I figured out from all those different things we did and see if you think I got it right.

Mary: OK.

Assessor: And I'll also try to answer the question you gave me at the beginning about why you can't stop the bedwetting.

Mary: Alright.

Assessor: So, Mary, I think the main thing I learned is that you have been really sad since your family moved from California, and that you are missing your friends and school a whole lot. Does that seem right?

Mary: (nods "Yes")

Assessor: That seems right? (*Mary nods.*) And I'm wondering if you stopped telling your parents how sad you are because they kept saying you'll "get over it" and just have to think about all the good things that came from the move. Is that part right too?

Mary: (*Looking to see parents' reaction*) Yes. They always talk about how nice our new house is and how the traffic is better here...Can I have my story now that you wrote?

5.   As the previous example shows, it is our experience that most children will not tolerate direct feedback for very long, so we think carefully about what we say and try to keep it brief and relatively simple. Then, we closely pay attention to the child's signals to sense when it is time to shift to indirect feedback. To repeat, with young children and older children who have not posed Assessment Questions, we may go directly to the fable at this point.

6.   Present the therapeutic fable. Provide paper copies for each person in the room, plus have an electronic copy open on the computer.

    a.   Let the child know that you wrote a special fable *just* for her or him.
    b.   Ask the child who she or he wants to read the fable (e.g., self, parent, assessor, each person a section, etc.).
    c.   Read fable out loud-with pauses for comments and reactions, if needed.
    d.   When the fable has been read, ask the child for reaction(s).
    e.   Ask the child if she or he would like to make any changes, making it clear that a new copy can be printed. If the child suggests changes, consider adding the child as a "co-author" on the title page.
    f.   Possibly invite the child (and parents) to illustrate the fable right then or to consider doing that at home.
    g.   Process the experience as a family by asking what they think about the fable, how they feel at the end of the assessment, and what was it like to share the experience as a family together.
    h.   Say thank you and good-bye to the child, reminding the child that this is the last session as the assessment has ended.
    i.   Say good–bye to the parents for the time being, knowing that they are invited to attend a Follow-up Session in about 6-8 weeks.

Case: Summary/Discussion Session With Henry and Parents

For me (Dale), the end of an assessment is a mixed bag of thoughts and feelings. There is some excitement when the assessment has gone well, and I am better able to understand the child and family. For me, there is nothing more satisfying than being part of a process that allows a child and family to adopt a different, more positive narrative. Sometimes when it has been a difficult assessment, I also feel relief, for example when: 1) it has been difficult to join with the parents in order for them to have a more systemic understanding of the problem; 2) my own schedule is over-crowded; or 3) it was difficult to form an alliance with the child. There are other times when I have feelings of loss. TA-C is such an intimate and intense process; it has taken time to complete, and relationships have developed. I have stepped into a family for a number of weeks, and then one day, our collaboration is over, and it is time to say good-bye.

With Henry and his parents, I wasn't feeling a loss yet because (as already discussed with the parents at the previous Summary/Discussion Session), I had recommended family therapy, and the parents knew I was available to be their family therapist if they wanted to continue with me. I knew we had worked well together, and thought it was likely that they would choose me as their family therapist. So, I had a sense of excitement and was feeling very positive about the outcome of what had been a difficult assessment. As I met with Henry, I was mindful that I might continue to see him in family sessions, but chances were that our individual time together was at an end. As I prepared for this meeting, I was reminded of how difficult it had been to witness and interact with Henry's unrelenting sadness; but I also appreciated his intensity, sense of humor, and intelligence. In addition, I was thankful for Barbara and David's willingness to participate in the TA-C and to reflect on themselves.

I prepared for this final session with Henry by again reviewing the assessment and thinking about how I was going to write the fable. I wanted the main character's name to reflect Henry's sadness but to also show his strength. I also wanted to make his sadness palpable. As I read over my notes from our sessions, I was reminded of Henry's words from the Fantasy Animal Drawing Game (discussed in Chapter 4). The first time I introduced the task, Henry drew an irregular rectangular shape that he named a "giant void of nothingness." He did not elaborate on it much but used it as a way to share his despair. On a subsequent day I tried the activity again, and he drew a dot—so small that I could hardly see it on the page. I saw both of these responses as an expression of his terrible loneliness and sadness. I decided to use these responses, Dot and Void of Nothingness, in the fable because I knew Henry would remember them from our time together. The fable was going to be set in the context of a family. I wanted to illustrate how his sadness may have started early on, partly because, as described earlier: 1) temperamentally, Henry seemed to be a highly sensitive child; and 2) at 18 months of age, when his brother was born, he had to deal with the loss of his parents' undivided attention. I also wanted the fable to include how children learn about feelings, why a child might stay focused on sadness, and what other feelings, like anger, might need to be expressed within Henry's family. I wrote the fable for Henry hoping that it would help him to have a new understanding of his situation and that it would reinforce for the parents things we had talked about in the last session. For various reasons, I didn't have time to write the fable collaboratively, but I shared the major points with Henry's parents before the upcoming session. I was confident that it didn't contain any material or messages that they would object to. Next, I prepared an answer to Henry's Assessment Question, "Why am I so sad all the time?" in language that was developmentally appropriate and understandable. You will see my approach in the dialogue below.

When Henry and his parents arrived for the session, I brought them all back into my office and checked in. We talked about how the last two weeks had gone, and all agreed that there weren't any major issues that needed to be addressed. Henry was working on the applications to the magnet schools and was doing that without a lot of help. We talked about how summer was approaching, and everyone looked forward to a reduction in the stress that comes with Henry being in school.

Then, I explained what would be happening for the next couple of hours.

Dale: What I would like to do today is answer the question Henry asked at the very beginning of our time together. Henry, do you remember your question?

Henry: Yes, "Why am I so sad all the time?"

Dale: Yup, that was it. I also wrote a special fable for you. I thought we could read it together first and then share it with your parents at the end of our time together. Is that OK? *I had decided to meet alone with Henry because I wanted to see how engaged he would be with the fable without the distraction of his parents. I was concerned that Henry might use the time to continue to highlight his sadness if his parents attended and miss the "lessons" in the fable.*

Henry and his parents agreed to the plan, and I asked the parents to return to the waiting room. I continued the session alone with Henry. I acknowledged that this would probably be our last time working alone together and how much I appreciated all his hard work and all that he shared with me. He was quiet and attentive as I talked. I noted that he didn't play with his ear or roll around on the couch, which earlier had been signs of his anxiety. In the spirit of collaboration, I asked him which he would like to do first, have me answer his question or read the fable together. He opted to hear the fable first and then get the answer to his question.

Dale: Ok. I just want you to know this is a special fable about a little boy who has a lot of feelings inside and really badly wants to figure out what to do with them. Ready?

Henry: Yeah.

We read the fable together the first time through. Henry didn't comment much on it but seemed quite attentive. Next, I presented the fable with a few sentences on each page leaving a blank space to allow for Henry to illustrate the story. After reading the first two lines, I asked if he might like to draw something to go with the fable. To my surprise and enjoyment, he agreed. We continued reading, and Henry illustrated every page. This was the most participatory Henry had been in terms of doing any creative activity with me. I took this as a positive sign that the fable was resonating with him. Here is the fable, along with some of Henry's illustrations.

The Dot People—A Fable for Henry

Once upon a time, a long time ago, there were two Dots. They each were having nice lives working and playing in a big city (see Figure 8.1).

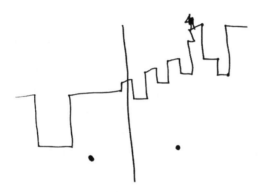

Figure 8.1 Fable Illustration #1.

Then, one day both Dots went to this party, where they met each other. They had a lot in common and they were very different, but they enjoyed each other's company. After a while, they decided to get married (see Figure 8.2).

Figure 8.2 Fable Illustration #2.

Like a lot of Dot people, they thought it would be so much fun and bring so much joy to have a little Dot. This little Dot, like all Dots, was born as a unique and amazing Dot. They named him Noble Dot.

All the big Dots' friends and family thought the new Dot was remarkable. He was a serious, sensitive little Dot and looked at the world with big eyes and wanted everything to be just right. He laughed and smiled and enjoyed himself.

The Big Dots were so glad they had Noble Dot that they decided to add another Dot to the family. This Dot was named Righteous Dot. Noble Dot loved Righteous Dot from the minute he was born.

However, Noble Dot noticed that all of a sudden, he had to share his time and the attention of the big Dots with Righteous Dot. This was not always great.

But Noble Dot grew and liked learning new things and was a very smart and complicated Dot. He didn't know that all Dot people are born with lots of Dot feelings inside. Some feelings are happy and positive, and some are not so happy, but rather sad (see Figure 8.3).

Figure 8.3 Fable Illustration #3.

He didn't know that Little Dots learn about their feelings from the Big Dots around them. But sometimes the Big Dots don't know what the feelings are inside their Little Dots. Sometimes the Big Dots forget to hold up a Dot mirror and say "Oh, you are running and jumping and smiling. You're happy (see Figure 8.4)!"

Figure 8.4 Fable Illustration #4.

On other days, maybe the Big Dots look at their little Dot and see he is sitting by himself. He looks sad and lonely. No Big Dot wants to see their Little Dot sad, so they try and cheer him up and hold up a Dot mirror that isn't quite right. They say, "Things are really wonderful here, look the Dot tree is blooming and the big Dot sun is shining and there are wonderful things in our world (see Figure 8.5)."

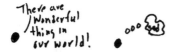

Figure 8.5 Fable Illustration #5.

But the Little Dot doesn't feel understood. He really wants to know what this little Void of Nothingness inside him is. It doesn't feel like the sun is shining. He just feels blah and nothing. He doesn't know that every Dot has some Voids of Nothingness inside at different times. It's just what happens with all Dots; sometimes they have feelings that aren't so great.

So, this is what happened with Noble Dot. He couldn't figure out what all of his feelings were. He just knew that there was this Void of Nothingness inside. He didn't quite know what to do about it. So, he began asking about it (see Figure 8.6).

Figure 8.6 Fable Illustration #6.

At first the Big Dots held up the mirror and said, "Yup, at times, all us Dots feel like there's a bit of nothingness inside. We call that sadness." But Noble Dot didn't really feel like the Big Dots got how really awful this little Void of Nothingness felt. He began to call the Void of Nothingness VON. And it began to grow. The Big Dots decided to take Noble to a feelings doctor, Dr. Dot, to see if she could help with his VON. Dr. Dot found out that Noble Dot was a sensitive Dot. The more the Big Dots didn't understand about VON the worse it felt. Noble Dot began to feel more and more alone.

So, he did what lots of Dots do when they don't understand something. He began talking about it all the time. The Big Dots really didn't know what to do then. They were afraid that if they held up the Dot mirror and talked about it all the time the VON would never go away (see Figure 8.7). So sometimes they talked about it and sometimes they didn't.

That really didn't help – the little VON became a giant VON because no one explained it or could stand holding up the Dot mirror for too long. Everyone kept trying to cheer Noble Dot up.

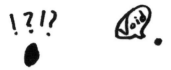

Figure 8.7 Fable Illustration #7.

They told him how smart he was. But he didn't believe it. They told him how talented he was. But he didn't believe it. They told him how funny he was. But he didn't believe it (see Figure 8.8).

Figure 8.8 Fable Illustration #8.

Noble Dot decided that if he could just be perfect, the giant VON would go away. But it didn't go away no matter how perfect he tried to be. Things weren't working out. Noble Dot started to think that he was responsible for all the disorder in the world.

So, what to do? It was not OK that what had grown inside was only the giant VON and not all the other Dot feelings (see Figure 8.9). The Big Dots were concerned, and they took Noble Dot to another feelings doctor to try and figure this out.

Figure 8.9 Fable Illustration #9.

This Dr. Dot really heard Noble Dot's dilemma. He could not understand or let other feelings grow inside until the Big Dots really understood how miserable he was and how scared he was of not being perfect (see Figure 8.10).

Figure 8.10 Fable Illustration #10.

Then, Dr. Dot and Noble Dot made a plan. The first step was to get the Big Dots to not be afraid of Noble Dot's VON.

The second step was to have Dot family meetings, so the Big Dots could understand Noble Dot a little better, and Noble might be able to understand the Big Dots a little better.

The third step was to continue with Noble Dot's other Dr. Dot, so he could understand all the feelings he had inside. They needed to make room for other feelings—not only VON. Both Dr. Dots thought that one of the other feelings might be anger.

Through talking with Dr. Dot and his parents, Noble Dot began to understand that not only how you're born affects things, but how you think affects things too. He noticed that once he talked about the VON to people who understood it and could listen about it, he started to feel a little better. He realized he had other feelings and thoughts inside as well (see Figure 8.11).

Figure 8.11 Fable Illustration #11.

He began to see that how he thought about things also affected how he felt. So, he decided to let other thoughts and feelings in. He decided to say something positive about himself each day (see Figure 8.12). He was going to be a scientist and experiment to see if that made the giant VON a little smaller.

Noble Dot began to realize that although the Dot sun did not shine all the time, neither did the giant VON have to be present all the time. It was just going to take a while for the VON to shrink (see Figure 8.13).

Figure 8.12 Fable Illustration #12.

Figure 8.13 Fable Illustration #13.

THE END

Interestingly, throughout reading the fable, Henry did not talk much or ask any questions. He was very intent on his illustrations. They were very simple and meaningful drawings. I was surprised at his willingness and focus on the drawings. I thought that he was engaged in a different more cooperative way, perhaps because the fable acknowledged and validated his sadness.

Dale:	What do you think? Good fable?
Henry:	Yeah, I like it. Are we going to read it with my parents? (*I took this as a positive sign that he wanted me to help his parents understand him better.*)
Dale:	Do you want to read it with your parents?
Henry:	Yes, but I'm not sure they'll like it.
Dale:	Why not?
Henry:	I don't know.
Dale:	I bet they'll really love your drawings. You know, I wonder Henry, if we used this story to think about why you might be so sad all the time, what would you say?
Henry:	Maybe that my parents don't listen to me?
Dale:	Well, I think that's part of it. Do they not listen to you or do they not listen about certain things?
Henry:	They hate it when I'm sad. And my brother hates it even more. He always tells me to stop talking.
Dale:	That must be really hard. I imagine it feels as if he doesn't care, if he

doesn't like the sad part of you. How hard! Should I try and answer your question now?

Henry: Yes!

Dale: You remember your question? "Why am I so sad all the time?" Well, I think you were born into this world as a sensitive kid. We all have different temperaments. Our temperament is biological. It is not something we decide to be but rather we're just born that way. Being sensitive is just one type of temperament. Your parents gave you lots of attention and love but then, when your brother was born, you had to share that attention with him. Sometimes, kids, especially those with sensitive temperaments, struggle a lot with sharing attention after a sibling is born. And I think you might have struggled with that. It was hard to share and then your mom had to go back to work. You missed her and your dad was still home, but he had to deal with two kids by himself, so there might have been less attention. Does that make sense?

Henry: Kind of. But why am I so sad now?

Dale: Well, parents help us to understand our emotions, and it's really hard for parents to see their child so sad, so they try and cheer the child up, rather than focus on the sadness. But then the child doesn't feel like anyone is paying attention to him and he feels more alone. I think that might have been a little bit of what happened to you. In order for things to get better, we need to help your parents listen more to your sadness, which will help you to feel not so alone with it. Then, everyone can also notice other feelings in the family like joy, or anger. Does that make sense, Henry?

Henry: Yeah, I guess. Do you think we could read the story with my parents now? *(I think Henry was excited to share the fable because it really reflected his truth.)*

Dale: Sure, I'll get them.

I brought Barbara and David back into the office and we all read the fable together. They both seemed to appreciate the story. They said how much love there was in the Dot family, and then David said how sad it was that Noble Dot was so sad.

Dad: Henry, do you think you're a little like Noble Dot?

Henry: Yeah, I guess.

Dale: *(I didn't want Henry to feel put on the spot, so I quickly interceded.)* I wonder, Henry, if it would be a good idea to share my answer to your question about "Why am I so sad all the time?" with your parents. What do you think?

Henry: Good idea.

From the beginning of the assessment, Barbara and David knew Henry's Assessment Question, and we had discussed already how I was going to answer his question during their Summary/Discussion Session. I knew there wasn't going to be any new information shared with the parents, but I wanted them to hear pretty much exactly what I had said to Henry in order for them to be able to reinforce my explanation. The parents listened and were quiet. I shared that I thought family therapy would be beneficial in helping everyone understand and share their feelings with each other. I again repeated how much I enjoyed working with Henry and how much he taught me about how important it is to have your feelings recognized by others, even when it was difficult for others to do.

Before they left, we all talked a little about the fable. David and Barbara thought it would be nice to read it together at home. I said I thought that was a great idea and asked Henry what he might like to do with the fable. He said he wanted to keep it and read it as a family, including Frank. I gave Henry his fable after I made a copy of it for his file, and we all said good-bye.

I felt pleased with how the session went. I appreciated Henry's attention and focus. He really seemed to enjoy me reading the fable to him and most importantly didn't reject my suggestion to illustrate it. I took this as a very good sign of how the fable must have resonated with him. I was initially surprised by him wanting to share it with his brother but then realized that this was totally appropriate since Frank struggled with Henry's sadness. I took it as Henry's way of explaining himself to his brother.

Collaborative Therapeutic Collage

As mentioned earlier, the Collaborative Therapeutic Collage method was initially developed by Marita Frackowiak for children who seemed too mature for a therapeutic fable. Quickly, however, Marita began to use collages at the end of TA-C with children who struggled with reading or verbal comprehension, were stronger visual-spatial learners, or simply preferred art or doing things with their hands over reading. Marita found that this method could be as creative and varied as clients and assessors. Below we present Marita's guide for preparing the collage, steps of the activity, and a case example from Marita's practice.

Preparing for the Session: Structure and Steps

The first step in the Collaborative Therapeutic Collage is to make a bullet point outline of the main findings of the assessment to be shared with the child. You won't share all of the results, but only the main points. Keep them short and organized as bullet point phrases. You should also attend to Levels of Information and not include findings that might be Level 3 for the child. Here is a sample list for a smart 11-year-old girl:

- Above average intellectual skills and special talent in solving visual puzzles
- Good attention at the beginning of a task, but difficulties staying focused over time

- Hard worker, excels at academics
- Very caring in relationships
- Good at reading people
- Quiet and reserved
- Longs to have more friends
- Feels sad a lot, but does not like to share her feelings
- Tends to try to solve problems on her own

Next, print the phrases in a large font on one page that you will bring into the session. Typically, this page is shared with parents to get their input and let them know what you plan to share with the child. The parents are informed that the next session will focus on constructing a collage based on the phrases, with the result being a final product that the child can take home. Also explain to the parents that their role in the session is to: a) support their child's art project by being helpful in various practical ways (e.g., cutting, gluing); b) verbally validate the strengths discussed (e.g., by offering specific examples of when they have seen the strengths in daily life); c) offer verbal support and understanding of the areas that need improvement/intervention; and d) help facilitate a child-centered, fun, and meaningful activity (e.g., by showing enthusiasm and doing the collage together, without taking over the activity). Ask the parents to help prepare for the session by gathering images from their own photos or from magazines representing the phrases (e.g., personal pictures of one of the child's achievements, or a photo of the child sitting alone in the garden) and to bring anything they think might resonate with the child and the activity (e.g., a marker of the child's favorite color, the tag from a beloved lost pet). In a sense, the parents are co- creators of the project by contributing to the materials the child uses.

Similarly, the assessor prepares for the session by gathering images representing metaphors discussed in the assessment process. For example, the child saw "a sad and lonely bird" on the Rorschach, which was discussed in more detail to understand how the child felt, and so the assessor cuts a photo from a magazine of a bird who is alone. Or on the Early Memory Procedure (Bruhn, 1992) the child might have told of being brave and facing her or his fear before a school's Spelling Bee. The assessor might find an image of a friendly or cartoonish bee that could represent the achievement, and also remind the child of how hard it was to be alone with those feelings. In addition to images, the assessor prepares and brings various art and craft supplies to the session (e.g., stickers, letters of different font and size, dried leaves, flowers, glue, pipe cleaners, colorful markers, scissors). One final thing the assessor brings is a large piece of posterboard or cardboard on which the collage will be constructed.

The goal of the collaborative preparation of the materials by parents and the assessor is to present the child with a thoughtful selection of images and craft options to mirror how the parents and the assessor have come to understand the child. The careful preparation also shows that the assessor paid attention and listened carefully during assessment sessions, and made special note of who the child is, what they like, and how she or he feels and think about the world. Selecting "special" images that represent discussions or metaphors used during the assessment also helps the child feel seen and understood. Typically, when the child first sees some of those images she or he smiles and looks at the assessor with a surprise and a bit of "this is our little secret language" expression on her or his face. The child also realizes that her or his parents participated in collecting the materials, and this gives them hope about being understood outside the assessment.

Conducting the Collaborative Therapeutic Collage Session

As usual in TA-C we start the session by welcoming the child and the parents. We let the child know that it is our last session concluding the assessment. We introduce the session as an opportunity to do a special activity together and to talk about the assessment findings. We then introduce the activity of the collage, stating that this is going to be a joint effort between the child, parents, and assessor. We let the family know that the assessor's role is to talk about different test findings; the child's goal is to decide where and how in the collage they want to represent the findings with words and images; and the parents' role is to be helpers to the child, by cutting out pictures, gluing things, and following the child's instructions.

The assessor then proceeds to let the child know that one way to organize the test results is to divide the collage into two sections, one representing the child's strengths and another representing the child's areas of struggle. We typically let the child title the two sections. We can offer labels to help, like: "great strengths" and "work in progress" or "yay, I got this down" and "help, needed, please…." But quite often children will come up with their own "one-liners" to capture the spirit of the collage. Starting this way allows the child to anticipate both positive and potentially difficult ideas to be discussed, and it sets the stage to talk about the findings in a non-overwhelming, yet direct and accurate manner. We have found that children respond well to being talked to directly and honestly, yet in a developmentally appropriate manner. This activity offers such an approach, with the benefit of the art medium being distracting and self-soothing.

The next step in the process is for the assessor to begin explaining the findings (usually starting with strengths) while cutting out the statements on the summary page prepared prior to the session. As the assessor hands each statement to the child, everyone present discusses whether it is a strength or area of weakness. If the child agrees that the statement is accurate, then together with their parents they search for images to illustrate or embellish the statement. This process is repeated as many times as needed based on each of the prepared assessment findings. As each new piece of the story is revealed, the assessor checks in with the child, asks for examples from her or his life to illustrate various findings, and encourages the child to make personal notes (if she or he would like to do so) as the collage is assembled.

Parents are also invited to share examples, comment, validate feelings, and offer praise and support as the child, step-by-step, discovers each statement about her or himself. Typically, it is best to start with strengths and positive statements, then talk about more difficult findings, and end with something neutral or encouraging. As with most TA-C sessions, we stay attuned both to parents as well as children and change course, as needed, based on the child's or parents' response. We do not want to overwhelm the family system. However offering a calm, creative space to work together on a very personal art project can offer an emotionally moving experience for both the child and parents. In Marita's experience, the Collaborative Therapeutic Collage method has been an overwhelmingly positive, highly appreciated family experience, even with the moments that are moving or sad.

Case Example

Let me (Marita) share a brief case example that illustrates the power and enjoyment of the Collaborative Therapeutic Collage. Aiden was a 12-year-old, very bright boy who was referred for TA-C due to multiple social and behavioral problems at school. He was academically advanced, but struggled to make friends, follow teachers' requests, and respect school rules. Aiden loved to "argue" with his teachers and almost always "insisted" on getting an explanation of the rules, which he then proceeded to "evaluate" and "prove" wrong. Needless to say, the teachers were exhausted by this behavior, and other kids were not interested in his typical conversations. Aiden loved science, art, science fiction, drawing comics, and nature. One of his parents' Assessment Questions was, "Why does Aiden struggle so much socially?" Aiden really wanted to know his IQ. A comprehensive assessment revealed that:

a. Aiden's IQ was in the top two percent across all domains for his age group.
b. Aiden analyzed information by talking aloud and easily connected various topics across domains.
c. Aiden's social/emotional/behavioral difficulties with peers and adults were consistent with a diagnosis of Autism Spectrum Disorder (ASD); yet he did not meet all of the criteria for ASD.
d. Aiden and the rest of the family (as was discovered in the FIS) were grieving the death of a beloved pet who had died a year prior, yet nobody in the family wanted to talk about emotions.
e. Aiden used his intellect to stay away from painful feelings, and he expressed his underlying anger and anxiety through his oppositional behavior and argumentativeness.
f. Underneath Aiden's outer presentation of being a know-it-all, he was a tender-hearted boy who felt insecure and misunderstood and wanted connection. One way Aiden sought comfort was through his connection with nature.

I decided to do a collage with Aiden as I felt sure he would react poorly to a fable as being "beneath him." His parents were eager to help and gathered various images and materials; I prepared my outline of statements. When I explained what we would be doing in the session, Aiden was very excited about the activity, but very quickly asked me if I didn't want to tell him his actual IQ and instead wanted to distract him with art. I thought this was a funny and a clever way to engage, so I immediately responded by reassuring him that I would start with his IQ, and would even tell him about various other scores he obtained on the intelligence test. He was relieved and agreed to participate.

One of the metaphors Aiden and I developed during the assessment, when discussing his tendency to think aloud, was that his brain was like a tree with many branches and leaves. He liked this image a lot. When I began talking about his IQ scores, one of my summary statements read: "extraordinary intelligence skills across many cognitive domains." Aiden was very pleased. He was even more delighted when at this point, his mother presented him with a picture of a brain in a shape of a tree, labeled "The Amazing Tree Brain." The parents told Aiden that using this metaphor helped them understand how complex his thinking is and how frustrating it must be for him to be so often misunderstood by others. He agreed, and we extended the metaphor of the "tree brain" to discuss how "pruning" what one says is an important skill in social situations. Aiden liked the discussion and wrote: "pruning needed when with people so they don't get bored or mad" on one side of the giant "tree brain" picture. He had divided this picture in half to represent that there were both strengths and weaknesses to having a "tree brain." He proudly marked: "bragging rights" next to his IQ score, adding that he was going to tell his older brother.

We continued step by step, following my outline of statements, with Aiden engaged in both the discussion and creating a collage. He responded very well to my suggestion that his "tree brain" was excellent at many things, but naming feelings was not one of them. Hence, that was the area he could improve by working with an individual therapist. Again, Aiden agreed, as he did with my suggestion that because his feelings are not easily accessible for him, he expressed them with his behaviors and argumentativeness instead. For example, he might often be irritated instead of understanding the more nuanced feelings he might be having, such as sadness, loneliness, regret, guilt, etc. Aiden then pointed out that my observation about his being argumentative was not true in our session because he was agreeing with me a lot. We both laughed, and he made a note under the summary statement I had prepared, "Tendency to be argumentative to avoid feelings," that said: "except when the therapist is right."

At the end, both Aiden and his parents shared how much they enjoyed the collage activity and how great it was for Aiden to have the direct, but kind feedback about his social struggles. As I typically do, I made a copy of the collage for my file before he left, and encouraged him to take the original with him. I received an email later that week from his mother thanking me for the activity as it was fun and meaningful for them all. She added that Aiden was keeping the collage by his desk.

As mentioned earlier, Collaborative Therapeutic Collage can offer a meaningful experience of summarizing the results of the assessment, sharing a pleasant family moment, and leaving the child with a personalized transitional object at the end of the process. We believe that it offers a strong therapeutic option to the fable, and we encourage you to consider both options, as well as others you may think of, for giving feedback to children.

References

Aschieri, F., Fantini, F., & Bertrando, P. (2012). Therapeutic Assessment with children in family therapy. *Australian and New Zealand Journal of Family Therapy*, 33(4), 285–298.

Booker, C. (2019). *The seven basic plots: Why we tell stories.* London: Continuum.

Bruhn, A. (1992). The Early Memories Procedure: A projective test of autobiographical memory: II. *Journal of Personality Assessment*, 58, 326–346.

Engelman, D. H., Allyn, J. B., Crisi, A., Finn, S. E., Fischer, C. T., & Nakamura, N. (2016). "Why am I so stuck?": A Collaborative/Therapeutic Assessment case discussion. *Journal of Personality Assessment*, 98(4), 360–373.

Frackowiak, M. (2016). *Little bear's cup and saucer.* Manor, TX: Dover Creek Publishing.

Handler, L. (2007). The use of therapeutic assessment with children and adolescents. In S. Smith & L. Handler, (Eds.), *Clinical assessment of children and adolescents: A practitioner's guide* (pp. 53–72). Mawah, NJ: Erlbaum & Associates.

Hansson, A., Hansson, L., Danielsson, I., & Domellöf, E. (2016). Short- and long-term effects of child neuropsychological assessment with a collaborative and therapeutic approach: A preliminary study. *Applied Neuropsychology: Child*, 5(2), 97–106.

Mercer, B. L., Fong, T., & Rosenblatt, E. (Eds.) (2016). *Assessing children in the urban community.* New York: Routledge.

Purves, C. (2016). Surface ripples or deep water? Finding the level for children's feedback stories. In Mercer, B. L., Fong, T., & Rosenblatt, E. (Eds.) (2016). *Assessing children in the urban community* (pp. 134–139). New York: Routledge.

Tharinger, D. J., Finn, S. E., Wilkinson, A. D., DeHay, T., Parton, V., Bailey, E., & Tran, A. (2008). Providing psychological assessment feedback with children through individualized fables. *Professional Psychology: Research and Practice*, 39, 610–618.

Tharinger, D. J., & Pilgrim, S. (2011). Child and parent experiences of neuropsychological assessment as a function of child feedback by individualized fable. *Child Neuropsychology*, 18, 228–241.

9 Phase IV: Written Communications: Reports and Parent Letters

Having completed the Summary/Discussion Sessions, where we provided oral feedback to the parents and oral/fable feedback to the child and parents, we move onto written communications. While some assessors only provide oral feedback, we feel it is important to include written feedback in the assessment process. We understand that for some assessors, report writing and other means of written communication can be a difficult and at times, an impersonal task. It is different than face-to-face contact during the assessment and it can feel daunting to organize and put in writing all they learned about the child in the context of the family. We empathize with these struggles, as without a doubt, each of us has been challenged in our own ways with writing up the findings and making meaning of an assessment. We hope the framework provided in this chapter, consistent with the values of TA-C, offers a more personal, meaningful, and pleasant approach to capturing the assessment process.

Throughout the assessment and as we begin the writing process itself, we ask ourselves three questions: 1) Why are we writing this up? 2) Who are we writing this for? 3) What's the best format to use?

Why Are We Writing This Up?

As noted by Lance and Krishnamurthy (2003), a combination of oral and written feedback has the greatest impact on clients and is better than either oral or written feedback alone. The authors posited that having continued access to the written word helps clients solidify new learning about themselves. We have certainly seen this to be true in our clinical practices.

It may be tempting for a busy assessor to not produce any written document and rely solely on oral feedback or an audio/videorecording of the Summary/Discussion Session. But there are other practical reasons for producing a written document at the completion of the assessment. Sometimes, perhaps even years later, parents may ask for a written document for a specific purpose like disability eligibility or admittance to a residential treatment program. In these situations, it is often difficult for the assessor to resurrect the case and write a meaningful document without taking a lot of time and

DOI: 10.4324/9781003000174-9

effort to review the case. Hence, we recommend that assessors produce some form of written feedback for every TA-C at the time of the assessment.

Who Is the Intended Reader?

In any assessment the audience for the written document can be varied and needs to be considered. In TA-C, first and foremost, parents have access to every written document that arises from the assessment, so their perspective is always taken into account. In some assessments, parents will be the only readers of the written feedback. In other cases, written feedback is drafted with additional readers in mind, e.g., teachers; current and future mental health professionals; and occupational, physical, speech, and language therapists.

For example, in Henry's case, a full psychological report was prepared after the assessment, intended for current and future professionals who would be involved with Henry. In addition, a personal letter was given to Barbara and David focusing on the family dynamics and their Assessment Questions. We say more about these documents below.

What Is the Best Format to Use?

Depending on the intended audience the format of the written product may vary. We have found that traditional reports often do not take into account parents' perspectives and how vulnerable they feel when reading a written document about their child. What might it be like to read a report that is written in the third person, with lots of statistical data, that doesn't interpret the data in the context of the child and family? Writing a letter to the parents, instead of a traditional report, has been a unique contribution of TA-C to the field of assessment with children. It is a personal, unique, and often treasured document that parents receive about their child and family. The goal of the letter is to answer the Assessment Questions, to have written documentation of the assessment process and, in many cases, to review major findings. We strive to communicate to the parents what they have experienced, what has been learned from the TA-C, and what the next steps are. This letter is usually very personal, and parents may not want to share it with service providers. This is when a report comes in handy.

In TA-C, we have been disappointed with many traditional reports. Often, they are written in a format consistent with a medical model, that is, they are formal, jargon filled, and not very engaging for the family and many other professionals. Such reports often do not reflect the context of the assessment or family. In response to these shortcomings, we have developed our own methods and standards for written reports. We refer to our product as a Therapeutic Psychological Report, reflective of the values and process of TA-C.

Commonalities Between the Parent Letter and the Therapeutic Psychological Report

Both the letter and the report are written in a more personal and accessible manner. We refer to ourselves in the first person ("I" and "we") rather than in the third person ("the examiner", "the assessor"). This style acknowledges a basic view of TA where assessors are participant-observers in the assessment process. While we may like to think that we are objective reporters of fact, the test data, assessment process and results are viewed through our subjective lenses. We may as well be transparent about that. We do not want the data presented in such a way as to obscure the human interaction.

Within both the Parent Letter and the Therapeutic Psychological Report, we remind or tell the reader the amount of time spent face-to-face with the clients and the tests that were administered, and we make mention of the participation of both the parents and the child. When discussing a test, we briefly explain its goals and procedures so those unfamiliar with the test know why it was given, as well as the findings. We avoid jargon because it does not consider the reader's perspective when they are not psychologist. For example, what is it like to for someone to read: "Rorschach findings showed that the child's oral dependency scale was elevated, indicating unmet primitive needs" vs "The results of the Rorschach suggested that John was longing for more nurturance and affection. While he might not be fully aware of those needs and thus be unable to express them with words, some of his behaviors, such as taking toys from his younger sister, could be a way he signals those needs."

In writing both letters and reports, we try and link the test data to the child's everyday life. We believe that the most useful way to help parents remember the meaning of the assessment findings is to connect the test data to their life and behaviors. We make these connections in the Summary/Discussion Session with the parents, but equally importantly we include some examples in the written communications. For example, "Johnny's scores on both self-report tests and on the performance-based test like the Rorschach, suggest that he experiences a lot of anxiety. I think he distracts himself by talking to his neighbors in class and asking to go to the restroom multiple times in the hour. While this is disruptive behavior it alleviates some of his concern about not being able to participate fully in class."

We write "suggestions for next steps" rather than "recommendations." We feel this is a more respectful stance. It is really up to the recipient of the report or letter to decide how they want or can proceed. We also believe that "suggestions" reflect the spirit of the therapeutic collaboration, by not taking a "one-up" stance in telling parents what to do. We often prioritize the list of suggestions from most to less important, helping parents make decisions about what steps to pursue after the assessment. And we always try to include suggestions that parents can work on alone, as well as suggesting getting help from other professionals.

Specifics about the Parent Letter

The idea for writing a letter to parents rather than a report came from Finn (1997) who believed, that in situations where parents were the only readers, a letter format would make more sense. Also, when a Therapeutic Psychological Report is provided along with a letter, the letter can serve as a supplement to address the parents' specific Assessment Questions and touch on information that parents don't want to share with general readers. The letter is very personal and often includes what the assessment meant to the assessor and what they have learned from the process.

As has already been discussed, the letter is written after the Summary/Discussion Session and closely follows the outline written for that session. The letter can include new information discovered during the session, as well as the parents' perspectives on what was discussed. The information gleaned during that session can enrich the letter. For example, "Jim, you shared just how much Max shut down emotionally after your cat died and did not talk about his feelings with anyone until he broke down. That was a good example of what his testing shows about his tendency to dismiss his feelings and focus on his school and sports. However, as we discussed, it does not mean that Max is not feeling his feelings deeply inside. He needs help putting words to them and expressing them before they overwhelm him." The letter also can be personalized with comments about parental reactions, such as, "Julie, you seemed very relieved when we discussed Mary's cognitive findings in our session."

The letter to Henry's parents that Dale wrote to supplement the Therapeutic Psychological Report follows.

Dale Rudin, Ph.D.
Licensed Psychologist

4310 Medical Parkway, Suite 101, Austin, TX 78756

May 1, 20XX

Dear Barbara and David,

I hope you are both doing well. This letter accompanies the report that summarizes the results of the Therapeutic Assessment we did together. The report was written for you and for school and mental health professionals. This letter mainly addresses your Assessment Questions.

Before getting to your questions, I want to appreciate how willing you were to take part in Henry's assessment. You provided me with lots of information about yourselves and your families of origin that allowed me to get to know you both and Henry in a deep and authentic way. As we discussed in one of our last sessions, psychological assessment is a vulnerable process for parents, and you were already exhausted from living with Henry's depression and negativity. So, I doubly appreciate your participation and commitment to the process. I think your dedication speaks to how much you love Henry and want to help him in any way you can.

I also want to acknowledge how puzzling and difficult it can be to interact with Henry, and I completely understand why you said at the beginning of the assessment that you were at your "wits' ends." There were times during the assessment sessions where I found myself also getting frustrated with his incessant negativity. I think it took the test results and your open disclosures for me to begin to understand Henry and the family. I am hopeful the assessment, the report, and this letter will be useful as you deal with the concerns that brought you to my office. And, I believe that you all can get to a better place with appropriate support in part because of the psychological strengths you all have. For example, I was struck by both of your ability to "hang in there" with Henry even when it gets tough. And I really enjoyed Henry's sense of humor and quirkiness when he allowed me to see them.

Answers to Your Assessment Questions

Now, let me turn to your questions.

Is Henry clinically depressed or is it situational?

I think when you asked this question you were wondering if Henry's reporting of his sadness was happening more because of pressure at school, his difficulty doing homework, and the upcoming transition to middle school. Perhaps your thoughts had been that once summertime comes and the decision is made about which middle school to attend, he will no longer be depressed. I don't think school stressors are enough to explain Henry's current difficulties, nor that things will get better if those stressors go away. As described in the report, many of the psychological tests we did show that Henry is very depressed. Remember how his Rorschach indicated that he has a damaged view of himself and that he is anxious? His sadness is pervasive and it can overwhelm his thinking. For example, he can be doing well in school but think everyone is doing better than him. His perfectionism only adds to the negative view of himself and his circumstances. His depression might be magnified because of the difficulties of his present situation, but even if he did not have the external pressures of school and transitioning to middle school, I think he would still be depressed.

What are Henry's intellectual strengths and weaknesses? Is there a disharmony among them? What kind of learning environment is best for him?

As explained in the psychological report, I did the gold standard cognitive test for children, the WISC-V, to help answer this question. As we discussed, I think the cognitive test results are likely an underestimate of Henry's "true" potential—because of the emotional issues that are affecting him--but they do give us a window into how he is doing at this moment. On this WISC-V, Henry scored in the above average range on the Verbal Comprehension Index (VCI=113), Visual Spatial Index (VSI=119) and Fluid Reasoning Index (FRI=112). If these were accurate measures of Henry's intellectual functioning (which is doubtful), they would suggest that Henry has the ability to get A's and B's, at a moderately difficult middle school if he is able to study and work relatively hard. However, the other two WISC-V Indices were in the average range--Working Memory Index (WMI=97), and Processing Speed Index (PSI=98). The WMI measures a child's ability to hold verbal and visual information in mind and work with it. Think about going to the store when you have $5.00 to spend and you're trying to figure out if you have enough money for 3 items. You have to get the prices of each item (visually or auditorily) and hold them in mind while you do a mental calculation. Henry's score suggests that this would not be a super easy task for him. The PSI measures how slow or fast a child thinks and processes, especially using visual information in a paper-and-pencil task, but also with other kinds of cognitive challenges. For example, let's think about Henry being in school and writing notes from the board or while the teacher is speaking, on his own paper. Can he keep up with the task of writing while thinking about what he has to write? Again, his scores suggest this would not be a super easy task for him. To repeat, the PSI and WMI indices probably don't tell us Henry's true potential, as they are most affected by depression as compared to the other WISC-V indices. But they do suggest that Henry would likely struggle keeping up in a demanding middle school. As I described in the report, Henry was engaged in the WISC-V and tried hard, but once things got more difficult, he seemed to deflate and give up. I think Henry would benefit from a low-pressure, but stimulating, learning environment. I suggest you look for a school that is challenging but supportive, with teachers who can be authentically positive and encouraging.

Why does Henry make provocative statements to us?

I must say, when you gave me this question, I was curious whether I would get to witness Henry being provocative during the assessment. Then, do you remember the first session we had all together? I couldn't engage Henry in having a positive response to *anything* I said. At times it felt like he was purposefully testing us--pushing to see if we would fall into despair with him or get angry and reject him. When I wondered how that felt for you both, you said it was both a relief that he was showing me how negative and provoking he could be and also upsetting to see him interact so negatively with a person he had just met.

During the testing, I got to see how challenging Henry could be and what big emotions he can provoke in others. Do you remember, when he was completing the BASC-3, he responded negatively to everything except for a couple of the items? And then, he asked if I thought he did it accurately. I was noncommittal, and he said he wanted to change some of his responses. I said, "Sure," thinking he would move some in a more positive or neutral direction. Instead, he made several of the neutral responses more negative. I felt myself getting really irritated, but I also was amazed at how effective Henry's behavior was in seeing if I would reject or shame him.

After a particularly challenging session, where Henry was really negative, I thought about the feelings he brought up in me and what they might tell us. Several things came to mind:

A. Often, I felt angry with Henry. I started to wonder, "Is Henry really angry with himself, and getting other people to 'hold' it for him because it is too scary for him to feel and express directly?" This made me wonder about how anger was processed in your family. Was it OK to be angry? Did anger come out of nowhere? Did people contain anger until they couldn't any longer and then explode? How could Henry safely share that he was angry with the two of you? This reminds me of our family session, where Henry shared how upset he was that you, David, got angry about his not taking his bath and dragged him into the bathroom. Henry was startled and hurt by that incident, but also still angry about it.

B. Henry's ongoing negativity also made me feel helpless. I'm a psychologist in part because I want to help people feel better, and this didn't feel possible with Henry. I found myself wanting to change his attitude, rather than empathize with it. I thought about what you, his parents, might feel after hours of this unrelenting negativity? Like every parent, you want your children to be happy, but Henry doesn't let this happen. And often, helplessness can turn to anger or real sadness. I started to feel what a struggle and worry Henry's behavior and emotions must be for you.

C.   When Henry wasn't testing me with his extreme negativity and instead was genuinely sad, I found it painful to really be there for him, because I felt the depths of his pain and had to work to not be "sucked into" it. If I, a person outside the family, could feel overwhelmed by Henry's pain, I could only imagine how difficult it would be for you, his parents, who love him and care for him. I can see how you might want to dismiss or minimize Henry's pain to keep your own bearings.

So, let me return to your question about why Henry might be provocative. I think he is unconsciously "testing" the two of you to see if you can manage emotions that he doesn't know how to handle. We didn't talk about this directly in our Summary and Discussion Session, but I thought more about this afterwards and wanted to share something about this idea of "testing." The test has two parts. First, will you join him in sinking into massive hopelessness and despair and agreeing that life is not worth living? A part of Henry wants to see that you can feel and empathize with his depression and not be over-whelmed by it, so you can show Henry how to handle it. Second, I think Henry wants to see if he can provoke you to be angry with him and reject him and shame him, or again whether you can manage your own anger in a way where you set limits but don't lose control. The testing suggests Henry needs this example from you because he is holding a lot of anger that he doesn't know what to do with. He doesn't feel safe expressing his anger, so he directs it at himself, but this provides a way for him to "poke at" other people, which is his safe way of expressing anger.

We might ask, who or what is Henry angry at? Basically, I think he feels you are not passing his "tests," and this leads to his being scared and angry. First, because of your own backgrounds, it has been hard for the two of you to sit with his deep sadness and helplessness, and to appreciate how much he wants to be taken care of. (Remember how hard this was for me, and I'm not Henry's parent!) Barbara, you survived a very chaotic family of origin by learning to "pull yourself up by your bootstraps" and take care of yourself. David, although you are sensitive, you don't show your emotions very easily. As a result, Henry may not feel heard or seen by either of you as much as he needs. He'd prefer to see you angry about his being provocative rather than feel left alone with his feelings. Second, I think Henry is unconsciously provoking anger in both of you to see if you can handle it in a good way: by setting limits and being firm without being punitive, explosive, or shaming. This is hard for the two of you because you didn't get a lot of support or models for handling your own anger. But you have managed to find this "magic spot" with Henry several times, for example when you limited his "sad talk" to a certain period every evening. Third, the testing suggests that there is a part of Henry where he feels worthless and damaged. He is also testing the two of you to see if you will shame him and reject him, or find a way to love and cherish him, even when he pushes the two of you to your limits. What a hard and difficult situation this creates for the two of you. I know I wouldn't be able to handle Henry well as a parent without a lot of outside support.

Has Henry experienced an unknown trauma that has adversely affected his self-image and how he engages with the world?

This is an interesting question. Before our family session, I would have said that as far as I knew, there was no big "T" trauma, but there might be a lot of small "t" traumas that have contributed to Henry's current struggles. What does this mean? Big "T" traumas involve one or more incidents that are overwhelming and terrifying, such as physical, sexual, or emotional abuse from which the person can't escape. As hard as it may be to believe or hear, if we look at the family session, the event that Henry described in which David dragged him to the bathroom seems to be a big "T" trauma for Henry; it sticks in his mind as a very shocking and frightening event, in part because you, David, so rarely express your anger directly. I think our work in the family session is the beginning of healing from this incident, but there is more work to do.

Also, I think there were small "t" traumatic experiences that probably influenced Henry's development. Often these smaller traumas have a bigger impact on a child than a parent might be aware of. I think one these might have been when you, Barbara, went back to work and David became the primary caregiver. The household organization and routine changed, Henry was used to your (Barbara's) warmth and expressive demeanor, and suddenly he was left more with you David, and your more retiring personality. As we talked about previously, you don't give a whole lot away through your facial expression and can be difficult to read. I imagine this might have been a huge change for Henry. Also, while both of you agreed on the new family arrangement, Barbara, you had a lot of feelings about going back to work and starting a business. I'm wondering if some of the resentments you might have felt toward David affected the emotional tone in the family, which then created less safety and more negative feelings for Henry. I imagine this might have been a difficult time for Henry and that you might not have picked up on this fully or known what to do if you did notice.

In addition, I wonder about the intergenerational transmission of trauma. Barbara, you described a lot of trauma in your family of origin. Your mother was mentally ill and suffered a lot at the hands of her first husband and children. Your father, although very dear to you, was an alcoholic and that takes a toll on children. Your sister suffered tremendously with depression, and you were her main support person. You are a sturdy survivor but lived under the cloak of trauma both with a capital "T" and lower case "t." There are times when this trauma gets transmitted through the generations, unbeknown to anyone. David, it's less clear what happened in your family growing up, but somehow you learned to keep your feelings to yourself and not show much. While this presumably helped you growing up, it probably wasn't helpful to Henry who was trying to make sense of his own emotions.

How do we prevent Henry from becoming further anxious and depressed?

When considering how to support kids Henry's age who are anxious and depressed, I think about what internal and external support is needed. If we turn first to what he needs from you, what we've learned is that Henry longs for positive attention and attunement from you both. That means you have to be able to mirror his feelings and let him know that whatever he feels can be seen, tolerated, and accepted by you. This means there is extra pressure on both of you to be exquisitely aware of feelings, which will require you to first be aware of your own feelings. In other words, you must become more comfortable with a wide range of your own feelings so that Henry can better understand his feelings. As you make progress in this endeavor, you will be able to respond in a more helpful way to Henry and he will learn how to regulate his own emotions better. This is not going to be easy. You will have to become real masters at validating his feelings, especially those that "push your buttons" and that you were not allowed to express when you were growing up. You will need to model sharing your own feelings appropriately, especially anger, and using your anger as a cue to set limits in a firm but non-reactive way. Henry will be watching to see if you can do this not only with him, but in your relationship with each other.

Then, thinking about what Henry needs internally, I believe he needs ongoing support outside the family from an "emotions expert" who can help Henry name his feelings and express them in a more direct way. As Henry gets acceptance and support for his feelings, I believe they may become less extreme and will be easier to handle within the family. In our last session, Dr. Jagger said she is willing to continue working with Henry, and I strongly advise that you stay with the individual psychotherapy.

How can we help Henry feel confidence and loved?

It is important to have a balance where Henry feels cherished and also contained. Barbara, I remember you talking about how much you cherish your children. I think you said it was like carrying them around on a linen cloth. I got the image of them being carefully, delicately revered. So, I know you cherish Henry. The testing shows that right now he has a lot of intense dependency needs and is longing to be taken care of. Be available when he needs you without impatience towards his needs. Validate his wide range of feelings, clearly show him when you enjoy him, help him realistically appraise his schoolwork, reward his persistence in trying rather than focusing on the product, and set appropriate limits. I think limit setting is difficult for both of you, but it is essential, and you managed to do it when—with the support of Dr. Jagger—you limited Henry's sad talk time. For the health and well-being of the entire family, this limit needed to be set, but you successfully balanced it with validating Henry's sadness and letting him know there would be a time to really talk about how bad he feels. It might be interesting to take this example as a model and think of other situations where Henry is needing a firm, gentle limit.

Suggestions for Next Steps

1. Continue Henry's individual therapy, with a focus on helping him name his feelings and learn how to comfort and soothe himself.
2. Begin family therapy, with the following goals:

    a. family members learning how to express and respond to each others' feelings, especially anger,
    b. the two of you learning how to set firm but kind limits with Henry,
    c. learning to repair events from the past where Henry felt hurt or left alone,
    d. discovering if Henry is "holding" feelings for other family members, and if so, how to reclaim these so Henry doesn't bear the burden.

3. Decrease pressure at school. Make sure that Henry has similar 504 Accommodations that we negotiated with his elementary school as he enters middle school. I strongly recommend a school that is not as competitive as the magnet school he has applied to.
4. Provide a tutor for academic support to help Henry stay on top of assignments. This may have as much to do with emotional as with academic support. Therefore, a tutor who: a) is empathic but firm, b) can help with emotional self-regulation, and c) understands how to respond to negative self -talk without being dismissive,

would be most beneficial. In addition, it would be helpful if the person could coordinate with Henry's individual therapist.

5. Obtain a sensory integration evaluation by an Occupational Therapist to see if they can suggest ways to use the sensory system to decrease anxiety.
6. Consult with a psychiatrist to see if medication might be helpful for Henry.
7. Continue to get support to understand how your own family experiences and life traumas have affected you, and inevitably, Henry and his brother.

I hope this letter is informative and helpful in providing you with an understanding of the assessment results and answers to your Assessment Questions. It truly was a privilege to work with you all, and Henry certainly kept me "on my toes"—which was challenging and also rewarding. I wish you all the very best as you move forward from here.

If you have any questions about this letter and the assessment, please do not hesitate to contact me. I will call you at the end of the month to schedule a Follow-up Session with the two of you, free of charge. This is a chance for us to discuss how things are going, address any new questions you have, and fine tune the suggestions. I think it will be better if Henry does not come for this session.

In closing, I have a favor to ask of you both. I'm enclosing several forms that I use to get feedback about my assessments. Would you be willing to fill these out and return them to me (separately, if you like) in the enclosed stamped envelope? Your honest reactions will help me improve my ability to work with other children and families.

Warm regards,
Dale Rudin, Ph.D.
Licensed Psychologist
Licensed Specialist in School Psychology
Encl: Parent Experience of Assessment Questionnaire
Parent Feedback Questionnaire

Specifics about the Therapeutic Psychological Report

One of the most important purposes of a psychological report is to summarize the information gathered in the assessment process in an organized, reader-friendly way to offer continuity of care between various professionals and settings in which the child functions or might function in the future (e.g., current school, new school, day treatment program, inpatient hospital, etc.). In other words, a psychological report can serve the role of getting everyone involved on the same page.

The report serves as a snapshot in time of what is going on in the life of the child and family. Over time, it can reflect changes in the child's developmental abilities and challenges. In cases when the child is first assessed at a very young age and receives interventions throughout their childhood, a psychological report can serve as a baseline point of comparison as the child develops. In addition to its important clinical and developmental role, psychological reports can have a powerful impact on parents and caregivers. Because of the stated importance, writing a psychological report is a crucial part of the assessment process and, in TA-C, is usually written in addition to a personalized parent letter.

A Therapeutic Psychological Report follows the structure of a traditional report with headings and sections, but it is written (as stated above) in a more personal TA style using first person with less jargon. Below we provide a generic report format and what is included under each section. This format generally follows that laid out by Fischer (1985/1994).

Outline for Therapeutic Psychological Report

Therapeutic Psychological Report

NAME

Date of Birth:
Grade:
Dates of Assessment:
Date of Report:
Assessor:

Referral

Opportunities for Assessment

Test battery
Amount of direct interaction with parents, child, and family
Interactions with other professionals

Relevant Background Information

Context for referral and specific history of concern
Developmental History
Educational History

First Impressions and Comportment During the Assessment

Assessment Findings

Organized by themes with testing results and real-life examples integrated throughout the theme
  Describe a person rather than test results
  As needed explain the test and what it measures
  Offer specific examples from client's life to illustrate findings

Summary and Conclusions

Can include Diagnostic Impressions

Suggestions

Appendix

The Appendix includes lists of relevant test scores

Therapeutic Psychological Report for Henry's Family

We now provide the Therapeutic Psychological Report that Dale wrote for Henry's family. At the end of the Report we include an annotation. The annotation is meant to highlight and explain aspects of it for readers who are mainly familiar with traditional psychological reports.

Dale Rudin, Ph.D.
Licensed Psychologist

4310 Medical Parkway, Suite 101, Austin, TX 78756

Therapeutic Psychological Report

HENRY TAYLOR

Date of Birth: 08-27-2006
Grade: 5th at Martin Luther King Elementary School in the Liberty Independent School District
Dates of Assessment: 11-9, 11-15, 11-22, 12-2, 12-8, 12-9, 12-12, 12-19,12-12, 12-19, 12-21, 12-27-20XX, 1-6, 1-12, 1-27, 2-1, 2-13, 2-17, 3-2, 3-10-20XX

Date of Report: 4-27-20XX
Assessor: Dale Rudin, Ph.D.

Referral

Henry Taylor is a 10-year-8 month-old boy referred for a Therapeutic Assessment (TA) by his parents, Barbara Baker and David Taylor, at the recommendation of Henry's therapist, Dr. Diane Jagger. All three were concerned about Henry's sadness, negativity, and suicidal ideation. Henry has been talking more and more about his sadness and negative outlook this year, and his mother said that last summer, before he entered 5th grade, Henry started saying extremely alarming things about wanting to suicide and wishing he could be "erased."

Opportunities for Assessment

We began the Therapeutic Assessment in November, with Barbara, David, and me meeting to generate questions they wanted to have answered through the assessment.[a] Therapeutic Assessment (TA) is a client-centered, collaborative form of psychological assessment, designed to help clients gain new insights and make changes in their lives. In TA with children, the goal is to help parents understand their child's problems in the context of the family, and the process is guided by questions the parents generate at the beginning of the assessment.[b]

A test battery was chosen that would help answer Henry's parents' questions. The tests included:

Behavior Assessment System for Children – 3 (BASC-3): Parent Report, Teacher Report and Self-Report
Fantasy Animal Drawing Game
House-Tree-Person Drawings
Kinetic Family Drawing
The Rorschach Inkblot Test (R-PAS adminstration and scoring)
The Wartegg Drawing Completion Test (WDCT) – Crisi Wartegg System (CWS)
Roberts Apperception Test, Selected Cards (RAT)
Individualized Sentence Completion Task
Wechsler Intelligence Scale for Children-Fifth Edition (WISC-V)

Scores from many of these measures are provided in the Appendix at the end of this report.

I met with Henry for 14 hours on 11 separate occasions; all of these sessions were videotaped so they could be shown to and discussed with the parents. I met with Barbara and David together for about 9 hours on 5 separate occasions, and I met with Henry and his parents together for 6 hours on 4 separate occasions. During the parent meetings we reviewed test results, watched and discussed videos of Henry as he was engaged in the testing, and problem-solved school concerns as they arose. In addition, Barbara and David completed the Minnesota Multiphasic Personality Inventory-2 (MMPI-2) on themselves, and we reviewed these results and their implications for parenting Henry. I spoke with Dr. Jagger a couple of times to discuss Henry's therapy and her referral questions. I also had several conversations with Henry's school counselor and attended a 504 Accommodations Meeting at the school. One of the final parent sessions was devoted to discussing the test results and addressing the parents' assessment questions. In addition to this written report, the parents received a feedback letter that described the process of the TA, answered their assessment questions and provided them with suggestions to address the family's and Henry's needs. In one of the final sessions with Henry I gave him a written fable that synthesized the assessment results in metaphor for him. In the last session Henry, his parents, and I read the fable together.[c]

Background Information

Presenting Issues[d]

Henry's parents reported that when he was in the second grade, he began to talk very negatively about himself. He would tell them he wanted to die, disappear, or erase himself. They said that for months Henry would cry himself to sleep. Both Barbara and David said that they couldn't figure out what, if anything external, was triggering Henry's sadness and negative feelings about himself. They sought professional help, and Henry began to see Dr. Jagger individually through third grade, once or twice a week. Primarily, Dr. Jagger did play therapy with Henry, and also provided some parent coaching during this period as needed. After about 18 months, Henry's negative self-talk and sadness disappeared, and by fourth grade he seemed to be doing a lot better. The parents and Dr. Jagger thought Henry was doing well enough to discontinue therapy. In the summer before the fifth grade, his parents reported that Henry began saying alarming things again, so they contacted Dr. Jagger. They described feeling like Henry "was sad and wanted to stay sad."

Barbara reported that when Henry is clearly having fun, if his parents notice or comment on it, Henry denies it. Both Barbara and David said they are worn down by all of Henry's negativity and very depressive talk. They didn't feel that talking about his sadness all the time was helpful, so, with the help of Dr. Jagger, they made a rule to allow Henry "sad talk" time before bed for a certain amount of time. This strategy was initially helpful in allowing them to respond in a way that they felt less burdened.

Developmental History

Barbara reported that she had a full-term pregnancy with no complications. However, she was in labor for 55 hours, and Henry was born by C-section. (Henry has come to interpret this birth story as meaning that he really just didn't want to be born.) Most developmental milestones were achieved within the normal time frame. His mom remembered how even when he was less than a year old, Henry sat in his high-chair and was very serious. For example, Barbara said after drinking from a cup he would set it down very carefully, not throwing it down like other toddlers.

David reported that Henry was a little delayed in talking. He had a speech and language evaluation at 22 months that indicated his expressive language was about 3 months delayed, while his receptive language was 4–5 months advanced. Henry's brother, Frank, was born 20 months after Henry, at which time, 1 month earlier, Henry was weaned. He was toilet trained at about 3 and ½ years of age. The family moved from New York to Texas around this time. Barbara was a stay-at-home mom until Henry was about 5 and ½ years old when she started her own business and was very busy with it.

School History

Henry went to pre-school a couple of times a week when he was about 14 months old, with no problems reported until the family moved. After that he stayed at home with his brother until elementary school began. He did well in school but there were a couple of teachers that he didn't think were very nice. When he started to share how sad he was, he also began to complain about going to school.

Presently, Henry has a tight group of friends but has been very stressed about school. He worries about homework and his grades. He reports not doing well even though he has gotten good grades. Also, Henry shared how overwhelming some of his classes can be, especially during transition times when the classroom is chaotic and loud. During the assessment I shared with Henry's parents that I thought he would be eligible for Special Education services under the Individuals with Disabilities Education Act (IDEA). We discussed the difference between Special Education and 504 Services covered under Section 504 of the Rehabilitation Act. The latter is a civil right's law that provides support to students with a disability. It is not part of special education and is commonly thought to be less comprehensive and accountable than special education. The parents decided they wanted to pursue 504 Services, and a meeting was scheduled with the school in April, 2017 to see if Henry was eligible. Services were recommended and Henry's accommodations consisted of him being able to: 1) leave class when anxious and complete work in the counselor's office, 2) have regularly scheduled meetings with the counselor, and 3) have extra time on projects.

During the assessment, I was aware that this is a particularly stressful time because a number of educational decisions must be made. First, the family must decide if Henry should transition to middle school or stay at Martin Luther King Elementary School through the sixth grade. If they decide to move to middle school, then a decision must be made about whether Henry would go to his home school or apply to one of the magnet schools. Presently the family is leaning towards applying to a specific magnet school.

This is a highly competitive school, and there is concern that Henry will not fare well with the added pressure. However, Henry really wants to go to school with his present group of friends, all of whom are applying to that magnet school.

First Impressions and Comportment During the Assessment

When I greeted Henry and his parents in the waiting room I noticed a fair-haired boy that was leaning into his mother. He looked up when I said hello but his facial expression did not change nor did he acknowledge me. I wondered if he were shy or anxious or maybe just hesitant about what was to come. I invited them back to my office and Henry came willingly.[d]

Initially Henry was hard to actively involve. In our first session alone, without parents around, he laid on the couch, slouching, and played with his ear, turning the lobe inside out. I later learned that at school, this particular habit was an indicator of stress and worry. He had a hard time thinking about what he might like to learn about himself. I tried to engage him as best I could but most importantly, he was anxious, as evidence by his playing with his ear, and wanted to tell me how awful he was and how terrible he felt.[f] In later sessions, as we got to know each other better, Henry shared more of himself. For example, he became animated when showing me the video game he was playing. On other occasions he shared his concern about how much work one teacher was giving. His question for the assessment was, "Why am I so sad all the time?" He said that the only time he seemed not to be sad was, "…while I'm playing video games because they seem to relax me and while I'm eating something sweet."[e]

Throughout our time together Henry continued to seem intent on making sure I knew how awful he felt. While he was generally cooperative when presented with a new task, he used each activity to share how sad and miserable he was. When we were able to engage in some playtime, towards the end of our sessions, he let his guard down and seemed to have a good time.

Henry had a difficult time with any story telling task that was attempted (e.g., the Roberts Apperception Test) and said that he wasn't able to do what was asked. Interestingly, his parents said he had a good imagination and was able to tell stories easily. During the WISC-V, the cognitive test I gave, Henry was attentive and focused. However, he tended to give-up as we got to the more difficult items on each subtest. He didn't risk answering when he was uncertain about an answer, refusing to guess and he became more reticent and unresponsive. My impression was that Henry was afraid to make a mistake.[g]

Assessment Findings

Henry Is Intent on Presenting Himself as Sad and Depressed

As already described, Henry was persistent throughout the assessment in presenting himself as very sad, hopeless, and feeling badly about himself. Not unexpectedly, this showed up also in his psychological test responses. For example, on the BASC-3, where Henry was asked to rate himself on face-valid items capturing problems and strengths, he endorsed items like: "I feel good about myself" (False), "I never seem to get anything right" (True), "I feel sad" (Almost Always), "I feel depressed" (Almost Always), "I feel like my life is getting worse and worse" (Almost Always), and many other negatively oriented statements. His resulting score of 111 on the BASC-3 Depression Scale is at the 99th percentile, which is much worse than his level of daily functioning. In fact Henry's scores on this self-report measure were so extreme in a negative way that, according to usual guidelines, they must be interpreted with great caution.

Also, on the Wartegg Drawing Completion Test (WDCT), where Henry was asked to turn small marks in 8 boxes into "drawings that mean something," he immediately produced very sad or damaged images. His eight drawings were: "a sad face crying, a lopsided face sticking out its tongue next to a sad face crying, a giant staircase, a robotic sad face crying, an upside down sad face crying, a sad face with a unibrow crying, a snowman upside down sad face crying, and a plain old sad face crying." As an experiment, I let Henry know that I understood how very sad he was, how much pain he was in, and that I really "got it." Then I invited him to do the WDCT again without having to repeatedly tell me how sad he was, because I already knew. Henry then completed a WDCT that was more diverse and representative of himself as a whole, and which was more in line with his functioning and with other test results. This experience led me to hypothesize that Henry's exaggerated negative presentation is in part the result of him feeling that others don't take his sadness seriously. When he felt "heard," Henry was no longer as relentless in sending the message that he was incredibly sad.[h]

Henry is in Fact Depressed and Anxious, With Underlying Anger

Given Henry's exaggerated negative self-presentation, others understandably may wonder if he is malingering or just being provocative to get attention.[i] In fact, various psychological test scores showed that Henry is suffering with very significant low self-esteem, a sense of inadequacy, depression, and a damaged view of himself—even if these are not to the level that Henry asserts.

First, supporting evidence for Henry's depression comes from how others close to Henry rate his behavior on the BASC-3, both teachers (Cortez T = 77, Smoot T = 87) and parents (Dad T = 88, Mom T = 98) rated Henry as being significantly depressed. Second, performance-based tests, which are extremely difficult for children to influence, Henry did show significant signs of depression. On the Rorschach Inkblot Test, Henry's R-PAS scores suggested he felt stressed and helpless (m=117, Y=118), had a damaged and negative self-view (MOR=129), and that he tended to worry and ruminate excessively (FD=117). On the repeat administration of the WDCT, which was scoreable, the results showed that Henry was depressed (IST=5), was feeling a great deal of stress and (m=3), fearfulness (T=83) and social anxiety (T=75), and had limited energy for overcoming even minor obstacles (Box 3=D).

In addition to validating that Henry was depressed, the performance-based tests also indicated that Henry has a significant amount of underlying anger that he did not express on the self-report measures (R-PAS AGC=119). I wondered[j] if this anger was more palpable at home than at school, as Henry's teachers did not rate him as at all angry (BASC-3 Aggression = 43T; both Perez and Hall), while his parents—and especially his mother--rated him as angry (BASC-3 Aggression = 69T (mother) and 60T (father). The parents' scores are consistent with their believing that Henry's need to continually talk about his sadness is provocative and intended to frustrate them. Both parents reported that they try to stay patient, but their frustration and anger can boil up unexpectedly at times. Their report was supported by several of Henry's responses on the Sentence Completion Task: When I am with my dad... "if I make one small mistake, he'll get angry and yell at me." When I am with my mom… "she won't listen to anything I say that's negative. She'll say she doesn't want to hear it and leave the room or get super frustrated."

Henry Has Cognitive Strengths, But These Are Hampered by His Anxiety and Depression

To assess Henry's cognitive strengths and weaknesses, I administered a standard test of intellectual functioning, the Wechsler Intelligence Scale for Children (WISC-V). The results indicated that Henry is bright: On three of the five major ability indices he scored in the High Average range. On the Verbal Comprehension Index (VCI), a measure of word knowledge and verbal concept formation, Henry's score of 113 is equal to or better than 81% of children his age. This ability is essential in being successful in school, as material and directions are often presented in a verbal format.[k]

His score on the Visual Spatial Index (VSI)—a measure of non-verbal reasoning—was 119, at the 90th percentile. And on the Fluid Reasoning Index (FRI), which assesses the ability to interpret and work with novel information, Henry scored 112 (79%). Importantly, Henry scored significantly lower—in the Average range—on the two other major indices: Processing Speed (PSI)—which involves the ability to perform simple tasks accurately and quickly (98, 45%) and Working Memory (WMI; 97, 42%)—which measures the ability to hold information in mind and remember it accurately. Looking more closely at Working Memory, Henry did better on a test of visual memory (Picture Span=12, High Average) than he did on a test of verbal memory (Digit Span=7, Low Average). How can we understand Henry's relatively worse performance on Processing Speed and Working Memory? These indices are known to be more affected by anxiety and depression than the other indices; Thus, my hypothesis is that Henry's scores on PSI and WMI are lower-bound estimates of his true abilities, although they give us an important window into how he is functioning at this time.

Henry's insecurity and anxiety were palpable throughout much of the testing. For example, I asked Henry to rate his feelings before and after each of the cognitive testing sessions, using a horizontal line going from "Very Sad" to "Very Happy." He consistently came into the session feeling "Neutral" or above and unfailingly ended up in the "Very Sad" range at the end of the testing session. His self-rating appeared related to his insecurity about his cognitive abilities and his tendency to compare himself negatively to his peers. When I interviewed her, Ms. Gallos, one of Henry's teachers, said, "He compares himself often to his friends and gets really down on himself, even though his grades are fantastic!" Also, Henry's father reported that Henry, "believes he is getting the worst grades of all his friends, even though his grades range from B+ to A+."[l]

Henry Longs to Be Taken Care Of, But Doesn't Trust Others

The testing also suggests that in part, Henry's requests for others to bear witness to and discuss his sadness are because he wants them to comfort and care for him. He scored extremely high on a Rorschach score related to dependency (ODL%=133), indicating that Henry longs to be taken care of in a way that is more typical of children much younger than he is. This Rorschach score is often associated with very early failures in emotional attunement from caregivers. This finding also fit with Henry's mother report that, "Henry has a sort of Peter Pan thing going. He doesn't want to grow up." Perhaps Henry hopes that if he doesn't grow up, he can get some of his earlier dependency needs met. Poignantly, the Rorschach results also indicate that overall, Henry has a negative view of other people (PHR/GHR=118) and is hypervigilant (R-PAS VCOMP = 119). These scores suggest that Henry faces a painful internal dilemma—of wanting to be close and be taken care of, but not trusting others to meet his longing. This might result in his asking for care in a way that potentially also pushes most people away, e.g., going on and on about how miserable he is.[m]

Henry's Coping Mechanisms Are Overwhelmed

Findings from the performance-based testing indicate that Henry is under a significant amount of stress and is experiencing a lot of distress (Rorschach: m=117, PPD=116; Wartegg: M/m=0/3, IIT-1 Adj=1.00, IIT-2 Adj=.7/7.3; WIP=D, Beta). In particular, the Rorschach suggests that although Henry has an age-appropriate capacity to reflect on himself and his experiences (M = 97) and to deal with life's challenges (MC = 94), the stressors he experiences currently overwhelm his coping skills. In fact, the imbalance between Henry's coping and his emotional stressors (Rorschach: MC-PPD = 79) suggests that he would have difficulty coping with everyday situations where he experiences helplessness and/or anxiety (Wartegg: WIP=D, Beta). His responses on the Sentence Completion Task indicate that Henry has a lot of anxiety about school. He said he felt like a nervous wreck when he "answers wrong on any kind of test." He gets scared when his "teacher gives an assignment and assigns less than two weeks to do it." The school has tried to respond to Henry's needs by allowing him to leave the classroom when he is overwhelmed and anxious, but clearly, this has other costs in terms of his engagement in the class.

Henry Has Some Idiosyncratic Thinking, Without Evidence of a Thought Disorder

One of Henry's mother's concerns was that her son might have some sort of psychotic thinking. This is in part due to the mental health issues in Barbara's family of origin. She was also concerned that when Henry became focused on his sadness, he had trouble acknowledging the reality of the times when he appeared happy. To her, it felt like Henry was really distorting reality.[n] Both the Rorschach and Wartegg results indicate that Henry does not have a psychotic thought disorder (Rorschach: TP Comp=98T; EII=112T; Wartegg: Disturbance of Thought Process=56T). However, both tests suggest he does have some unique, idiosyncratic ways of viewing the world (Rorschach: FQu %=90T; Wartegg: Inadequate Reality Testing=65T). Furthermore, it seems that Henry is more likely to perceive things in a unique way when he is upset and full of emotion, and that his perceptions are an attempt on his part to make sense of his confusing, upsetting feelings. One example would be when he made sense of his insecurity during the WISC by concluding that he had "done terrible."[o]

The Family System is Stressed and In Need of Support[p]

David and Barbara were very cooperative and participated in the assessment as requested, even being willing to be tested themselves to see how their personalities might influence their parenting. Results of the Minnesota Multiphasic Personality Inventory-2 (MMPI-2) indicated that David is not aware of any distress, while Barbara experiences anxiety and stress, but optimistically keeps on going. In our discussions, both the parents and I became aware that each has a lot of past trauma that is impacting the present. Barbara came from a very difficult background and is used to dealing with very depressed and psychotic people. She can minimize Henry's behavior and at times has doubted if he is depressed. David shows little affect externally, and Henry believes he is angry a lot. Henry's parents indicated that when they try to be present for Henry's feelings, the sadness and negativity do not abate. They worry that attending to Henry's negative feelings actually intensifies his sadness and is unhelpful; thus, it is hard for them to know how to support Henry. They are also worried about Frank, Henry's brother, who is witness to Henry's sadness and feels angry and upset with his brother. When I asked Henry to rate emotions of each family member, he always put himself on the opposite end of a continuum from other family members. For example, when we discussed anger, Henry put Frank, Mom and Dad all together as being "Most Angry" while he was alone in a different spot. This configuration was true of all other emotions we rated: lonely, stressed, happy, and guilty. These ratings reflected Henry's sense of being rejected and scapegoated in the family and of feeling alone and unsupported.

Summary and Conclusions

Henry is a 10-year-old, 5th grade student who has been intermittently seriously depressed and anxious since the 2nd grade. He has been in individual therapy since the time he first expressed his sadness and suicidality. The treatment was effective until more recently. His therapist, Dr. Jagger, recommended a Therapeutic Assessment, and Henry's parents, Barbara Baker and David Taylor, contacted me shortly thereafter. By the time Barbara and David sought out the assessment, they were worried, frustrated, and reported being "at their wits' end."

The assessment results show that Henry is very depressed but is not comforted easily. Henry doesn't know why he feels so badly and longs for affirmation and understanding of his sadness However, because of past experiences, Henry is full of shame and expects rejection and abandonment from close others. Thus, Henry presents his sadness to his parents, especially to his mother, in a very exaggerated and insistent way. It is almost as if Henry is saying, "Please help me sort through my anger and sadness, and show me that you can handle these feelings." Unfortunately, Henry's parents—due to their own backgrounds—have difficulty managing their own or Henry's sad and angry feelings. As a result, they feel depleted, frustrated, and worried, and Henry perceives this and escalates further--to the point where his moods control the family. This vicious cycle leaves Barbara and David feeling depleted, frustrated, and worried, while Henry feels anxious, lonely, and more ashamed. Henry and his parents will need increased professional help to interrupt this destructive cycle.[9]

Henry is a bright child who excels in school but has a lot of worry and stress about his school performance. He compares himself negatively to his peers and doesn't believe he is doing as well as they are. When anxious he is unable to concentrate and stay in the classroom. Henry is getting accommodations under Section 504 of the Rehabilitation Act. This arrangement allows him to leave the classroom, when needed, and to get support from the school counselor. Henry will be transitioning to Middle School next year. This upcoming change is placing added stress on him and the family. He wants to apply to a very competitive middle school in order to stay with his friends, but the extra school work and competition at this school will be a source of anxiety for him, likely more than he can manage on his own.

Suggestions[r]

1. Continue Henry's individual therapy. It would be helpful to focus on validating Henry's perspective and feelings as well as providing him with more resources to address his depression. For example, teaching Henry relaxation exercises specifically geared for children may provide him with a specific strategy for dealing with stress.

2. Barbara and David are under a lot of stress while trying to support both of their children who have different needs. Parent coaching would be helpful. Henry needs containment as well as validation. This can be difficult to do especially when Henry is being provocative. In addition, Henry's parents would benefit from the support of other parents whose children are also struggling. Brave Parents is an organization that provides peer support and resources to families in need.

3. I believe family therapy will be necessary to address the underlying family system issues that are creating the vicious cycle in which Henry and his parents now find themselves. Initially, the focus might be on the expression of affect, especially anger, and how it is received and expressed by each family member. It will be helpful for Henry to not always be in the role of the identified patient. Barbara and David would also benefit in understanding how their own backgrounds influence the way they respond to Henry.

4. Henry is anxious about school. He is bright, but I believe the additional stress of a competitive school is likely to be too much for him. I suggest looking into a smaller private school that provides more individualized support for their students. If the cost is prohibitive, then a public school with supportive 504 services is recommended. If it is decided that Henry should stay with his friends and go to the more competitive school, I suggest having tutoring available at the start of the school year to provide emotional, as well as organizational and academic support.

I appreciated the opportunity to work with Henry and his family. Please feel free to call me if you have further questions.

Respectfully,
Dale Rudin, Ph. D.
Licensed Psychologist

Appendix of Scores

Wechsler Intelligence Scale for Children – Fifth Edition (WISC-5)

Composite Scores	Score	Percentile	95th % Confidence Interval
Verbal Comprehension	113	81	104-120
Visual Spatial	119	90	110-125
Fluid Reasoning	112	79	104-118
Working Memory	97	42	90-105
Processing Speed	98	45	89-107
Full Scale	110	75	104-115

Verbal Comprehension Subtests

Subtest Scaled Scores

Similarities	13
Vocabulary	12
Information	1

Visual Spatial Subtests

Block Design	13
Visual Puzzles	14

Fluid Reasoning Subtests

Matrix Reasoning	11
Figure Weights	13
Picture Concepts	8

Working Memory Subtests

Digit Span	7
Picture Span	12

Processing Speed Subtests

Coding	11
Symbol Search	8
Cancellation	4

Behavior Assessment Scales for Children – Third Edition (BASC-3)

Parent Report

Subtests	T(mom)	T(dad)
Hyperactivity	47	53
Aggression	69*	61*
Conduct Problems	42	48
Externalizing Problems	53	5✓
Anxiety	73**	80**
Depression	88**	98**
Somatization	68*	86*
Internalizing Problems	81**	87**
Learning Problems	n/a	n/a
School Problems	n/a	n/a
Atypicality	60*	62*
Withdrawal	58	65*
Attention Problems	35	40
Behavioral Symptoms Index	63*	68*
Adaptability	29**	25**
Social Skills	38*	35*
Leadership	33*	38*
Functional Communication	45	39*
Activities of Daily Living	57	48
Adaptive Skills	39*	35*

*At-Risk
**Clinically Significant

Behavior Assessment Scales for Children – Third Edition

(BASC-3) Teacher Report

Subtests	T (Cortez)	T (Smoot)
Aggression	43	43
Conduct Problems	43	48

(Continued)

Subtests	T (Cortez)	T (Smoot)
Externalizing Problems	42	44
Anxiety	72**	80**
Depression	77**	87**
Somatization	50	78**
Internalizing Problems	71**	-91**
Learning Problems	39	45
School Problems	39	49
Atypicality	67*	55
Withdrawal	51	77**
Attention Problems	40	53
Behavioral Symptoms Index	54	62*
Adaptability	51	40*
Social Skills	55	41*
Leadership	57	38*
Study Skills	61	52
Functional Communication	49	47
Adaptive Skills	55	43

*At-Risk
**Clinically Significant

Behavior Assessment Scales for Children – Third Edition (BASC-3)

Self-Report

	T-score	Percentile
Attitude to School	80	99**
Attitude to Teachers	90	99**
School Problems	89	99**
Atypicality	66	82*
Locus of Control	93	99**
Social Stress	91	99**
Anxiety	96	99**
Depression	111	99**
Sense of Inadequacy	103	99**
Internalizing Problems	104	99**
Attention Problems	67	94*
Hyperactivity	58	80
Inattention/Hyperactivity	64	90*
Emotional Symptoms Index	111	99**
Relations with Parents	14	1**
Interpersonal Relations	10	1**
Self-Esteem	12	1**
Self-Reliance	15	1**
Personal Adjustment	10	1**

*At-Risk
**Clinically Significant

Personality Inventory for Youth (PIY)

Scale	Standard Score	Scale	Standard Score
VAL	69	COG	86*
INC	08	Cog1	72*
FB	90+*	Cog2	82*
DEF	47	Cog3	75*
ADH	52	DLQ	45
Adh1	49	Dlq1	48
Adh2	57	Dlq2	42
Adh3	49	Dlq3	50
FAM	66	RLT	68*
Fam1	77*	Rlt1	60
Fam2	57	Rlt2	76*
Fam3	53		
SOM	82*	DIS	88*
Som1	82*	Dis1	75*
Som2	77*	Dis2	90*
Som3	66*	Dis3	76
WDL	83*	SSK	82*
Wdl1	68*	Ssk1	75*
Wdl2	90*	Ssk2	82*

*Clinically Significant

Rorschach Inkblots (R-PAS Scoring)

Scores are in Standard Score Format (mean of 100, standard deviation of 15)

Engagement and Cognitive Processing	Perception and Thinking Problems
Complexity = 107	EII-3 = 112
R = 95	TP-Comp = 100
F% = 92	WSumCog = 112
Bln = 109	SevCog = 106
Sy = 101	FQ-% = 96
MC = 94	WD-% = 100
MC-PPD = 79	FQo% = 90
M- = 97	FQu% = 117
M/MC = 104	P = 107
(CF+C)/Sum C = NA	
W% = 126	
Dd% = 87	
SI (Space Integration) = 115	
IntCont = 90	

(Continued)

Engagement and Cognitive Processing	Perception and Thinking Problems
V = 94	
FD = 117	
R8910% = 71	
WSumC = 92	
Mp/(Ma+Mp) = NA	

Self and Other Representation	Stress and Distress
ODL% = 133	YTVC' = 117
SR (space reversal) = 90	m = 117
MAP/MAHP = NA	Y = 118
PHR/GHR = 118	MOR = 119
M- = 91	SC-Comp = NA
AGC = 119	PPD = 116
H = 84	CBlend = 118
COP = 90	C' = 108
MAH = 90	V = 94
SumH = 92	CritCont% = 115
NPH/SumH = 122	
V-Comp = 109	
r =134	
p/(a+p) = 99	
AGM = 106	
T = 119	
Per = 92	
An = 88	

Wartegg Drawing Completion Test--Crisi Wartegg System (CWS)

BOX 1 = C	BOX 2 = C	BOX 3 = D
BOX 4 = AD	BOX 5 = C	BOX 6 = AD
BOX 7 = D	BOX 8 = NC	M/m = 0/3
E.C.+% = 50	IIT-1 = 0.625	SIG% = 25
AQ+% = 44	IM = 0.13	ARC% = 13
FQ+% = 88	AI = .50	AS% = 13
A/F = 1.5/3.5	IIT-2 = 3.0: 5.0	ICE% = 13
P% = 0	WIP = D, Beta	I.I.T.-2 = 3/5
P+% = N.D.	M/m = 0/3	AP = 3
O% = 13	H% = 0	m = 1
O+% = 50	OBJ% = 38	MI = 3

Annotation of Henry's Therapeutic Psychological Report

[a] The TA-C report is written in first person ("I" and "we") rather than third person ("the examiner...") to make it more readable and to reflect the collaborative stance of TA-C as opposed to the more impersonal tone of many traditional psychological reports.

[b] A short explanation of Therapeutic Assessment is provided to orient any reader who is unfamiliar with the model.

[c] This section gives a detailed account of all the interactions the assessor had with the child and parents, referring professional, and other collateral professionals.

[d] The Presenting Issues are discussed first because they are the most relevant to the Assessment Questions.

[e] By sharing vivid first impressions the assessor helps readers get a sense of the client as a unique person in relationship to the assessor.

[f] By describing her interactions with Henry, Dale creates a bridge to other readers who know him who may have had similar experiences.

[g] Dale's description of Henry's behavior during the testing sessions helps put his test scores in context.

[h] By labeling this idea as a hypothesis rather than stating it as a conclusion, Dale opens the door for other readers to form their own opinions.

[i] By openly raising this question, Dale speaks to people in Henry's life who wonder if he is truly depressed.

[j] By using phrases like "I wondered..." or "the test results suggest..." Dale recognizes that her interpretations are not set in stone nor are they the only possible way of viewing these data.

[k] Dale ties the meaning of test scores to how they are likely to appear in real life.

[l] Here Dale ties together information from three sources—the mood rating activity she did with Henry in sessions, the report of his teacher, and David's comment—to explain her hypothesis about the anxiety she witnessed in the testing sessions.

[m] You can see here how Dale is using the test scores to help readers become empathic to why Henry acts in ways that people can experience as off-putting.

[n] These initial sentences give the family context about why Dale assessed Henry's reality testing and thinking and why this content is a major finding of the TA-C.

[o] Dale provides a clear example from the testing sessions of how these test scores might show up in behavior.

[p] This entire section demonstrates how TA-C applies a family systems perspective to understand the child.

ᑫThis paragraph captures the systemic case conceptualization and presents it succinctly for the reader.

ʳThe report includes suggestions relevant to the various professional readers of the report. More personalized suggestions for Barbara and David are included in the letter.

Final Procedures

Typically, both the Therapeutic Psychological Report and the Parent Letter are mailed to parents 2–4 weeks after the Summary/Discussion with the child and parents where the fable is presented. At the end of the Parent Letter, we encourage parents to contact us immediately if they find any errors in the report (e.g., incorrect historical information) or if they have urgent questions. Otherwise, we remind them of the upcoming Follow-up Session, where questions and reactions to the written feedback can be discussed in detail. If parents have asked us to share the report with other professionals, we may also include Release of Information Forms to be signed and returned to us. Last, we typically also include two forms for Parents to give us feedback about the TA-C: 1) the Parent Experience of Assessment Questionnaire (PEAS: Austin et al., 2018) and the Parent Feedback Questionnaire (see Appendix D). (You can find the PEAS and scoring materials on the TAI website.) We let parents know that they can complete and mail these to us before the Follow-up Session, bring them with them when they come to that session, or complete them after the Follow-up Session. If the assessor is continuing with the family in treatment after the TA-C, the timing of the written feedback (and Follow-up Session) may be different than what is written here.

References

Austin, C. A., Finn, S. E., Keith, T. Z., Tharinger, D. J., & Fernando, A. D. (2018). The Parent Experience of Assessment Scale (PEAS): Development and relation to parent satisfaction. *Assessment, 25*(7), 929–941.

Finn, S. E. (1997). *Collaborative child assessment as a family systems intervention.* In S. E. Finn (Chair), "Collaborative assessment of children and families." Symposium presented at the annual meeting of the Society for Personality Assessment, San Diego, CA.

Fischer, C. T. (1985/1994). *Individualizing psychological assessment.* New York: Routledge. (Originally published by Brooks Cole.)

Lance, B. & Krishnamurthy, R. (2003, March). *A comparison of the effectiveness of three modes of MMPI-2 test feedback.* Paper presented at the Midwinter meeting of the Society for Personality Assessment, San Francisco, CA.

10 Phase V: The Follow-up Session

At this point, we have one more Phase in the model of Therapeutic Assessment with Children (TA-C); the Follow-up Session with the parents. This step usually occurs about 2 months after the Summary/Discussion Session (although there are exceptions, addressed below). In this chapter we discuss the goals and benefits of Follow-up Sessions and how to conduct them, with examples. We then turn to Henry's case.

Before jumping in, we want to clarify why we invite only the parents to the Follow-up Session. Attachment theory is one of the guiding theories of TA-C. It informs us that reestablishing contact with a child post assessment could potentially reactivate the child's attachment to the assessor. As described in the previous chapter, we work mindfully during our last session with the child, offering a personalized fable or other creative means of child feedback and saying goodbye. The child knows that this session is the last contact with the assessor, unless the assessor continues in a therapeutic relationship with the child and/or the family. Thus, inviting the child to the Follow-up Session is likely to reactivate the child's attachment to the assessor and then create another, potentially distressing separation. For this reason, even when asked by parents if they can bring their child, we politely decline and explain to them why it is better that the child not attend. This explanation gives another opportunity to help parents gain more empathy for their child.

Goals and Benefits of Follow-up Sessions

We have several goals and benefits in mind for this session: 1) for the parents to feel "held" and "remembered"; 2) to see how the family is progressing with the new narrative and suggestions that came out of the assessment; 3) to reinforce messages and insights derived from the TA-C; and 4) to satisfy our own desire to know how TA-C is useful and how it might be able to be improved. In terms of the first goal, we remember that many parents form a unique and deep attachment to the assessor during a TA-C. For some, the assessment is the first time that they have felt understood and appreciated for their challenges as a parent, and some parents tell us they never found previous mental health interventions as helpful as TA-C. In addition, the

DOI: 10.4324/9781003000174-10

collaborative working relationship between assessor and parents that is cultivated in TA-C, especially when an assessment takes place over 2 to 3 months, leaves parents with the feeling of having been part of team with a joint objective: to help their family do better in the world. Given all this, we don't want parents to feel "dismissed" or abandoned at the end of a TA-C, and the Follow-Up Session is an opportunity to show that we have not forgotten them and are still holding them in mind. The keen interest the assessor shows about how the family is doing and what new things the parents have learned often provides a sense of relief and comfort to the parents and reminds them that they are not alone.

The second major objective of this session is to assess how the child and family are doing from the parents' perspective, and how they are adapting, adjusting, and accommodating to their life challenges given what they learned in the TA-C. Simply put, a Follow-up Session can tell us if and how the parents and child are benefiting from the new family narrative co-created in the TA-C and whether they have been able to maintain their "new way of viewing" after returning to their normal lives and interacting with the other people and systems who may not share this new perspective. Some parents seem to have been "talked out of" their new narratives by family members and friends who were not involved in the assessment. Other parents find reinforcement and support for their new views. In either case, the Follow-up Session is a chance for the assessor to discuss how the family is doing and answer any new questions that may have arisen since they last were seen.

Third, the Follow-up Session serves as an opportunity for the assessor to reinforce or even strengthen the new family narrative derived from the TA-C. In this sense, we think of the Follow-up Session as a "booster" intervention session, and as reported in Chapter 2, there is research evidence that some families show positive changes immediately after this session (Smith et al., 2010). Some parents can't wait to tell the assessor about changes they have made based on the work done together, and the assessor can applaud the parents for putting new understandings into practice. Other parents tell the assessor about new challenges that have arisen, ways the new narrative hasn't seemed to fit, or suggestions that have not worked out that well. The assessor can then empathize, show curiosity, and help refine the earlier suggestions or explore others that were not discussed before.

Fourth, Follow-up Sessions benefit us, as assessors. Without such an encounter, we rarely know what happened to the families we work with and how the TA-C impacted them. It might be one of the most unsatisfying aspects of our work as psychologists or assessors to not know if and how the client progressed, what changes they made, and how the assessment affected them. Thus, a Follow-up Session offers closure for the assessor as well. Furthermore, by conducting Follow-up Sessions we learn about our own work with the TA-C model. We consider this final session to be a unique opportunity to receive feedback about what we did well and what we might have done differently. We can evaluate what changes to consider making in the future and how to continue to fine-tune the TA-C model with different types of families. Some of us have joked that we find Follow-up Sessions so useful, that we would pay families to come to them.

Finally, a word about families that continue to work with the assessor in an ongoing intervention after the TA-C is finished. In such instances, follow-ups can be threaded throughout the subsequent therapy, holding in mind the findings from the TA-C. We have also found that even when the family and clinician continue to meet after the TA-C, it can be useful to set aside a session during the ongoing intervention to serve as a structured Follow-up Session. This gives the therapist and family a chance to gauge the family's progress and reflect back on the assessment process, findings, and proposed next steps. As you will see, this is the approach that Dale used with Henry and his parents, because they opted to see her for family therapy after the TA-C.

Conducting the Session

We now provide practical guidelines for conducting a Follow-up Session. As always, we present the most typical approach, but we encourage you to be flexible and respond to the needs of individual families. For example, we have found that parents from more "collectivist" cultures (e.g., Latinx, Japanese, or Chinese families) may ask to bring extended family members, such as grandparents or aunts and uncles, to Follow-up Sessions. Often, these extended family members have read the Therapeutic Psychological Report or Parent Feedback Letter and have questions or observations of their own they want to share with the assessor. We don't have a fixed policy about such requests and typically explore with parents the advantages and disadvantages of including these other people in the session. But when this arrangement makes the most sense in the parents' culture, we are happy to follow their cue.

Scheduling

As mentioned in Chapter 2, we typically invite parents for a Follow-up Session about 2 months after the presentation of the fable to the child. By then, we hope that the family will have had time to integrate some of the therapeutic work of the TA-C and to try out the suggestions for next steps. The parents will have received the feedback letter and/or the report, and should have had enough time to read it, think about it, and develop questions to bring up. As mentioned in Chapter 7, sometimes we schedule Follow-up Sessions with parents at the time of the Summary/Discussion Session, and then contact them as the time gets closer to make sure the timing still fits. Occasionally 2 months is too long for parents to wait to check back in and get support, and they contact us to set up an earlier meeting. In contrast, in other instances 2 months are too soon for parents to meet for a follow-up and they express a lack of readiness or ambivalence about coming in. In our experience, such delays typically mean that the family needs more time to work on the post assessment integration before coming together with us. If so, we either set up a meeting in the future or offer to contact the family the following month to see if they are ready to schedule. Staying relational and flexible about the timing of the Follow-up Session, while keeping the invitation open, communicates to the parents that we continue to hold them in mind. Last, of course, sending a reminder to busy parents several days before the scheduled Follow-up Session also shows that we are eager to see them and encourages them to come.

Steps in the Follow-up Session

The Follow-up Session is, to a great extent, shaped by what parents "bring" to the meeting. Flexibility here is just as important as in all other TA-C sessions. Even so, we find that having a general outline to fall back on can be useful. Therefore, we suggest that you:

- Review the file prior to the meeting and re-familiarize yourself with the test findings, Assessment Questions, and written feedback. Taking this time leaves assessors well prepared and helps them provide parents with the sense, mentioned earlier, that they are remembered and held in mind. Again, if parents have questions about the written feedback or test results, the assessor has recently reviewed them and can address questions easily.
- Offer a warm welcome when you greet the parents, appropriate to their culture and personalities. These first few minutes are an opportunity for a bit of small talk, reconnection, and expression of interest and pleasure to meet the parents after not seeing each other for several months.
- Ask the parents how they feel about coming to the Follow-up Session.
- Ask if the parents have any particular goals for the meeting. If so, their goals become the priority and provide the structure for the session. For example, the parents might want to ask questions about the Therapeutic Psychological Report or Parent Letter, share new observations of their child that seem inconsistent with the assessment findings, tell how their child is responding to the changes they have been making, or report on suggested next steps that have not panned out. Any need that parents express takes priority in the structure of the session, and we flexibly change our plan to meet their goals. If, however, parents don't have specific goals for the Follow-up Session, we continue with the following structure.
- Ask the parents about any changes or lack of changes in their life post assessment. As parents share the positive changes in their life, listen attentively to mirror and praise the positive striving. If possible, connect

the positive changes to what parents learned during the TA-C. For example:

Mother: One thing that's better is how long the temper tantrums last. They still happen, but they are shorter and less intense than before. Sometimes I still get so upset when Mary acts like that, but often I have been able to remember what you said about her brain getting flooded with emotions. It's been easier for me to stay calm when I think about that.

Assessor: That's great, I am so glad that our discussion about her emotional flooding helped you. It's impressive that you were able to use this information to manage your own emotions. It's such a key to helping Mary.

Mother: Yes, it's been easier. I do this thing with my hand to remember the "flip the lid" thing you told us about. That's been a lifesaver; I even told my friends about it to help them with their kids. When I remember it, and I don't always, I can stay calmer and can help her calm down instead of getting so mad at her and yelling the way I used to.

Assessor: That makes a lot of sense, Kim. As you might remember from our discussions, kids like Mary need a lot of help regulating their emotions before they can do it on their own. It sounds like you are making a great impact by staying calm yourself. I imagine that it is not always easy, but what an important step to take from our work together. Thank you for sharing this with me. Are there any other things you have been able to shift? What about you, Jeff?

However, as we would expect there might be ongoing struggles reported or failed efforts to make changes, or perhaps short-lived changes that the family was not able to sustain. When parents report such frustrations, we suggest that the assessor empathize with the difficulty and get curious about what else might be going on in the family as a system. Imagine the following scenario:

Mother: We have tried to do the self-esteem building thing you taught us, to join her self-doubts instead of telling her that she is wonderful and shouldn't say those ugly things about herself. Well, we tried and tried, but it's not working anymore. It worked at first but not anymore.

Father: I lose my patience when she says these things and I tell Susan to take over. I tried the approach you suggested but I can't do it. I get so frustrated because we try, and it's not helping.

Assessor: You are right, that sounds very frustrating. It sounds like you both have been trying your best and it's not making a difference. I am so sorry to hear that. I know how hard you both worked in the assessment, so I don't doubt you are trying to make these changes and working hard now.

Father: To be fair, we were really good right after the assessment, but lately it's been harder to have the patience. I am traveling a lot again so when I get home, I want things to be smooth; I want Susan to deal with Lucy. I know we should do it together, but it's hard.

Assessor: So, it was easier when you were in it together, but with time it's been harder and harder to keep up the team work, and you are worn out. Susan, it's a lot to handle Lucy's needs and the home when Scott is out of town. And, I imagine Scott, you want to help Susan, but you are worn out as well from working hard and all the travel you do. No wonder it's been harder to keep up, that makes sense. Would it help if we talked a little about how to get you on the same page again? What might you need from each other to help Lucy? I remember we talked about these suggestions in our last session, but it was a while ago, so maybe it would be helpful.

- Ask the parents for their reactions to the Therapeutic Psychological Report and/or Parent Letter. This conversation can be general and can start with the assessor inquiring what it was like for them to receive the letter and/or report, and whether they have any questions about their contents. Typically, parents find the assessment letters very useful, personal, and moving, as they are written in a warm, but informative, therapeutic tone. Occasionally, however, parents find parts of the letter unclear or even upsetting. For example, parents may have reacted well to Level 3 information in the Summary/Discussion Session, but then found it difficult when they read it in the Parent Letter. If so, the Follow-up Session provides an opportunity to discuss their reactions. Therapeutic Psychological Reports are even more sensitive, in our experience, as the implication that they will be read by others (not necessarily true of the parent letter) can elicit parents' concern and even shame. We encourage parents to let us know if there is material in the report that they would prefer we omit (of course, within certain bounds), or we help them think through if they want to limit the people with whom they share the report. Not infrequently, parents also have delayed reactions to the therapeutic fable. In one family, the child asked the parents to read the fable to her every night for 1 month. When the parents arrived for the Follow-up Session, they said that as a result of this, they had grasped new levels of the assessment results that they had only partially understood before.
- Ask the parents if they have any new questions that have come up after the assessment. Sometimes parents have entirely new Assessment Questions, and the assessor explores whether the test data and other

information gathered can offer insights into new puzzles the parents might have about their child. Again, in such instances the assessor tries to engage the parents in collaboratively addressing the new questions, providing scaffolding as needed. Here is an example:

Mother: One thing we noticed since the assessment that does not make sense to us is her coming up with stories and lies. Maggie has always had a vivid imagination, but now these stories are constant, and she tells them as if they were real. She tells them to friends at school and often they include some kind of lie. I am worried that when her friends find out her stories are not true, she will lose them and it will make her feel bad. She can't go on doing this again and again. Is there anything in the testing that could explain why she is doing it? This seems like the kind of thing that a younger kid would do, not a 10-year-old.

Assessor: How interesting, and you are right this is a new behavior. I am not sure why Maggie is telling these stories, and there is nothing specific in the testing that speaks to that. However, we can talk about why children lie and maybe the testing can help us understand it for Maggie. Do you have any ideas?

Mother: Yes, I know from the assessment that she has low self-esteem and I wondered if she lies to make herself feel better. Maybe that's her coping mechanism, but that doesn't explain why she doesn't just tell the truth when I ask her a simple question like: "Did you brush your teeth?" and she says: "Yes," knowing well that she did not. That I don't understand.

Assessor: Yes, that's different than making up stories about herself to friends. Do you think that maybe she lies because she does not want to face your reaction or consequences of telling the truth? What would happen if she told you that she did not brush her teeth?

Mother: I would get upset because she knows she is supposed to do it every night. She is 10-years-old. But I don't think that's it, because she knows I will get upset if she tells me the lie and I always know because her toothbrush is dry. So, either way I get upset because she is not doing what she is supposed to do.

Assessor: So maybe in the end it does not matter to her, since you are likely to get upset either way. Have you tried a different approach other than getting upset? And, don't get me wrong, I think she needs to brush her teeth. I am just wondering if anything else could work better…

Mother: I know what you mean. I remember what you said to me in the assessment about her self-esteem and how she does things to provoke me to have a negative reaction to her and then it makes sense to her because she already feels bad about herself. At first, I didn't understand this idea, but it helped when you said, "Kids who feel bad inside do things that make them look bad in the world, which leads people to tell them that they are bad, and that is what reinforces their feeling bad." It's like a circle of feeling bad.

Assessor: Exactly. I wonder if this is what's going on with Maggie. Maybe if you can try a different reaction, however hard it might be, you could break the circle of her feeling bad. Do you know what you might be able to do differently in the teeth brushing situation?

Mother: To be honest, I was thinking of finding a video about teeth and hygiene and having her sit and watch it with me. She knows better, but I was thinking about making it a learning experience, and if it takes away from her time watching other movies maybe she will just brush her teeth (*laughs*).

Assessor: (*also laughs*) I like this idea, and it sounds much more positive than you getting upset. Maybe you can even make it a mother/ daughter special time for as long as she does not brush regularly and on her own. Another possibility, you could write her a note from her teeth asking to be brushed and expressing their upset feelings when she does not brush them. Remember, we talked about these silly ideas to turn misbehaviors into a silly thing to laugh and connect about rather than fight about?

Mother: Yes, I did this during the assessment when you suggested it. I wrote her a letter from her room about being so messy. It was great, I put a funny note from each piece of furniture and in the end, she was laughing so hard she forgot how upset she was about having to clean up. I forgot about these strategies. You are right, these positive, silly strategies work better with her. I just forget and get upset because she is old enough to know better, but I need to remember all the things you said about her self-esteem and her being younger than her age.

- Ask the parents about the suggestions from the assessment and discuss which ones they were able to implement and with what level of success. A conversation like this can offer insights into what the family was able to process or integrate from the assessment and what additional support they might need. You might also ask about how referrals to other professionals have worked out, and offer additional resources, if needed. Imagine the following scenario.

Assessor: I understand that the family therapy with Dr. Smith did not work out, is that right? Can you tell me what happened?

Mother: Well, we went a couple of times and Carly seemed to like her, but then we were not able to make several appointments because we

	had family in town and then somehow, we stopped going. I am not sure if we need to go back or not, especially now that things seem better.
Father:	I am not sure we need family therapy. I like the therapist Carly sees on her own. She met with us alone twice and it seemed like it was kind of the same thing, except Carly was not there so we were able to talk about our concerns, and she gave us some suggestions. I didn't like going to the family therapy because it usually ended with Carly and Elena crying or fighting with each other.
Assessor:	Wow, Jeff, thank you for saying this. It sounds like family therapy was difficult. Elena, do you feel the same way?
Mother:	I was fine going, but yes, it was hard. Carly would get very upset each time, and it was hard to recover from it, go to work after, and try to be normal at home. Maybe that was a part of why we stopped going.
Assessor:	Yes, that sounds very hard. I can understand not wanting to go if it impacted your life so much after. I am so sorry to hear that. Jeff, you mentioned that meeting with Carly's therapist was good. Elena, do you agree with that?
Mother:	Yes, she is very nice, and Carly seems to like her.
Assessor:	I wonder if she would be willing to meet with you occasionally to offer specific parent coaching ideas based on how she knows Carly and what Carly needs. It's not atypical, given Carly's young age, to have regular check-ins with her therapist to see what you can work on as a family. What do you think?
Father:	I would be open to that. That last meeting with her was good, and she seems to understand Carly, so we could try.
Mother:	I can ask if she does that kind of thing, but if she doesn't, what should we do?
Assessor:	Well, based on all of the work we did during the assessment, it seemed that Carly's progress is to a great extent impacted by how well you work as a family unit, which is why we thought family therapy would be important. I would say that a combination of individual therapy and parent coaching could be a good alternative to give you some support as a family in the changes you are trying to make with Carly. If she can't do the parent coaching piece, let's see if we can find someone else who might be able to do it. Dr. Smith might have a suggestion about this as well, so you could ask her opinion, or I would be willing to call her if you want.
Mother:	That's a good plan, I would be interested in doing the parent coaching. I think it might be better than family therapy, at least right now.
Father:	I agree. But would you be willing to talk to Dr. Smith in any case?
Assessor:	I can do that and then give you all a call.

- Establish a framework for any future contacts. While we assume that the Follow-up Session marks the final contact between the assessor and the parents, many parents want to know if they may contact you in the future if they need. For example, parents may request that you provide ongoing consultation to the primary treating professional, stay connected to the family via occasional check-in sessions in case future questions come up, or re-assess their child at an older age.

- Before the session comes to a close, there is one more step: metaprocessing (i.e., jointly reflecting on and discussing) the TA-C with the parents and saying goodbye. We typically initiate this step by saying something like, "Now that you have some distance from the assessment, may I ask what was helpful, what was hard or not helpful, and how we could improve our assessments for future families?" We then listen closely to what parents say and ask follow-up questions. Here is a brief example:

Mother: I thought the whole process was helpful because we were able to learn things about Suji we did not know before that he was not able to tell us. You can't help your child if you don't know what's going on. Now, at least we have more information to follow.

Father: I wasn't so sure at first when you said it would take several weeks, but now I understand why. I liked how comprehensive the assessment was.

Assessor: Yes, I know. It took us a long time, and you both were very patient in the process, even when it seemed like it was going on and on (*all laugh*). I really appreciated that about you. Was there anything during the assessment that stood out the most to you or was most helpful to your family?

Father: For me it was the session when we met alone, and you showed us the video of him talking about all of those sad stories about the pictures and missing his cousins and grandparents. Everyone in those stories was sad and crying and then you asked him if he ever felt that way (*father gets choked up*). It broke my heart. I went home and cried that night because I really did not know he was feeling so bad.

Assessor: I remember that session and how moved I was by your reaction. You both were feeling so much for him. I know there is nothing more painful than to see your child in pain.

Mother: I actually remember that you teared up in that session, and it felt good to see you also felt the sadness Suji feels. I was sad for him, but I was also feeling good because I thought you were really understanding him and you said you would help us cope with his depression. We don't have family here. They are all abroad and we had been feeling so alone and homesick and also sad. I think Suji helped all of us feel our sadness.

Assessor: He is a very special boy; you know, he will have a soft spot in my heart forever *(all smile)* as will you, of course.

Meta-processing the assessment experiencing is not just a way of assessors getting feedback on their work. As Fosha (2000) has emphasized, meta-processing therapeutic work and our relationship with clients adds another level of integration of the clients' experience and increases emotional and cognitive benefits. Framed in the language of attachment theory, meta-processing makes the *implicit* experience of the therapeutic relationship *explicit* by capturing it in words. Asking clients to reflect on what the experience was like for them, as well as assessors judiciously sharing some of their personal experience, offers an opportunity for both parties to uncover thoughts and feelings they might not have been fully aware of, provides closure to the relationship, and promotes a cohesive narrative of the full therapeutic experience.

Finally (assuming you and the client are not continuing to work together) we suggest you explicitly say good-bye to the parents. Many clients have few experiences of authentic and acknowledged endings in relationships. The Follow-up Session is a chance to offer clients such an experience, which can have therapeutic benefit in and of itself.

Before we turn our attention to Henry's case, we want to again encourage assessors to conduct a Follow-up Session at the end of a TA-C. As stated previously, this unique opportunity offers many benefits to the family as well as to the assessor.

Let's now turn our attention to the case of Henry and Dale's work.

Case: Follow-up Session with Henry's Parents

Three weeks after the final Summary/Discussion Session with Henry and his parents, Barbara called to make an appointment for family therapy. We had previously discussed this possibility in our Summary/ Discussion Session. I suggested that we wait until after I finished the Therapeutic Psychological Report and Parent Letter, but Barbara said they didn't want to lose the momentum of the assessment and preferred to get started as soon as they could. I scheduled a family session for the following week and suggested Henry's brother Frank join us as well. I had met Frank a couple of times during the assessment so I didn't think him joining us would be problematic. I wanted the whole family present to be able to focus on systemic family change.

I am going to share a bit about the first few family therapy sessions as they relate to the Follow-up Session. During the first session we talked about why the parents had decided to do family therapy, and what each member might like to get out of it. Henry and Frank were noncommittal and both parents indicated they wanted the family to "work better together." (*I took this as a positive sign because the focus was on the family and not on Henry as the identified patient.*) Toward the end of the session, we played a spirited game of Slapjack. For those unfamiliar with the game, it is played with a regular set of cards. Each player gets the same number of cards, and takes turns flipping a card over sequentially to make one stack of cards. The first person to notice a Jack slaps the pile and takes all the cards in the pile into their hand. At the end of the game, one person has all the cards and is declared the winner. Frank was upset and pouted when he didn't win. At the end of the game, he decided to sit in the chair Henry was occupying. It looked like they were playing, and then Frank suddenly, perhaps playfully bit Henry, who did not defend himself or say anything. Neither parent intervened or said anything. (*I was surprised by this because, during the assessment, both parents shared that Henry could become aggressive with Frank, who they felt was more easy-going than Henry.*) I softly asked Frank if he was angry at Henry. He said, "No, I was just playing."

At the next session I asked the family to make a large family drawing in a particular way. Each person would have 30 seconds to draw something. When I called time, the person who was drawing would stop, and the next person would add to the drawing. Each time it was Henry's turn he added a sad representation to some part of the drawing. This clearly bothered Frank, who tried to negate Henry's representation by putting a happier representation into the drawing. There was tension in the room that was palpable as Henry insisted on injecting sadness into the drawing, which others clearly saw as "spoiling" the drawing, and Frank pushing back. Again, no one said much about Henry's additions except Frank, who was clearly exasperated. As we talked and processed a bit about the session, Frank kicked Henry. I don't think either of the parents saw the interaction, but they heard Henry get upset with Frank. David quietly told Henry to stop complaining. I didn't intervene, wanting to see if either of the boys would respond. Nothing else was said. (*I wondered how often Henry was blamed for something and whether that was a result of being the eldest child, or because his parents were unconsciously angry at Henry for being so sad all the time.*)

The third week we played *The Talking, Feeling & Doing Anger Card Game* (Childswork/Childsplay, 2004). This is a game where people take turns, throw a dice that lands on a number that corresponds to a card, which then instructs the player to talk, feel, or do something that has to do with anger. This game allows the family to "play" with anger. At one point Henry responded to one card by sharing how he felt when his father got angry with him and picked him up and dragged him to the bathroom. David didn't respond spontaneously, and Frank said something about the incident not being that scary. (*At this point it was clear that Frank was allied with the parents in the family dynamic of minimizing Henry's distressing feelings.*)

Within these first three weeks of family therapy, the anger was palpable in the room, although mainly between Frank and Henry. I decided this would be a good time to meet alone with Barbara and David to discuss the family therapy, weave in the assessment results, and do some processing of the TA-C as it related to the family work. While this is not the typical Follow-up Session discussed above, I anticipated it would allow us to integrate the work we were doing in therapy with the assessment. I started with an open-ended question about how they thought things were going.

Barbara:	I'm surprised that Frank seems so comfortable in the sessions since he doesn't really know you. But he's our easy kid who can pretty much go with the flow. I noticed how much he wants Henry to be happy!
Dale:	Yes! That was so clear when we did the family drawing.
David:	Yes, I was surprised by that. I know Henry's negativity really bothers Frank but was shocked when he kept trying to change the sad faces into happy faces.
Dale:	What did you all make of that?
Barbara:	I guess he's as sick of Henry's sad talk as much as we are.
Dale:	I noticed that no one really commented on it or said anything about it.
Barbara:	What can we really say? It's so draining.
Dale:	I know, it's so hard as we try to enjoy ourselves, to have one person always being Eeyore. Do you remember how you were feeling during that time?
David:	Frustrated.
Barbara:	Irritated.

We discussed their feelings and how this was one of the times when it felt like Henry was being provocative.

Dale:	Yes! This takes us back to the assessment. Do you remember what we said about that question—the one about why he makes such provocative statements?
David:	Kind of. He may not feel like he is allowed to express his anger and he can only do it indirectly.
Barbara:	Yeah, we talked about how anger wasn't expressed on our families, and we don't really know how to do this until the anger becomes bigger than it needs to be.
Dale:	Yes, and he is testing you to see if you can you deal with his sadness or, will you get angry and shame or punish him. So, what happened in the session?
Barbara:	I think we just tried to ignore it and not focus on it.
Dale:	Right. And how do you think that felt for Henry?
David:	Don't know, maybe lonely.
Dale:	Yes, how else do you think?
Barbara:	Isolated? Angry? Sad?

Dale: We didn't talk about this directly during the assessment, but I mentioned it in the letter. Do you think you passed his tests?

A conversation ensued about passing Henry's unconscious tests and what that might look like in family therapy. We discussed the possibility of them setting a limit or asking Henry how sad he was feeling during the activity or acknowledging the anger that was present during the session. We also talked about them containing Frank, so he wasn't in the role of expressing anger for the whole family at Henry. We spent more time talking about this and how we might handle anger when it came up again in family therapy.

The weaving together of the assessment results with the process of what was going on in the therapy seemed to be a positive way of having a Follow-up Session. Within the first few months of the family therapy, I met with Barbara and David several times to focus on the sessions, do some parent coaching, and tie what we were doing back to the TA-C. In reviewing this case, I am sure now that I could have done a more traditional Follow-up Session (e.g., by asking that we use one of the scheduled meetings to discuss the written feedback and the TA-C). But the way I followed up happened organically and served to thread together the assessment results with the problems in daily living that the family members were experiencing.

During these sessions with the parents, I did ask about how they experienced the TA-C. Several times we discussed how they understood more and more about how family members' feelings went underground and weren't necessarily validated. We talked about how hard it is to make behavioral changes in a family even after people are more conscious of the family dynamic. We discussed that it takes time, patience, and perseverance to change a family system that has been in place for a number of years.

References

Childswork/Childsplay. (2004). *The Talking, Feeling & Doing Anger Card Game.* Bohemia, NY: Creative Therapeutics, Inc.

Fosha, D. (2000). Meta-therapeutic processes and the affects of transformation: Affirmation and the healing affects. *Journal of Psychotherapy Integration, 10,* 71–97.

Smith, J. D., Handler, L., & Nash, M. R. (2010). Therapeutic Assessment with preadolescent boys with oppositional defiant disorder: A replicated single-case time-series design. *Psychological Assessment, 22*(3), 593–602.

11 Adapting the Therapeutic Assessment with Children Model to Various Settings

As mentioned in Chapter 2, a cornerstone of Therapeutic Assessment (TA) is that its procedures always should be adapted to particular clients and different professional contexts. In this chapter, we sketch out various adaptations, based on our own and other colleagues' experiences. We first discuss brief Therapeutic Assessment with Children (TA-C), then build on this discussion to review TA-C done remotely, TA-C in inpatient and residential treatment facilities, TA-C in outpatient community mental health centers, and finally, TA-C bridged to schools and school assessments.

Brief TA-C

We believe that the full TA-C model, with all the steps that have been presented and illustrated in Chapters 3–9, has the most therapeutic power to help a child and family address persistent problems and be able to handle difficulties that may arise in the future. However, we recognize that it may not always be feasible or even advisable for assessors to implement the full TA-C model. Let us review several situations in which assessors may choose to use a briefer model that includes only some of the steps.

The Presenting Concerns Are Mild and/or Relatively Acute

When the problems that bring a family for a TA-C are not severe or are relatively recent in nature, and there are many other signs of good family functioning, it may not be necessary to do a full TA-C. For example, Finn and Chudzik (2013) reported on the case of a 7-year-old boy brought for a TA-C because of treatment-resistant enuresis that had developed after his close uncle suddenly died from AIDS. After an initial session with the parents, a drawing from the Fantasy Animal Drawing Game, and another loosely structured activity with the boy—with parents observing—it became clear that the boy was distressed that the family was not really grieving the uncle's death, in part because of the intense shame they felt over the uncle's illness. The parents came to realize they had not helped the boy grieve and collaborated with the assessor to organize a Family Intervention Session (FIS) in

DOI: 10.4324/9781003000174-11

which members of the extended family acknowledged the uncle's death and celebrated his life. The boy's enuresis stopped immediately. Through the brief assessment, the parents learned that they had avoided their grief and buried themselves in their careers; afterwards they began to work less and spend more time with their son.

In this instance, factors that suggested that a brief TA-C might be effective included: 1) the parents and child had many positive psychological resources and good family support, 2) the presenting issue (enuresis) was relatively circumscribed, 3) prior to the enuresis, there were no noted problems, 4) there were no apparent early attachment disruptions, 5) the level of projective identification was not severe, e.g., the parents were able to "buy back" their split-off grief when it became apparent in the boy's assessment materials, 6) the assessor found it easy to ally with both the parents and the child, and 7) the boy easily used the assessor and the assessment activities to clearly lay out the family's dilemma of change. Importantly, if unsure of what was needed, the assessor could have proceeded with a brief TA-C and then added more sessions/steps if the family needed more time or scaffolding in order to shift.

Parents Are Unable to Participate in a Full TA-C and/or Resources Are Limited

Sometimes, even when it is apparent that a full TA-C likely would be the ideal intervention for a child and family, various factors make this impossible. It may be that one or both parents are unable or unwilling to attend multiple assessment sessions, a full TA-C would be too costly and there is no financial support available, or the assessing clinician or sponsoring agency does not have the time or staff available to do a full TA-C.

Where to Cut Back

There are various ways to shorten a TA-C. Let us share our thoughts about which steps to keep or modify when a brief TA is warranted.

Initial Sessions

In our minds, initial sessions should always be part of a brief TA-C, as they are crucial for building alliance, establishing the scope of the assessment, and inviting parents' collaboration. When time and resources are short, it may be tempting to try to streamline the initial session by sending parents beforehand extensive developmental history questionnaires to complete. We recommend against this, as we have found that one gets very different information on such questionnaires once parents feel some connection with and trust in the assessor. After the initial session, however, it can be useful to ask parents to complete such forms and this can save time vs. collecting the information orally. In addition, if one or both parents are unable to attend an initial session for whatever reason, we have found that tele-health sessions can work well—either with both or one parent being present by phone or web conference.

Standardized Testing Sessions and Parent Observation

One of the steps that is most flexible and hence most adaptable to brief TA-C is the standardized testing. In our experience, many of us are most comfortable drawing conclusions from an assessment when we give many tests, often tests of the same constructs. Within reason, this has many advantages because we get to see how children perform in different contexts and on different measures (Cf. Meyer et al., 2001). But, "when push comes to shove," often we could get by with fewer tests, especially if we are clear with parents at the end that we are presenting a considered "best guess" about what is going on with a child, and that more testing could be done in the future if the next steps we have laid out are not successful.

For example, during his psychology internship, Steve served as a psychological consultant to a pediatric neurology clinic in a large community hospital. Steve spent one day each week seeing children and parents with one of the pediatric neurologists, and typically there was very limited time to assess each child. Often, as part of the initial visit, Steve would ask the child to complete a House-Tree-Person drawing (Buck, 1948) or a Kinetic Family Drawing (Burns & Kaufman, 1972) with parents and neurologist in the room, and then everyone would discuss the results. Steve was surprised by how many children would "send messages" to the assessment team through their drawings of their emotional state (e.g., drawing a dead tree if they were depressed) or of important family dynamics (e.g., drawing parents fighting and the child isolated in his room). This simple assessment task certainly did not provide all the information Steve would have liked to have about the child and family, but it suggested themes that could then be collaboratively discussed and followed up on. Sometimes, a complete psychological assessment was undertaken afterwards, but it most instances it was not.

In cutting down the number of tests administered, we have found it useful to ask ourselves: 1) What are the most important questions to be addressed in the assessment?; 2) What tests can I give that are most central to those questions?; 3) Are there any alternative measures that are briefer or easier to give?; 4) Even if I can't myself eliminate competing hypotheses from the test results, can I collaborate with parents in weighing the possible conclusions instead of doing more tests?; and 5) Would intervention strategies be that different from each other even if I could eliminate competing hypotheses?

As mentioned in Chapter 4, one other way to simplify the testing process in TA-C is to eliminate or greatly limit direct parent observation of child testing, and perhaps to videotape assessment sessions and share excerpts with parents at a later time, such as at the Summary/Discussion Session. And when videotaping is impossible for any reason, it can also be effective to read parents their child's assessment responses in detail, for example, stories from the Roberts Apperception Test for Children-RATC, (McArthur & Roberts, 1982) or item responses from the Wechsler Intelligence Scale for Children-WISC-V, (Wechsler, 2014) as a way to help them "get in the shoes" of their child.

Family Intervention Sessions

It certainly is possible to eliminate FISs as a way to achieve a briefer TA-C, and this may be appropriate for families where systemic issues are less central to the child's problems. However, as mentioned in Chapter 2, research suggests that eliminating the family component of TA-C makes it less effective (e.g., Hansson et al., 2016) and that FISs can be crucial in changing family narratives (e.g., Smith et al., 2011). Thus, we urge that assessors try to keep this step in a brief TA-C and consider shortening the assessment in other ways, if possible.

Summary/Discussion Sessions

Like Initial Sessions, Summary/Discussion Sessions with parents are crucial to the TA-C model, and should always be included if at all possible. As with other parent sessions, however, we and other colleagues have conducted such sessions over the telephone or by web conference when necessary, and our impression is that they can still be effective. Another practice used by some assessors, which may shorten Summary/Discussion Sessions, is to first provide parents with a written report and feedback letter, and then meet with them after to address their questions and reactions. Our sense is that this approach can work in situations where the assessor is not presenting any Level 3 Information, and where parents are healthy enough to manage Level 2 Information on their own until they can meet with the assessor.

Parent Feedback Letters and Written Reports

As discussed in Chapter 8, the written documents we produce for parents and other professionals at the end of a TA-C are one of the most time- and energy-consuming parts of the model. Thus, for brief TA-C we strongly advise assessors to consider what kinds of written feedback are necessary and most useful. Possibly, a letter written to parents also will serve the needs of a referring therapist, and there is no need to write a separate letter. Alternatively, a formal psychological report—if written in an accessible and clear way—may be enough to remind and inform parents of the major findings of the TA-C. If time and resources are short, we have found that many parents are very happy with a list of plainly written "bullet points" of major assessment findings and answers to Assessment Questions, which can be shared at the Summary/Discussion session, and which parents can refer back to for understanding a more formal report needed for other contexts (e.g., a school). One other time saving practice is to invite parents to audio-tape Summary/Discussion sessions; for some parents this may preclude the need for a written feedback document.

Child Fables

It is possible to eliminate writing a child fable at the end of a TA-C in order to save time or reduce cost; however, we worry that this might leave some children feeling incomplete or possibly imagining negative results from the assessment. For this reason, if no fable is written for the child, we urge as-sessors to give them some oral feedback. Still, if at all possible, we urge as-sessors to retain this step in a brief TA-C. We remind you of the research by Tharinger and Pilgrim (2011) mentioned in Chapter 2 and 8 that showed that adding a child fable to an otherwise traditional assessment significantly enhanced the assessment experience for both children and parents. Two middle-ground approaches might be to: 1) write very short fables and/or 2) write a fable for the child, but give it to the parents to share with the child at home, rather than scheduling an additional session with the assessor present.

Follow-up Sessions

Follow-up Sessions likely are the most expendable step in the TA-C model, although we believe they help families carry forward what they have learned in the TA-C (Kamphuis & Finn, 2019). When time and resources are limited, we suggest assessors not routinely offer Follow-up Sessions, but let families know that another meeting can be scheduled if they have questions about the written feedback or have difficulty implementing the next steps outlined at the end of the TA-C. Another option is to check in with families by telephone or email 6–8 weeks after an assessment to see how they are faring and assess if there is any need to meet in person.

Case Example of Brief TA-C Due to Agency Limitations

The case described earlier, of the boy with enuresis, was appropriate for a brief TA-C because the problem was relatively circumscribed and the family was high functioning. Let us present another case where a brief TA-C was done because of limitations in resources.

Ruling-out ADD

Mr. and Mrs. Patel scheduled their 12-year-old son, Anik, to be assessed at a local Child Guidance Center to see if he might have ADD. Because of limited resources and high demand, the Center routinely conducted brief

TA-Cs consisting of 3 to 5 two-hour sessions. Families needing more were sometimes referred for longer evaluations. In the Initial Session, the assessor gathered background information and the parents' main Assessment Questions: "Does Anik have ADD?" and "If not, what is responsible for his grades dropping so much?" She learned that the family had moved recently from another state due to Mr. Patel's work, and that Anik had always done exceptionally well in school before the move. The Patels also explained that academic achievement was very highly valued in their Indian-American family, and that a teacher had suggested Anik might benefit from Adderal or another stimulant medication. The parents had considered going directly to their pediatrician, but decided to have Anik assessed before doing that. The assessor thanked the parents for their openness and asked them to complete the Behavior Assessment System for Children (BASC-3; Reynolds & Kamphaus, 2015) before they left that day and to bring Anik to the next session. Both parents' BASC-3s had clinical elevations on the Attention Problems and Depression scales.

At the next session, the parents observed over a video link as the assessor and Anik worked on the Individualized Sentence Completion Task (see Chapter 4). He appeared downcast and quiet during the session and in his responses to the Incomplete Sentences, Anik expressed a great deal of distress about the family's move. He said he missed his old friends and did not feel comfortable in his new school, where he was the only Indian-American student. While Anik sat in the waiting room, the assessor met with his parents. They all discussed the BASC-3 results and the Patels' surprise at how unhappy Anik was about their move. The parents explained that they had already talked to Anik numerous times and underlined the many positive reasons why they had come to their new city. At one point, Mrs. Patel shared that she too missed the strong Indian-American community they had left, but was determined to make the best of their new home. Mr. Patel was a bit defensive at first, but with the assessor's support, he became more open and wondered aloud what he/they could do. Should they move back to their old city? Everyone agreed another disruption was not for the best, and the assessor asked if Mr. and Mrs. Patel were open to coaching about helping Anik adjust. They were. The assessor scheduled a FIS, and asked the Patels to bring pictures of their former house, city, and friends.

At the beginning of the next session, the assessor met with the parents alone and provided psycho-education about the importance of joining with a child's feelings of loss before affirming positive aspects of a situation. Otherwise, the assessor explained, Anik might still feel sad but also bad for feeling that way. The parents easily understood and accepted this frame. Then Anik was brought in and, at the assessor's suggestion, the family used the photos they had brought to talk first about all that they missed about their previous city and home. In this part of the session, Anik seemed relieved to know that he was not alone with his sad feelings. Then, to his parents' surprise, Anik himself initiated a discussion of all the things that were better since they moved. For example, Anik liked his bigger bedroom in their new home, had already connected with several of his teachers, and was excited about the chess club he had joined.

The fourth TA-C session (two weeks later) was a Summary/Discussion Session with the parents alone. The assessor and parents talked about the FIS, reviewed the BASC-3 results, and discussed the parents' original Assessment Question of whether Anik had ADD. The parents had already concluded that Anik did not, and said that Anik had greatly improved since the family session, and was already studying hard and getting his homework done. They related that Anik had asked several times that they talk again about what they all missed about their previous life and what they liked about their new situation, and that they had done this, finding new things to add to their lists. The assessor validated the parents' conclusion that Anik did not have ADD and explained it was very unlikely given Anik's excellent academic performance before the move.

At the end of the session, the assessor showed the parents a therapeutic fable she had written for Anik, and they suggested several changes to make the story fit him better. The assessor reprinted the fable and gave it to the parents to take home to Anik. They sent the assessor an email the next day saying that Anik had loved the fable.

One week later the assessor sent the parents a 3-page letter summarizing the assessment process and what had been learned. She invited the parents to contact her if they had any questions and said she would contact them in 3–4 weeks to see how things were going. One month later, the assessor emailed the parents to set up a brief follow-up phone call. When they spoke, the parents reported that Anik was doing really well in school, and that they had successfully connected with several other Indian-American families in the area. They thanked the assessor for her help, and she let them know they could contact the Center if they needed any more support in the future.

Tele-assessment and Remote TA-C

As we write these pages, the world is in the middle of the 2020 COVID-19 pandemic, and many aspects of life have changed, including the practice of psychological assessment. With many of us in or just starting to open up from quarantine, and with the possibility of more waves of infection in the future, mental health professionals in many disciplines have begun to work with clients via telephone or internet platforms that allow video and voice transmission. This is also true for psychological assessors. In fact, the American Psychological Association responded quickly to the novel coronavirus crisis by publishing a set of general guidelines for the practice of psychological tele-assessment (Wright et al., 2020). APA also worked with a group of neuropsychology organizations to prepare a set of resources for tele-assessment in general and remote neuropsychological assessment in particular, including a summary of the research on the equivalence of in-person and remote test administration (Inter Organizational Practice Committee, 2020). Last, many individual test publishers have provided guidance on remote use of their particular instruments, e.g., the Rorschach Performance Assessment System (2020). We urge you to be familiar with all these resources and to consult them for specific questions on tele-assessment. Here we share our thoughts about remote TA-C, whether it is done in response to a pandemic or because of other limiting circumstances, e.g., assessing a child and family in an isolated village where there are no psychologists.

Remote TA-C

Many aspects of TA-C are well suited to tele-assessment, and traditional assessors who need to assess children remotely could benefit from learning about the principles and practices of TA-C. For example:

The Importance of the Assessor-Client Relationship

As we hope has been clear throughout this book, Therapeutic Assessment has always emphasized the enormous importance of the relationship between assessors and clients in gathering useful information, reaching new understandings of clients' challenges, and making use of what is learned through an assessment. In remote testing, the assessor-client relationship is even more important, and we are encouraged by our experience that it is indeed possible to develop a safe, trusting relationship with assessment clients when working online. What are the essential elements for building a good relationship when you cannot meet with clients in person? In our minds they are: 1) showing clients that we see them as unique, separate individuals and we will put their needs equal to or above our own, 2) constantly working hard—even from a distance—to "get in clients shoes" and understand how they experience the world, thereby helping clients get curious about themselves, 3) demonstrating that we will not judge clients or shame them, no matter what they show or tell us, and 4) being willing and competent at helping clients manage the emotions that come up during a psychological assessment. With children, we also find that flexibility and creativity is extremely important in helping them engage with us over a remote connection, and these are also core aspects of TA-C.

Involving Parents as Collaborators

When working remotely with young children to do psychological testing, it is usually essential that parents assist us and manage not only the online technology (e.g., the computer set up and internet connection) and the testing situation (e.g., providing a quiet, non-distracting environment), but also the test materials themselves (e.g., test forms, pencils, and some stimulus materials). For example, the Crisi Wartegg System (a performance-based test administered to Henry—see Chapter 4) can be administered to young children remotely (Crisi & Palm, 2020); but, there are many steps where parents must be involved. These include arranging the camera so the child's drawings can be seen by the assessor, opening the envelope the assessor has mailed with the test materials, making sure the child has an appropriate pencil, mailing the response form back to the assessor, etc. Fortunately, involving parents in this way is only a small step beyond what we normally do in our offices when we have parents observe child testing sessions in TA-C. For this reason, we have not found it difficult to collaborate with parents during remote assessment. Of course, assessors must brief parents on what is required for each test used, and also debrief parents afterwards about what they observed. But again, as explained in Chapter 4, we already do these things and thus, the modifications needed for online testing are relatively minor.

Remembering That Test Scores Are Not "True"

Understandably, psychologists conducting remote psychological assessments are concerned about the equivalency and validity of tests administered online compared to those administered in person (Wright et al., 2020). We appreciate this concern and applaud research being done on this topic. Yet, we also affirm that psychological tests and assessment can be used to help understand children and families, even if they are administered under less than ideal circumstances. In TA-C we do this by holding test scores "lightly" rather than as absolutely "True," and helping consumers of test scores situate their meaning by richly describing the assessment context and a child's behavior. Fischer (1978) reminds us that in our earlier understanding of science, test scores were viewed as objective and more real than actual experience and behavior, whereas in collaborative models of assessment test scores are viewed as derived data, secondary to behavior and experience.

Keeping Context in Mind

This leads to another fundamental aspect of TA-C that is highly pertinent to remote testing of any kind and in particular to assessments done in the middle of a global pandemic: the importance of context. In TA-C, we see a psychological assessment as a detailed "snapshot" of a child and family in a particular setting at a certain point in time. Test results collected remotely during a COVID-19 lockdown are inevitably influenced by that highly unusual context, and most likely in ways we can never fully know. Still, this doesn't mean online assessments are not helpful, because we can dialogue with parents and children about their context and explore implications for any test results. For example, imagine we attempt to test a child remotely and he is inattentive and uncooperative on a certain day. We find out later that he has had five hours of online schooling before the testing session, and is most likely exhausted. Discussing the situation with the parents afterwards, we come to understand a dilemma we had not grasped earlier: the parents don't want the child to miss any school, because he is already falling behind academically; but they also don't want to postpone the assessment because they believe he needs special accommodations. After a discussion with the parents, we agree to do some testing in the mornings, before the child has done any schooling, to see if that influences his ability to pay attention. Such collaborative "experiments" can lead to direct recommendations about how to help that particular child deal with the specific challenges of online instruction.

Showing Respect and Humility in Reporting Assessment Results

While acknowledging our own expertise as skilled assessors, we also strive to show humility about the limits of remote assessment and to help consumers of our assessment reports and letters avoid interpreting test scores in "absolutist" ways. For example, the following might be an appropriate qualifying statement in an assessment report about the child mentioned above: "Samuel scored in the average range in all areas on a standardized test of intellectual ability. However, as described earlier, this test was administered remotely on a Zoom platform, on two different days. On both days Samuel had attended multiple hours of online classes already, was clearly tired, and had trouble staying on task, even with his parents supporting him. Samuel's parents said that in their eyes, on those days he was more distractible than usual during the testing sessions. Thus, Samuel's scores on the intellectual testing are most likely an underestimate of his potential. This conclusion is supported by the fact that on a standardized test of academic achievement, which Samuel and I did one morning before he began his online classes, Samuel scored in the high average range in all areas, except for on math reasoning…"

In conclusion, we suggest that psychologists conducting remote assessments become familiar with the principles and techniques of TA-C.

TA-C in Inpatient and Residential Treatment

Although TA-C is still relatively new, we are aware of its being successfully applied in inpatient and residential treatment settings. Let us address these two types of settings separately.

Child Inpatient Treatment

Pagano et al., (2019) gave recommendations about how to adapt TA-C to child inpatient settings and presented three case examples of using the model on an inpatient child psychiatric unit in a community teaching hospital. As the authors explained, contemporary inpatient treatment of children is focused largely on brief stabilization, typically after children report serious suicidal ideation or make a suicide attempt, and the average length of stay for children in the US is about 7 days. Perhaps not surprisingly, after such brief treatment many children require re-hospitalization soon after they are discharged--perhaps 30–40%, depending on the length of the follow-up (Blader, 2004). Pagano et al. assert that TA-C makes child inpatient treatment more effective and decreases readmission rates because it creatively integrates work with families into child-focused interventions. However, they also acknowledge that it is generally impossible to implement the full TA-C model in inpatient units because psychologists have such limited time to address the needs of children and their families.

In effect, the case examples described by Pagano and his colleagues demonstrate the power of *brief* TA-C as an inpatient intervention. Pagano et al. (2019) recommend the following steps of TA-C be used: 1) Initial sessions with children and parents in which Assessment Questions are collected and a working alliance is established. In addition, Assessment Questions may be solicited from nurses, psychiatrists, social workers, and other hospital staff treating the child. We would add here that parent rating forms such as the BASC-3 could easily be included at this stage. 2) Very targeted psychological testing of the child, using performance-based tests like the Rorschach, TAT (Murray, 1943), CAT (Bellak & Bellak, 1976), or projective drawings. Pagano et al. felt these were often extremely useful in helping parents and staff become more empathic to children's emotional experiences. 3) A FIS, which Pagano et al. felt was crucial to the success of inpatient TA-C. They recommended the same structure and techniques described in Chapter 6. 4) Providing written feedback to staff, parents, and at times, to children in the form of a therapeutic fable. We urge interested readers to review Pagano's and his colleagues' three case examples, from which they concluded that TA can quickly guide professionals involved in helping children and families and also address the individualized needs of children in inpatient treatment as well as those of their parents.

Child Residential Treatment

As far as we know, there are no published accounts of TA-C in long term residential treatment, but we have conducted and supervised such assessments. In our experience, TA-C can be useful at several different points: 1) prior to admission, as a way of defining a focus for treatment and of helping children and families be prepared, 2) mid-treatment, especially as a way of addressing problems or concerns that have arisen during the treatment, and 3) just prior to discharge, as a way of documenting progress, identifying areas that need ongoing work, and planning for outpatient follow-up.

There are several unique factors to using TA-C as part of residential treatment: 1) In this setting, typically assessors do not have the time constraints that exist with inpatient treatment; thus, generally it is possible to have weekly meetings and to use as many standardized tests as seem appropriate. Staff at many facilities are more used to traditional psychological assessment, where a child is tested all at once over the course of a single day. But in our experience, when TA-C is explained, most staff adapt to a more extended assessment such as we typically use. 2) Depending on whether the TA-C is done prior to admission, parents may be more or less accessible. For example, if a child is at a treatment facility far from home, it may not be possible for parents to directly observe assessment sessions. In such instances assessors may still videotape the testing sessions and share excerpts with parents online to get their input. 3) For mid-treatment assessments, we often involve the staff of the group home or residential treatment facility as essential collaborators, much as parents are involved in outpatient TA-C. For example, we generally collect Assessment Questions from treatment staff, ask for their input and collaboration as the TA-C proceeds, and invite them to tell us how a child has been in between assessment sessions. 4) In fact, TA-C can be highly integrated with other treatment components in residential treatment, with assessors informing individual and group therapists about what happened in each weekly assessment session, and treatment staff informing the assessor of important events in the community that might be affecting the child. 5) Again, depending on parent accessibility, a FIS may not be possible. Sometimes such sessions can be scheduled when parents are visiting the facility. In addition, our experience with remote TA-C gives us hope that online FISs may be useful and productive when parents and child cannot be in the same room. 6) Similarly, parent Summary/Discussion Sessions may be conducted online or by telephone, and typically involve other treatment staff. 7) Last, it is not uncommon for a child's individual therapist to be present when the child is given the fable at the end of the TA-C.

TA-C in Community Mental Health Centers

A great deal has been written about the use of TA-C in community mental health centers, where children and families are often economically disadvantaged, racially and culturally diverse, and have high levels of trauma. As discussed in Chapter 2, many of the accounts of TA-C with such clients come from WestCoast Children's Clinic (WCC) in Oakland, CA (Finn, 2011; Guerrero et al., 2011; Haydel, et al., 2011; Lipkind & Mercer, 2017; Mercer, 2011, 2017; Mercer et al., 2016; Purves, 2012, 2017; Rosenberg et al., 2012). In addition, a recent issue of *The TA Connection*, the newsletter of the Therapeutic Assessment Institute, focused on TA in community mental health centers and includes descriptions of how TA-C has been implemented in four community mental health centers across the US: 1) WCC (Lipkind & Mercer, 2019); 2) Child Haven, Inc. in Solano County, CA (Miller, Novotny et al., 2019); 3) Washburn Center for Children in Minneapolis, MN (Miller, Shah et al., 2019); and 4) the Center for Behavioral Health at the University of Missouri in St. Louis (Smith et al.,2019). Although there are some differences as to how TA-C was adapted for each of these settings, there are common elements that stand out about using TA-C in community mental health centers:

It Is Crucial to Have Buy-in From Clinic Administration and From Funding Sources

Staff at all four sites said they could not have succeeded in implementing TA without a great deal of support from clinic administration, who then secured the buy-in from funding sources (typically, county mental health contracts or outside grants). In part the support of clinic administrators was secured because of existing research data on the efficacy of TA; but it also came from an alignment the staff felt with the core values of TA and some of its theoretical underpinnings (humanism, attachment theory, and trauma theory). In each instance, however, enthusiastic adoption of TA-C in each setting only occurred after one or more "trial" TA-C cases had demonstrated the model's applicability and effectiveness with the clinic's clients. It is worth noting that funding was needed not only to cover the client sessions, but in many cases for the purchase of assessment materials and test scoring.

Expert Outside Training and Supervision May Be Necessary to Successfully Implement TA

Given that TA is relatively new, all four sites found it necessary to "import" TA experts to conduct supervision and training. Fortunately, they were able to do so and were able to overcome confidentiality hurdles so outside the experts could consult about clients. While initial trainings were crucial for providing an overview of TA-C (both for assessors and other clinic staff), regular case supervision was essential for dealing with the complex clients who are served at community mental health centers.

Student Trainees Can Be Used as Assessors With Close Supervision

As TA-C is time intensive, all of the mental health centers relied heavily on graduate student clinicians, who were closely supervised by licensed psychologists to conduct the TA-Cs. This arrangement not only provided needed services for clients, but also valuable experience to student trainees. As has been reported elsewhere (e.g., Smith & Egan, 2015) learning TA is a transformative experience for many trainees, and this was evident in the accounts from all four centers.

It May Be Necessary to Modify the Structure of the TA-C to Accommodate Diverse, Underprivileged, or Highly Overwhelmed Families

All of the centers were able to flexibly adapt TA-C for their diverse, un-derprivileged, and stressed families. For example, some families were unable to come weekly for the 7-8 sessions often needed for a full TA-C with complex Assessment Questions. Thus, some centers arranged for fewer, but longer (e.g., 4-hour) sessions. Again, as described in Chapter 4, it can be difficult to get both parents, particularly fathers, to attend sessions. Thus, an emphasis was placed on trying to have both parents present for Initial Sessions, FISs and Summary/Discussion Sessions. Some centers were also able to provide childcare for siblings, who often could not be left at home when the parents attended TA-C sessions.

Assessors Have to be Sensitive to Not Overwhelm Traumatized Families

As mentioned earlier, many clients in community mental health centers are low-resourced and have extensive histories of medical and mental health problems and multiple traumas. In working with such clients, assessment teams learned to adapt TA-C procedures so as to not overwhelm clients. For example, at WCC we learned that if parents and children both had high levels of trauma, one had to be cautious about having parents observe certain standardized testing sessions with the child. Children might respond to narrative tests such as the Roberts Apperception Test for Children (McArthur & Roberts, 1982) or the Children's Apperception Test (Bellak & Bellak, 1976) by telling horrific stories that resembled traumatic events they might have experienced. Parents watching the session could become over-whelmed and re-traumatized themselves. Staff learned to anticipate such occurrences, and to videotape those assessment sessions, knowing they could select afterwards which portions of the videotape would be helpful to show to parents.

It Is Important to Closely Collaborate With Referring Professionals

Because the clients treated at community mental health centers were so complex, they often had multiple providers involved—often both within and outside the clinic. Assessors learned early on that it was crucial to involve and collaborate with referring therapists, psychiatrists, social workers, occu-pational therapists, and others to ensure the best outcomes from TA-C. For example, sometimes referring therapists would be invited to observe child testing sessions with parents, or to attend FISs. Such collaborations were found to reduce splitting, help treatment team members come to a common understanding, and make use of the different skills, insights, and experiences of the various professionals. Clients also were greatly helped and reassured by their sense of a team of caring professionals all working together.

TA-C Can Be Extremely Helpful in Conceptualizing Complex,
Multi-Problem Families

In almost all instances TA-C was appreciated because it greatly helped clinic staff understand complex, multi-problem families, and to engage those families in the clinics' services in a new way. As staff understood the power of TA-C, one issue that frequently arose was how to address a large increase in requests for TA-C.

TA-C Can Empower Children and Families Who Traditionally Feel
Disrespected, Powerless, Misunderstood, and Unseen

Last but not least, it was apparent that TA-C was an effective method with the types of clients typically seen in community mental health centers, who frequently have had experiences with medical and mental health professionals that have left them confused, hopeless, diminished, and feeling unseen. The core values and practices of TA-C have much to offer to populations who feel disenfranchised and disrespected.

In summary, existing clinical evidence strongly supports the use of TA-C in community mental health centers, and we urge that the model be taught and adopted in those settings.

TA-C in the Schools

We address several ways to transport aspects of TA-C into the schools. We focus on our knowledge of such adaptations in the United States, aware that different approaches are taken in other countries where TA is practiced.

Bridging the TA-C Model to Schools

Often, it can be useful for psychologists practicing TA-C in the private sector to invite the school a child client attends to take part in the assessment, in either a minor or major way. In some cases, the parents have requested a TA-C privately, and the assessor believes it would be useful to get input from the school to understand how the child acts and is viewed outside the home. Thus, the assessor may contact the child's teachers, conduct brief phone interviews, ask teachers to complete comprehensive behavior checklists, and perhaps even follow-up with additional queries.

Consulting to Both Parents and Schools

In other cases, the contact is more extensive. For example, the parents or child may have included concerns about the child at school in one or more of their Assessment Questions. The questions may concern the fit of the school for the child, a recent change in the child's grades or behavior or attitude at school, or a significant clash between a teacher and the child (and perhaps parents). In such situations the assessor is more involved with the school personnel and may meet with teachers and/or administrators at the school to gather information. With the parents' permission the assessor may even invite school personnel to ask Assessment Questions to be addressed by the TA-C. The nature of interviews, tests and informants used is decided on a case-by-case basis, depending on the Assessment Questions. Often, parts of the TA-C focus on the child and the school as a system or the relationship between the child/family system and the school system. Although the parents and child are the primary clients of the assessor, the assessor also develops relationships with the school and functions as a bridge between the parents and school personnel. This role requires diplomacy to balance the needs of both sides while being employed by the parents. Fortunately, there is usually a common goal that both sides agree on--doing what is best for the child—and the assessor helps the two sides come together by consulting on how to achieve this goal. To "be the bridge" the assessor needs administrative support from the school and permission from the parents.

Let's consider an example of such a collaboration by looking at the case of Mary, age 11, who was referred for a TA-C by her parents to one of the co-authors of this book, Marita Frackowiak. Mary struggled at school, not only academically but also socially. She had undergone three previous evaluations at the school under the umbrella of Special Education (addressed more thoroughly in an upcoming section) that pointed to a variety of disabilities and learning differences, including possible Autism, emotional regulation problems, and cognitive weaknesses across multiple cognitive domains. Mary was receiving services through Special Education. However, her parents felt the school was not offering Mary sufficient resources and the school had recently suggested that Mary's needs would be better met in a lower level resource class. The parents felt she was more capable if the right support resources were in place. They worried that moving Mary to a lower level class would impact her self-esteem as well as future educational opportunities. They seemed to want the private assessment, at their expense, to "prove" to the school that they were right.

It became clear in Marita's initial session with the parents that collaboration with the school, rather than confrontation, would likely be a more effective option. Marita suggested she take on the role of being an advocate for the family, but also a collaborator with the school. The parents agreed. The first steps included setting up a school observation, scheduling a meeting with two of Mary's main teachers and her parents, and asking teachers to fill out BASC-3 behavior rating scales to offer their perspective on Mary's behavior and learning. The tone of the meeting was collaborative, affirming that Mary's case was complex and would need everyone to work together to figure out what was best and possible for Mary. During the conversation, it became clear that Mary was withdrawn in the classroom and seemed to struggle to follow instructions. Both teachers expressed praise for Mary's polite and kind behavior, but repeatedly stated that getting Mary involved in the content of class was very difficult. By the end of the meeting, the teachers felt validated and understood, while the parents felt heard and responded to. The assessment process that followed provided an outside perspective on what was best for Mary. The results of the assessment Marita conducted showed that both parents and teachers were "right" in their perspectives of Mary. Marita's goals were to "bridge" those perspectives by offering a shared narrative and then to collaborate on possible solutions.

One tool used in the assessment was videotaping of testing sessions. As we know, a picture is worth a thousand words. During the videotaped administration of Mary's WISC-V, not only did her performance vary but so did her stamina and engagement. Some sections of the video showed Mary able to answer questions reasonably well, while other sections showed her confusion and slow processing. Yet others showed the patience needed by Marita to encourage Mary to verbalize the responses after initially whispering them or quickly shutting down when she felt she didn't answer correctly. When Marita shared the video with the parents it was eye opening but also heartbreaking for them to see Mary's struggles. It was also validating, however, to see her achieve a higher score when she was approached calmly and with patience and encouragement.

A discussion of Mary's needs in the classroom followed and the parents began to understand how difficult it must be for her teachers to offer her the needed support, while also attending to many other children. The parents also felt validated seeing some of Mary's strengths. They felt that these were often dismissed by the teachers, and Mary was categorized as an "unable" student. The test results also supported the observation (and teachers' concerns) of Mary's very slow processing speed, but also showed her ability to reason thoughtfully when given the time and offered hints.

At the end of the assessment, a joint meeting was set between school administration, teachers, and Mary's parents. Marita was invited to attend as Mary's advocate to collaborate efforts and bridge the perspectives between the parties. The meeting started by validating both sides (the teachers and the parents), letting them know that they interacted with and experienced two different aspects of the same complex, kind, hardworking, but struggling student. It followed with acknowledging that both parties were right and each perspective was important in helping Mary. Test results were shared to explore what services Mary would benefit from, but most importantly short clips from the videotaped WISC-V session were offered to demonstrate both Mary's strengths and weaknesses. This was the moment the "bridge" was built, when parents and teachers together watched this quiet, shy child take a painfully long time (almost 5 minutes) to process a WISC-V perceptual reasoning problem and minutes later show her thoughtful, focused response when she was invited to elaborate a definition of a word on the Vocabulary subtest.

Parents and teachers were moved, validated, humbled and joined in their determination to help Mary. Without taking sides or confronting either perspective, Marita was able to present the data and use it to bridge the two different understandings by encouraging empathy for Mary. The parents were able to appreciate the teachers' efforts and understood their frustration in the classroom with limited resources, and the teachers could empathize with the parents' wanting to make sure their daughter was accurately understood for her abilities as well as struggles, which the parents saw when working with her at home in a one-on-one setting. A middle ground solution was created to give Mary additional services, including one-on-one support in her current classroom and after school, private tutoring, financially supported by the parents. The possibility of moving her to a lower level resource class was temporarily put on hold, much to parents' satisfaction.

As illustrated by this case, methods of TA-C have a lot to offer in helping various parties involved in children's lives come to a shared agreement and maybe even a shared narrative about who the child is and what they might benefit from. The spirit of collaboration and humility, embedded in the model, helps to build the bridge rather than polarize the perspectives.

Using TA-C Results to Address School Programming

Another way that TA-C can involve schools is when assessment results are used to tailor school programming. Sometimes we advise parents about what elective courses might be best for their child, or whether an optional summer school program might be helpful. In other instances, such as we saw with Henry, findings from the TA-C can be used to seek accommodations for the child, perhaps even while the TA-C is still in process. As explained in Chapter 9, Dale wrote a letter based on Henry's assessment results documenting the disabling aspects of his depression and anxiety, and this was sufficient to secure accommodations for Henry under 504 Regulations. Specifically, Henry was allowed to leave class and go visit the school counselor whenever he felt overwhelmed or despondent. In other private TA-C cases that bridge to schools, findings may suggest that the child might meet the criteria for a disability that significantly impacts educational performance. Parents may then use the results of the TA-C to pursue an evaluation at the school to determine if the child might be eligible for Special Education Services.

Infusing School Assessments for Special Education With
TA-C Values and Methods

Another application involves assessments conducted in the schools by a school psychologist for Special Education consideration. Our focus in these situations is how the values and methods of TA-C can best infuse the highly regulated, legally mandated methods of assessment in the public schools under the auspices of Special Education. The laws and regulations come from both the federal and state levels, and there are variations among states and across districts within a state; however, the basics are very similar.

Typically, comprehensive evaluations are conducted after interventions have not been successful. The major goal is to determine if a student meets 1 of 13 disabilities and if that disability adversely affects a student's educational performance. Many different specialists are involved in the overall evaluation, each doing assessments based on their specialty. A school psychologist is most likely to be called in when there are concerns that the student's disability might be Seriously Emotionally Disturbed, Specific Learning Disability, Intellectual Disability, Autism, or Other Health Impaired (usually for ADHD or possibly anxiety). Using TA language, such assessments in the schools are guided by the school's main Assessment Question: "Does the student meet the criteria for a disability that impairs their educational performance?" A secondary question is usually, "What services need to be in place to adequately address the child's needs?" These needs focus primarily on academic achievement benchmarks, but also can include social, emotional, and behavior challenges.

This highly regulated system in the US may at first seem to restrict the integration of therapeutic approaches to assessment. We do not agree. We maintain that the values of TA and the use of selected TA-C methods can be infused with the procedures required in school-based assessments for Special Education. We further believe this integration can greatly enhance the process, outcome, and subsequent impact of psychological assessments in the schools.

From our professional experiences providing TA-C workshops, consulting with assessors in schools, and practicing in schools, we are aware that school psychologists (and diagnosticians in some states) are curious and interested in using aspects of TA-C in their work. At the most basic, we encourage them to embrace Finn's (2007) description of "therapeutic assessment" as an attitude of respect for the relationship with the client, where the goal is more than gathering information to inform understanding and intervention with the child. The goal is to create an assessment experience that is positive and results in positive changes for the child and family.

This goal has universal value and fits the intent of assessment in the schools, which is to positively impact the student, teachers, and parents to support the student's educational performance. Further, the core values of TA, if embraced, have the potential to further influence the tone and process of assessments in the school. These include: a) actively collaborating with students, teachers and parents; b) respecting students, teachers and parents and their diversity; c) having humility about our expertise and the power of our assessment tools; d) having compassion for students, teachers, and parents and their situations and treating each with sympathy and kindness; e) being open and curious about ourselves in relation to students, teachers, and parents and how that might impact the assessment; and f) being open and curious about how each student has developed as a unique individual.

We see many benefits from embracing the values of TA in school assessments: 1) enhanced relationships between the assessor and all other parties involved, including teachers and parents; 2) a greater likelihood that the student will have a positive experience of the assessment; 3) an opportunity for parents, in particular, to experience a favorable view of the Special Education Program, and, if it has been bumpy earlier, to initiate a repair; 4) an enhanced likelihood that the student will come to understand themself better, as will their teachers and parents; and 5) the opportunity for school psychologists to have a richer, more rewarding experience that promotes morale and a sense of having their work viewed as effective and appreciated.

Almost two decades ago, Deborah Tharinger introduced our ideas about TA-C and Special Education assessments in a chapter entitled: *The Development and Model of Therapeutic Assessment with Children: Application to School-based Assessment* (Tharinger et al, 2010). In the chapter Tharinger and her co-authors described the comprehensive model of TA-C, made recommendations for what was most applicable for school psychologists to include from TA-C to enhance their Special Education assessments, and provided four case studies where graduate students implemented methods and techniques of TA-C into school assessments to good result. Here is a list of the authors' main recommendations: 1) embrace a collaborative stance toward assessment; 2) construct Assessment Questions with the child, parent, and teachers; 3) use process testing techniques, such as Extended Inquires; 4) actively collaborate with the child, parents, and teachers throughout the assessment; 5) consider multiple theoretical perspectives during case conceptualization; 6) carefully plan and deliver feedback to parents and teachers, including organizing findings by Assessment Questions and Levels of Information; and 7) develop a fable or use another creative method to provide feedback to the child.

Case Example

We now present a first-person account of an assessment by the first author of this book, Deborah Tharinger, that was featured recently in the *TA Connection*, the newsletter of the Therapeutic Assessment Institute (Tharinger, 2019). At the time, Deborah was working as a school-based school psychologist.

Robert, a 7-year-old second grader (his name and various details have been altered to protect his identity) was referred for a comprehensive evaluation for Special Education consideration due to: 1) academic underachievement and 2) his tendency to "shut down" when reading and doing writing assignments that he perceived as too difficult, both at school and at home. Several teachers at the school thought Robert's challenges were exacerbated by his academic failure in 1st grade, followed by a short-lived (6 week) retention in 1st grade during the current school year.

I was told that Robert was extremely distressed during the time of his retention. His behavior declined significantly, going from "shut downs" to "melt-downs." He was subsequently placed, at his mother's insistence, in 2nd grade, and his extremely distressed behavior stopped (although his challenges with independently producing schoolwork and shutting down when frustrated continued). I hypothesized that the retention experience had a very negative and possibly traumatic impact on Robert and his sense of himself as a learner, member of his class, and member of his community. I also had to take into account that this trauma and conflict with the school might impact our ability to build a relationship, to complete a valid assessment, and for me to establish trust with his mother. I felt that a therapeutic assessment approach would go a long way toward repairing the empathic failure Robert (and his mother) had experienced at the beginning of the school year.

I worked collaboratively with the teacher, mother.and Robert. I supported Robert through a shutdown in the first session with me, involved his mother in supporting our work, and checked in with his teacher often about the nature of his shutdowns in the classroom over the course of the assessment.

I worked to show respect and attunement to cultural beliefs (in the family and the school). In Robert's culture, feelings are private, often even within the family. I felt strongly that his withholding of challenging feelings was getting in his way both at home and at school. He was revealing some of these feeling to me. I supported his expression and with his explicit permission shared his feelings with his mother and teacher during the assessment.

I addressed previous hurts and school-related traumas by showing empathy and compassion for Robert's experiences. For example, when we first met, I assured Robert that he would be staying in his second-grade class. I let him know that I was interested in how we could support him in second grade. I also acknowledged that not starting the year in second grade had been very hard and sad for him, and he agreed; I felt this interchange strengthened our relationship.

I worked with Robert, his mom, and his teacher to construct Assessment Questions. *School's Question*: Would Robert meet criteria for a disability that could be shown to be adversely impacting his educational performance? *Teacher's Questions*: Why did Robert have such severe and variable melt-downs when he was retained? Why does he still look so sad sometimes? *Mother's Question*: Why does Robert get mad and shut down when she tries to help with his homework? *Robert's Question* (provided late in the assessment): Why didn't my mother know how upset I was about the changes at home?

I used process assessment methods (Extended Inquiry methods) following standardized administration of tests with Robert. For example, Robert endorsed two items on the BASC-3 that I further explored: "in trouble at school" (when inquired, he responded "for shutting down") and "sad at home" where he elaborated, when questioned, "that something was not working right at home." Robert did not expand further but suggested I ask his mother about what was going on at home. Robert later told me that his parents broke up last year and that he was sad.

I looked closely at agreement and lack of agreement across the multiple informers and used the marked inconsistency to highlight how well Robert hid his feelings. My aim was to enhance empathy and compassion for Robert by revealing his feelings. For example, on the Conners 3-Student Self-Report Anxiety Screener (Conners, 2008), Robert indicated that very often he was nervous or jumpy or worried; had trouble controlling his worries; and often was irritable. In contrast, both his mother and teacher indicated very little concern in this area. On the Revised Children's Manifest Anxiety Scale (RCMAS); Reynolds and Richmond (1985) (which only has a student version), Robert endorsed the following items (all are on the Physiological Anxiety Sub-Scale): "Often I feel sick to my stomach;" "I have too many headaches;" "I get mad easily;" "It is hard for me to get to sleep at night;" "I am tired a lot;" "My hands feel sweaty;" "I have bad dreams;" and "It is hard for me to keep my mind on my schoolwork."

It was apparent when I spoke with Robert's teacher and mother about my findings that they were both unaware of the level of anxiety he was experiencing. A similar experience occurred on the Conners' Depression Screener. On that measure Robert endorsed that very often he felt worthless, sad, gloomy, irritable and low on energy. In contrast, his mother endorsed no items on this screener and his teacher endorsed two items, indicating some awareness of Robert's subjective experience. These findings are similar to the results on the Children's Depression Inventory (CDI-2; Kovacs 2011), where Robert rated himself at the clinically significant level (T = 71), his teacher rated him at the At-Risk level (T = 67), and his mother rated him in the average range (T = 52). When I shared these combined findings about anxiety and depressive symptoms with Robert's teacher, she was taken aback. She immediately expressed compassion and empathy for Robert. I subsequently noticed significant changes in her actions toward Robert in the classroom, all positive and supportive.

I had multiple sessions and contacts with Robert and his teacher over the course of the assessment. This allowed for Robert to get comfortable with me and for us to form a trusting relationship. It also allowed for the teacher and me to strengthen our relationship and collaborate in implementing interventions in the classroom, including a behavior plan. Unfortunately, it turned out to be difficult to meet with Robert's mom as often as I would have liked, as she had a new baby to care for and significant other family responsibilities.

I considered multiple frameworks in devising a case conceptualization. I focused on Robert's emotional functioning and strategies he had developed to protect himself from embarrassment and shame. I hypothesized that the combination of his learning disabilities that were not understood or addressed in kindergarten and first grade, the break-up of his parents that was not adequately explained or addressed in his family, the trauma of being retained in first grade, and the cultural tendency to not express feelings combined to grow his anxiety and depression and strengthen his protective strategy of shutting down.

I provided feedback to the mother and teacher along the way, so they were informed before the formal meetings. At the Eligibility and Placement meeting and the Individual Educational Plan meeting, through the comprehensive assessments provided by multiple professionals (he was also assessed by the Diagnostician and the Speech and Language Pathologist), it was agreed that Robert met eligibility for Special Education services with a primary disability of Specific Learning Disability. It was recommended that he receive services from the pull-out resource teacher to assist him with his academics. It was also evident from my work with him that he was struggling emotionally and had developed a strategy that was not conducive to his learning (i.e., shutting down). Thus, it was decided that he would benefit from individual pull-out counseling services, as well as direct services in his classroom from me. I also provided ongoing teacher consultation to support her newly found empathy for Robert.

I wrote and presented Robert with an illustrated fable about a puppy that was sad and worried about things at home and his struggles at school. With help from a wise dog, his mother and teacher came to understand the puppy better because they didn't know he was so worried and sad. The puppy learned that sharing his feelings with others helped him reduce his frustration and shut downs and he felt more understood and much happier. (You can access the complete fable, with illustrations, in *The TA Connection*, Tharinger, 2019).

I also conducted a brief follow-up to gather information on how Robert was doing four months later, at the end of the school year. Robert's teacher reported that he participated more in class, no longer had "shut downs", persisted on classroom tasks, and had made significant academic gains. I also readministered self-report measures that I had used during the assessment. Robert showed a significant decrease in levels of anxiety and depression that went from the clinically significant range to the average range.

So, what was the impact of using TA-C values and methods in Robert's case? Without them, Robert likely would have stayed shut down and not revealed his concerns about the retention and his parents' separation. And without the strong alliance developed between Robert and myself, it is also likely that he would not have endorsed the symptoms of anxiety and depression on the various self-report measures. I felt strongly that Robert would not have been understood through a traditional assessment and subsequently would not have received the social-emotional interventions he needed, both at school and at home. Grounding my work in the values and methods of TA-C seemed to pay off well for Robert, his teacher, and his mother and I felt very satisfied.

Final Thoughts

In this chapter, we have illustrated how TA-C can be adapted to different settings and to clients with different needs. Again, we emphasize that modifying TA-C to make its procedures more useful and acceptable is a basic feature of the model. Furthermore, recent research on Therapeutic Assessment with adults suggests that the most important and therapeutic aspects of TA are its core values and attitudes (Durosini & Aschieri, 2021), and we suspect this is also true of TA with children and families.

References

Bellak L., & Bellak, S. S. (1976). *The Children's Apperception Test (CAT)*. Larchmont, NY: C.P.S.

Blader, J. C. (2004). Symptom, family, and service predictors of children's psychiatric rehospitalization within one year of discharge. *Journal of the Academy of Child and Adolescent Psychiatry, 23*, 440–451.

Buck, J. N. (1948). The H-T-P technique: A qualitative and quantitative scoring manual. *Journal of Clinical Psychology, 4*, 317–396.

Burns R. C., & Kaufman S. H. (1972). *Actions, styles, and symbols in Kinetic Family Drawings (KFD)*. New York: Brunner/ Mazel.

Conners, C. K. (2008). *Conners Third Edition (Conners 3)*. Toronto: Multi-Health Systems.

Crisi, A., & Palm, J. (2020). *Guidelines for remote administration of the WDCT according to the CWS*. Rome, Italy: Italian Institute of Wartegg.

Durosini, I., & Aschieri, F. (2021). Therapeutic Assessment efficacy: A meta-analysis. *Psychological Assessment.* 10.1037/pas0001038

Finn, S. E. (2007). *In our clients' shoes: Theory and techniques of Therapeutic Assessment*. Mahwah, NJ: Lawrence Erlbaum Associates.

Finn, S. E. (2011). Therapeutic Assessment "on the front lines": Comment on articles from WestCoast Children's Clinic. *Journal of Personality Assessment, 93*(1), 23–25.

Finn, S. E., & Chudzik, L. (2013). L'Evaluation Thérapeutique pour enfant: théorie, procédures et illustration. [Therapeutic Assessment with children: Theory, techniques, and case example.] *Neuropsychiatrie de l'Enfance et de l'Adolescence, 61*, 166–175.

Fischer, C. T. (1978). Dilemmas in standardized testing. In J. S. Mearig (Ed.), *Working for children: Ethical issues beyond professional guidelines* (pp. 115–134). San Francisco, CA: Jossey-Bass.

Inter Organizational Practice Committee (2020). *Tele-neuropsychology during the COVID-19 pandemic*. Downloaded from www.iopc.online on June 1, 2020.

Guerrero, B., Lipkind, J., & Rosenberg, A. (2011). Why did she put nail polish in my drink? Applying the Therapeutic Assessment model with an African American foster child in a community mental health setting. *Journal of Personality Assessment*, *93*, 7–15.

Hansson, A., Hansson, L., Danielsson, I., & Domellöf, E. (2016). Short- and long-term effects of child neuropsychological assessment with a collaborative and therapeutic approach: A preliminary study. *Applied Neuropsychology: Child*, *5*(2), 97–106.

Haydel, M. E., Mercer, B. L., & Rosenblatt, E. (2011). Training assessors in Therapeutic Assessment. *Journal of Personality Assessment*, *93*, 16–22.

Kamphuis, J. H., & Finn, S. E. (2019). Therapeutic Assessment in personality disorders: Toward the restoration of epistemic trust. *Journal of Personality Assessment*, *101*(6), 662–674.

Kovacs M. (2011). *Children's Depression Inventory 2 (CDI 2)*. North Tonawanda, New York: Multi-Health Systems.

Lipkind, J., & Mercer, B. (2019). Integrating Therapeutic Assessment and community mental health. *The TA Connection*, *7*(2), 11–16.

McArthur, D., & Roberts, G. (1982). *Roberts Apperception Test for Children-- Manual*. Los Angeles: Western Psychological Services.

Mercer, B. L. (2011). Psychological assessment of children in a community mental health clinic. *Journal of Personality Assessment*, *93*, 1–6.

Mercer, B. L., Fong, T., & Rosenblatt, E. (Eds.) (2016). *Assessing children in the urban community*. New York, NY: Routledge.

Mercer, B. L. (2017). Making unbearable feedback bearable: You can't "half-ass" attachment. *The TA Connection*, *5*(1), 14–18.

Mercer, B. L., Fong, T., & Rosenblatt, E. (Eds.) (2016). *Assessing children in the urban community*. New York, NY: Routledge.

Meyer, G. J., Finn, S. E., Eyde, L. D., Kay, G. G., Moreland, K. L., Dies, R. R., Eisman, E. J., Kubiszyn, T. W., & Reed, G. M. (2001). Psychological testing and psychological assessment: A review of evidence and issues. *American Psychologist*, *56*, 128–165.

Miller, J. D., Shah, T. D., Brooks-White, C., & David, R. (2019). Implementation of Therapeutic Assessment in a community mental health training site: Potential barriers, implications, and benefits for adolescents and their families. *The TA Connection*, *7*(2), 19–25.

Miller, L., Novotny, D., Cotas-Girard, A., & Gromoff, C. (2019). Therapeutic Assessment at Child Haven. *The TA Connection*, *7*(2), 4–10.

Murray, H. A. (1943). *Thematic Apperception Test Manual*. Cambridge, MA: Harvard University Press.

Pagano, C. J., Commins Blattner, M. C., & Kaplan-Levy, S. (2019). Therapeutic assessment with child inpatients. *Journal of Personality Assessment*, *101*(5), 556–566.

Purves, C. (2012). Collaborative Assessment of a child in foster care: New understanding of bad behavior. In S. E. Finn, C. T. Fischer, & L. Handler (Eds.), *Collaborative/Therapeutic Assessment: A casebook and guide* (pp. 291–310). New York: Wiley.

Purves, C. (2017). Collaborative Assessment with adolescents in juvenile hall and group homes. *The TA Connection*, *5*(2), 13–17.

Reynolds, C. R., & Richmond, B. O. (1985). *Revised Children's Manifest Anxiety Scale Manual*. Los Angeles: Western Psychological Services.

Reynolds, C. R., & Kamphaus, R. W. (2015). *Behavior Assessment System for Children* (3rd ed.). Bloomington, MN: Pearson.

Rorschach Performance Assessment System (April, 2020). Recommendations concerning remote administration of the Rorschach. Downloaded from www.r-pas.org on June 1, 2020.

Rosenberg, A., Almeida, A., & Macdonald, H. (2012). Crossing the cultural divide: Issues in translation, mistrust, and co-creation of meaning in cross-cultural Therapeutic Assessment. *Journal of Personality Assessment, 94*, 223–231.

Smith, D., Darling, A., & Frackowiak, M. (2019). Incorporating TA in a community mental health clinic. *The TA Connection, 7*(2), 26–29.

Smith, J. D., & Egan, K. N. (2015). Trainee and client experiences of Therapeutic Assessment in a required graduate course: A qualitative analysis. *Journal of Personality Assessment, 99*(2), 126–135.

Smith, J. D., Nicholas, C. R. N., Handler, L., & Nash, M. R. (2011). Examining the clinical effectiveness of a family intervention session in Therapeutic Assessment: A single-case experiment. *Journal of Personality Assessment, 93*, 149–158.

Tharinger, D. J. (2019). Assessing children in public schools using Therapeutic Assessment values and methods. *The TA Connection, 7*(1), 11–16.

Tharinger, D. J., Krumholz, L. S., Austin, C. A., & Matson, M. (2011). The development and model of Therapeutic Assessment with children: Application to school-based assessment. In M. A. Bray & T. J. Kehle (Eds.), *Oxford Press handbook of school psychology* (pp. 224–259). Oxford University Press.

Tharinger, D. J., & Pilgrim, S. (2011). Child and parent experiences of neuropsychological assessment as a function of child feedback by individualized fable. *Child Neuropsychology, 18*, 228–241.

Wechsler, D. (2014). *Wechsler Intelligence Scale for Children* (5th ed.). Bloomington, MN: Pearson.

Wright, A. J., Mihura, J., Pade, H., & McCord, D. M. (2020). Guidance on psychological tele-assessment during the COVID-19 crisis. Downloaded from www.apaservices.org on June 1, 2020.

12 Learning and Practicing Therapeutic Assessment with Children

We hope that at this point you are impressed with the therapeutic potential of Therapeutic Assessment with Children (TA-C) and are interested in integrating it into your clinical activities. In this chapter we present logistics and guidance about how to learn and practice TA-C.

Becoming Competent in TA-C

Becoming Skilled with Tests

Since Therapeutic Assessment uses psychological tests as empathy magnifiers and opportunities for discussion with children and families, one central competency in practicing TA-C is to become highly skilled with a variety of psychological tests. TA-C can be done with any type of test, but you will want to learn tests that are relevant to the problems and strengths of children and caregivers who typically seek help in your setting. For example, if you work in a pediatric neurology clinic, probably you will need to learn a number of cognitive and neuropsychological tests. If you work in a school evaluating students for learning disabilities, you will need to be skilled with cognitive, achievement, and behavioral/emotional tests. If you work in a child guidance clinic or in private practice, you will want to learn many different tests—both cognitive and behavioral/emotional, although you may decide to refer to specialists (e.g., a child neuropsychologist) for certain parts of your assessments. We have found it interesting and useful to collaborate in TA-C with certain colleagues with assessment knowledge that we may not have.

In general, in TA-C we recommend that you become highly competent with multiple categories of tests. Table 12.1 lists these categories along with sample tests. (Please note, this list is not exhaustive.) Also, as discussed later, to become certified in TA-C by the Therapeutic Assessment Institute, you must be highly skilled with each of these categories of tests.

What is the best way to become expert with different psychological tests? Hopefully the basics of some of the tests listed in Table 12.1 were taught in your graduate school courses or internship. Often test publishers offer basic

DOI: 10.4324/9781003000174-12

Table 12.1 Types of Tests Typically Used in TA-C

Type of Test	Examples
Broad Self-report Scales for Children	Behavioral Assessment System for Children, 3rd edition (BASC-3) Child Self Report (Reynolds & Kamphaus, 2015)
	Personality Inventory for Youth (PIY; Lachar & Gruber, 1995)
	Millon Pre-Adolescent Clinical Inventory (M-PACI; Millon et al., 2009)
	Child-Behavior Checklist-2 Youth Self-Report (YSR; Achenbach & Rescorla, 2001)
Specific Self-report Scales for Children	Child Depression Inventory 2 (CDI 2; Kovacs, 2011)
	Revised Children's Manifest Anxiety Scale, 2nd ed. (RCMAS-2; Reynolds & Richmond, 2008)
Broadband Rating Scales for Parents and Teachers	Behavioral Assessment System for Children, 3rd edition (BASC-3) Parent and Teacher Reports (Reynolds & Kamphaus, 2015)
	Child-Behavior Checklist-2) Achenbach & Rescorla, 2001)
Specific Child Rating Scales for Parents and Teachers	Conners, 3rd edition (Conners 3; Conners, 2008)
Broad Cognitive Measures for Children	Wechsler Intelligence Scale for Children, 5th edition (WISC-5; Wechsler, 2014)
	Woodcock-Johnson IV Tests of Cognitive Abilities (WJ IV COG; Schrank et al., 2016)
Broad Achievement Measures for Children	Woodcock-Johnson IV Tests of Achievement (WJ IV ACH; Schrank et al., 2016)
	Kaufman Test of Educational Achievement, 3rd edition (KTEA-3; Kaufman et al, 2014)
Broad Standardized Performance-based Personality Tests	Crisi Wartegg System (Crisi, 2018)
	Rorschach Performance Assessment System (R-PAS; Meyer et al, 2011)
	Rorschach Comprehensive System (RCS; Exner, 2003)
	Roberts Apperception Test, 2nd edition (RAT-2; Roberts & Gruber, 2005)
Broad Self-report Inventories for Adults	(Minnesota Multiphasic Personality Inventory-2 (MMPI-2; Butcher et al, 1989)
	Minnesota Multiphasic Personality Inventory-3 (MMPI-3; Ben-Porath & Tellegen, 2020)
	Personality Assessment Inventory (PAI; Morey, 2007)

workshops or webinars to help you learn new tests or keep up with new research or new versions of tests. Apart from these opportunities, we strongly recommend that you seek consultation from colleagues who are expert with various tests, discussing the test results of clients you are seeing in your setting. If individual consultation is too costly, supervision groups led by experts are often more accessible, or you might seek or form a peer assessment consultation group (see Evans & Finn, 2017).

Learning to Work with Children and Families

It goes without saying that working with children and families requires different skills than working with individual adults. If you wish to practice TA-C you will want to have supervised experience in child play therapy and also in family therapy with children and parents. Again, such experiences may begin in your graduate training, continue in your psychology internship, and then go further in your post-doctoral training. We have found that clinicians who learned traditional models of child assessment often do not think systemically. We believe it is important to have enough training in family therapy to make the cognitive shift to thinking systemically, that is, coming to see children and parents as parts of a larger system where the individuals mutually influence and respond to each other. We believe it is also very important for people who practice TA-C to learn about attachment and child development, and if you have not studied these areas you may want to seek out courses at a local university, read extensively, or take courses online.

Becoming Skilled at TA-C

Once you have good skills in child assessment, child intervention, and family therapy, you can put these elements together to practice TA-C. (Of course, you can learn TA-C at the same time as you are learning these basic elements.) We hope that this book will help you understand the TA-C model and its individual components, and besides what we have offered here, there are now a number of case examples of TA-C published over the past 20 years in articles and chapters. Appendix E contains a list of published cases of TA-C and of collaborative child assessments. In addition to reading these on your own, consider forming a TA-C reading/study group with like-minded colleagues, so you can discuss the various case examples together and think about how they apply to your own clients and settings.

Besides reading, we suggest you attend workshops on TA-C sponsored by the Therapeutic Assessment Institute (TAI) and presented by TAI faculty and TAI members. These trainings are listed on the TA website: *www.therapeuticassessment.com*, and are also announced through the TA list serve that is available to TAI members. As a result of the recent pandemic, there are now more online trainings—both at an introductory level, where videos of TA-C sessions with real clients are shown—and also "live TA" workshops, where participants watch an actual TA-C with clients as it un-folds. As travel becomes more possible, the TAI plans to reintroduce its "TA Immersion Course," where participants come together for five days of lectures, videos, and role plays of TA-C with "actor clients." Many participants have told us that the Immersion Course is life changing.

In our experience, to become highly skilled in TA-C you will also want to receive close supervision from someone who is expert in the model and who has been trained to do supervision. At first, you may find it useful to simply talk about your clients with the supervisor, discuss test results, construct a case conceptualization, get help planning Family Intervention Sessions and Summary/Discussion Sessions, and review Therapeutic Psychological Reports, Parent Letters, and fables. As soon as you are able, we encourage you to videotape your TA-C sessions and show them to your supervisor. Although sharing videos is anxiety provoking for most of us, there simply is no better way to truly become expert in TA-C. Also, TAI Faculty are trained to handle the anxiety and shame that can arise when clinicians show videos to a supervisor, and Faculty apply the same core values and collaborative approach to supervision that they use with TA in general. Finn (2019) and Handler (2008) have written about the process of supervision in Therapeutic Assessment.

You may wonder, how does one approach clients about videotaping TA-C sessions and allowing you to show the videos to a supervisor? We have been struck by how many clients are willing to give permission when assessors explain that they are involved in advanced clinical training and would like to show videos of their work with clients to increase its effectiveness. It can also help to explain that you routinely videotape sessions with the possibility of reviewing them together with clients at some point in the TA-C. In Appendix F, we give a sample videotape permission form that you may modify for your own use. Last, even if you don't show videos of your sessions to a supervisor, it can be very helpful to review them yourselves. We strongly believe that "the proof of the effect of an intervention is in how the client reacts." So, when watching your videos, look closely to see if clients seem more relaxed and open after you speak, or more tense and closed. Pay special attention when clients look down and become silent after you speak, as this can be a sign that what you said elicited shame. When Stephen Finn was developing Therapeutic Assessment, he spent hours reviewing videos of his sessions with clients and gradually honed many of the procedures we use today.

Formal Certification in TA-C

The Therapeutic Assessment Institute (of which all four authors are founding members) offers a certification process in TA-C for licensed clinicians who want formal recognition of their competence in TA-C. To quote from the TAI website, certification in TA was developed to: "1) provide a "marker" for practitioners who wish to know that they are practicing TA with fidelity and competence, 2) insure that research on TA is done using practitioners who are well trained in the model, 3) provide a structure for advanced training in TA, 4) provide direction for clients who wish to work with assessors trained in TA, and 5) build a community of assessors who have common language and training, who can promote the development of TA in years to come" (TAI, 2021).

You will find details about the TA-C certification process on the TA website, *www.therapeuticassessment.com*. In short, full certification involves working with a TA Faculty Member who watches your videotaped TA-C sessions, gives you feedback, and helps prepare you for certification. There is an online multiple-choice exam you must take about the theory, research, and practices of TA. Passing this gives you "Level 1 Certification" in TA, attesting to your basic knowledge of TA. Next, one or more certification "judges" reviews your client videos and case materials on one or more TA-C cases. The judge(s) assess how competent you are with various psychological tests and rate your sessions according to a number of specific certification criteria. (The most up-to-date criteria are listed on the TA website under the "Training" tab.) You rate yourself on the same criteria. Then you and the judges discuss their and your ratings of the TA-C sessions, and if you "pass," they recommend to the TAI Board that you be granted certification. Typically, if the ratings on one of the steps are not high enough, you may redo that step with another client and submit a video to the same judge(s). Once you are fully certified, your name is added to the list of fully certified clinicians on the TA website, which facilitates clients finding you. Because TA is a rapidly evolving field, certificates are granted for 5 years, after which to maintain your certification, you must demonstrate that you have continued to develop your skills in TA-C.

We recognize that many practitioners will not choose to become formally certified in TA-C, and we want to state clearly that you DO NOT need to be certified to effectively practice TA-C. In fact, we hope this book will help many clinicians understand and use TA-C in a variety of settings, and we encourage you to take away whatever is useful to you and your clients and to know that you have our blessing. That being said, many colleagues have told us that going through the certification process in TA not only improved their work and increased their confidence, but that it helped them grow personally. For those of you interested in engaging in this growth process, we hope this book will help you do so, and you can get more training if you wish.

Marketing

Once you become competent in TA-C, a next step to successfully practicing it is to develop a client base. Here we share some thoughts about marketing TA-C.

Good Work Is the Best Advertisement

In private-practice, and even in institutional settings, we have found that the best source of referrals is satisfied clients and satisfied referring professionals. We state this because we hope it is comforting to know that "if you build it"—*and do excellent work*—"they will come." This maxim fits not only our own experience, but the experience of many colleagues around the world who have begun to practice TA-C. Initially, they worried about finding an adequate number of clients, but after six months they had to start a waiting list. Truly, once clients and referring professionals start experiencing TA-C, it seems they often can't wait to tell others.

Differentiate TA-C From Traditional Child Assessment

A general tip (touched upon in Chapter 3), whether you are marketing to potential clients or referring professionals, is make sure you explain to stakeholders how TA is different from traditional psychological assessment. Unfortunately, we have found that many potential referring professionals (e.g., psychiatrists, pediatricians, social workers, psychotherapists) have negative associations to psychological assessment, typically from having referred clients for assessment and discovering that the results and report were not all that useful. Sadly, the same is often true of parents who have previous experiences with psychological assessments of their children. It is not uncommon for them to be reluctant to invest in another assessment that may yield another incomprehensible psychological report that doesn't help them or their child.

Thus, in promoting your work, we suggest you emphasize how TA-C is both an assessment and a therapeutic intervention, how caregivers are involved throughout the process, and how TA-C strives to help people with the problems they struggle with in daily life. The caregiver Information Sheet we discussed in Chapter 3 emphasizes these factors for parents, and you may find it helpful to develop a similar information sheet for referring professionals who inquire about your services. (Finn & Martin, 1997, presented a sample information sheet for professionals regarding adult TA that you may easily adapt to TA-C.) Of course, you may also put all this information on your website. If you are willing, another good marketing tool is to offer a free TA-C for the client of a well-connected referring professional—perhaps one of those professionals who is skeptical or completely uninformed about TA-C. Once that clinician sees TA-C close up, including its positive effects on a client, you are likely to get more referrals from that person and their colleagues.

Give Talks and Presentations

Although Therapeutic Assessment is becoming more widely known, it is still a best-kept secret in many areas of the world, and therefore, especially when entering a new community, it can be helpful if you give short talks and presentations about TA-C. These talks can be to professionals, for example at a local psychological association lunch, or to a group practice of psychiatrists, or, you may even present a paper at a local or state professional conference. We have found that speaking to groups of Masters-level counselors and psychotherapists is especially helpful in building a referral base, as many of them are looking for ways to get support in treating difficult clients. TA-C not only helps families, but can also provide guidance and support to those professionals responsible for helping them. Apart from speaking to professionals, it is also ethical for you to directly inform potential clients about your work, for example by giving a talk at a church, PTA meeting, or even a Rotary or Lions Club meeting. Whether speaking to professionals or to the public, remember that you may focus directly on TA-C, or you could speak about related topics such as child depression, or ADD, or Autism Spectrum Disorder and demonstrate in your presentation how TA-C can be useful with these specific issues. Some years back, Stephen Finn gave a public lecture entitled, "How to Raise Responsible Children without Toxic Shame." In it he spoke briefly about TA-C, and immediately after, he had a number of inquiries from parents interested in getting a TA-C for their child and themselves.

Educate Administrators and Other Professional Stakeholders

In practicing TA-C, you may be called upon from time to time to educate not only clients and referring professionals, but also the administrators or gate-keepers who oversee how services are provided in a workplace or who determine which services clients are allowed to use. For example, if you work in a clinic or hospital setting where you are allowed to practice TA-C, you may need to explain to your boss why your assessments (done with the TA-C model) take slightly more time than those done by your colleagues (who do all traditional assessments). Or you may need to advocate for time to do Summary/Discussion Sessions or to write fables for children. Alternatively, you may need to talk to the gatekeeper of your client's insurance provider to explain why you need more hours pre-approved for your ADD assessments than are usually granted. (Below we say more about working with insurance companies.) Again, we have found that the key in such interactions is to: 1) be empathic to the questions or outright resistance that responsible administrators have about the value of psychological assessment. They probably are only familiar with traditional assessment, and have never heard of TA-C. 2) Patiently and carefully explain the differences between TA-C and traditional child assessment, using research, case studies, or your clinical experience to back up your claims. (There are many articles you can download about TA-C from the Therapeutic Assessment website, and the research on TA-C is reviewed in Chapter 2.) 3) Seek permission to "give it a try" by doing a demonstration TA-C that is closely followed, and collect outcome and satisfaction information from the clients (perhaps by giving the PEAS to parents—see Chapter 9). Evidence is continuing to accrue that even brief TAs can have lasting effects and can make subsequent treatments more effective (See Durosini & Aschieri, 2021; Kamphuis & Finn, 2019; Smith et al., 2014).

Billing for TA-C

Of course, to successfully practice TA-C, you need to get paid. You may find this section more or less relevant, depending on your work situation. If you are on salary at a community mental health center, clinic, or university counseling center, you may not be billing clients or insurance companies yourself. Still, some of our comments may be useful for the administrators or billing personnel in your institution. Also, if you are in private practice, there is a huge difference depending on whether you bill clients directly or must deal with insurance companies and managed care gatekeepers in order to be paid. But let us start with a general issue that touches upon all these settings.

Charging for Your Time

In our experience many clinicians have come to act as if psychological assessment is a second-rate professional activity that is worth less than psychotherapy or consultation. In short, they are willing to accept less money (per hour)—often MUCH less—for the time they spend doing psychological assessment than they are for doing psychotherapy. We understand that the underpinnings of this situation are complex, and rely in part on larger market factors, Medicare reimbursement rates, and psychology as a whole's complacence for many years about the need to show that psychological assessment has added value. (See Finn, 2007 and Evans & Finn, 2017 for more complete discussions of the undervaluing of psychological assessment.) In addition, however, we believe assessment psychologists in general have suffered from a kind of "inferiority complex" about their work, seeing assessment as less valuable, less prestigious, and more an activity for clinicians who are "better with numbers than with people." As you can tell from this book, we believe the opposite—that psychological assessment can make a unique, highly valuable contribution to understanding clients' situations, is best done by practitioners with expertise in both assessment and psychotherapy, and that when practiced according to a collaborative model, assessment can change lives.

Hence, in practicing TA-C we encourage you not to "undersell" yourself by routinely charging greatly lower rates for your time or by not billing for the hours you spend on an assessment report. We realize this approach may feel risky, and you must gauge your own level of risk-taking. But, we believe that if clinicians are not compensated at their therapy rate for the majority of the hours they do assessment, either: 1) they will eventually stop doing psychological assessment (and we have seen many instances of this), or 2) they will start taking shortcuts such as writing boiler-plate reports that are not very useful, spending little time on case conceptualization, or having graduate students or psychometricians do most of their testing.

Fortunately, there is more and more recognition that TA is different than traditional assessment, and that it involves both assessment and intervention. Therefore, if you are skilled at TA-C you may find it easier to bill more for your assessments, have more hours pre-approved by managed care gatekeepers, and have your bosses accept that you will complete somewhat fewer assessments in a year than colleagues practicing traditional assessment. Fortunately, there is also more flexibility billing for TA-C than for many assessments, as we will detail now.

How to Charge and Bill for TA-C

After years of discussing how to charge for TA-C with experts in billing, insurance, and ethics, it is now clear to us that in most settings it is permissible to bill TA-C exactly for what it is—a mixture of assessment and psychotherapy. (Of course, you should always check your billing practices with administrators and companies with whom you have service contracts.) In the United States, different clinical services are connected to official CPT "billing codes." Typically, the Initial Session with parents can be billed as a Diagnostic Evaluation (CPT 90791), assessment sessions with the child can be billed as a combination of Test Administration (CPT 96136 and 96137) and Psychological Evaluation (CPT 96130 and 96131), later parent sessions—including the Summary/Discussion Session--can be billed as Family Therapy without patient (CPT 90846), and Family Intervention and Fable Sessions can be billed as Conjoint Therapy (CPT 90847). Last, report- and letter-writing hours are billed as Psychological Evaluation (CPT 96130 and 96131). David (2013), Finn (2007), and Finn and Martin (1997) have all published sample bills for TA that are easily adapted to TA-C and to the most current CPT codes.

Also, David (2013) and Finn and Martin (1997) have written extensively about how to approach managed care gatekeepers for pre-authorization for Therapeutic Assessment sessions. In brief, they recommend getting authorization for an Initial Session, where Assessment Questions are formed with the client. Then, the clients' questions are used as the basis of a treatment plan that justifies the tests that will be used (i.e., explains their "medical necessity") and the purpose of other sessions such as Family Intervention and Fable Sessions. The treatment plan is submitted to the managed care gatekeeper along with information explaining Therapeutic Assessment and the research that backs it up. (If you have developed an information sheet for referring professionals, you can share that same one.) We have also found that telephone discussions with gatekeepers are very helpful if you can arrange them, in which, once again, a major goal is for you to explain how TA-C is different than traditional psychological assessment and how clients typically benefit. Over time, you may even develop an ongoing relationship with certain gatekeepers, and future discussions/negotiations may become much easier.

Getting Support While Practicing TA-C

A final recommendation for practicing TA-C is "Don't Work Alone!" TA-C is an intense process for both clients and assessors, and we believe strongly that you will need a community of like-minded colleagues for support in order to avoid burn-out while doing TA-C over time. As mentioned in Chapter 2, parents who seek TA-C are often those whom other providers have not been able to help. Typically, such families are in the throes of intense projections and psychological conflicts that have developed over generations and are not easy to interrupt and resolve. It is not at all uncommon for assessors to experience intense emotions as they work with such families, and to be pulled into being "rescuers" (e.g., taking parents' calls at all times of the night and day), "victims" (e.g., sitting silently as a father berates us that we are not helping his child), or "persecutors" (e.g., shaming parents about the way they have been treating their child). Finn (2014) has written about these types of enactments and how to avoid them, including the importance of having support and getting consultation. Last, TA seems to intensify the engagement and emotions assessors experience, because—as one colleague put it—we have "taken off the protection of our white coats." We four authors count ourselves lucky to have worked together at the Center for Therapeutic Assessment in Austin, where we have experienced the incredible value of support from our colleagues while doing TA-C. Each of us feels that this support has been essential to our practicing TA-C at a high level. We urge you to consider forming group practices, peer consultation groups, and/or to seek support from TA faculty even if you achieve certification in TA-C. One consequence of the core value of "humility" in TA is our belief that each of us should seek supervision/consultation for our work throughout our careers. In keeping with this belief, the TAI offers monthly supervision groups to help support the TA community, and we all are committed to developing other ways to sustain and encourage TA practitioners around the world. Please feel free to let us know how we can help.

References

Achenbach, T. M., & Rescorla, L. A. (2001). *Manual for the ASEBA School-Age Forms & Profiles*. Burlington, VT: University of Vermont.

Ben-Porath, Y. S., & Tellegen, A. (2020). *Minnesota Multiphasic Personality Inventory-3 (MMPI-3): Manual for administration, scoring, and interpretation.* University of Minnesota Press.

Butcher, J., Dahlstrom, W. G., Graham, J., Tellegen, A., & Kaemmer, B. (1989). *MMPI-2 manual.* Minneapolis: University of Minnesota Press.

Conners, K. (2008). *Conners 3 manual.* Bloomington, MN: Pearson.

Crisi, A. 2018. *The Crisi Wartegg System (CWS) manual.* New York: Routledge.

David, R. M. (2013). Billing health insurance for Therapeutic Assessments. *The TA Connection, 1*(2), 13–17.

Durosini, I., & Aschieri, F. (2021). Therapeutic Assessment efficacy: A meta-analysis. *Psychological Assessment.* 10.1037/pas0001038

Evans, F. B., & Finn, S. E. (2017). Training and consultation in psychological assessment with professional psychologists: Suggestions for enhancing the profession and individual practices. *Journal of Personality Assessment, 99*(2), 175–185.

Exner, J. E. (2003). *The Rorschach: A comprehensive system* (4th ed.). Hoboken, NJ: Wiley.

Finn, S. E. (2007). *In our clients' shoes: Theory and techniques of Therapeutic Assessment.* New York, NY: Routledge.

Finn, S. E. (2014, March). *Learning to navigate Karpman's triangle: The healing potential of assessing traumatized clients.* Paper presented at the annual meeting of the Society for Personality Assessment, Arlington, VA, as part of a symposium, "Countertransference and Trauma: Therapeutic Uses of Self in Collaborative/Therapeutic Assessment," Diane H. Engelman (Chair). Available from the author.

Finn, S. E. (2019). Supervision of Therapeutic Assessment. In A. J. Wright (Ed.), *Essentials of psychological assessment supervision* (pp. 221–242). Hoboken, NJ: Wiley.

Finn, S. E., & Martin, H. (1997). Therapeutic Assessment with the MMPI-2 in managed health care. In J. N. Butcher (Ed.), *Objective psychological assessment in managed health care: A practitioner's guide* (pp. 131–152). Oxford University Press.

Handler, L. (2008). Supervision in therapeutic and collaborative assessment. In A. Hess, K. Hess, & T. Hess (Eds.), *Psychotherapy supervision: Theory, research, and practice* (2nd ed., pp. 200–222). New York, NY: John Wiley & Sons.

Kamphuis, J. H., & Finn, S. E. (2019). Therapeutic Assessment in personality disorders: Toward the restoration of epistemic trust. *Journal of Personality Assessment, 101*(6), 662–674.

Kaufman, A. S., Kaufman, N. L., & Breaux, K. C. (2014). *Kaufman Test of Educational Achievement–Third Edition (KTEA-3) (Technical & interpretive manual).* Bloomington, MN: Pearson.

Kovacs, M. (2011). *The Children's Depression Inventory 2 (CDI-2).* Bloomington, MN: Pearson.

Lachar, D., & Gruber, C. P. (1995). *Personality Inventory for Youth (PIY) manual.* Los Angeles: Western Psychological Services.

Meyer, G. J., Viglione, D. J., Mihura, J. L., Erard, R. E. & Erdberg, P. (2011). *Rorschach Performance Assessment System: Administration, codisng, interpretation, and technical manual.* Toledo: Rorschach Performance Assessment System.

Millon, T., Tringone, R., Millon, C., & Grossman, S. (2009). *Millon Pre-adolescent Clinical Inventory: M-PACI.* Bloomington, MN: Pearson.

Morey, L. C. (2007), *The PAI professional manual.* Lutz, FL: Psychological Assessment Resources.

Reynolds, C. R., & Kamphaus, R. W. (2015). *Behavior Assessment System for Children* (3rd ed.). Bloomington, MN: Pearson.

Reynolds, C. R., & Richmond, B. O. (2008). *Revised Children's Manifest Anxiety Scale, 2nd edition (RCMAS-2)*. Torrence, CA: Western Psychological Services.

Roberts, G. E., & Gruber, C. (2005). *Roberts Apperception Test for Children: 2 (RAT-2)*. Los Angeles: Western Psychological Services.

Schrank, F., Mather, N., McGrew, K., Wendling, B., & Woodcock, R. W. (2016). *The Woodcock-Johnson IV*. Rolling Meadows, IL: Riverside Insights.

Smith, J. D., Eichler, W. C., Norman, K. R., & Smith, S. R. (2014). The effectiveness of Collaborative/Therapeutic Assessment for psychotherapy consultation: A pragmatic replicated single case study. *Journal of Personality Assessment, 97*(3), 261–270.

Therapeutic Assessment Institute. (2021). *Certification in Therapeutic Assessment*. Accessed from www.therapeuticassessment.com on July 20,2021.

Wechsler, D. (2014). *Wechsler Intelligence Scale for Children* (5th ed.). Bloomington, MN: Pearson.

Wechsler, D. (2020). *Wechsler Individual Achievement Tests* (4th ed.) Bloomington, MN: Pearson.

13 Closing Thoughts

As we promised in the preface, in the preceding pages, we have laid out and illustrated in detail a new paradigm of child psychological assessment that is collaborative, client-centered, systemic, and culturally sensitive, and which can accomplish all the purposes of traditional psychological assessment (diagnosis, treatment planning, placement, and treatment monitoring) while also serving as a brief therapeutic intervention for children and families. We understand that our model, Therapeutic Assessment with Children (TA-C), while expanding, is not yet widely accepted, and we hope that this book will help remedy that situation. Still, we have written and presented about TA-C enough to have noticed resistance to and/or disinterest in its core concepts and methods. Rather than bemoan this situation, we have become curious about the "restraining forces" (see Chapter 2 on Complexity Theory) influencing TA-C adoption. We share our thoughts here, as they may be useful to others who are attempting to implement TA-C.

Factors That Restrain TA-C Implementation

Overwhelm

People cannot learn new things when they are overwhelmed and stressed, and unfortunately many child assessors work in settings where the service demands are high and they have little time to write therapeutic fables or letters to parents or even to include parents as active collaborators during an assessment. If you find yourself in this situation, we sympathize and we encourage you not to pressure yourself to adopt practices illustrated in this book that will make your life harder. Perhaps brief TA-C would be feasible in your setting, or perhaps even that is too much, and you can simply gather Assessment Questions or write a therapeutic fable for the child. In addition, we firmly believe that simply bringing the underlying core values of TA-C to your assessments can be therapeutic. That is, by showing respect, compassion, and humility to clients during your assessments, you can help them immensely, even if you can't formally do TA-C.

DOI: 10.4324/9781003000174-13

Insecurity

When we teach TA-C to professionals or graduate students, a relatively frequent comment we hear is, "I don't know how to do what you are asking." Or, as one participant in the TA Immersion Course told us, "Learning TA-C is a whole doctoral program by itself!"

We understand completely that TA-C may seem daunting, and that assessors need skills in psychological testing (adult, child, self-report, performance-based, cognitive, and learning), psychotherapy with children, family therapy, case conceptualization, and in several styles of writing to practice TA-C at a high level. What a tall order! If you have this reaction, we want to reassure you that is ok (to use a TA-phrase) to take "half-steps", and that if you start with the tests you know and psychotherapy skills you have, while staying humble and open to clients' input, you will gradually learn and grow. One of the benefits of TA in general is that it helps assessors become more skilled with tests and with interacting with clients. (See Finn, 2005 for a discussion of this phenomenon.) Another thing that comforts us when we feel insecure is that because we collaborate with clients, we don't always have to be right—for example in discussing the potential implications of a test score. The client can always correct us if we are wrong, and certainly this has happened to each of us.

Lack of Support

We have also seen colleagues and graduate students become excited about TA-C, begin to implement it in their work, and then stop pursuing it. What seems to differentiate these clinicians from those who keep practicing TA-C is the amount of collegial and institutional support they have. As we wrote in Chapter 12, we believe TA-C is too difficult to practice without like-minded colleagues to talk with about our work. Because TA requires us to "get in clients' shoes" during an assessment, we find ourselves full of anger at times, incredibly sad at others, and heartbroken when we can't find a way to help our clients suffer less. All of these feelings are natural in a model where assessors are participant-observers rather than "objective cataloguers" of traits and diagnoses, and they are part of what makes TA-C successful. Still, we urge you again to form a peer support or study group, join a Therapeutic Assessment Institute (TAI) consultation group, or seek individual consultation with a TAI supervisor. It will pay off in the end for both you and your clients.

Restricted Ideas about "Science"

The previous restraining forces applied mainly to clinicians interested in practicing TA-C. There are other restraining forces that keep people from even seeing its potential value. Of these, the first is a view that psychological assessment must be "scientific" according to a logical positivistic or deterministic philosophy of science—where the task of the psychologist is to measure real "traits," "temperaments," and "inborn characteristics" of in-dividuals (e.g., intelligence, extraversion, and neuroticism) as "objectively" as possible, using assessment "instruments" that are "empirically validated" and "free from bias." This point of view, which is less dominant in modern psychology than in the past, still seems to underpin the training and practice of many assessment psychologists in the United States and other parts of the world. Within this framework, TA-C is too subjective, too "constructivist," and "not empirically-based" enough to be of value. In our minds, the key to addressing these objections is first, to not throw the baby out with the bathwater. In other words, we affirm the value of scientific research, stan-dardized tests, that traits and temperaments do exist, and that it is important to consider potential bias in interpreting test scores. But we also think that human beings are incredibly complex, influenced by context and culture as well as genetics, and that our views and our tests are inherently limited—even if they have value as starting points for discussions with clients and as ways to compare clients in similar contexts to others in hopes of understanding their dilemmas. In TA-C, we use standardized procedures, normative data, and our knowledge of personality, psychopathology, and behavior genetics to begin to answer clients' Assessment Questions. But we also believe that children's play, answers to Individualized Sentence Completions, or Fantasy Animal Drawings can be valuable tools in under-standing them. And we continue to be astounded by clients' capacity to rewrite their own narratives and defy predictions that might come from non-contextualized interpretations of their test scores.

Desire to Remain an "Expert"

When Constance Fischer first began to write about Collaborative Assessment based in what she termed "human science psychology," many of her original articles were rejected as "unscientific" and "speculative." One journal re-viewer went a step further, however, to say that if Fischer's assessment model gained footing, it would "destroy" the field of psychological assessment by "demystifying" it and undoing psychologists' role as "experts" (Fischer, 1985/ 1994). We see this argument as a sign of the insecurity we all feel operating in a profession where: (1) we feel responsibility for helping complex suffering people whom other professionals often have not been able to help, (2) the medical model is dominant and determines not only how we and are services are judged, but also how we are paid, and (3) we are asked to be "oracles," both by clients and by other professionals (see Schafer, 1954). In fact, the longer we practice TA-C, the less anxiety we feel about acknowledging our limitations and humanity and inviting clients to "figure things out with us," bringing their perspectives together with our knowledge of psychology, as-sessment, and human relations. And in fact, it almost always happens that clients look up to us and feel immensely grateful for our experience, while also feeling deeply respected.

The Challenge of Thinking Systemically

Another "catch" if you will that keeps some people from adopting TA-C is its emphasis on systemic thinking, contextual and culturally informed case conceptualization, and assessing children in the context of their families. In fact, several times when we have presented the family prototypes discussed throughout the book (Figure 2.2) at workshops, irate professionals have criticized us for "blaming parents" and not understanding that parental behavior is "largely determined by children's innate temperaments." In fact, we want to appreciate how difficult and unnerving it can be (especially in individualistic Western cultures) to start thinking intersubjectively and seeing the human world as one where we are all mutually influencing and responding to each other. Stolorow and Atwood (1992), developers of intersubjectivity theory, wrote about the "unbearable embeddedness of being," and of how thinking systemically can lead to a sense of vulnerability, feeling less in control, and being less sure of who you are. We acknowledge how difficult such feelings can be. However, we find that thinking systemically and intersubjectively helps us feel more connected to our clients and more effective as clinicians. We believe you will find that a systemic perspective and clinical approach will make you more successful in understanding and helping children and families.

Hierarchy and Privilege

In this era of increased awareness of social justice issues, it seems important to name one other block we have encountered to TA-C being more widely accepted. That is, the TA-C model challenges established cultural and professional institutions that are based on distinct definitions of who is "sick" and who is "well," who is an "expert professional" and who is a "patient," and who is responsible for the widespread suffering in our societies. Because we use tests as empathy magnifiers and work hard to get in clients' shoes, it is difficult to practice TA-C and emerge unscathed after listening deeply to clients traumatized by existing cultural structures of privilege and hierarchy that diminish so many people. TA-C teaches us, as elegantly expressed by Harry Stack Sullivan, that "everyone is much more simply human than otherwise" (1953, p. 32). As such it is revolutionary, and while this helps us understand the challenge of practicing TA-C, it also makes us more resolute to keep teaching, writing, and practicing it.

Ideas for Future Research

Having discussed restraining forces to TA-C, we close with our thoughts about an important potential driving force, future research about TA-C. We hope this section will be of help to graduate students and professionals who wish to join us in continuing to develop TA-C.

As already discussed in Chapter 2, we believe a combination of both qualitative and quantitative studies would be beneficial, with qualitative studies focused on reaching in-depth understandings of clients' experiences during and after a TA-C. One model might be the study by De Saeger et al. (2016), where adults clients who experienced a full TA were interviewed afterwards. This publication led both to further quantitative research on TA and also to advances in understanding why TA works (e.g., Kamphuis & Finn, 2019). Regarding quantitative studies, both group comparison studies and additional time-series analyses would be helpful. Those time-series studies of TA-C already completed have yielded interesting insights into the anatomy of client change. (See Chapter 2.) And quantitative studies that lend themselves to cost-benefit calculations would be extremely helpful (e.g., Does TA-C done before or as part of child inpatient treatment provide fiscal benefits to various stakeholders?).

There is also a need to research TA-C with children and families with specific problems in living, such as eating disorders, separation anxiety, ADHD, atypical gender identities, and so on. Published case studies of TA-C suggest that it can be helpful for these and other problems, but empirical research could help us both generalize and understand the mechanisms of change in TA in clients with these struggles.

To date, only two steps of TA-C have been examined in isolation to see how much they contribute to its efficacy: Family Intervention Sessions (Smith et al., 2011) and individualized Therapeutic Fables (Tharinger & Pilgrim, 2011). Other steps/methods that are ripe for research are (1) gathering Assessment Questions in an initial session, (2) asking parents to observe child testing sessions, (3) providing assessment feedback to parents using the Level 1, 2, 3 schema, and (4) Parent Letters and Therapeutic Psychological Reports. As in the Tharinger and Pilgrim study, it would be helpful for both child and parent outcome variables to be assessed.

Last, much more research is needed examining the acceptability and accessibility of TA-C with clients of diverse backgrounds. As described in Chapter 2, a series of papers and case studies from clinicians at WestCoast Children's Clinic in Oakland (e.g., Mercer et al., 2016) has illustrated how useful TA-C can be with disadvantaged clients and those from racial and ethnic minority groups. Still many questions remained unanswered, e.g., in what ways should TA-C be adapted for clients from diverse backgrounds, what aspects of TA-C are most appreciated or most difficult for underprivileged clients? We hope future researchers will take up some of these questions.

In closing, we look forward to collaborating with all of you readers in the future to further understand TA-C. We invite you to take any elements of this model that resonate and inspire you and bring them into your personal and professional life and continue to develop them further. Then let us know what you have learned, and please pass it on your clients, students, colleagues, and the children and parents in your life.

References

De Saeger, H., Bartak, A., Eder, E. E., & Kamphuis, J. H. (2016). Memorable experiences in Therapeutic Assessment: Inviting the patient's perspective following a pretreatment randomized controlled trial. *Journal of Personality Assessment, 98*(5), 472–479.

Finn, S. E. (2005). How psychological assessment taught me compassion and firmness. *Journal of Personality Assessment, 84,* 27–30.

Fischer, C. T. (1985/1994). *Individualizing psychological assessment.* Mawah, NJ: Routledge. Originally published by Brooks Cole.

Kamphuis, J. H., & Finn, S. E. (2019). Therapeutic Assessment in personality disorders: Toward the restoration of epistemic trust. *Journal of Personality Assessment, 101*(6), 662–674.

Mercer, B. L., Fong, T., & Rosenblatt, E. (Eds.) (2016). *Assessing children in the urban community.* New York, NY: Routledge.

Schafer, R. (1954). *Psychoanalytic interpretation in Rorschach testing: Theory and applications.* New York: Grune & Stratton.

Smith, J. D., Nicholas, C. R. N., Handler, L., & Nash, M. R. (2011). Examining the clinical effectiveness of a family intervention session in Therapeutic Assessment: A single-case experiment. *Journal of Personality Assessment, 93,* 149–158.

Stolorow, R. D. , & Atwood, G. E. (1992). *Contexts of being: The intersubjective foundations of psychological life.* Hillsdale, NJ: Analytic Press.

Tharinger, D. J., & Pilgrim, S. (2011). Child and parent experiences of neuropsychological assessment as a function of child feedback by individualized fable. *Child Neuropsychology, 18,* 228–241.

Appendix A
Published Case Examples of Family Intervention Sessions

Aschieri, Fantini, and Bertrando (2012).

> *FIS with an 8-year-old girl and her parents. Family puppet play was used to help the parents see how their daughter's separation anxiety was related to their marital conflict.*

Chudzik, Frackowiak, and Finn (2019).

> *FIS with a 10-year-old boy and his parents. Consensus storytelling and parent coaching was used to help the parents understand how their relentless positivity and desire to fix their son's sadness was related to his depression.*

Fantini, Aschieri, and Bertrando (2013).

> *FIS with a 4-year-old girl and her parents. Projective drawings were used to help the parents learn to mirror their daughter's emotions and to see that they had difficulties tolerating their own emotions.*

Finn and Chudzik (2013).

> *FIS with a 7-year-old boy who became enuretic after his close uncle died from AIDS. The family failed to acknowledge the death due to their shame. In the session—designed by the boy as a memorial for the extended family—the family grieved the uncle's death. The boy's symptoms disappeared almost immediately.*

Guerrero, Lipkind, and Rosenberg (2011).

> *FIS with an 11-year-old girl with acting-out behaviors, her aunt, and her mother with mild intellectual disability. The family collaborated in telling stories to cards from the TAT and RAT. The highly frustrated aunt began to understand that her niece's problematic behaviors were partly due to her frustrations at school and anger over having been neglected by her mother.*

Hamilton, Fowler, Hersh, Hall, Finn, Tharinger, Parton, Stahl, and Arora (2009).

> *FIS with an 8-year-old girl and her parents in which the parents were coached in child-centered play. The parents discovered that their daughter's problem behaviors decreased when they gave her attuned, positive attention.*

Haydel, Mercer, and Rosenblatt (2011).

> *FIS with a mother and her 6-year-old son, who was refusing to do school work. Semi-structured play and parent coaching were used to help the mother discover that through a combination of positive mirroring and firmness, she could help her son be more open to attempting and completing his school work.*

Pagano, Blattner, and Kaplan-Levy (2019).

> *1st Case. FIS with a 12-year-old girl on an inpatient unit and her mother using a family sculpture exercise to inform the Assessment Question "How can I improve my relationship with my mother." The exercise brought emotions, thoughts, and dynamics into vivid relief, allowing the assessors to guide the mother and daughter toward a more functional style of communication.*

> *2nd Case. FIS with a 12-year-old boy in an inpatient unit and his mother and younger brother. The goal was to encourage positive interaction between the client and his younger brother while the client taught his brother to play Jenja. The experience was a success and demonstrated many of the client's positive qualities, allowing the mother to regain hope and compassion about her son and offset the dominance of the boy's negative and disturbing behaviors.*

> *3rd Case. FIS with a 13-year-old girl in an inpatient unit with depression and her grandmother. The goal was empathy development and relationship repair. The pair told stories to picture cards, which allowed the grandmother to validate the hurt and abandonment her granddaughter had felt when she provided care to a young relative who entered their household after the loss of his parents. The grandmother reached out and was received, beginning the reparative process between the two of them.*

Smith, Finn, Swain, and Handler (2011).

> *FIS with an 11-year-old boy and his parents using consensus story-telling and consensus family memories. The boy was referred because of episodes of confusion and disorientation that had no medically identified cause. The boy's parents come to realize that their son was unable to identify and express many basic emotions.*

Smith, Nicholas, Handler, and Nash (2011).

> *FIS with a 12-year-old boy and his father. The boy had grandiose and unrealistic ideas about his competence, which were supported by the father's inaccurate view of him. In the intervention session, the father came to see his son more realistically and then—through parent coaching—helped the boy see himself that way. This led the boy to improve his performance on the Bender Gestalt Test.*

Smith, Wolf, Handler, and Nash (2009).

> *FIS with a 9-year-old boy, his mother, and stepfather. Through a parent-child drawing task, the parents learned that the boy's aggression was tied to their impatience and to his feeling alone.*

Tharinger, Finn, Wilkinson, and Schaber (2007).

> *FIS with an 11-year-old girl and her custodial grandparents, who were very frustrated with her "disobedient" behavior. The three of them had an enjoyable interaction playing a board game in the session, which helped shift the grandparents' view and changed how they treated their granddaughter.*

Tharinger, Fisher, and Gerber (2012).

> *FIS with a 10-year-old boy, his mother and his stepfather. Through supported play, the family had positive interactions that began to repair their broken trust in each other.*

Tharinger, Matson, and Christopher (2011).

> *FIS using projective drawings with a 9-year-old boy and his mother concerning how they expressed anger. At the following session, the mother reported feeling more empowered in her role as parent.*

Wilkinson-Smith (2019).

> *FIS done by tele-health with a 10-year-old girl and her parents. The girl had been exhibiting possible psychotic symptoms related to painful affect states her parents could not listen to. Consensus storytelling and parent coaching were used to help the parents tolerate and support their daughter's painful emotions.*

Appendix B
Outline for Summary/Discussion Session with Henry's Parents

B. I Check-in

Nice to see you all. I just want to check in and see how things have gone for the past couple of weeks.

(Interested to see if they would spontaneously bring up the FIS.)

B. II Review Plan

Let me remind you of what we will be doing today. While I know you have a lot of information already about the test results, I want to synthesize it all and provide you with answers to your questions.

We are going to proceed just as we did with the assessment—collaboratively. Please feel free to let me know if you agree or disagree with what I'm saying. Of course, if you have questions let's discuss them as we go. This is the part where I share results but they can still be modified by more information from you. Dr. Jagger, this goes for you too, of course. Any questions? Comments?

B. III Appreciations

Before we get to your questions and the assessment results, I want to thank you for your openness and participation in the assessment. I know how vulnerable parents can feel and you were both brave and trusting to take the MMPI. I think this speaks to how much you love Henry and want to help him in any way you can. This has been a challenging assessment given how persistent Henry is in sharing his misery. I can only imagine how hard that has been for all of you. I also came to understand how difficult it can be to have empathy when it feels like Henry is punishing you.

Dr. Jagger, I certainly appreciate you referring Henry for the assessment. I know you've worked with Henry and the family for a long time and have helped them and him through many difficult times. It also takes a lot of trust to refer a client. So, thank you.

B. IV Review of Assessment Results

What I'd like to do now is to review the test results, briefly. I just want to make sure we begin by all being on the same page. I have shared these results with all of you already so this is just a reminder. Then, what I would like to do is go over the answers to your assessment questions. How does that sound?

(Very brief overview of test results given.)

1. Henry was bright but very anxious and insecure about his cognitive ability. He had three composite scores that were in the above-average range (VCI = 113, VSI = 119, and FRI = 112) and his other two scores were in the average range (WMI = 97, PSI = 98). Given his emotional state, I believed the WMI and PSI were a lower estimate of his intelligence because they are most affected by depression.
2. Henry was determined to share how sad and depressed he was, and this came out in all our interactions, his self-report on the BASC, and sentence completions, as well as both projective tests.
3. Both teachers and parents saw him as depressed and anxious as reported on the BASCs.

Let's review your questions.

1. What are Henry's intellectual strengths and weaknesses? Is there a disharmony among them? What kind of learning environment is best for him?
2. Is he clinically depressed or is it situational?
3. Has he experienced an unknown trauma that has adversely affected his self-image and how he engages with the world?
4. Why does Henry make provocative statements to us?
5. How do we prevent him from becoming further anxious and depressed?
6. How can we help Henry feel confidence and loved?

Answers to the Assessment Questions

Let's begin with what I think is the most straight-forward question.

1. **What are Henry's intellectual strengths and weaknesses? Is there a disharmony among them? What kind of learning environment is best for him?**

I know we have reviewed this, but I want to make sure I've been clear and wonder if you might have any questions about it. As previously stated, Henry is operating in the average to above average range of intellectual functioning. The test we did (WISC-V) looks at five different areas of cognitive functioning. The areas in the above average range were: VCI = 113, VSI = 119 and FRI = 112; the other two scores were in the average range --WMI = 97,

PSI = 98. Again, I think the testing results are probably an underestimate of his ability, given his depression. He was engaged in the test and tried hard, but once things got more and more difficult, he seemed to deflate and give up. In general, when any of us are feeling down, blue or depressed we do not usually test as well. I imagine if his depression decreased his scores would increase, especially in the two areas that can be affected by depression—his scores on the WMI and PSI.

I believe his general overall ability can serve him well. However, part of doing well in school is being able to persevere even when the material is difficult. This is an area of weakness for Henry. His negative view of his abilities limits what he is intellectually capable of.

I think he would benefit from being in a low-pressure, but stimulating, learning environment. One that is challenging but supportive, with teachers that can be authentically positive and encouraging.

2. Is he clinically depressed or is it situational?

I think when you asked this question you were wondering if Henry's reporting of his sadness was happening more because of pressure at school, his difficulty doing homework, and the upcoming transition to Middle School. Perhaps your thoughts had been that once summertime comes and the decision is made about which middle school to attend, he will no longer be depressed. I don't think school stressors are enough to explain his current difficulties, nor that things will get better if those stressors go away. Henry is clinically depressed, although this might be magnified because of the difficulties of his present situation. Aside from how he presents himself, as you might remember, all measures—ones done by both of you, the teachers and Henry indicate that he is very depressed (show BASCs and Rorschach visuals that pertain to depression, share some of the clinical information—sentence completions, the dot).

3. Why does Henry make provocative statements to us?

I want to start by saying that when you brought up this question, when we first met, I was curious about it. I have certainly watched kids provoke their parents into behaving in ways that were less than positive. I wasn't exactly sure if and how this might manifest in the testing sessions. But after our first session with Henry I knew I would get to see it more and more. Do you remember that first session we had all together? I couldn't engage him in a positive response to anything I said. I wondered how that felt for you both. I think, in some ways it was a relief that he was showing me how negative he could be. But I also think it must have been upsetting to see him interact with a stranger like that.

Then during the testing I saw how perceptive and really good he is at provoking another person. Do you remember, when he was completing the BASC he responded negatively to everything except a few items. And then he asked if I thought he did it acurately. He said he didn't and then he went on to change each of the items he did in a positive or neutral direction to a negative one. That was brilliant!

After awhile his relentless negativity felt punishing. I thought about my feelings for a long while one day after our session. Several things came up:

1. Perhaps, underneath his negativity was a lot of anger. It made me think about how anger was processed in the family. Was it OK to be angry? Did anger come out of nowhere? Did people contain anger until they couldn't any longer and it exploded? How could Henry share that he was angry with his parents?
2. His ongoing negativity made me feel helpless. I found myself wanting to change his attitude, rather than trying to empathize with it. I thought about what you, his parents, might feel after hours of this unrelenting negativity. This really helped me to get in your shoes and feel what a struggle and worry this must be for you.
3. When Henry wasn't being provocative and was genuinely sad it was painful to really be there for him because I had to feel the depths of his pain. As a parent that would be really difficult.

So let's talk about his provoking behavior. I think he wanted me to get angry as a way of perhaps seeing and feeling how angry he really was. If we focus on him being angry, it's important to think about who or what is he angry at. An old psychodynamic theory was that depression might be understood as anger turned inward. I think he has had a lot of anger directed at himself and this kind of poking at other people is his safe way of expressing anger.

So what could he be so angry about? I'm not sure he has felt that you understood the depths of his sadness. It's difficult for a parent to be empathic to the sadness because it is so painful. And when it feels like no matter what you do or say, and the sadness doesn't decrease, then it is even more difficult. You have to feel your own feelings of heplessness. If you haven't provided him with an active response and mirroring, then this is a way for him to get your attention because any attention, even irritations, is better than none. He is dramatic because he wants and needs to get a reaction from you. This allows him to feel powerful and seen. He's dramatic because he doesn't feel like your responses are "big" or attuned enough. This makes sense when we think about your family of origin Barbara and how chaotic things were as well as how much you had to care for yourself. You know how stable you and David are in comparison and how much you focus on the kids, so at times it would be really difficult for you to get in Henry's shoes and recognize his longings to be taken care of when you know you do such a better job than your mom, Barbara. David, we've already talked about this in the past. While you are sensitive, you don't necessarily wear your heart on your sleeve. It's hard to know what you're thinking or feeling from your facial expression. As a result, Henry may not feel heard or seen by you as much as he needs. He'd prefer to see you angry about his being provocative rather than feel left alone with his feelings.

4. Has he experienced an unknown trauma that has adversely affected his self-image and how he engages with the world?

Well, this is an interesting question. Before our last session, I would have said that as far as I know, there was no big "T" trauma, but there were a lot of small "t" traumas that have contributed to Henry's current struggles. So, what does this mean? Sometimes we talk about trauma with a capital T. This usually indicates a specific occurrence that involves some sort of abuse or overwhelming, scary event. Neither you nor Henry identified any event that would qualify as trauma with a capital "T." But, if we look at our last session, as hard as it may be to believe or hear, the event that Henry described in which David dragged him to the bathroom can be considered a big "T" trauma for Henry. It remains in his mind as a very frightening event. I think our work in the last session is the beginning of healing from it, but there is more work to do.

There are also small "t" traumatic experiences that can influence a child's development. These are events that might have had a bigger impact on a child than a parent might be aware of. I think one such event occurred when you, Barbara, went back to work and David became the primary caregiver. The household organization and routine changed. Henry was used to your (Barbara's) warmth and expressive demeanor, and suddenly that was gone. He was left more with you David. As we talked about previously, you don't give a whole lot away through your facial expression and you can be difficult to read. While both of you agreed that this change was needed, Barbara, you had a lot of feelings about going back to work and starting a business. I'm wondering if some of the resentments you might have felt toward David affected the emotional tone in the family, which also might have affected Henry. I imagine this was a difficult time for Henry, and may have left him with emotional insecurities.

In addition, I wonder about the intergenerational transmission of trauma. Barbara, you described a lot of trauma in your family of origin. Your mother was mentally ill and suffered a lot at the hands of her first husband and children. Your father, although very dear to you, was an alcoholic and that takes a toll on children. Your sister suffered tremendously with depression, and you were her main support person. You are a sturdy survivor but lived under the cloak of trauma both with a capital "T" and lower case "t." There are times when this trauma gets transmitted through the generations, unbeknown to anyone.

5. How do we prevent him from becoming further anxious and depressed?

When thinking about how to support pre-adolescents who are anxious and depressed, I think about what internal and external support is needed. If we think about what's going on inside of Henry, what we've learned is that he longs for positive attention and attunement from you both. That means you have to be able to mirror his feelings and let him know that whatever he feels can be seen and tolerated by you. This places extra pressure on both of you to be exquisitely aware of feelings. So, the first step in this is understanding and being aware of your own feelings. Importantly, you must be able to claim your own feelings so that Henry can better understand his feelings. The challenge is for you to both become more comfortable with a wide range of feelings. As that happens you will be able to respond in a more helpful way to Henry and he will learn how to regulate his own emotions better. You will have to really become masters with validating his feelings, especially those that "push your buttons" and that you were not allowed to express when you were growing up. You will need to model sharing your own feelings appropriately, especially anger. It will also be important to set limits in a firm but non-reactive way.

6. How can we help Henry feel confidence and loved?

It is important to have a balance where he feels cherished and also contained. I remember you talking about how much you cherished your children, Barbara. I think you said it was like carrying them around on a linen cloth. I got the image of the children being so carefully, delicately revered. So, I know you do cherish Henry. Be available when he needs you without impatience toward his needs. Validate his wide range of feelings, clearly show him when you enjoy him, help him realistically appraise his schoolwork, reward his persistence in trying rather than focusing on the product, and set appropriate limits. Limit setting is difficult. I think you did this with the sad talk time. When you, with the help of Dr. Jagger, decided that the sad talk could happen at night. For the health and well being of the enitre family, this limit needed to be set, accompanied with validating his sadness and letting him know there would be a time to really talk about it.

B. V Review of Suggestions

1. Continue indiviudal therapy
2. Begin family therapy.
3. Decrease pressure at school. Not a good idea to go to the more competitive school.
4. Provide a tutor for academic support to stay on top of assignments especially if he ends up going to the magnet school. This may have more to do with emotional rather than academic support. Therefore, a tutor who: a) is empathic but firm, b) can help with emotional self-regulation, and c) understands how to respond to negative self talk without being dismissive, would be most beneficial. In addition, it would be helpful if the person could coordinate with Henry's individual therapist.
5. Obtain a sensory integration evaluation by an occupational therapist to see if they can suggest ways to use the sensory system to decrease anxiety.
6. Consult with a psychiatrist to see if medication might be helpful.

B. VI Metaprocessing: Ask for Questions, Reactions, and Feedback

I know this is a lot to take in all at once but I'm wondering if you have any questions, reactions, and feedback?

B. VII Closing

Discuss writing the fable for Henry, the characters and words from our work together—the dot and void of nothingness. Share how I would like to present it to Henry alone first and then read it all together and why.

Share how they taught me about love and resilience. Reminded me of the Zelda Fitzgerald quote "Nobody has ever measured, even poets, how much the heart can hold."

Say good-bye (or delay this if you will see the parents again soon).

Appendix C
Sparky the Unicorn and the Magic Force
A Fable for Yan

A long time ago, in a Magical Land far, far away, there lived a young Unicorn named Sparky. She was a smart, sweet, and fun unicorn. Everyone in her family loved her and said she was a joy to spend time with.

Sparky lived in the Enchanted Cloud part of the Magical Land with her unicorn mom, Pearl, her unicorn dad, Kai, and her older unicorn sister, Fen. The Enchanted Cloud was the capital of the whole magical land and there were many different things to do and learn. Sparky's mom and dad knew that she was a very talented unicorn. All young unicorns had to learn how to channel a special Magic Force, which made their mane turn into the colors of the rainbow, but it took a lot of hard work and learning at the Enchanted Academy before such a magical event took place.

Sparky was one of the young unicorns at the Enchanted Academy, and although she liked her teachers, she did not like school very much. She was quite smart and curious about things, but sometimes special unicorn training was hard for Sparky. She could feel the Magical Force all around her in her classroom and at home with her family, but she didn't know how to use it.

Some things Sparky's teachers asked her to do were easy for her, but others were hard. She just couldn't figure it out, even when she worked on it. Her parents and her teachers kept telling her to *use the Magic Force,* but she didn't really understand what that meant.

All Unicorns at the Enchanted Academy had to learn all about the mystical falls, clouds, and the never-ending forest; how to get along with other unicorns; how to solve problems of number magic; and how to read the ancient scrolls. Sparky was excellent at solving number magic problems, and she was very good at getting along with the other unicorns, but reading the ancient scrolls was difficult for her. Even when Sparky tried her hardest, she would get frustrated when she had to work on the ancient language, especially because it was different than the language she used at home with her mom, dad, and Fen. Equally hard was writing and solving riddles; it took a lot of special concentration. Sometimes, Sparky would look at a page with riddles and could not make any sense of it. That made her feel frustrated and sometimes sad because she knew she tried her best.

Sparky's parents really loved Sparky and wanted her to learn how to use the Magic Force so she could grow up to be a strong Unicorn with a colorful mane. They saw that Sparky was struggling with her ancient scrolls and riddle work, and they worried about their young Unicorn.

So, one day they decided to fly her in their red carriage to the Young Unicorns-in-Training Rainbow Clinic to work with Miri Shoma. Miri Shoma was said to have the special gift of working with young Unicorns. She believed that all young Unicorns were special and talented – even when they were having a hard time in some areas. Miri said that she was going to help Sparky and her parents understand how she could learn to use the Magic Force.

Miri Shoma asked Sparky to complete several mind drills. Some of the mind drills were kind of boring and hard, but others were okay. Sparky's favorite part was when she got to draw and play games. She especially liked to do secret drawings and not show her work until the very end. She had all kinds of great ideas and Miri always enjoyed seeing the colorful art Sparky created.

After Sparky completed her work at the Young Unicorns-in-Training Rainbow Clinic, Miri talked to her parents.

"I have learned two very important things about Sparky," she told her parents. "First, Sparky is a very smart Unicorn and she is very good at numbers, picture puzzles, and mind games, better than many other Unicorns her age. But, when it comes to reading the scrolls and writing the riddles, her brain works differently than most other young Unicorns' do."

"What do you mean?" asked Sparky's mom. "Can we do anything about it?" asked her dad. They wanted to help.

"Well, when Sparky looks at an ancient scroll, it's as if some of the letters jump at her and others move around or disappear. The rules for the scroll reading can be hard to follow so making sense of the sounds of the letters is very hard for Sparky. It's impossible to make sense of how the words come together. Sparky will need some extra mind drills with Amaya, the Purple Unicorn, so that these things can become easier for her. It's extra hard because she is learning the scrolls in the ancient language, which is so different than the one you speak at home. Now that we know more about the way Sparky's brain learns scrolls, we know what kind of teaching she needs."

Sparky's mom nodded. "I think I understand what you mean. Everyone's brain is so different and sometimes it can play all kinds of tricks on us." "I understand, too," added Sparky's dad. "This makes sense because Sparky is such a good learner. I did not know that her brain played these kinds of tricks on her. I am glad that we can take her to the Purple Unicorn. I hear that she helps young Unicorns with riddles and scrolls; things should be easier with time."

Miri also told Sparky's parents, "The second important thing that I learned about Sparky is that the Magic Force is very strong in her, as you already knew. She has the potential to become a very strong Unicorn. But right now, she has not yet learned to use the Magic Force. Learning to use the Magic takes lots of practice and experience. When Unicorns don't yet know how to use the Magic Force, they have a hard time feeling good about their learning and instead feel pretty badly inside. Sometimes they feel unsure about their work and might be shy to show others the things they make, draw, or write. They don't yet feel confident on the inside that the other Unicorns will understand and help them. Even with their parents they might not feel ready to say how they really feel on the inside and instead show pink and purple colors while really they are feeling kind of dark and grey instead."

"Hmmm," said Sparky's mother. "What can I do to help Sparky learn to use the Magic Force and feel more confident?" "Yeah, is there something we can do to help her feel like she can always tell us about the grey colors and not just the pink?" asked Sparky's dad.

Miri talked with Sparky's parents about some things they could do to help Sparky learn to use the Magic Force. Miri said, "She will need to start with small things and work up to bigger things. Continue to read the ancient scrolls with her and be very patient when she is trying to read them alone. Always notice when she works hard and maybe offer a small compliment about how hard she is working, not about how she is improving but about all the effort she is putting in. We know these kinds of compliments help much more than telling little Unicorns that they are doing a good job. It's not easy to do the extra work we are talking about!"

"But what about helping Sparky with her grey feelings inside when she feels so shy or worried and doesn't want to talk in front of others?" they asked. "Well, that can be bit tricky ... but here are some special words you can use to help Sparky feel better." Miri whispered the words into Sparky's mom and dad's ears' as they listened very carefully.

As they talked more, Sparky's parents started to understand how much practice it took to learn how to use the Magic Force. They explained to Sparky that it wasn't her fault that she couldn't use the Magic yet. Hearing this made Sparky feel better. As the darkness of the night fell on the Enchanted Cloud, Sparky went to bed feeling good about the days to come. She knew her mom and dad understood her and would help her learn to use the Magic Force and read and write in the ancient language.

Everyone knew that the best thing that happened to Unicorn Sparky was that her parents and all the Academy teachers agreed to work together to help Sparky learn to use the Magic Force. They all knew that Sparky was a very good young Unicorn, and that the Magic Force would one day turn her mane into all the colors of the rainbow. Her parents knew that they wanted to use the special words that Miri whispered into their ears to help the Magic grow inside their little Unicorn, as they loved her dearly and wanted the best for her. And Sparky the Unicorn knew it, too – and that made her feel loved, soft, and fluffy, just like her favorite little bunny!

Appendix D
Parent Feedback Questionnaire

1. How well did the assessment of your child meet your expectations?
2. What part(s) of the assessment did you find most valuable?
3. What part(s) of the assessment were least valuable?
4. What suggestions do you have for improving the way we do assessments?
5. What would you tell a friend who was considering getting an assessment from us for their child?
6. Please give any other comments. Use the back of the form if needed.

Appendix E
Published Case Studies of TA-C and Collaborative Child Assessment

Aschieri, F., Fantini, F., & Bertrando, P. (2012). Therapeutic Assessment with children in family therapy. *Australian and New Zealand Journal of Family Therapy*, 33(4), 285–298.

Becker, E., Gohara, Y. Y., Marizilda, F. D., & Santiago, M. D. E. (2002). Interventive assessment with children and their parents in group meetings: Professional training and storybook feedback. *The Humanistic Psychologist*, 30, 114–124.

Chudzik, L., Frackowiak, M., & Finn, S. E. (2019). Évaluation Thérapeutique et dépression de l'enfant: Faire du bilan psychologique une intervention familiale brève [Therapeutic Assessment and child depression: Using psychological assessment as a brief family intervention]. *Bulletin de Psychologie*, 559(1), 19–27.

Del Carmen Espinoza, M. (2020). The use of Collaborative/Therapeutic Assessment with Oppositional Defiant Disorder. *Rorschachiana*, 41(2), 200–222.

DuBose, T. (2002). Family-centered, strength-based assessments with special needs children: A human-science approach. *The Humanistic Psychologist*, 30, 125–135.

Fantini, F., Aschieri, F., & Bertrando, P. (2013). "Is our daughter crazy or bad?" A case study of Therapeutic Assessment with children. *Contemporary Family Therapy*, 35(4), 731–744.

Finn, S. E., & Chudzik, L. (2013). L'Evaluation Thérapeutique pour enfant: théorie, procédures et illustration. [Therapeutic Assessment with children: Theory, techniques, and case example]. *Neuropsychiatrie de l'Enfance et de l'Adolescence*, 61, 166–175.

Finn, S. E., Fischer, C. T., & Handler, L. (Eds.) (2012). *Collaborative/Therapeutic Assessment: A casebook and guide*. Hoboken, NJ: Wiley.

Fischer, C. T. (1985/1994). *Individualizing psychological assessment*. Mawah, NJ: Routledge.

Gart, N., & Williams, M. E. (2016). Considering the opportunity for therapeutic assessment: Values and practices in pediatric primary care. *The TA Connection*, 4(2), 10–14.

Gart, N., Zamora, I., & Williams, M. E. (2016). Parallel models of assessment: Infant mental health and Therapeutic Assessment models intersect through early childhood case studies. *Infant Mental Health Journal*, 37(4), 452–465.

Gorske, T. T., & Smith, S. (2008). *Collaborative therapeutic neuropsychological assessment*. New York: Springer.

Greenberg, L. A. (2016). Liberating the butterfly: Engaging the family and system in the therapeutic assessment and traumatized and gender non-conforming child. In

B. L. Mercer, T. Fong, & E. Rosenblatt (Eds.). *Assessing children in the urban community* (pp. 196–201). New York, NY: Routledge.

Guerrero, B., Lipkind, J., & Rosenberg, A. (2011). Why did she put nail polish in my drink? Applying the Therapeutic Assessment model with an African American foster child in a community mental health setting. *Journal of Personality Assessment, 93*, 7–15.

Hamilton, A. M., Fowler, J. L., Hersh, B., Hall, C., Finn, S. E., Tharinger, D. J., Parton, V., Stahl, K., & Arora, P. (2009). "Why won't my parents help me?" Therapeutic Assessment of a child and her family. *Journal of Personality Assessment, 91*, 108–120.

Handler, L. (1995). The clinical use of figure drawings. In C. Newmark (Ed.), *Major psychological assessment instruments* (pp. 206–293). Boston: Allyn & Bacon.

Handler, L. (2006). The use of therapeutic assessment with children and adolescents. In S. Smith & L. Handler (Eds.), *Clinical assessment of children and adolescents: A practitioner's guide* (pp. 53–72). Mawah, NJ: Erlbaum & Associates.

Handler, L. (2012). Collaborative storytelling with children: An unruly six-year-old boy. In S. E. Finn, C. T. Fischer, & L. Handler, *Collaborative/Therapeutic Assessment: A case book and guide* (pp. 243–266). Hoboken, NJ: Wiley.

Handler, L. (2014). The Fantasy Animal and Story-Telling Game. In L. Handler & A. D. Thomas (Eds.), *Drawings in assessment and psychotherapy: Research and application* (pp. 117–130). New York, NY: Routledge.

Haydel, M. E., Mercer, B. L., & Rosenblatt, E. (2011). Training assessors in Therapeutic Assessment. *Journal of Personality Assessment, 93*, 16–22.

MacDonald, H., & Hobza, C. (2016). Collaborative assessment and social justice. In B. L. Mercer, T. Fong, & E. Rosenblatt (Eds.), *Assessing children in the urban community* (pp. 69–78). New York, NY: Routledge.

Mercer, B. L., Fong, T., & Rosenblatt, E. (Eds.) (2016). *Assessing children in the urban community.* New York, NY: Routledge.

Miller, L., Novotny, D., Cotas-Girard, A., & Gromoff, C. (2019). Therapeutic Assessment at Child Haven. *The TA Connection, 7*(2), 4–10.

Mutchnick, M. G., & Handler, L. (2002). Once upon a time …: Therapeutic interactive stories. *The Humanistic Psychologist, 30*, 75–84.

Pagano, C. J., Commins Blattner, M. C., & Kaplan-Levy, S. (2019). Therapeutic assessment with child inpatients. *Journal of Personality Assessment, 101*(5), 556–566.

Purves, C. (2012). Collaborative Assessment of a child in foster care: New understanding of bad behavior. In S. E. Finn, C. T. Fischer, & L. Handler (Eds.), *Collaborative/Therapeutic Assessment: A casebook and guide* (pp. 291–310). New York: Wiley.

Smith, D., Darling, A., & Frackowiak, M. (2019). Incorporating TA in a community mental health clinic. *The TA Connection, 7*(2), 26–29.

Smith, J. D., Finn, S. E., Swain, N. F. & Handler, L. (2010). Therapeutic Assessment of families in healthcare settings: A case presentation of the model's application. *Families, Systems, & Health, 28*, 369–386.

Smith, J. D., & Handler, L. (2009). "Why do I get in trouble so much?": A family Therapeutic Assessment case study. *Journal of Personality Assessment, 91*, 197–210.

Smith, J. D., Nicholas, C. R. N., Handler, L., & Nash, M. R. (2011). Examining the clinical effectiveness of a family intervention session in Therapeutic Assessment: A single-case experiment. *Journal of Personality Assessment, 93*, 149–158.

Smith, J. D., Wolf, N. J., Handler, L., & Nash, M. R. (2009). Testing the effectiveness of family Therapeutic Assessment: A case study using a time-series design. *Journal of Personality Assessment, 91*, 518–536.

Tharinger, D. J., Christopher, G., & Matson, M. (2011). Play, playfulness, and creative expression in Therapeutic Assessment with children. In S. W. Russ & L. N. Niec (Eds.), *An evidence-based approach to play in intervention and prevention: Integrating developmental and clinical science* (pp. 109–148). New York: Guilford Press.

Tharinger, D. J., Finn, S. E., Arora, P., Judd-Glossy, L., Ihorn, S. M., & Wan, J. T. (2012). Therapeutic Assessment with children: Intervening with parents "behind the mirror." *Journal of Personality Assessment, 94*, 111–123.

Tharinger, D. J., Finn, S. E., Austin, C., Gentry, L., Bailey, E., Parton, V., & Fisher, M. (2008). Family sessions in psychological assessment with children: Goals, techniques, and clinical utility. *Journal of Personality Assessment, 90*, 547–558.

Tharinger, D. J., Finn, S. E., Wilkinson, A. D., DeHay, T., Parton, V., Bailey, E., & Tran, A. (2008). Providing psychological assessment feedback with children through individualized fables. *Professional Psychology: Research and Practice, 39*, 610–618.

Tharinger, D. J., Finn, S. E., Wilkinson, A. D., & Schaber, P. M. (2007). Therapeutic Assessment with a child as a family intervention: Clinical protocol and a research case study. *Psychology in the Schools, 44*, 293–309.

Tharinger, D. J., Fisher, M., Gerber, B. (2012). Therapeutic Assessment with a 10-year-old boy and his parents: The pain under the disrespect (pp. 311–333). In S. E. Finn, L. Handler, & C. T. Fischer (Eds.), *Collaborative/Therapeutic Assessment: A casebook and guide.* Hoboken, NJ: John Wiley.

Tharinger, D. J., Krumholz, L. S., Austin, C. A., & Matson, M. (2011). The development and model of Therapeutic Assessment with children: Application to school-based assessment. In M. A. Bray & T. J. Kehle (Eds.), *Oxford Press handbook of school psychology* (pp. 224–259). Oxford University Press.

Tharinger, D. & Roberts, M. (2014). Human figure drawings in Therapeutic Assessment with children: Process, product, life context, and systemic impact. In L. Handler & A. D. Thomas (Eds.), *Drawings in assessment and psychotherapy: Research and application* (pp. 17–41). New York: Routledge.

Troy, M., & Robinson, J. (2016). A developmental perspective on Therapeutic Assessment. *The TA Connection, 4*(2), 4–9.

Wilkinson-Smith, A. (2020). Uncharted waters: A case study of Therapeutic Assessment with a child using telehealth. *The TA Connection, 8*(1), 6–10.

Appendix F
Sample Informed Consent for Videotaping

I, _____, hereby grant permission to Stephen E. Finn, Ph.D., to videotape Therapeutic Assessment sessions with myself and/or my child _____ during the period from _____ to _____.

My initials indicate that I authorize the use of these videos for the following purposes:

(Please initial all that apply.)

_____ For Dr. Finn to review on his own and to show me to help with our work.

_____ For Dr. Finn to share with colleagues to get consultation/supervision, with the understanding that my name and that of my child will not be given, and that Dr. Finn will make every effort to protect our identity by not sharing unneeded information.

I understand that Dr. Finn will **not** provide me with copies of the videos, and that they will be destroyed when my work with Dr. Finn is completed.

I understand that I have the right to rescind my permission at any time in the future without negative consequences for this or future psychological assessments or psychotherapy.

I have read this form carefully and I sign it of my own free will. I have received a copy of this form for my records.

_____   _____
Signature   Date

_____   _____
Address   Telephone number

_____   _____
Witness (Signature)   Date

Index

Note: Page numbers in **boldface** refer to tables and *italics* refer to figures